Written as I Remember It

WOMEN AND INDIGENOUS STUDIES SERIES

The series publishes works establishing a new understanding of Indigenous women's perspectives and experiences, by researchers in a range of fields. By bringing women's issues to the forefront, this series invites and encourages innovative scholarship that offers new insights on Indigenous questions, past, present, and future. Books in this series will appeal to readers seeking stimulating explorations and in-depth analysis of the roles, relationships, and representations of Indigenous women in history, politics, culture, ways of knowing, health, and community well-being.

Other books in the series:

Indigenous Encounters with Neoliberalism: Place, Women, and the Environment in Canada and Mexico, by Isabel Altamirano-Jiménez

Standing Up with Ga'axsta'las: Jane Constance Cook and the Politics of Memory, Church, and Custom, by Leslie A. Robertson with the Kwagu'ł Gixsam Clan

Being Again of One Mind: Oneida Women and the Struggle for Decolonization, by Lina Sunseri

Indigenous Women and Feminism: Politics, Activism, Culture, edited by Cheryl Suzack, Shari M. Huhndorf, Jeanne Perreault, and Jean Barman

Taking Medicine: Women's Healing Work and Colonial Contact in Southern Alberta, 1880-1930, by Kristin Burnett

Written as I Remember It

Teachings (ʔəms taʔaw) from the Life of a Sliammon Elder

ELSIE PAUL

in collaboration with

PAIGE RAIBMON and HARMONY JOHNSON

UBC Press • Vancouver • Toronto

22 21 20 19 18 17 16 15   5 4

Printed in Canada on FSC-certified ancient-forest-free paper (100% post-consumer recycled) that is processed chlorine- and acid-free.

Library and Archives Canada Cataloguing in Publication

Paul, Elsie, 1931-, author
     Written as I remember it : teachings ([glottal stop] [schwa]ms ta[glottal stop]aw) from the life of a Sliammon elder / Elsie Paul, in collaboration with Paige Raibmon and Harmony Johnson.

(Women and Indigenous Studies series)
Title page: The symbols for glottal stop and schwa appear on the source of information.
Includes bibliographical references and index.
Issued in print and electronic formats.
Text in English; includes Sliammon narratives with English translations.

ISBN 978-0-7748-2710-2 (bound) – ISBN 978-0-7748-2711-9 (pbk.)
ISBN 978-0-7748-2712-6 (pdf) – ISBN 978-0-7748-2713-3 (epub)

     1. Paul, Elsie, 1931-. 2. Elders (Native peoples) – British Columbia – Sunshine Coast – Biography. 3. Comox Indians – British Columbia – Sunshine Coast – Biography. 4. Comox Indians – British Columbia – Sunshine Coast – History. 5. Comox Indians – British Columbia – Sunshine Coast – Social life and customs. 6. Legends – British Columbia – Sunshine Coast. 7. Oral tradition – British Columbia – Sunshine Coast. I. Raibmon, Paige, 1971-, author II. Johnson, Harmony, 1980-, author III. Title. IV. Series: Women and indigenous studies series

E99.C86P39 2014   971.1'310049794   C2013-908263-8
                                                  C2013-908264-6

Canada

UBC Press gratefully acknowledges the financial support for our publishing program of the Government of Canada (through the Canada Book Fund), the Canada Council for the Arts, and the British Columbia Arts Council.

This book has been published with the help of a grant from the Canadian Federation for the Humanities and Social Sciences, through the Awards to Scholarly Publications Program, using funds provided by the Social Sciences and Humanities Research Council of Canada, and with the help of the University of British Columbia through the K.D. Srivastava Fund.

UBC Press
The University of British Columbia
2029 West Mall
Vancouver, BC V6T 1Z2
www.ubcpress.ca

In memory of Molly and Iasa, Elsie's grandparents,

and all of those other Sliammon, Ḵlahoose, and Homalco Elders

and friends whom Elsie remembers so fondly

Contents

WHERE I COME FROM

CHILD

✿

CHI-CHIA (čičiyɛʔ)

Illustrations

A Note on
the Sliammon Language

Honoré Watanabe

The Sliammon language is Elsie Paul's mother tongue. In terms of its genetic affiliation, it is one of ten languages that make up the Coast Salish branch of the greater Salish language family. There are twenty-three Salish languages altogether, most of them with further dialectal variations. Salish languages have many unique sounds as well as rich and complex systems for word and sentence formation that have intrigued linguists for more than a century. Sadly, four of the Salish languages have already lost all their speakers, and the rest of the languages are highly endangered. This is a consequence of, above all else, the residential school system, a topic discussed by Elsie in the chapters that follow.

THE NAME OF THE LANGUAGE

The language that Elsie speaks is referred to in this book as "Sliammon." Determining the most appropriate name for it is not a simple issue. Two other peoples, the Homalco and the Klahoose, speak essentially the same dialect as the ɬaʔamin people.[1] All three of these peoples historically lived on the mainland of British Columbia.[2] Some speakers have stated that there are slight differences among the speech of the three peoples; however, no systematic research has been conducted on this issue, and it is now hard to determine for certain because so few speakers of the language are left. For the present purposes, it will be convenient to refer to Elsie's dialect as the "Mainland" dialect, as there is no other cover term for it. Another dialect of the same language, referred to as "Island Comox," was spoken on Vancouver Island by the Island Comox people; however, this dialect has no living speakers. Linguistic research clearly shows that the Mainland dialect and Island Comox are distinct dialects of the same language. (For example, the Mainland dialect has a *th* sound, as in English "thin," whereas Island Comox does not. Wherever there is a *th* sound in the former dialect, the latter has an *s* sound.) The Sliammon language has sometimes been called "Comox" in technical literature. However, "Comox" is not the term the ɬaʔamin people prefer because it is also the name of a town on Vancouver Island where an entirely different First Nations people reside. Some ɬaʔamin, Homalco, and Klahoose people call the language "ʔayʔaǰuθəm," which also means "to speak well." "ɬaʔamin-qin" ([ɬaʔamɪnqɛn]), literally "Sliammon-mouth/language," is sometimes, but not often, used to refer to the Sliammon language.

GUIDE TO THE PRONUNCIATION OF SLIAMMON

Although some sounds of the Sliammon language are either identical or similar to those of the English language, many are quite different. Overall, pronunciation of Sliammon is highly distinct from English and other European languages such as French, German, Italian, or Spanish, as well as from other languages like Japanese, Chinese, or Arabic.

The Sliammon language has been passed on for generations orally. Until quite recently, there had never been a conventional writing system, or orthography. (This is nothing unusual; the majority of the world's languages were or still are oral languages without an orthography.) Because the Roman alphabet is inadequate to convey the pronunciation of Sliammon, phonetic symbols, most commonly used by linguists, are incorporated into the orthography. The symbols represent each sound of Sliammon fairly well; however, because rhythm, speed, and intonation cannot be rendered on paper, the written forms are at best only approximations of the actual sound when it comes to longer words, phrases, or sentences. Throughout this book, the following symbols are used to write Sliammon as it is pronounced.

Consonants
The following consonants have equivalent or very similar sounds in English:

č   like the first sound in "change" or the last sound in "catch"
g   like the first sound in "gum"
h   like the first sound in "hello"
ǰ   like the first sound in "jam"
k   like the first sound in "cut" or "kiss"
kʷ the "k" sound but with the lips rounded, as in the first sound of "quiz" or "quick"
l   like the first sound in "light"
m   like the first sound in "meet"
n   like the first sound in "note"
p   like the first sound in "pin"
s   like the first sound in "sit"
š   like the first sound in "sheep"
t   like the first sound in "teacher"
θ   like the first sound in "thin"
tθ the "t" and "th" sounds simultaneously, like the last sound in "eighth"
w   like the first sound in "wine"
y   like the first sound in "yard"
ʔ   a silence created by closing the vocal cords, as in the middle of "uh-oh!" This sound is called a "glottal stop," or sometimes less formally referred to as "catch-in-the-throat."

The following consonant sounds are not found in English:

q   like the "k" sound as in "kick" but pronounced farther back in the mouth
qʷ the "q" sound above but with the lips rounded into an O shape
xʷ like the first sound in "who" but with much more friction in the mouth
χ   (also written x̣) like the "h" sound but with much more friction in the mouth, almost like the French "r"
χʷ (also written x̣ʷ) like the "χ" sound above but with the lips rounded into an O shape
ɫ   like a whispered "l" but with much more friction in the mouth; the tip of the tongue is touching the front teeth as air is blown out along the sides of the tongue
ƛ   the "t" sound and the "ɫ" sound in a quick sequence
č', k', kʹʷ, ƛ', p', q', qʹʷ, t', tθ   The apostrophe in these nine consonants indicates a certain "popping" effect. In the case of "p'," for example, the lips are closed as for "p"; the popping effect is made by holding the breath and then releasing the air in a burst.[3]

l', m', n', w', y'   These five consonants are their corresponding consonants in combination with the glottal stop (ʔ). Depending on
where they occur in a given word, they will be pronounced differently. If they come before another consonant or at the end of
a word, then the "l," "m," "n," "w," or "y" sounds are cut off
abruptly. If they are between two vowels, the "ʔ" comes before
the "l," "m," "n," "w," or "y."

Vowels
ɑ   like the *a* in "father"
a   like the French *a* in "patte"
ʌ   like the *u* in "up"
e   like the *a* in "aim"
ɛ   like the *e* in "pet" or "bell"
u   like the vowel in "choose" or "who"
ʊ   like the *u* in "put"
i   like the vowel in "beat" or "meet" but short
ɪ   like the *i* in "bit" or "hit"
ə   like the *o* in "lemon"

Also, two stress marks and two length markers may be used over or
following a vowel:

á   (acute accent) strongest stressed vowel of a word
à   (grave accent) stressed vowel but not the strongest one in the word
a: (long) long vowel
a· (half long) half long vowel

ABOUT THE FORMAT OF SLIAMMON NARRATIVES

The three Sliammon narratives in this book are excerpts of narratives
that were told in the Sliammon language by Elsie, recorded by me,
and subsequently transcribed and translated with the assistance of
Marion Harry. Further clarification was provided by Elsie.[4]

Elsie's Sliammon narratives are presented in sets of five lines. A set
usually corresponds to a sentence in English, or to a phrase or a "passage" that is separated by a pause. I hope that those who are not
familiar with the technical terms employed in the third line will still
review the fourth and fifth lines of each set to get an understanding

of the scope of the differences between the Sliammon and English languages.

Here is a passage from one of the narratives (p. 271):

1. [hʌhkʷaʔɪːt'ᶿʌč nɛʔkʷ ʔasq']
2. hə-hkʷ-ay'-it'ᶿa ͜č   niʔ   kʷ ͜ʔasq'
3. IMPF-hang-LIG-clothes ͜1SG.INDC.SBJ   be.there   DET ͜outside[5]
4. hanging.clothes ͜I   be.there   outside
5. 'I was hanging clothes outside.'

Line 1 is the Sliammon language transcribed as Elsie pronounced it in the recording. This is called "phonetic transcription" and is placed between brackets ([...]). Sliammon is written this way by some community members who have received some training in phonetic symbols. Sliammon words appearing in the English-language chapters of the book are phonetically transcribed.

Line 2 is an analyzed line representing Line 1 in an "abstracted" spelling (for example, [nɛʔ] is written niʔ) called "phonemic transcription." Linguists use this notation because certain patterns and rules emerge only by abstracting away from actual pronunciation.[6] Words are separated into meaningful segments (roots, prefixes, and suffixes) by hyphens. (Thus, the English word "unfriendliness" would be separated into "un-friend-li-ness": "un-" is a prefix, "friend" is the root, and "-li" and "-ness" are suffixes.) The pieces with an underhook (" ͜č" and "kʷ ͜") are those that usually do not occur on their own but must be pronounced as one group with the preceding or the following words. (They are called "clitics" in linguistics.)

Line 3 is for labelling (or glossing) each of the segmented pieces in Line 2. So, for example, in "hə-hkʷ-ay'-it'ᶿa ͜č," "hə-" indicates an ongoing act (imperfective aspect); "hkʷ" (the base form is "həkʷ" but the vowel is dropped here) means "hang," and it is the root of this word; "-ay'" is a suffix that connects the following suffix to the root; "-it'ᶿa" is a suffix that means "clothes"; and finally, " ͜č" indicates that the subject is "I" (the first person singular).[7]

Line 4 is more or less a word-for-word translation, provided in this book especially for non-linguists to get the gist of the Sliammon language. Note that one word in Sliammon often corresponds to more than one word in English. In such cases, the English words are connected with a period. Thus, "hə-hkʷ-ay'-it'ᶿa ͜č" is translated in this line as "hanging.clothes ͜I."

Line 5 is a free translation in English, enclosed between single quotation marks ('...'), corresponding to Lines 1 and 2 in Sliammon. The translations from Sliammon may not always be eloquently written in English because they are intended to reflect the Sliammon wording and phrasing as much as possible. It is worth mentioning that literary conventions vary widely from language to language; what may sound articulate or eloquent in English may not always sound the same in Sliammon and vice versa.

A Closer Look at the Sliammon Language: Differences between Sliammon and English

Translating between two languages is notoriously difficult, particularly when the two languages are as radically different as the two Elsie uses, Sliammon and English. Even though Elsie is fully fluent in English, she describes how she sometimes struggles to convey her thoughts, ideas, and especially the traditional teachings in English. Elsie often says that there is just no way to accurately translate from Sliammon to English.

The differences in pronunciation explained above are only the beginning. Many other layers of difference between the Sliammon and English languages are evident in the Sliammon-language narratives in this book. The following is a very brief sketch of how different these two languages are.

Word Order
In English, the verb is generally placed either in the middle of a sentence (e.g., "John *loves* Mary") or at the end (e.g., "The man *ran*"). In Sliammon, it comes at the beginning; for example, "hu ̣č" is literally "go I," meaning "I go."

Meaning of Words
The meanings of certain words in English do not correspond to any words in Sliammon and vice versa. Elsie's narratives told in Sliammon are full of concepts that require explanation using multiple English words. For example, "qiqti?" (p. 269) means "youngest child of a family" and "hiwtał" (p. 355) means "eldest child of a family" (this is the traditional name of Elsie's eldest son, Glen), whereas "children of a family" is "təgixʷał" (p. 269). There is also a word that refers to the children in the middle, "čuxʷčuxʷ." Another example is "hiqiθut"

(p. 383), which means "to pull out into water (in canoe or boat)"; in contrast, "ɬayiš" means "to go toward shore, come ashore."

Words that reflect particular objects or acts in ɬaʔamin culture likewise cannot always be translated in a word or two but call for longer explanations. Many such words are, of course, culturally important. The word "suhuθut" (pp. 282 and 379) is a good example. It is commonly translated as something like "to perform the traditional ritual on oneself," but its meaning is actually more specific. The ɬaʔamin people used to wake up before sunrise and go into a nearby river, and then, as the sun rose, breathe out, blowing air out hard toward the sun several times. When doing so, one's hands are held to each side of the mouth, and then in one motion, the arms are stretched out forward as if throwing one's breath toward the sun. This ritual has been practised with the belief that it would get rid of illness or maintain health, both physically and spiritually. It used to be practised even during winter; small children and elderly people alike would make their way into an icy river every morning at the crack of dawn. Clearly more than a few English words are required to convey the meaning of "suhuθut." For practical reasons, including space and accessibility, however, I have compressed this and many other words into short English phrases. But readers should be aware that much of the real meaning of many words – what they mean for Elsie – is almost entirely lost in translation.

Word Formation

Word formation in Sliammon is also quite different from English. For example, when Elsie began to speak about losing one of her children, she used the word "man'a-ʔuɬ" (p. 269) before she explained the incident. This word is composed of "man'a," "child," and a suffix that indicates the past, "-ʔuɬ." This suffix can attach to verbs to indicate past tense, as seen in numerous passages in the narratives, but when it is attached to nouns, it indicates "something or someone of past" – hence meaning "deceased" when attached to words that refer to people. Elsie could have simply said "man'a," but the use of this suffix immediately foreshadows the death of the child to the listener. Later in the same narrative, the same suffix is found in "čičiyaʔ-uɬ," "deceased grandmother."[8]

Another example of word formation in the Sliammon language is "čaɬ-aya," "three people" (p. 269). Here a suffix that means "people," "-aya," is attached to the root "čaɬ," which means "three." (The numeral "three" is "čalas," but its form changes when "-aya" is attached.) "Four people" is "mus-aya" ("mus" is "four"); "five people" is "θiyits-aya" ("θiyičis" is "five"). There are other suffixes for counting different concepts or objects. For example, "-us" "face, head, round object" is attached to numerals when counting money (dollars) or months: "čalas-us" – "three dollars, three months," "mus-us" – "four dollars, four months," – "θiyits-us" – "five dollars, five months," etc. Yet another example is "-igił," "canoe": "čalas-igił" – "three canoes," "mus-igił" – "four canoes," etc. It is important to keep in mind that although these words are written here with hyphens, they are all single words. The suffixes cannot be used by themselves, just like the English "-er" in "teach-er," "play-er," etc.

Verbs in Sliammon can be quite simple (like "hu," "go"), but they can also be quite complex. Let us take another look at our earlier example, "hə-hkʷ-ay'-it'θa," "to be hanging clothes." Again, this is one word composed of the prefix "hə-," the root "hkʷ" (or "həkʷ"), and two suffixes, "-ay'" and "-it'θa." None of these pieces of the word can be used by itself. The last suffix, "-it'θa," means "clothes," but there is another word that means "clothes" that can be used by itself ("ʔiʔagikʷ'").[9] Elsie could have used a different verb form without the suffix, that is, "hə-hkʷ-ət," "hanging it/them";[10] however, she chose to include "-it'θa" in the verb. Presumably, this is because clothes are not the central issue in the story, so the concept did not need to be expressed overtly by an independent word.

All the characteristics of Sliammon described here represent but a glimpse of the very rich, complex, and systematic nature of its grammar.

NOTES

1 Sliammon words in this section are written in phonemic spelling (see Note 6), unless they are between brackets [...].
2 Many of the Homalco people now reside on Vancouver Island.
3 In slightly more technical terms, the vocal cords in the throat are closed, trapping air in the mouth. One would then get the "popping" effect by increasing the air pressure in the mouth (by raising the larynx or Adam's apple) and releasing the closure at the lips.
4 I am grateful to Mrs. Marion Harry for generously sharing her knowledge of this language with me. I also thank Aidan Pine for his assistance in proofreading the translation and making editorial suggestions. However, the transcriptions, translations, and linguistic analyses in the Sliammon narratives reflect my own current understanding of this language, and I am solely responsible for any errors. I am also grateful to the ɬaʔamin community for allowing me to study their

language and to Elsie and other Elders for patiently teaching me this language. I would like to thank especially the following people, all of whom were Elsie's life-long friends: the late Mrs. Mary George, the late Mrs. Agnes McGee, the late Mrs. Annie Dominick, the late Johnny George. My research on the Sliammon language has been funded by various agencies, most recently by the Japanese Ministry of Education, Culture, Sports, Science and Technology (2011–2013) and also by funding awarded to ILCAA, Tokyo University of Foreign Studies (2008–2013; "Linguistic Dynamics Science Project").

5 Determiners (abbreviated as DET in Line 3) resemble articles in English ("a," "an," and "the"). There are five determiners in Sliammon. "tə" (non-feminine referential) and "łə" (feminine referential) are often translatable as the English definite article, "the." "kʷə" (non-referential) and "šə" (remote/hypothetical) can be translated as the indefinite "a" or "an" although their meanings only partially overlap. The fifth determiner is "łu" (plural); "łu͜X" means "X and other people" where X is always a noun referring to people. Articles are not written in Line 4 where they would be awkward or ungrammatical in English, as in this example ("an outside").

6 The phonemic spelling of Sliammon is different from the phonetic transcription in several aspects but most significantly in (1) vowels and (2) g' and ǰ':

1 The wide range of phonetic vowels is analyzed into just four phonemic vowels: a, i, u, ə. The phonemic vowels are realized according to their sound environment, that is, what they are next to in a word. The rules are fairly complex but are systematic and generally as follows:

- a is pronounced as [ɛ] following č, č', ǰ, ǰ', š, y, y', k, k'; as [a] following ł, ƛ, ƛ'; as [ʌ] when unstressed; and as [ɑ] elsewhere
- i is pronounced as [i] next to č, č', ǰ, ǰ', š, y, y', k, k', g, g', kʷ, kʹʷ, xʷ, w, w'; as [ɛ] next to q, q', x̱, qʷ, q'ʷ, x̱ʷ, ʔ, h; as [ɪ] when unstressed; and as [e] elsewhere
- u is pronounced as [u] next to č, č', ǰ, ǰ', š, y, y', k, k', g, g', kʷ, kʹʷ, xʷ, w, w'; as [ʊ] when unstressed; and as [o] elsewhere
- ə is pronounced as [ʌ] next to q, q', x̱, ʔ, h; as [ʊ˞] ([ʊ] but close to [o]) next to qʷ, q'ʷ, x̱ʷ; as [ʊ] next to kʷ, kʹʷ, xʷ, w, w'; as [ɪ] next to č, č', ǰ, ǰ', š, y, y', k, k', g, g'; and as [ə] elsewhere.

2 g' and ǰ' are pronounced as [ʔg] and [ʔǰ] in actual pronunciation, but they need to be recognized as one unit for the purpose of linguistic analysis.

7 The following symbols and abbreviations are used in the Sliammon narratives: A.INTR – active-intransitive; APPL – applicative; AUX – (unidentified) auxiliary; CAU – causative; CJR – conjectural; CLF – cleft; CLT – (unidentified) clitic; CNJ – conjunctive; CTR – control transitive; DEM – demonstrative; DET – determiner; DIM – diminutive; EPEN – epenthesis (h and ʔ); ERG – ergative; FILLER – rhetorical filler; FUT – future; IMP – imperative; IMPF – imperfective; INC – inceptive; IND – indirective; INDC – indicative; INDP – independent form; INTR – intransitive; INTRR – interrogative; LIG – ligature; LV – link vowel; MDL – middle; MTG – mitigator; NEG – negative; NOM – nominalizer; NTR – noncontrol transitive; OBJ – object; OBL – oblique; PASS – passive; PAST – past; PERF – perfective; PL – plural; POSS – possessive; QN – question marker; QUOT – quotative; RCP – reciprocal;

RDPL – reduplication/reduplicant; RFL – reflexive; RLT – relational; SBJ – subject; SBR.PASS – subordinate passive; SG – singular; STV – stative; TR – transitive (transitivizer); - reduplication and affix boundaries; ‿ clitics; <...> enclose infixes; < <...> > enclose English words used in Sliammon sentences.

8 I invite interested readers to do a little bit of detective work and look for other words with this suffix, which sometimes appears as "-ułł," "-ʔu," or "-ʔuw," depending on the preceding or following sound. Look also at the gloss in Line 3 to see if it is labelled as PAST.

9 [ʔɛʔɑgikʸʷ] in phonetic writing.

10 The suffix "-ət" attaches to the root "hang" to make the verb transitive – a verb form that can take an object ("it/them").

Acknowledgments

For many years, Elsie intended to develop a book to tell her life story and impart her knowledge of ɫaʔamɪn teachings and history. This was only made possible through the first practical steps taken by Arlette Raaen and her husband, Chris McNaughton. Arlette in particular invested many hours in undertaking recordings with Elsie, drafting the original typescript and providing advice, thoughts, and a generous and gentle spirit of support throughout the life of this project. We are also grateful for the work of Janet May, who spent many hours with Elsie and Arlette recording much of the content for this book.

We would like to thank Marguerite Pigeon for her careful and respectful transcription of Elsie's words. Our thanks also to Eric Leinberger for creating the maps.

Many scholars generously shared their time and expertise in discussing aspects of this work with Paige. In this regard, we would like to thank Julie Cruikshank, Paul Kroeber, Dana Lepofsky, Bruce Miller, Leslie Robertson, and Patricia Shaw. Jean Barman, John Roosa, Susan Roy, Coll Thrush, and Honoré Watanabe read drafts of the introduction and provided insightful feedback. Courtenay Booker's close reading improved the introduction in crucial ways. We would also like to thank Wilbert Wong, Eric Wright, and Aidan Pine for their work as research assistants.

Anonymous readers for UBC Press and members of the UBC Press Publications Board provided positive and helpful reports on this manuscript. We appreciate their time and their depth of understanding of this work; family members were moved by their comments. We are grateful to Darcy Cullen and Lesley Erickson at UBC Press, to Sarah Wight for copy-editing, and to Cheryl Lemmens for proofreading and indexing.

We gratefully acknowledge financial assistance from the Social Sciences and Humanities Research Council of Canada and the University of British Columbia Faculty of Arts.

Many members of the Paul family contributed to this project in a number of ways, including reviewing various drafts and providing feedback, particularly in terms of hearing "Chi-chia's voice" on the written page. Elsie's daughters Jeannie Bassett and Marlane Christensen provided much practical assistance in coordinating various details and required support between Vancouver and Sliammon. Elsie's grandson Davis McKenzie developed the descent chart and collated the photos. Honorary Paul family member Honoré Watanabe very generously lent his time and expertise for all the Sliammon-language elements of this project.

Our thanks also to Marion Harry, Elsie's lifelong friend and fellow mother-tongue speaker of the language, for her work with Honoré to transcribe and translate the Sliammon narratives included in this book.

Each of us is grateful for the support of our friends and families on this multi-year journey. Special mention to Joe Gallagher, Benjamin Gallagher, Hart Caplan, Asha Raibmon, Trudy Raibmon, and particularly all Elsie's children, grandchildren, and great-grandchildren.

DESCENT CHART: ELSIE PAUL

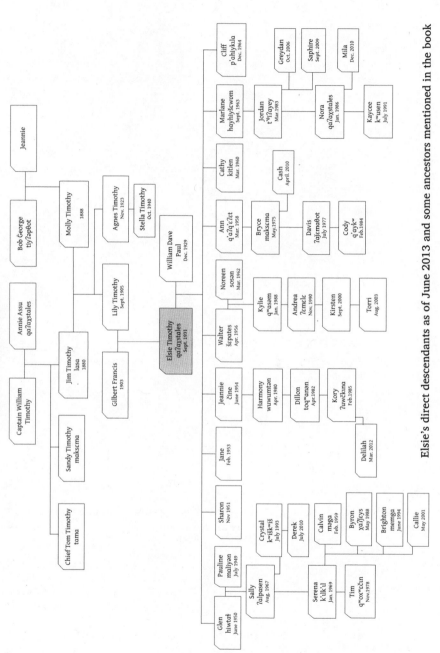

Elsie's direct descendants as of June 2013 and some ancestors mentioned in the book

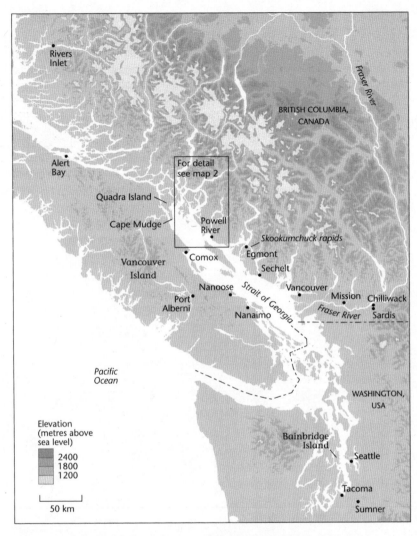

Southern British Columbia and northwestern Washington State, showing ɬaʔamɩn territory and other places mentioned in this book

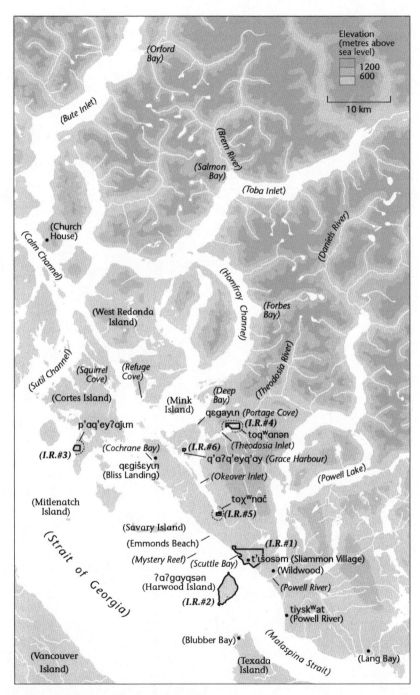

łaʔamɪn territory and surrounding area

Written as I Remember It

Introduction:
Listening to ʔəms taʔaw

Paige Raibmon

"The history written as I remember it," said Elsie, expressing her sense of this project. It was December 2011, and we were in North Vancouver at her granddaughter Harmony's house, visiting and working on this book. We were playing around with potential titles, and earlier that day, Harmony and I had suggested "Chi-chia's Teachings." "Chi-chia," which means "grandmother" in the Sliammon[1] language, had seemed a logical word to include in the title: many people call Elsie "Chi-chia," not just her biological grandchildren; moreover, Elsie's own Chi-chia has always been important to her. "Teachings" is the word Elsie uses to refer to the ɬaʔamın ways, beliefs, values, and practices that she recounts in this book. But to Elsie's ears, "Chi-chia's Teachings" sounded didactic and overemphasized her as an individual. The teachings, she reminded us, do not belong to any individual; they are "ʔəms taʔaw" or "*our* teachings." ʔəms taʔaw are, as she later explained, "the very essence of our well-being." The phrase "the history written as I remember it" was not Elsie's suggestion for a title but was instead part of her extended explanation of the problems with our proposal. The phrase stayed with me, however, and I jotted it down. I felt slightly clever, as though I had salvaged a fragment of verbal ephemera. Several months later, in need of a working title to submit to the press, I shared my notes with Harmony, and we decided to use "The History Written As I Remember It." Good thing I wrote that down, I thought, feeling slightly cleverer. A short time later, however, while reviewing

3

interview transcripts that I had read before, I was surprised to read Elsie's words to a journalist friend in 2006: "I've always wanted to write this – to document the history as I remember it." I realized then that what I had thought of as an off-the-cuff remark was, in fact, Elsie's carefully considered and precisely articulated conceptualization of this project.

I relate this incident here to illustrate two points that are relevant for readers. The first is the consistency, reliability, and authority of Elsie Paul's voice.. People familiar with expert storytellers and the practice of oral narrative will not be surprised at this story, yet many people remain skeptical about the reliability of orally narrated memories. In 2006, Chi-chia had not yet begun work on this book, and since that time the project has passed through many hands and multiple iterations. My point is not that she necessarily remembered in 2011 the exact turn of phrase she used in 2006. It is rather that a five-year interruption did so little to alter her sense of what it meant to record ʔəms taʔaw in book form that she repeated herself nearly verbatim. This is typical of the precision that Chi-chia brings to speech, particularly to storytelling. As Harmony and I studied the transcripts, we discovered depths to her narrative abilities that we had previously not fully appreciated. No matter how often phone calls, visitors, or interlocutors interrupted, Chi-chia never strayed from her train of thought. Unfailingly patient and courteous in her response to the interruption, over and over she returned without missing a beat to where she had left off. When Harmony and I struggled to connect disparate pieces of transcript, our efforts ended, time and again, with the humbling realization that our laboriously reached solution had been there all along, inherent in the logic of Chi-chia's original tellings. Long before she learned to tell stories like this, she learned to listen to them. The care and attention with which Elders taught Elsie to listen as a young girl is an important part of her skill at speaking now that she is an Elder herself.[2] Chi-chia is a serious storyteller, and by this I do not mean there is any shortage of laughter or lightness in her words. She is a serious storyteller because she avoids conjecture, speaks with clear intention, and selects words with care. She does not tell stories to mislead or harm. She takes the power of words seriously, and so tells stories in order to impart helpful, potentially healing, knowledge.

My second point, related to the first, is about listening, particularly transformational listening. By this I mean listening in ways and to voices that have the power to unearth sociopolitical assumptions and intellectual foundations. That afternoon in 2011, I listened carefully enough to catch something important about Chi-chia's meaning, while at the self-same moment I misconstrued my act of listening. Although I had read/heard Chi-chia utter those words before, I had neither taken in their significance initially nor remembered them later. I eventually came to understand that by describing the work as "the history written as I remember it" in response to our questions about whether "Chi-chia's Teachings" was an appropriate title, Elsie revealed her sense of connection between "the teachings" and "the history." The teachings as she learned them from her grandparents *are* ɬaʔamɩn history as she remembers it. For Elsie, the teachings and the history are inextricable; a book of teachings *is* a book of history. This realization took time to dawn on me: time to reread the transcripts, time to talk with Harmony and Chi-chia, time to think. Had I not returned to reflect on Chi-chia's words in the transcripts, I likely would have retained my self-satisfied sense that I had recorded a fleeting gem of a phrase and, in so doing, missed the opportunity to deepen my understanding of how Chi-chia positions past, present, culture, and knowledge in relation to one another. This story brings into focus the often hidden barriers to transformational listening. On the face of it, Chi-chia's accounts seem plain enough and not particularly cryptic. Yet much of what she has to say is rooted in a radically different paradigm from that which many readers, including myself, bring to this book. To get a sense of this paradigm, readers must bring to her words a continual openness to learning something new and unknown, rather than the certainty of having "got it" that overconfidence in one's intellectual ability, empathetic ear, or good intentions so easily produces.[3] Listening/reading in this way is very much like the way Chi-chia's Elders taught her to listen to stories as a child. As she describes in Chapter 3, Elders taught her to remain receptive to new meanings and lessons regardless of how many times she had heard a story before, and they frequently asked her to explain what she had learned from a particular telling. In this spirit, Elsie, Harmony, and I invite readers to take in not only the content of her words but the method and intention, as well. This task is not necessarily easy, particularly for those like me who have been steeped in print-based learning rather than in oral traditions.

Transformational listening entails particular difficulties for readers/ listeners who want to "unsettle the settler within," to borrow the scholar Paulette Regan's phrase.[4] My own experiences and reflections as a non-Indigenous scholar lead me to believe that those of us working to be, in Regan's terms, "settler allies" may be most susceptible to the dangers of certainty when we least expect it, when we already believe we have opened our eyes, ears, and minds, extended our empathy, and elicited stories from the dispossessed, disadvantaged, and marginalized.[5] This susceptibility matters a great deal because it has become nearly a platitude that listening to a multiplicity of voices – particularly in the form of first-person testimony – triggers the transformative effects of decolonization and reconciliation. In recent decades, settler states have institutionalized and thus sanctioned the important practice of listening to "other" voices in a number of contexts. The process of giving testimony and bearing witness are cornerstones of the Truth and Reconciliation Commission's procedures in Canada, for example, as they were in South Africa.[6] The historian Bain Attwood dubs this the "age of testimony" and is among those who doubt that autobiographical forms usher in reconciliation.[7] While I agree that hearing autobiographical testimony does not inevitably set the settler-witness on a one-way street to reconciliation, I differ with Attwood's conclusion that testimonial or autobiographical narratives are problematic impediments to "true" understanding. Indigenous individuals who share their testimony – whether as formal evidence to a commission or court, or as personal narrative for a public audience – offer listeners an important gift.[8] Whether and how audiences are able to receive and appreciate that gift depends very much on the particular way that they listen.

Attwood's position relies upon the same assumption as the positions he critiques: that listening to testimony erases the distance – or difference – between subject and witness, creating an overidentification (what Attwood, following Freud, calls "transference") between the two. He sees this as a problem because he believes it impedes objective, dispassionate analysis. I suggest instead that first-person narratives do not necessarily eliminate distance at all. On the contrary, first-person accounts can preserve distance – that is, difference – *more* effectively than supposedly objective historical methodologies that shoehorn Indigenous narrators' words into Western paradigms. Elsie's narratives presented here are a case in point. At the same time, first-person narratives, including this one, can easily give the *illusion* of erasing distance or difference between the narrator and the witness. And herein lies the danger of certainty. The anthropologist Julie Cruikshank noted as much more than twenty years ago when she wrote, "one obstacle hampering the analysis of autobiography is the very real human tendency to make implicit comparisons between the account heard or read and one's own life."[9] Having tuned its ears to diverse autobiographical keys, the challenge for settler society is to strain to continue listening for difference rather than to succumb to a comforting but disproportionate sense of commonality.[10] This effort means, in part, resisting the urge to overidentify with the sympathetic narrator and perhaps forcing oneself to identify with historical ancestors whom one might rather disavow.[11] But it does not mean listening with less emotion or sympathy. The emotions that testimonial accounts evoke are an undeniable part of their power; where the listener goes with the emotional response can be problematic, however. To assume, after hearing or reading a moving testimony of a residential school survivor, for example, that I now know what it was like to be in that narrator's shoes would prematurely close down my understanding, when in fact I ought to listen in the spirit of an ongoing relationship, an open investigation toward further insight. This sort of active, open-ended listening has the potential to bring enduring assumptions out of the taken-for-granted background, to bring into relief otherwise hidden suppositions that undergird twenty-first-century colonial attitudes and power imbalances.[12] Absent this, settler society's sympathetic listening is laden with unjustified certainty: certainty that it is listening for the right reason, at the right time; that it is on the right side; that listening *is* reconciliation. Such certainty precludes facing up to the need to transform not only attitudes but also relations of power. It precludes addressing the material, as opposed to the merely rhetorical, changes that must be part of any meaningful process of reconciliation or decolonization. Such certainty fosters listening that reinforces rather than challenges the status quo of settler colonialism. How and to whom we listen is thus inherently political. As one historian points out, "true citizenship ... involves not only getting to speak (i.e., having 'a say' or 'a voice'), but also being actively and attentively heard."[13] Learning to listen for unsettling differences, however subtle, is a difficult process with serious stakes that requires self-conscious and dialogical responsiveness to the words of people who are not the beneficiaries of settler colonialism.[14]

The degree to which listeners assign authority to particular voices very much affects how listeners hear those voices. Rather than suggesting, as Attwood does, the need to reauthorize professional historians as the only ones capable of upholding the necessary distance for critical thought, knowledge acquisition, and an understanding of difference, Elsie, Harmony, and I suggest quite the opposite.[15] We invite all listeners to regard this text as a collaboratively authored historical analysis, a secondary source in its own right, and Chi-chia as a ɬaʔamɨn historian in *her* own right.[16] Both the open-ended listening discussed above and the recognition of the expertise of Indigenous Elders and knowledge keepers are important elements of the Indigenous methodology we have followed in producing this book, and as authors we hope readers will be willing to invest in our approach. Audiences commonly treat first-person life histories as anecdotal, and researchers approach them as primary sources to be mined for evidence. Doing so relegates the narrator to the status of "informant," however, and reserves interpretive authority for readers, particularly scholarly ones.[17] Attwood advocates this very approach because to do otherwise, he claims, imperils the very nature of historical understanding and inquiry by leading us into a morass of emotion and sentiment.[18] But rather than retreating to a safe "distance," I suggest that readers take advantage of the close-up view that Chi-chia offers. The voice of this text is obviously different from that in Western secondary sources. But instead of this difference disqualifying the text as authoritative, we hope it helps readers tune in to multiple forms of authority and knowledge. If you listen – that is, read – carefully, you will hear that Chi-chia does more than offer anecdotes from days gone by. She takes what scholars might conceive of as "primary sources" – her own life experiences – and situates them within the interpretive context of the teachings. That is, she uses detailed evidence to present an argument in terms of her own world view. In so doing, she interprets ɬaʔamɨn history and teachings for a broad audience, one that includes but is not limited to her family and community members. Her status as one of the last mother-tongue speakers of the Sliammon language adds dimension and poignancy to her interpretive act. In the chapters that follow, Chi-chia shares many of the details that are typically presented in an introduction such as this. Therefore I have not provided a mini-biography of where and when she was born, or provided a gloss on the history of colonialism and Indian policy in twentieth-century British Columbia. I hope that you, as readers, will be patient if such information does not appear in the order that you might expect. I provide suggestions for additional context on the many topics that Chi-chia discusses in the "Additional Readings" section at the end of the book.

Before undertaking this project, Chi-chia herself was an "informant" for numerous scholars and knowledge producers. Her involvement in such work – the sharing of knowledge between peoples and across "distance" – is a family tradition. Her great-grandfather Captain Timothy worked and travelled extensively on a schooner providing navigational assistance to newcomers. He later guided the reserve commissioner Peter O'Reilly throughout the territory.[19] One of Captain Timothy's sons, tama Timothy or "Chief Tom," was the primary ɬaʔamɩn informant to Homer Barnett, the first ethnographer to enquire about ɬaʔamɩn culture. And Chi-chia's grandmother translated Catholic sermons from Chinook into the Sliammon language when she was a girl. Chi-chia herself has patiently and generously shared the teachings, history, and language with linguists, filmmakers, archaeologists, historians, journalists, and university students who have asked her questions about everything from resource extraction to slavery to prepositions. Her experiences with researchers have usually been very positive, yet Chi-chia wishes, though she would not quite put it this way, that the knowledge she shared crossed disciplinary boundaries more easily. For example, before beginning this book, she collaborated for two decades with the linguist (and now good friend of many years) Honoré Watanabe in his meticulous documentation of the Sliammon language. This technical work, of great value for linguistic analysis and language preservation, by its very nature did not reach a wide audience. When related material was needed for another purpose – for treaty, court, or education, for example – Chi-chia noted, "A year later someone else is asking you the same questions again! So you don't know where it's going!" She hopes that this book will make the history and teachings available for all these purposes.

Relatedly and as importantly, she wants to present the teachings and history within her own narrative framework, a framework that treats knowledge holistically rather than a framework that parses it into separate disciplinary boxes. Chi-chia has, at times, been frustrated by the assumptions that frame the questions of even well-intentioned researchers, and she (always politely) resists attempts to shoehorn her answers into someone else's paradigm.[20] She implicitly understands the need to alter not only the content of the historical record, but its epistemic structure. In this she shares the perspectives of Indigenous scholars who demonstrate that oral history cannot be treated "like any other documentary source" and who critique the intellectual foundations of the academy at large.[21] She also echoes the work of feminist scholars who have long challenged grand, often male-centred, narratives, particularly through their use of biography and autobiography.[22] With this collaboratively authored, told-to project, Chi-chia recounts the history and teachings "written as she remembers them" rather than as someone else has represented them. Long regarded by many recognized "experts" as a knowledgeable and trustworthy "informant," she presents her words here under her own authority. In this book, she is an author rather than an informant. Understanding Chi-chia as a historian within her own tradition is a step toward learning to really listen to – rather than merely incorporate or assimilate – multiple voices within the academy and public sphere.

A further step in this direction is bringing awareness to *how* and *when* and *why* we listen. I listen to Chi-chia as a settler-ally of Indigenous people living in a colonial nation-state. I believe it is important to align with agendas set by Indigenous people for decolonization and healing. When Indigenous individuals seek input from collaborators in order to share their knowledge and histories in written forms, I believe it is both intellectually justified and ethically imperative to employ scholarly platforms to amplify their voices. I also listen as a historian who has long been inspired by histories of individuals. From my earliest research projects as an undergraduate to my ongoing work today, I have felt drawn to explore broad historical patterns and meanings through the stories of individuals.[23] Undoubtedly, this interest also drew me to working with Chi-chia on this book. In her narratives, I see dozens of points of engagement with various scholarly conversations, a few of which I detail below. More personally, I listen to Chi-chia as a mother. I began working with her words at a time when I was particularly in need of hearing them. After the loss of my first child in 2006, I struggled to find motivation to do much of anything. Yet when Elsie invited me to help, I agreed without hesitation. I had known that she wanted to produce such a work for many years and I had always been enthusiastic about its potential significance. It was difficult but ultimately profound to spend so much time with her teachings around grief and her stories about the loss of two daughters. Each of the many hours I spent working with Chi-chia's words was rewarding. Although I was present to hear her tell only a small portion of the stories reproduced here, I read and reread – usually and most enjoyably in Harmony's company – the entirety of the transcripts again and again. I always looked forward to sitting down and immersing myself in Chi-chia's knowledge, line by line, word by word. Every time I did so, I learned something new. Today, her words accompany me in my daily life. It is a gift to have participated in this book's production.

BOOKS, LIKE INDIVIDUALS, have life histories. What follows in the rest of this introduction is the life history of this project written as I remember it. Since I have betrayed above that I do not always pay attention as well as I would like, readers can be reassured that I have benefited from the notes and assistance of other collaborators. I have also relied extensively on Chi-chia's own words in order to explain her motivation for writing this book. I recount this textual life history in acknowledgement of scholars' calls for attention to process in the production of told-to narratives. Recently, the literary scholar Sophie McCall identified collaborative texts, broadly defined, as models for other forms of collaboration in settler societies working out the meanings of reconciliation.[24] In order for told-to narratives to realize this potential, however, there are a number of prerequisites. One is the self-critical and open-ended listening by audiences discussed above. Prior to that, however, is the matter of ensuring that the collaborative process is conducted with integrity. No told-to narrative, regardless of how positive in intention, innovative in structure, or original in content, can meaningfully model or contribute to reconciliation if this condition is absent. Accordingly, historians, anthropologists, and literary critics alike have argued that the *process* of collaboration is as important as the final multi-authored result.[25]

In recent decades, scholars have raised important questions about power and ethics in collaborative writing processes. As McCall notes, "Historically, non-Aboriginal recorders and editors have maintained tight control over structuring, editing, introducing, interpreting, and publishing versions of Aboriginal oral expression under their own name."[26] As a result, told-to narratives have been critiqued as colonial appropriations of Indigenous voice.[27] Scholarly collaborators themselves have engaged in extensive self-reflection, revealing details of their methodologies, exploring non-conventional layouts, and incorporating multiple voices.[28] Yet many of these self-critical efforts toward developing ethical collaborative practices address concerns raised by scholars rather than the concerns of narrators or their communities. In part, this is because significant amounts of time and distance intervene between the so-called fieldwork of recording the narratives and their eventual publication. In the interim, the scholar often assumes control over the shape of the final product and, in a sense, comes to treat the transcribed words as primary sources distanced from the narrator.[29] Although this approach does not necessarily entail an intent to appropriate the narrator's words, it can easily result in appropriation because it tends to obscure the fact that narrators bring their own ethical frameworks and agendas to told-to projects – frameworks and agendas that are distinct from those of their scholarly collaborators.[30] We still know surprisingly little about the wishes of many narrators with regard to the final published form of their words.[31] For example, after decades of wrestling with ethical qualms regarding representation and voice, the anthropologist Kathleen Mullen Sands settled on an experimental format for presenting the life of the Tohono O'odham man Theodore Rios. The published volume appeared only after Rios' death, and so we cannot know whether her innovative format achieved his goals.[32] Even when the narrator is still alive, collaborators and critics often do not place her wishes at the centre of their work. In thousands of pages devoted to the controversy surrounding the life history of Rigoberta Menchú, for example, one is hard-pressed to find someone who prioritizes Menchú's self-expressed view of the situation.[33] When scholars fail to explicitly address and incorporate the narrator's views, they imply that the narrator's perspectives are unsophisticated, underdeveloped, or simply not worth considering. They thus cast into doubt their own claims to ethical practice. We cannot engage in an ethical collaboration with someone if we do not respect their capacity and judgment. Scholars and readers who do not attend to the points of view of Indigenous narrators remain caged (however unwittingly) within a nineteenth-century, salvage mentality that once again freezes idealized Indigenous voices, albeit now in twenty-first-century postmodern poses.[34] This tendency to undermine narrators' authority is inadvertently reproduced in the policies of some university behavioural ethics review boards in Canada that routinely ask researchers to acquire a band council resolution before conducting research on-reserve. This requirement implies that the individual in question is naive and unable to give informed consent. Although informed consent may occasionally be impossible,[35] such policies assume a generalized lack of capacity among Indigenous people and thus reproduce the Indian Act's historical positioning of Indians as minors vis-à-vis the Canadian state. For Elsie, a grown woman and respected Elder, it is insulting to be treated as a ward of the band council who needs protection from her own judgment. In the wake of decades of scholarly, activist, and artistic criticism of colonial appropriations of Indigenous voices, would-be allies today must do better than self-correcting in whatever way they *assume* is in the best interests of Indigenous speakers. They must instead listen to what Indigenous voices say, and then take up ethical models that align with and respect

Indigenous epistemologies and ontologies. Admittedly, as I discussed above, this endeavour is trickier than it might seem on its face, because it requires engaging in active self-criticism of not only *what* is heard, but *how* to listen.

Harmony and I worked from our certainty that Chi-chia capably and reliably articulates her wishes and concerns. Accordingly, we took those wishes seriously. Consequently our methodology favoured a pragmatics of process rather than an abstract end – of narrative purity or dialogical representation, for example. Our central concern as co-authors has not been to produce something that critics might approve in postmodern jargon as a multivocal, culturally pluralist synecdoche for remediated colonial power imbalances. Instead, we sought above all to ensure that both our means and end aligned with Chi-chia's vision. This approach required us to revisit our plans frequently and to consult with Chi-chia regularly. That said, we played decisive roles in composing this text, and we do not shirk our responsibility as co-authors for what follows.

CONCEPTION: THE IDEA

We produced this book through a multi-authored, collaborative process. A number of people worked with Chi-chia at various points in time, and multiple draft manuscripts were produced in the process. Chi-chia's desire to make ɬaʔamɩn history and teachings accessible in written form has been a constant feature. Accessibility is a key goal for Chi-chia, and I return to it repeatedly in my discussion below. She was not motivated by a salvage mentality to document the history and teachings for the archives. She instead wanted to produce an account of ɬaʔamɩn ways that future generations could draw upon, learn from, and heal through.[36] In this desire, she is much like Elders before her, who taught that ʔəms taʔaw are not a set of abstract ideas but principles for living that should be practised and passed on. The teachings have provided her with a sophisticated context for living. They have been and remain a practical means for addressing all stages and aspects of life, including but in no way limited to the material and psychological impacts of settler colonialism. Chi-chia expressed these points eloquently in a conversation she had with a friend, the journalist Janet May, in 2006. Harmony, Chi-chia, and I originally discussed presenting the transcript of that conversation as Chi-chia's own introduction to this book, but Chi-chia felt that a stand-alone introduction by her was unnecessary. Instead, I engage below in a kind of dialogue with that transcript in order to highlight the constellation of language, teachings, history, and colonialism that lies at the heart of this book.[37]

For Chi-chia, the multiple instances of silencing imposed upon Indigenous people by colonialism are a crucial context for the act of sharing ɬaʔamɩn history and teachings. Reflecting on the passing of her lifelong friend Sue Pielle, who devoted herself to teaching ɬaʔamɩn culture, legends, and language in the public schools, she said to Janet, "You know, she was from a generation that lived a part of that life and is able to bring it forward to the young people. 'Cause a lot of people, like, my age, her age, have gone on. And the older people that we have today are not able to bring that forward. They have a lot of memories, even a generation older than I have a lot of those memories. But they were brought up in a time when it was not appropriate for us as a people, or it was not expected, to share those kinds of things, to bring awareness of the way we are as a people, to talk about our history. Our history was being smothered. It was like, 'Don't talk about that!' So a lot of the older people found it really difficult to share their memories, their history, to non-Native people. So that's been a real hurdle for us as a people."[38]

As Chi-chia continued, she equated language with history: the prohibition of the Sliammon language simultaneously silenced people from recounting ɬaʔamɩn history. "'Cause you're told, 'You forget about being Indian! You forget about your culture! Forget about the language!' So we were forbidden. Our people were forbidden to speak the language. So a lot of the young people today don't know the language at all. They're struggling to learn it. It's difficult. It's a difficult language to learn. You have to have been speaking it from the time you were a child. That was your language. And when the families were separated, the children were all taken out of the homes and brought somewhere else for school. You didn't see them for ten months out of a year. And they're told when you're there, 'This is the language you're now going to speak. You cannot use the language you've been growing up with.' So they were restricted. So that generation grew up being taught that their language was not acceptable? You will only learn English. So we have a lot of people in that generation now who lost their language, who were *robbed* of the language. And the culture! Because we came from a rich culture. We *come* from a rich culture."

In Chi-chia's framing, history, language, and culture are so deeply intertwined as to be inseparable. Consequently, the ramifications of language loss are immense: "And it makes such a difference when you're telling stories and legends, if it's told in the language. It's got more depth, it's got more meaning. And it's much more interesting to the listener if they understand the language. But if you tell the story in English, it's so different! 'Cause a lot of it, when told in the language, is gestures, the tone of your voice, just the whole presentation is *so* interesting – it was made so interesting. Because you understood the language! So it captured your interest. But when it's told in English, like when I tell a story in English, I struggle in the presentation. And to find the right word to use in telling the story. So it's quite a challenge! *[chuckles]*" Chi-chia's characteristic humility is apparent here; to my eyes and ears, the struggle she describes is imperceptible. Yet for her, the experience of narrating in English entails a palpable sense of loss and difficulty. As she explains it, narrating ɬaʔamɪn history in English, the language of the colonizers, is nearly a contradiction in terms. Yet she has chosen to do just that in an instance of what literary scholar Sophie McCall terms "impossible necessity."[39] Colonialism's assault on Indigenous language is at the heart of why "a lot of the older people found it really difficult to share their memories, their history, to non-Native people." It is why "that's been a real hurdle for us as a people." Yet Chi-chia undertook long ago to clear that hurdle. She began sharing ɬaʔamɪn history with audiences many years before she started this project. And she did so in English. She did not contemplate producing this book in Sliammon and for reasons of accessibility was initially reluctant even to include Sliammon-language sections.

Elsie's overriding concern with accessibility mirrors that of other Indigenous Elders, such as Harry Robinson, Angela Sidney, Annie Ned, and Kitty Smith – all fluent speakers of their Indigenous languages who chose to narrate told-to histories in English. Each of these Elders came to their decision in the wake of the near-annihilation of their mother tongue at the hands of residential schools and other colonial policies. They knew they would reach a much smaller audience if they presented their stories in a linguistic orthography with literal translations than if they were to, as Julie Cruikshank put it, "provide their own English translations."[40] It is a tragedy that any Elder willing to share valuable knowledge must choose between reaching an audience and communicating in her mother tongue. And it is important to respect whatever decision the Elder reaches as a result of this difficult, even painful, cost-benefit analysis. To second-guess their decision reproduces the long-standing pattern that I referred to above, in which settlers perennially discount Indigenous people's capacity to know their own interests. Archaic standards of purity would not be far behind, with their implication that "real" oral narratives can be told only in languages hardly anyone can understand and even fewer can read, an implication that would ensure the marginal status of these narratives in perpetuity. Elsie and these other narrators are all gifted storytellers in English. Just as the anthropologist Bruce Miller points out that contemporary Coast Salish people "are not simply lesser versions of their ancestors,"[41] stories told in English are not simply lesser versions of those told by earlier generations.

Chi-chia makes the considerable effort required to share the history and teachings in English, because she believes doing so can help those working to heal some of colonialism's damage.[42] As she explained later in her conversation with Janet, the institutions of school, church, and government inculcated ɬaʔamɩn and other Indigenous people with profoundly negative self-images that continue to reverberate: "And there's been a stigma placed on Indian people. You know, the 'natives,' like we were wild, we were running around naked. We had to be civilized. And all those *negative* kinds of messages. On the children. After they've been transformed or taught something *totally* different. How the government had the power to do that is beyond me. You know, in a short period of time, to change people's thinking of how we think about ourselves as a people, to become ashamed of who we were, of who we are. You know. And that's exactly how it was! You were all of a sudden ashamed to be Indian. It's not good to be Indian. If you're Indian you're dirty, you're lazy, you don't know nothing, you're dumb! And that went into the school system. It went to the churches. That's how the government enforced that. When I used to work, I've seen correspondence going way back, how the Department of Indian Affairs viewed us as a people: 'Those lazy good-for-nothing Indians. Those bums. Blah blah blah.' And that just used to make me *so* angry. It's like somebody came with the ugly brush and painted us over. And we are *all* lazy. We're *all* dependent on the system. Well, who made us dependent on the system? They did. You know? But that was not good enough. Now they're gonna take us and reshape us and remould us. So it's quite a challenge because once you've gone so far down this path, where from a child – maybe in my mother's time – especially the older generation have been brainwashed. That it's not good to be Indian: 'Now you are going to be this way.' And taking away *our* beliefs, our culture, our spirituality, our respect for the Creator. We've been told, 'What are you honouring the tree for?

You're stupid? What are you honouring the sun for? You're stupid? What are you honouring that salmon for? That's stupid!' You know? All of those things were, like, cut off. Those kinds of beliefs that my ancestors grew up with, to be respectful to *everything* around you. And all of a sudden you're told – your children are told – that's a no-no. That's ridiculous. So you're brainwashed not to be doing those things, not to think that way. Or that it's a sin. It's all these things, you know, 'This is the way now you're going to believe. You believe that this way, you're going to go to hell for sure!' They just totally rearranged our thinking, our lifestyle."

Chi-chia then drew a direct connection between recovering from the impact of these degrading messages and taking pride in one's history. Taking pains to point out that everyone has a right to know and treasure their own history, she said, "I know we can never go back and live our lifestyle we used to. But I think in order to take pride in our history as a people – which we all should! – I don't care if we're First Nations people, we're Chinese, we're Japanese, we're German, we're whoever we are, we all need to take pride in our own history. I'm not saying we're the only ones, as First Nations people, that we should be proud of our history. We *all* should have that. To be who we are. To be proud of our ancestors. Of where they came from, our history, our rich history. We each bring something to this world of ours. And one should not come along and say, 'No! You don't count. Your ancestors don't count.' Just like those trees in the forest. You know, you've got all kinds of different trees and growth in whatever have you up there. The cedar tree's no better than the other trees out there, or the alder tree is no better than any other tree. *Every one of those* serves a purpose. And you compare that to people. That's what we are. We're a mixed bag of people. But one should not overtake the other. There may be more bad weeds, I don't know! *[laughs]*"

Chi-chia's direct experience of these colonial attacks on her practice, belief, and history fed her desire to write a book. As she explained to Janet, she wanted to offer her grandchildren a counternarrative to these negative colonial stereotypes: "I've always wanted to write this – to document the history as I remember it. It's just that I've never really had the time, or, I guess, the know-how to write a book. You know, and I've said that to different family members of mine. They say, 'Yeah, we have to do that.' But they're so busy too with their jobs and other things. My grandson Davis is a really a smart young man. Him and my granddaughter Harmony. She's really smart. She's just very educated, but yet she has so much respect for who she is. Both Davis and her are part – their dads are non-Native. So, but they have a lot of respect for their – for the Native culture. And I'm *really* proud over that fact. That they're both from both worlds. One is just as important as the other. And they always want to learn more about. So we quite often sit and talk about, you know – they're really wanting to understand. Because I think the things they learn through school and university are sometimes biased. And so they come back to me and they want to know *my* version, or how I remember. So we sit and talk about that and compare. And, 'Yeah! We have to do a book! We really need to do this!' And then we don't. They get busy. Davis just went back to school. He's done four years of university. He's gone back to school again, just started back last week. So I'm really glad he's doing that. He wants to go in the teaching area. And Harmony's working and very busy. And my grandson Dillon – that's Harmony's brother – he's good at the language. He remembers a lot of the words that he learned while going to school. And when he comes home, you know, we'll exchange words. He remembers! He doesn't forget. So there are some that will probably want to carry on and carry the language and use it. But it's hard to use it when you got nobody to talk to. And then you start to lose it."

Coming full circle here to the question of language, Chi-chia then explained to Janet her belief that for those now living with the reality of the loss of Sliammon as a mother tongue, the history and teachings narrated in English can be carried forward as a kind of proxy: "But even if our children don't speak the language fluently as my grandparents did, I think as long as they know the history, as long as they know that there was a rich history, that we come from a rich history – this is the *true* history of our people, you know. It's not what's in a lot of books or whatever written document. This is the true history of who we are as a ɬaʔamın people. I think that's what they need. It's not to say we're better than anyone else. It's just that here is the true history. Because you know, there are books in the school about ɬaʔamın people or the coastal people. But it's not really detailed. So how do you condense the history, to bring out the things that need to be reported? Yeah. I think that there *is* a history. That there is something good, how people lived and how they lived with what they had. How they survived. The tools they had. The things they worked with. It's the same, I would say, with other cultures. Like even the farmers in Alberta or Saskatchewan – how did they survive? There's books about that. They had a hard life too. When they first lived there.

How did they survive? You know? What kind of tools did they have? What kind of food did they have? Where did they go to school? All those things. That's their history. There are generations of them now, there. So *we* also have a history." The deceptively simple statement that ɬaʔamɪn people have a history constitutes Elsie's refusal to accept the stigma cast by generations of colonizers. She makes the powerful assertion that ɬaʔamɪn people's lives and stories are not worth less than those of settlers.

This claim to equal worth, of the right to a history, is what she means by "the true history." In making this claim, she challenges the priests, schoolteachers, and Indian Affairs employees whom she encountered throughout her life, men and women who, though they did not understand ɬaʔamɪn ways, pronounced upon them nonetheless. Furthermore, she challenges scholars who write histories based upon colonial sources without consideration of Indigenous perspectives. Chi-chia's own narration of ɬaʔamɪn history, in contrast, derives from her direct experience of events as she lived them and of teachings as she learned them. The result is what she refers to as the "true history." She does not, however, make a claim to an objective or universal truth, and she would not want to be misunderstood as doing so. Her comparisons with the history of other peoples (the Chinese, Japanese, Germans, Prairie farmers) and her metaphor of so many trees in a forest demonstrate her sensitivity toward this issue and clarify that her bid is for the equality, not superiority, of ɬaʔamɪn history. Moreover, she uttered these statements about "the true history" moments after specifying that she wanted to write a book that would document "the history as I remember it." Where some might see dissonance between her claims to relate the "true history" and "the history as I remember it," for Chi-chia, there is no contradiction. The history as she remembers it *is* true history because she experienced and learned it directly. By making a truth claim for the value and validity of her experience as a ɬaʔamɪn woman, Chi-chia refuses colonizers' claims to know more about Indians than Indians know about themselves. Moreover, she does not claim to know the truth for all ɬaʔamɪn people, who, in her view, have their own lived experiences and thus their own true histories to narrate. Elsie literally speaks back to colonial messengers of the last century with this true history as she remembers it. She does so because, as she puts it, family and community members "need" the possibility to know and live the teachings. Members of the non-Indigenous public need the opportunity to see that ɬaʔamɪn people have history and teachings that are of value and that work for them. And all audiences need to overturn old colonial stereotypes and to heal their damage. These outcomes are not automatic, of course, but depend upon the successful practice of transformational listening by audience members.

Chi-chia's ideas as she recorded them in 2006 with Janet were the product of many years of thought about a project such as this. She had long discussed the idea with family, friends, and scholars. She and Harmony, in particular, spent a lot of time talking about it after Harmony came home to live with Chi-chia after graduating from Simon Fraser University with an English degree in 2004. Over the next year, Harmony's job with the Sliammon First Nation's culture and language program entailed working with Chi-chia on language recordings and cultural classes, work that fostered ongoing conversations about the possibility of a book. But in 2005, Harmony moved back to Vancouver, and collaborating on the book at such a distance seemed unmanageable.

In 2007, Chi-chia took the first concrete steps to begin work on the book. While reminiscing at a wake with her friend Arlette Raaen, then principal of Malaspina University-College in Powell River (now Vancouver Island University), she reiterated her desire to write a book. Arlette's husband, Chris McNaughton, piped up and volunteered Arlette's assistance. She was thrilled when Elsie accepted. Elsie subsequently made plans with Arlette to begin recording and asked Harmony to collaborate too. Janet meanwhile offered the use of her digital audio recorder. The book project was born, and with it an extended journey of learning and friendship that would draw in not only these four women but also other members of Elsie's extended family and me.

INFANCY: RECORDING THE STORIES

Chi-chia, Arlette, and Janet began their work together in June 2007 and continued over the next year and a half. They made audio recordings when Janet was available to bring her equipment. Arlette remembers a sense of urgency to the work because Elsie was experiencing some health difficulties. Consequently, when Janet – and by extension, her recording equipment – were unavailable, Arlette and Elsie continued, with Arlette taking detailed notes on her laptop while Elsie narrated. Arlette subsequently created a typescript of each session, based on either her notes or the audio recordings. The resulting texts were close approximations of Elsie's words but not verbatim transcripts. Arlette and Harmony discussed possible ways to organize the material into chapters, and the subsequent draft manuscript was shared with some of Elsie's children and grandchildren. In reviewing the manuscript, the family shared an overall observation that it didn't "sound" like Chi-chia. Reading her spoken words written on the page, they realized they wanted themselves and future generations of readers to hear Chi-chia's voice, and to get a sense of her character, tone, and sense of humour from the book. Harmony suggested to Chi-chia and Arlette that they ask my opinion, and Chi-chia gave permission to send me a copy of the draft text.

Harmony and I had stayed in touch since she was an undergraduate in my history classes at Simon Fraser University, and I had met her grandmother a number of times – first at Harmony's graduation ceremony and later when I interviewed her about her experiences of seasonal migration and mobility. From my perspective, the draft manuscript was full of important and fascinating historical information. Although I was unaware of the discussions the extended family had been having about voice, I also noticed that the text did not sound like Elsie when I read it. I replied to Harmony by email with a set of questions about the goals of the book, how Elsie wanted her voice represented, and what audiences she wanted to reach.

Elsie and her family's interest in representing the orality of her words on the written page had emerged as the project progressed to the point of a first draft. After further discussion, the participants agreed to foreground Chi-chia's voice in the next draft. To that end, Harmony volunteered to become more actively involved, and soon afterwards, Elsie, Harmony, and Harmony's mother, Jeannie, visited me at home in Vancouver. Elsie asked whether I would work with Harmony to revise the existing manuscript and help get it published. I agreed, naively confident that we could complete the project in a few months. I then met with Elsie, Harmony, and Arlette to discuss Elsie's wishes for the book in greater detail. I brought a few autobiographical and told-to narratives so Elsie could consider some possible formats.[43] She reacted visually to the texts: she disliked the look of books with a lot of orthographic symbols; she liked the look of those with ample photographs. She also explained her frustration with the challenge of fully expressing the teachings in English, and we discussed including some stories in Sliammon. She was very clear about accessibility being a priority for her. She also set the tone for the collaborative process to come. She felt she had done the hard work by telling the stories. Now, she wanted the rest of us to hurry up and get the book done. Although everyone wanted the project completed as quickly as possible, we agreed on the need to work from verbatim transcripts in order to ensure that the book sounded like Elsie. Representing oral speech on a written page requires someone with a talented ear who can interpret which punctuation best conveys the sound, spirit, and intent of the oral telling. Transcription is closer to the creative process of translation between languages than we usually recognize.[44] Indeed, oral speech and the written word can be conceived of as different languages. For this task of transcription, we hired the writer and poet Marguerite Pigeon, whose transcription of my earlier interview with Elsie, all of us agreed, captured the sound of her voice beautifully.

Having sent the existing audio recordings to Marguerite, Harmony and I planned a trip to Sliammon to work with Chi-chia and Arlette to make audio recordings of the previously told stories that had been documented solely with notes. I was eight months pregnant with my third child and had my two-year-old daughter in tow. I watched her play with friends on the beach from the shade of Chi-chia's enclosed front porch, where Chi-chia, Harmony, Arlette, and I worked. We began these recording sessions by asking Elsie to talk about one of the subjects she had previously narrated to Arlette. By this time, we had a provisional chapter structure in mind, and we organized our sessions along those lines. For example, Harmony prompted, "And we're recording for Chapter 9 on community work. So we probably, Chi-chia, wanted to start with, like, your earliest kind of work that you were doing for paid wages." Elsie launched easily from such prompts into lengthy accounts of the same stories she had previously narrated. After speaking for a while, she often concluded with a general statement: "Yeah, so all that is history." At such points, we sometimes asked her to elaborate upon something she had mentioned in passing, particularly if Arlette's notes indicated she had previously narrated it in greater detail. This technique worked well, and over the course of a few days, we recorded all the unrecorded subject matter that Chi-chia had previously shared. When these new audio recordings were complete, we sent them to Marguerite for transcription.

A number of times during the recording sessions, one of us asked Chi-chia about topics that she had not discussed in the original sessions with Janet and Arlette. Harmony was curious about certain stories she had heard growing up. I was interested in topics that spoke to gaps in the academic historiography. Chi-chia's responses to such inquiries were rich but almost invariably off the record. The one exception was her response to a question posed by Harmony about what Chi-chia refers to as her grandfather's "predictions" – that material now comprises Chapter 5. In every other instance, Chi-chia deemed the information inappropriate as content for this book. At first I believed this was because the information was politically – or personally – charged, and sometimes this was true. But more fundamentally, I came to realize, these stories did not further the goal of sharing ʔəms taʔaw. When Elsie selected content, the principles of respect and self-care were paramount. Speaking in ways that might harm would be in accord with neither. Nor would telling stories that were not fully hers to tell. The tremendous care and intention with which Chi-chia had narrated the first round of stories for the book became even clearer to me at this point. Through subsequent recording sessions, she remained committed to communicating ʔəms taʔaw, declining to include material that was at cross-purposes with this goal. As she narrated, she was not only sharing the teachings; she was living them.

Storytelling always involves an audience. In theory, all of Chi-chia's audio recordings had the same audience: the imagined reader of an eventual book. In practice, however, she told these stories to various combinations of Arlette, Janet, Harmony, me, and occasionally other friends and family. Not surprisingly, then, she varied her storytelling style. In the early recordings Chi-chia used few Sliammon words, but in later sessions she frequently invoked Sliammon terms and phrases. Perhaps this was because of our interim conversations about a bilingual component of the book; perhaps it was because she felt more comfortable speaking Sliammon in front of Harmony; perhaps a bit of both. When Chi-chia did not provide an English translation for these Sliammon words and phrases herself, we have done so in the notes. Chi-chia also spoke at greater length in later recordings. Perhaps we asked fewer or different questions at that stage; perhaps she felt more fluent in front of Harmony; perhaps a bit of both. She also sometimes personalized the stories for Harmony, pointing out, for example, that such and such happened when "your grandfather," that is, Chi-chia's husband, was young. Chi-chia also tended to situate herself in time and place. All her references to "here" or "this place" or "over there" are in relation to her home on the Sliammon reserve. And comments to the effect of "like I was talkin' about before" refer to previous conversations – some recorded, others not – which do not necessarily appear in this book in the order in which they occurred. When she situated herself in time more specifically – e.g., "last week" – we indicated the specific date in the notes. Harmony and I decided to retain these personal, geographical, and temporal references in order to remind readers (rather than ask you to forget) that these stories were recorded with a range of participants over a lengthy period.

Working on this project taught me several times over never to underestimate the barriers to transformational listening. Harmony's and my visit to Sliammon coincided with the hundredth anniversary of the founding of the Powell River townsite. Chi-chia had been invited to speak at a public event associated with the celebration. When we noticed that the local magazine, *Powell River Living,* had devoted its latest issue to the anniversary, we all thumbed through it, at first with interest and then with frustration. In the entire issue, there was no mention of the ɬaʔamɪn people upon whose territory the townsite was established in 1910. There was no mention of tiyskʷat, the ɬaʔamɪn village that the Powell River townsite displaced. There was no mention of the ɬaʔamɪn inhabitants of tiyskʷat or of the legal challenge to their alienation from the site that was still ongoing a century later. Instead, the anniversary issue evoked images of an empty place, a wilderness that lay dormant until ambitious and heroic pioneers arrived to develop it. We were dismayed and surprised at this erasure. This magazine frequently features sensitive and informative articles about ɬaʔamɪn people and history, and Chi-chia has even appeared on its cover! But when it came to Powell River's *history,* ɬaʔamɪn people and territory somehow vanished.[45] Never had Chi-chia's desire to convey the fact that *"we* also have a history" seemed more relevant.

Shortly after this, the difficulties of listening, being heard, and knowing we've been heard became apparent to me again from a new angle. Under Canadian law, Janet held the copyright to the original audio recordings because she had operated the recording device.[46] I suggested that Chi-chia get a written release in anticipation of future publication. I contacted Janet, and our brief conversation revealed that she and Chi-chia held different assumptions about how licensing for the recordings might work going forward. Both women were surprised and dismayed to learn of this gap in understanding. After dozens of hours of talking and listening, a sense of mutual trust had grown, yet each woman still took away distinct understandings of what that trust implied with respect to the use of the recordings. Each felt – for her own particular reasons – invested in the material, and both were hurt to learn that their assumptions and goals were not shared. Beyond hurt feelings, this situation jeopardized the book project; without clear copyright, Elsie could not use the material she had recorded with

Janet in a book. Fortunately, in terms of Elsie's ability to use the recordings, this story of mishearing has a happy outcome. After a number of conversations variously involving Elsie, Harmony, Arlette, and Janet, Janet released copyright to Elsie without retaining a licence or rights to use the recordings for her own purposes as she had hoped to do. The priority that Janet placed on her relationship with Chi-chia is, I think, the reason the situation was resolved as it was. In this instance, the project collaborators were able to arrive at a mutual agreement through respectful dialogue. Such an outcome should not be taken for granted. There is, unfortunately, a long history of researchers in many parts of the world holding steadfastly to the belief that they should retain control over "data" collected from Indigenous "informants" in the name of a greater good. Many researchers consciously or unconsciously refuse the opportunities for transformational listening that their work provides. Consequently, they conclude their time in the field with their underlying assumptions – about power, responsibility, and capacity – intact. Preventing such situations is admittedly the intention of the university ethics review policies discussed above that require a band council resolution (BCR). However, a BCR would not necessarily have prevented the misunderstanding between Janet and Elsie. Moreover, Chi-chia's response to the miscommunication with Janet was not to wish that somebody or something had protected her. She saw the situation as an interpersonal one that she had the right and ability to attempt to resolve herself. She still finds insulting any suggestion that she needs a BCR to protect her. The ethical question here turns not on the need for policies or institutions to "protect" Indigenous people – something the Indian Act was, after all, also designed to do – but on the need for researchers to respect Indigenous people's rights to make decisions for themselves. Engaging in a respectful relationship is a precondition for – yet is no guarantee of – communication across difference. The disappointment and frustration that grew from this episode reminds me more than ever of the elusiveness of transformational listening.

THE TODDLER YEARS: COMPOSING A NARRATIVE

Elsie's words had already undergone one translation: from oral to written form. Roughly thirty-six hours of audio now existed as 350 single-spaced typescript pages, or over 273,000 words. (In fact, this was the second translation, if we recall the self-translation entailed in her English narration.) Now Harmony and I began the next translation: turning the transcripts into a format accessible for readers. Extending the life history metaphor to refer to the "toddler years" here might seem a conceit. And I do not want to be misunderstood: I am not suggesting that the interventions Harmony and I made with the transcripts bestowed "maturity" on Chi-chia's words or helped earlier phases of the work "grow up." My metaphor refers to how the nature of the work changed as the project reached its next life stage. Just as, after the first draft, a new priority had emerged with respect to voice, now the priority of readability required attention. Just as toddlers change as they learn to interact with a wider circle of people beyond their immediate families, at this point we worked to facilitate the circulation of Chi-chia's stories beyond her family and friends – to an interested reading public, students, and scholars.

Harmony and I continued to seek Chi-chia's input and guidance at this stage. Chi-chia stressed that the transcripts needed to be "organized," as she put it, so as to be accessible to readers in a way that verbatim transcripts are not. Those who knew Chi-chia could "hear" her voice clearly in the verbatim transcripts, but we all realized that readers who did not know her personally would feel differently. Students to whom I assigned a selection of minimally edited transcripts complained that the literalness of speech on the page was frustrating to decipher. Chi-chia emphasized that she wanted a readable final product in which her voice came through clearly. Specifically, she directed us to remove verbal distractions such as "uh" and "um" and to ensure she did not appear to repeat herself. But she refrained from becoming involved in the composition of chapters. She made it clear that this was the work she expected of Harmony and me, and she nudged us to hurry up. Claims by collaborators that the narrator asked them to make decisions have been dubbed a "drama of ritual abdication" by one critic, and they are frequent enough features of introductions to told-to narratives that they attract charges of disingenuousness.[47] But Chi-chia's preferred division of labour did not at all imply that she was "unconcerned with the textuality of the published work"[48] – she simply wanted us to do our share.[49] She would review and provide feedback once we had something more polished to show her.

Writing about the textualization of oral narratives, scholars sometimes lament each adjustment to the spoken word as an incremental loss, a distancing from and an act of violence against the purity of the original utterance.[50] And, in a certain sense, they are correct: the written page cannot replicate an oral performance. At the same time, the translation from oral to written might be more usefully seen as a trade-off rather than an absolute loss. Gains can also be achieved in the process of turning oral speech into text. These might include sharing knowledge with a wider audience, and the oft-cited and debated benefit of "preservation." Of course these gains exist as such only if the narrator judges them so. Elders themselves are aware of the potential trade-offs, and they weigh the pros and cons of written formats just as they do when deciding whether to narrate in English. For example, although the renowned Lushootseed Elder Vi Hilbert called printed oral histories "shallow versions" of the originals, she pursued a vigorous agenda to publish them.[51] In Chi-chia's case, her desire to share the teachings was paramount.

Because we respect Chi-chia's oral style and voice a great deal, Harmony and I found it daunting to work with her words to compose a written narrative organized into chapters. Risking the extension of the toddler metaphor a bit further, we were wobbly on our feet as we started to look for the appropriate path – one that preserved the orality and style of the original narration while achieving readability. The work we did with the transcripts at this stage is often termed "editorial," a term I avoid because I find it misleading. Our work was more compositional than editorial, much closer than I had first anticipated to the process of crafting a historical argument. Essentially, we set to work to use the collected transcripts to elaborate an argument. Historians do this work all the time using an array of sources including documents, images, material objects, and oral interviews. The difference here was that Harmony and I were not attempting to answer a research question that either of us had set individually. Instead, we worked to craft a narrative that bent to the arc of Chi-chia's desire to share ʔəms taʔaw. Working in this way required us first to understand the teachings and then to convey them through the composition of the manuscript. This necessarily dialogical process required Harmony and me to remain in conversation not only with each other, with Chi-chia, and with the transcripts, but also with our own underlying assumptions. This method was not so dissimilar from how I would study the underlying and implicit meanings in any historical source, except for the crucial collaborative dimension that required me to focus on a shared rather than an individual goal. I was still very much doing my accustomed work as a historian, but following what scholars have termed an "Indigenous methodology," that is, a methodology that proceeded from and remained rooted in tribally specific knowledge.[52] For example, as a historian, I was at first drawn to what seemed to me the obvious historical relevance of the events of Elsie's life: attending residential school, working as a migrant labourer, socializing in racially segregated pubs and theatres. But over time, I came to understand that these life history events were inseparable from, and indeed subordinate to, the teachings. Chi-chia returned again and again – in the transcripts and in our ongoing conversations – to self-care, respect, healing, and spirituality. These were not topics about which I would have ever envisioned writing a book on my own. In retrospect, it took me much longer than I care to admit to understand what this book is *really* about.

The challenges of first reaching a common understanding among ourselves, and then finding an effective means to communicate that understanding to readers, meant that sometimes Harmony and I assessed certain material as extraneous only later to realize its relevance. Sometimes, a "good" idea suddenly became a "bad" one, as when I realized that a chapter structure I had proposed cast the historical events and the teachings as distinct categories and thus undermined the argument of the book as a whole. On other occasions, apparent contradictions in the transcript resolved themselves when, after speaking with Chi-chia, Harmony and I realized that the "contradictions" were the result of *our* misperception rather than Chi-chia's inconsistency. Over the lengthy process that ensued we went through the transcripts line by line and experimented with many chapter structures and textual arrangements. We tried our best to forestall potential misreadings as we carefully considered the implications of numerous approaches to structure, content, and editing. I discuss each of these areas in turn below, although in reality they intersected in complex ways and our decision-making process was more spiral than linear.

Chapter Structure
Structurally, we sought to highlight four narrative threads in this book. We attempted to embed their multiple interconnections in the book's architecture by interspersing them throughout. Chronologically organized chapters form one thread. In these chapters, Chi-chia narrates events from her life history. A second (though not secondary) thread consists of ʔəms taʔaw around particular topics: education, prenatal and neonatal care, grief, and spirituality. Although they are nominally divided into separate chapters, there is no clear line between the life history and the teachings, as I've noted above. Chi-chia narrates many life history events as examples of the teachings, and for her,

the teachings and the history are inextricable.[53] A third narrative thread comprises a specific form of teachings that Chi-chia refers to as legends. These are not archaic myths or children's fables;[54] as Chi-chia puts it, "They are what guided my life." We placed the legends where they overlap thematically in some way with the preceding chapter. That said, because multiple potential meanings can be taken from the legends, other textual arrangements were equally feasible and would have highlighted different connections. The fourth thread is made up of stories told by Chi-chia in the Sliammon language. These are selections from longer recordings made during her many years of collaboration with the linguist Honoré Watanabe.[55] We situated the Sliammon-language narratives in proximity to related stories told in English and presented them in a bilingual format, which is explained in the user-friendly "A Note on the Sliammon Language," which appears in the preliminaries of this book. Please take the time to consult it. The Sliammon-language narratives are not intended for the benefit of linguists alone. Chi-chia, Harmony, Honoré, and I hope that readers will not skip over them but instead will consider them carefully. The English translations provide a glimpse of the differences between English and Sliammon syntax and style. We hope that the presence of the Sliammon language on these pages reminds readers that the conversations with grandparents and Elders that Elsie recounts occurred not in English but in her mother tongue, that Elsie grew up immersed in a Sliammon-speaking world that conveyed ɬaʔamɩn ways of being and knowing that can only be approximated in English. Thus, we also hope these Sliammon-language narratives give readers a small sense of the tremendous act of translation that Chi-chia undertook in order to narrate these stories in English.

For similar reasons, we have, after a tremendous amount of consideration, decided to represent the Sliammon words that appear throughout this book in a linguistic writing system, or orthography. Until the penultimate stages of the project, we intended to limit the orthography to the Sliammon-language sections, and to use the Roman alphabet to create phonetic approximations for Sliammon words in the other chapters. Although such a practice would have been less scholarly, we believed it would be more accessible to general readers. However, our attempts to avoid orthography proved unsatisfying. Sliammon words have no standard spelling in the Roman alphabet, and family members themselves had varying ideas on how to write Sliammon words and names. Moreover, the lesson that the historian

Susan Roy learned from the Musqueam Elder Fran Guerin seemed increasingly relevant: "The phonetic representations of the language gave the speaker a false sense that they were pronouncing words properly. It was better to represent Aboriginal languages in all their complexity."[56] Recall that understanding difference, rather than erasing it, is an essential part of transformational listening. Accordingly, we have used the linguistic orthography for all Sliammon-language words and names. The one exception to this is "Chi-chia," a term that family members commonly use and write this way. Please refer to the pronunciation guide in the "Note on the Sliammon Language" for assistance with sounding out these words.

Chapter Content

In terms of the content of the chapters, our ideal was to leave the flow of Chi-chia's oral presentation uninterrupted. However, alternative versions of the same story contained different and often complementary details. Chi-chia was clear that she did not want to appear to be repeating herself, so including multiple versions of stories was not an option. At the same time, omitting significant points of illustration or information did not seem desirable either. This problem resolved itself as we studied Chi-chia's narrative style. We saw that whenever she told a particular story, she used not only very similar phrasing, but similar structure as well. In several stories about baskets, for example, she first noted what beautiful baskets her grandmother and other women of her generation had made, then talked about the technical challenges of root digging, and then connected that work to ʔəms taʔaw. We felt we could retain Chi-chia's narrative structure while combining multiple tellings of the same story in a version that was either clearer or more complete than any single recorded version. We did this as sparingly as we could and found it more necessary in some chapters than others. Ultimately, we did not follow abstract principles so much as we adjusted to the pragmatics of using diverse material recorded at different times with different people. The result is that some chapters consist of two or three long selections of narrative while others are pieced together from many different tellings. Within given chapters, we organized material thematically rather than chronologically for the most part, because this fit better with how Chi-chia tells the stories.

Some audio recordings contained a great deal more dialogue than others, but even when this was the case, we have not included that dialogue here. Scholars from Bakhtin onwards have stressed that a dialogical form is itself constitutive of and cannot be separated from content. Thinking through this principle, Harmony and I considered including at least some of the questions in the text. We did not do so first and foremost because a question-and-answer format did not fit Chi-chia's vision of how the book should look on the printed page. Second, Harmony and I noted that time and again, after responding to a question or engaging in a side conversation, Chi-chia returned to precisely where she had left off. The shape and selection of her stories was not influenced by the questions and comments that arose during recording sessions. Chi-chia narrated her life history and teachings with a firm, clear, and consistent intention, an intention from which interruptions did not sway her. In short, she did not speak without first thinking, and once she began to speak, she did not lose her train of thought. Ultimately, we feel that rather than feigning fluent oration where none existed, removing the questions will help readers detect her narrative flow more easily than if they were to read the verbatim transcripts.

Line Editing

The next stage was the line editing. With the content blocked into chapters, we focused on the details of Chi-chia's oral speech. In order to maintain some of the orality of the original tellings without creating too much distraction, we kept many of her most characteristic oral markers, particularly phrases such as "you know" and her tendency to complete stories or thoughts with "yeah." We have also preserved her tendency to use a rising intontation at the end of important statements to seek agreement from the listener. In written form, these moments are punctuated with question marks, although they are not true questions. They do not indicate uncertainty on Chi-chia's part. Rather, they represent moments when she wants to stress the importance of what she is saying and, so, checks in with the listener, as if to say, "Am I making myself clear?" or "Do you know what I mean?" We retained incomplete phrases or thoughts in places where she was clearly working through her ideas out loud. We occasionally inserted non-verbal markers in square brackets, such as "*[laughs]*," to clarify the emotional tenor. Italics indicate heavy emphasis on a particular word or phrase. Ellipses have been used to indicate a pause in speech and not as indicators of where material has been removed. On rare occasions we clarified the subject of a sentence by checking with

Chi-chia on her preferred wording and replacing "he" or "she" with a more specific descriptor such as "my husband." At her request, we removed incidental expressions such as "uh" and false starts. The reactions of family members have been our touchstone for evaluating the voice embodied in this written text, and we have been gratified that those who know Chi-chia well say they hear her on the pages that follow.[57] We authors hope you will feel likewise after reading the book, even though you may have never met Chi-chia in person.

With a full version of the manuscript assembled, Harmony and I travelled to Powell River in the summer of 2012 so Chi-chia could evaluate what we had done. The three of us discussed this introduction, possible Sliammon narratives to include, and, once again, the title of the book. It was at this point that Chi-chia expressed to us the importance of ʔəms taʔaw being part of the book's title. She read through the entire manuscript, marking it up with sticky notes to indicate her changes, all of which we subsequently made. These changes varied from clarifications of meaning to adjustments of word choice to removal of content. Arlette and other family members also reread the manuscript at this stage and provided feedback.

ADOLESCENCE AND ADULTHOOD: SHARING THE STORIES WITH READERS

Adolescence and adulthood are life stages when an individual enters the world independently. In the case of a book, this occurs after publication when it begins to circulate within popular and scholarly circles. As with our children, we as authors cannot know for certain what journey this book will take or how it will be received in various circles. But again as with children, we can orient it toward destinations where it may live its (we hope, extended) textual life. In my listening, Chi-chia speaks particularly to readers interested in the Coast Salish, in understandings of tradition and history, in women's history, and in reconciliation, healing, and Indigenous resurgence. I discuss these topics in turn below.

Living Coast Salish, Living ɬaʔamɩn

All of us involved in writing this book hope it moves widely among readers interested in Coast Salish peoples and places. Chi-chia's detailed experiential and geographically situated knowledge of ɬaʔamɩn practices and teachings has much to offer Coast Salish studies, a field that has flourished in recent decades.[58] As a ɬaʔamɩn Elder and as a woman, she speaks into multiple spaces within this literature.

The historical trajectory of scholarly attention to ɬaʔamɩn people is in many ways a microcosm of the trajectory of Coast Salish scholarship more broadly. Recent scholars have paid less attention to ɬaʔamɩn people and their neighbours than they have to central and southern Coast Salish peoples, much as earlier generations of scholars paid less attention to Coast Salish–speaking peoples than to other, particularly Wakashan-speaking, Northwest Coast peoples. In 2007, the publication of an edited collection, *Be of Good Mind: Essays on the Coast Salish,* simultaneously honoured both the influence of Suttles's 1987 watershed publication *Coast Salish Essays* and the intervening twenty years of rich scholarship on the Coast Salish that Suttles's work helped inspire. Scholarly interest in the Coast Salish over these decades focused on southern and central Coast Salish peoples, particularly the Stó:lō.[59]

Scholarly interest in the ɬaʔamɩn has been longer in coming. While their language has been amply documented and analyzed, Sliammon, Klahoose, and Homalco peoples have remained nearly absent from scholarly literature. Like so many Northwest Coast anthropology stories, this one has something to do with Franz Boas, or in this case, his absence. Boas conducted considerably less work with Coast Salish communities than with the "Kwakiutl," as he famously termed them.[60] Within his body of Coast Salish work, the closest he came to an investigation of Sliammon was his documentation of legends and vocabulary among the Island Comox, who spoke a dialect of the same language as the ɬaʔamɩn.[61] The historical accident of which communities Boas studied and which he did not has had a lasting influence on Northwest Coast anthropology and ethnohistory. Simply put, where Boas went, others often followed. It is not, after all, just historians who follow the archive.[62] Linguists have followed up the early work by Boas and Edward Sapir to generate a significant literature on the both the Island Comox and Mainland dialects.[63] Yet the ethnohistorical literature on the ɬaʔamɩn, Klahoose, and Homalco peoples has remained slight, despite the expanding number of studies on many other Coast Salish peoples.[64] Two studies constitute very nearly the entirety of the ethnohistorical corpus on ɬaʔamɩn people in the twentieth century. In 1936, Homer Barnett, a doctoral student in anthropology at the University of California Berkeley, conducted fieldwork at Sliammon for his dissertation, "The Coast Salish of British Columbia," which was published as a monograph in 1955.[65] The next anthropologists to work with ɬaʔamɩn individuals were Dorothy Kennedy and Randy Bouchard in the 1970s as part of the British Columbia Indian Language Project. Kennedy and Bouchard published an ethnography of the Island Comox, Klahoose, Homalco, and ɬaʔamɩn peoples – all of whom share a common language – titled *Sliammon Life, Sliammon Lands* in 1983.[66] Theirs is the only published, book-length scholarly study of any of these peoples. Relatively compact and accessible to a general audience, it is richly illustrated with photographs and includes a detailed list of place names. No further ethnohistorical work on the ɬaʔamɩn people was published before the turn of the twenty-first century.[67] Since then, a master's thesis and a number of scholarly articles have appeared.[68] More recently, an archaeological literature has emerged, and in 2012 and 2013, graduate students in an ethnohistory field school at Sliammon conducted research toward the goal of publishing a ɬaʔamɩn historical atlas.[69] Chi-chia's words thus move out toward readers at a moment of burgeoning scholarly interest in Coast Salish peoples in general, and in the ɬaʔamɩn people in particular.

Her contribution of a woman's knowledge and life experience is particularly valuable. Although Coast Salish women have been involved in extensive publishing projects of legends and oral narratives, they have not generally recorded their own life histories.[70] Most of the relatively few life histories of Coast Salish people are by or about men (none of whom are ɬaʔamɩn).[71] More broadly, scholars have recognized the need for more Indigenous women's narratives and oral histories.[72] Small as it is, the scholarly literature specifically on the ɬaʔamɩn still bears traces of the tendency to cast male experience as normative. Homer Barnett worked exclusively with male informants, and his resulting publication, *The Coast Salish of British Columbia,* extrapolated from men's knowledge and experience to make generalized claims about Coast Salish culture. Symptomatic of this, for example, is Barnett's general and rather cursory treatment of food and basketry, topics to which Chi-chia devotes extensive time, providing detailed, geographically specific accounts of how to preserve salmon, catch and dry herring, and harvest and prepare cedar roots. On the other hand, Chi-chia says little about hunting or salmon fishing, topics that preoccupied Barnett and that his informants discussed in detail.[73] Although Barnett seemed to sense that – with the interesting exception of Elsie's great-uncle Chief Tom – his informants lacked detailed ethnobotanical expertise, he did not connect this to his all-male sample.[74] Barnett was of his time, and his gendered emphasis on what

Wayne Suttles referred to as men's "food-getting methods" over women's equally important "food-storing methods" endured as a bias in the literature at least into the late 1960s, when Suttles commented on it.[75] Scholarly inquiry into ɬaʔamɪn women's knowledge in particular did not come until the 1970s with the work of Kennedy and Bouchard, work that has not been built upon until now.

As a life history, this book's format also makes a contribution to our understanding of Coast Salish peoples. Life narratives are particularly important to studies of the Coast Salish because individuals and families are the building blocks of Coast Salish societies. Coast Salish societies cohere over time through interconnected, gendered geographies of individual and family relationships. The Stó:lō oral historian Sonny McHalsie situates "family as a basis of nation."[76] Similarly, the networks of marriage, resource use, and labour that Chi-chia details are more than her personal life experiences; they are constitutive components of the ɬaʔamɪn people's territory and sovereignty. Her explanations of territory are stories about specific places where individual family members lived, and her explanations of the historical functioning of ɬaʔamɪn self-government are stories about discipline within the family unit. Thus, stories that might initially seem to be micro histories of families and individuals living in and throughout the territory in fact exemplify the macro category "Coast Salish." The accretion of such highly localized yet interconnected family histories is what renders the very category "Coast Salish" meaningful.

At the same time as Chi-chia expands and enriches our understanding of Coast Salish peoples, she also reminds us of some potential pitfalls of overrelying on categories such as "Coast Salish" as organizing principles. Such pitfalls date from the nineteenth century, when anthropologists first conceived of using culture and language areas as heuristic devices for studying Indigenous peoples. Influenced by the Boasian model of diffusion, early-twentieth-century Northwest Coast scholars cast Coast Salish peoples as inhabitants of a "receiver area" who had adopted their culture from the peoples of the more northerly, supposedly "core" areas. This logic misinterpreted unique aspects of Coast Salish life as absences or lacks; rather than possessing distinct forms of social organization, for example, Coast Salish people "lacked" the matrilineal clans documented among "core" peoples.[77] Moreover, as the historian Susan Roy notes, the historical recontextualization of "collected objects" – and, arguably by extension, of collected knowledge – "in anthropological exhibits and texts emphasized the category 'Coast Salish' and de-emphasized local identities, histories, and cultural meanings."[78] Roy's concern is with the work that early anthropological categorization performed upon specific Indigenous communities, in this case, the Musqueam. For people like the ɬaʔamɩn who were not studied by that first generation of anthropologists on the Northwest Coast, the implications of her point are no less acute. Indeed, Chi-chia has felt them in her own life. Throughout this book, she stresses the distinctiveness of ɬaʔamɩn ways when she explains leadership, governance, territory, spirituality, and power, topics discussed in the existing literature on the Coast Salish with almost exclusive reference to the central and southern peoples.[79]

Chi-chia's insistence on the distinctiveness of ɬaʔamɩn ways mirrors that of her grandfather's brother, tɑmɑ Timothy or "Chief Tom," Homer Barnett's main informant at Sliammon in 1936. In his monograph, Barnett commented on Chief Tom's wealth of knowledge, describing him as one of the four most knowledgeable informants with whom he had worked in a dozen Coast Salish communities across southwestern British Columbia.

> Three men were worked with at the Slaiäman or Powell River reserve. Two ... were finally abandoned in favor of Chief Tom to whom, along with Tommy Paul, Westly, and Mitchell, I am especially grateful for what little understanding I have of Salish culture. He was probably eighty years old. He still held to the traditional patterns, not desperately but for the honest good he found in them. A descendant of one of the most illustrious families in this region, he was conscious of his position as the leading representative of his people. Despite his years, he ... was ready to demonstrate enthusiastically the things of which he spoke.[80]

This characterization reveals the admiration Barnett came to feel for Chief Tom over time. Barnett's field notes, however, reveal that the working relationship between the two men was often characterized by frustration born of Chief Tom's refusal to accommodate Barnett's expectations for a normative Coast Salish culture. Well trained at Berkeley in the cultural diffusion approach of the day, Barnett approached his Coast Salish fieldwork expecting to find particular cultural practices in particular places, and he expected the people at Sliammon to dance, sing, wear masks, and potlatch in quite specific ways. Just as broader scholarly trends of the day positioned the Coast Salish as lacking "core" (i.e., monumental) elements of "Northwest

Coast culture," Barnett in turn viewed the ɬaʔamɪn through a lens that suggested they lacked "core" elements of "Coast Salish culture." This did not jibe with Chief Tom's world view. Reading Barnett's field notes today, it is apparent that although Barnett was listening to Chief Tom, Chief Tom knew he was not being heard, while Barnett was not hearing what he wanted.

Barnett's candid field notes contain emphatic, and sometimes amusing, expressions of the confusion and disappointment he felt when he could not find the Coast Salish practices that he believed should have been at Sliammon. For example, early on in his fieldwork there, Barnett recorded his interpretation of Chief's Tom's explanation of practices for honouring salmon by writing *"No first salmon rite."*[81] Barnett had the southern and central Coast Salish practice for welcoming sockeye in mind here. Chi-chia makes it clear that ɬaʔamɪn people welcomed salmon and other fish whenever they arrived.[82] Yet for Barnett, absent the description of a first salmon ceremony as he had heard related in other Coast Salish communities, the ɬaʔamɪn *lacked* a first salmon ceremony.

The mutual frustration between Barnett and Chief Tom escalated in their conversations about spiritual practices. Barnett was confused and disappointed at what he saw as a lack of "sacred" expression among the ɬaʔamɪn. He pressed Chief Tom repeatedly for information about practices that anthropologists had documented among other Coast Salish peoples, as well as among the Kwakwaka'wakw: masked winter dances and competitive gift exchanges. He asked Chief Tom leading questions and showed him photographs from elsewhere as illustrations of what he was looking for. Chief Tom's answers confirmed his familiarity with the ways of other peoples and his insistence on the distinctiveness of ɬaʔamɪn ways. On the question of whether the ɬaʔamɪn distributed blankets by throwing them from a platform in a "scramble," Barnett wrote: "Showed him the pictures of Cowichan potlatch from platform – *'not here,* Cowichan, Nanaimo.'"[83] And on the question of whether the ɬaʔamɪn practised a version of the hamatsa for which the Kwakwaka'wakw were better known, "Asked about the hamats he gave this ... *summertime, not winter* as he recognizes the Cape Mudges do."[84] Continuing to emphasize his surprise, Barnett wrote: *"No winter names* seems to know it as Cape Mudge – at least says he understands what I mean."[85] Chief Tom was well positioned to understand the distinctions between the "Cape Mudges" (the southernmost Kwakwaka'wakw) and the ɬaʔamɪn because his mother, qaʔaχstɑles, was from Cape Mudge and his father, Captain Timothy, was from Sliammon, as Barnett knew. After more than a dozen hand-written pages documenting Chief Tom's "lack" of expected response to his questions, Barnett concluded, "Either Tom is off his base or winter had little of the sacred to these people."[86] Barnett soon real-ized, however, if he had not already, that Tom was most certainly not "off his base." Barnett returned for further sessions with Chief Tom, remarking in his field notes that Chief Tom volunteered a great deal of detailed information without any prompting. Throughout these sessions, Barnett remained ever hopeful that the right information would emerge if he asked the right question in the right way. Chief Tom meanwhile, remained steadfast in his refusal to accommodate Barnett's expectations. The resulting climax of Barnett's frustration was something akin to ethnographic comedy: "Tom is all screwed up on winter dances or I am – *he says no winter spirit* singing. I can't get him to admit that a person ever sang his dreamed song or danced it. Says that's Cowichan. He is set upon the secrecy attaching to one's dreaming – but what the hell good is a song if you can't sing it?"[87]

By this point, Barnett admitted the possibility that his own lack of understanding clouded the situation. Nevertheless, he could not escape his own paradigm, which continued to cast the data that Chief Tom provided in terms of what it *lacked*. Barnett judged ɬaʔamɩn practices inadequate because they were unaccompanied by the expected com-plement of cultural expressions – "what the hell good is a song if you can't sing it?" – and ultimately characterized the winter ceremonial initiation rite of the Klahoose and ɬaʔamɩn as "but a partial imitation of the one to the south."[88] Subsequently, it was a short leap from Barnett's construction of this lack to the assumption by others that it represented a loss. If certain traits were normative for the Coast Salish, then their absence among the ɬaʔamɩn indicated that the ɬaʔamɩn had lost them – presumably because of the influence of the Church or other colonial forces.[89] Here again, the trajectory of scholarly assump-tions about the ɬaʔamɩn duplicates those toward Coast Salish peoples more broadly; many long believed they were too assimilated to be of scholarly interest.[90] For Barnett in particular, what stands out today is how strongly his disciplinary paradigm determined what he was able to hear. Although he wanted very much to listen to Chief Tom, whom he held in high regard, Barnett remained unable to grasp much of Chief Tom's meaning. His best efforts still did not enable him to hear in ways that contradicted his own intellectual framework.

Although unaware of Chief Tom's work with Barnett until this manuscript neared completion, Chi-chia has long been familiar with the contours and implications of Barnett's perspective on the Coast Salish. Reading his field notes aloud with Harmony and Chi-chia at Sliammon in June 2012 produced peals of laughter because they identified with the frustration that their ancestor clearly felt. Each woman has found herself in situations where she had to explain that a particular Coast Salish way is not the ɬaʔamɪn way, situations where she faced knowing looks or words from those who presumed to know better and assumed that the ɬaʔamɪn had lost their ways. Harmony and Chi-chia do not view ɬaʔamɪn ways as better than those of other Coast Salish peoples, but they are weary of the view that certain practices are normative for Coast Salish peoples. In the following chapters, for example, Chi-chia discusses winter dances and sweat lodges in this context. Wind-drying salmon and paying quarters to witnesses are other practices that she and Harmony have seen some people incorrectly generalize as universally Coast Salish. Having always insisted upon the specificity of ɬaʔamɪn ways, and having emphasized this point in her audio recordings, Chi-chia was gratified to see this same insistence on ɬaʔamɪn ways in the words of her ancestor.

Chi-chia speaks to what we could call the "separate but equal" nature of ɬaʔamɪn ways in more than one sense. She does so implicitly through the care and precision she brings to each account of ʔəms taʔaw as passed down to her by her grandparents and Elders. She does so explicitly when she distinguishes between the ɬaʔamɪn and other First Nations peoples. This distinction matters greatly to her because cultural sovereignty is linked to political sovereignty. For example, when Harmony and I asked her to speak about her understanding of territory, she launched into a remarkable narrative during which she spoke uninterrupted for nearly half an hour. (Those words open Chapter 1.) At one point, she moved from talking about territory to talking about cultural distinctiveness, and I mistakenly thought at first that she had moved on to a new topic: "Yeah, so when we talk about territories, I think it's really important to remember that, for me anyway, that I'm from the coast – I'm a Coast Salish person. But all Coast Salish people are not all the same. We're different. We all have our unique language, our dialect from other Coast Salish people, like the West Coast people or the people from Saanich or the people from North Island or way up north, Kingcome Inlet and all of these other groupings of people. They all have their own dialect. Along the coast here, like, Campbell River people have a different language from us. So we're not all Coast Salish in how some people see us to be. I'm Coast Salish. But I'm a ɬaʔamɪn person. And it's unique that we are three groupings of people, Klahoose and Homalco, that speak the same dialect."

She continued by specifying her audience, addressing those unfamiliar with the human and geographical landscape of the British Columbia coast. Conscious that the ways of some other Coast Salish peoples are better known than those of the ɬaʔamɪn and are thus sometimes taken as normative, she cautioned against undue conflation: "And I think that's really important to know – 'cause I think to a person that doesn't know, or is a non-Native person, or is a visitor from elsewhere – that we do not all speak the same dialect 'cause we're brown! You know, 'Oh yeah, that's an Indian person. They must be like this or like that, or they must speak this language.' And we're not. We have different traditional practices, styles of practices. We use different tools in how we practise our traditional ways. Our spiritual kinds of ceremonies is different in how we do it where I come from, through the teachings of my ancestors, my grandparents especially. That we practise differently than other tribes or bands of people. Theirs is different, different style, but unique to them. And it's important to remember to respect all of the other practices and how they do it, the tools they use."

To illustrate her point, she drew on the example of spiritual practices associated with the longhouse – often referred to as "winter dancing" or "spirit dancing" in scholarly literature. In so doing, she unknowingly echoed Chief Tom's insistence that this was never the ɬaʔamɪn way: "The longhouse. We don't have that in Sliammon. We never have. We never did. Ours was more the cleansing, the self-care, the taking care of yourself and getting your power, your spirit, by going off and living on your own off the land for as long as it takes." Then, tying her example explicitly back to the theme of territory, she clarified what she meant by "ours": "The same for Homalco and Klahoose people – we were the different grouping of people in the way we practise. Yeah." The ɬaʔamɪn, Klahoose, and Homalco were, in her words, "one people" before the bureaucratic colonial interventions of reserves and band lists. She distinguishes them from other Coast Salish peoples and, in so doing, demonstrates how language, territory, and practice converge to create community.

Chi-chia thus offers a nuanced and historicized commentary on categories of identity that are all too easily taken for granted. She reminds the reader that certain historical processes – the creation of Indian bands and band lists, for example – severed important connections, while at the same time she points out that other historical processes – the creation of "Coast Salish" as a category, for example – masked important distinctions. Over time, the bureaucratic interventions of the colonial state both divided and conflated, multiply misrepresenting ɬaʔamɪn people and ways. She reminds us that Indigenous people draw their physical and social boundaries in ways that will surprise us if we have come to rely too heavily on lines drawn by colonial bureaucrats (be they surveyors, Indian agents, or academics). Her account of colonialism's contradictory ramifications offers a case study of circumstances that have affected Indigenous peoples in multiple settler societies. Closer to home, she enriches and diversifies understandings of Coast Salish peoples by contributing her knowledge of ɬaʔamɪn ways. If we can listen carefully enough, more carefully than Barnett could, we will understand these ɬaʔamɪn ways as distinct unto themselves, as ʔəms taʔaw.

Living Teachings, Living History

In her accounts of ʔəms taʔaw, Chi-chia delineates change and continuity in similarly nuanced ways and in so doing speaks to debates about tradition, modernity, and culture. We should not mistake Chi-chia's insistence on "our" teachings – ʔəms taʔaw – for chauvinism or xenophobia. She has no objection to the adoption or adaptation of new practices. She is, in fact, deeply interested in other people's teachings and in attempts to adapt and apply them, particularly toward the goal of healing. But she promotes an understanding of new practices as the innovations that they are, rather than as resurrections of an imagined ɬaʔamɪn past. Her insistence on "the longhouse" as a foreign practice is a case in point. She is aware of the high stakes attached by many people to identifying fixed traits as characteristic of a given culture. And although Chi-chia is an expert on what we might call ɬaʔamɪn "culture," she rarely uses the term. She refers instead to "the teachings" or "our teachings," ʔəms taʔaw. In her careful detailing of specific ɬaʔamɪn practices – from basket weaving to salmon preservation to spiritual cleansing – she consistently foregrounds the actor's *intention*. When she describes the appropriate steps to take after a funeral, she stresses that whether one plunges into the river or goes home to have a shower, the most important thing is to think about washing away the grief and sadness. Similarly, when she talks about basketry, she emphasizes the need to express gratitude for the materials to the tree and to the Creator. Once that is done, it is less important whether the weaver uses maple leaves or rusty nails to dye the roots and bark. In these accounts of ʔəms taʔaw, internal intentions endure across time while outward practices evolve. In this view, the marrying of intention to appropriate action enables self-care and healing. The teachings – the ideas, values, and intentions – are what is crucial. Although the practices themselves are not insignificant, Chi-chia locates their importance historically: they matter because they are part of the history, part of how the Elders lived the teachings in their day, not because they need to be retained as they were. Practices can and will change over time; the teachings are constant. Chi-chia thus suggests that what is enduring about tradition or culture is not necessarily located in the physical practices where many may expect to find it, or in the texts and artifacts long collected by salvage anthropologists.

Thinking about the location of culture in this way is useful – even necessary – for situating Chi-chia's life in historical context. Nominally, a survey of early colonial history for the ɬaʔamın might read as a series of first encounters: with European ships and diseases in the eighteenth century, with the Hudson's Bay Company in the 1830s, with Roman Catholic priests and nuns in the 1860s, with settlers and provincial and federal Indian Affairs officials (but notably not with treaty commissioners) in the 1870s, with ethnographers in the 1930s, with modern-day treaty negotiators in the 1990s, and so on.[91] Such an account, however, tends easily toward a declensionist narrative of successive losses from a supposedly pure point of origin. Readers steeped in the popular notion that "tradition" and "modernity" are polar opposites might be drawn to interpret Chi-chia's childhood as traditional and her adulthood as modern; her childhood as ɬaʔamın and her adulthood as colonial.[92] Many told-to narratives inadvertently appear to replicate this dichotomy. Whether through the interventions of scholarly collaborators and editors, the choices of narrators themselves, or, most likely, some combination thereof, autobiographies of Indigenous women tend to emphasize women's roles as wives, mothers, and preservers of cultural practice (as basket weavers, language teachers, and button-blanket makers, for example).[93] To be sure, Chi-chia too talks a lot about these topics; readers will readily recognize caring for babies, drying salmon, and weaving baskets as ɬaʔamın women's work. But in focusing so heavily on a narrow conception of the ethnographic value of the narrator's life, many autobiographies and told-to accounts minimize the narrator's work in the paid labour force, and implicitly position her on a precarious fulcrum between tradition and modernity, as "the last of her kind."[94]

Such a gloss on Chi-chia's life, however, misses something enormously important in her telling. For Chi-chia, the entire book is about ɬaʔamɪn ways of living. ʔəms taʔaw are consistent features of her life, and thus hers is a ɬaʔamɪn life through and through. At the same time, because of the historical period, her life history is *also* about colonialism. This is true not only in the obvious places, where she discusses residential school, the segregation of bars and movie theatres, and discrimination at the hands of the RCMP. It is also true where she discusses her childhood on the land, travelling through the territory with her grandparents. In so doing, she portrays distinctly mid-twentieth-century ɬaʔamɪn geographies, formed, as ɬaʔamɪn geographies have always been, out of specific historical processes.[95] Taking the *very* long view, for example, her tremendous, site-specific knowledge of chum salmon is a form of historically specific expertise, a historical transformation from earlier generations' reliance on herring as a keystone species for thousands of years.[96] In Chi-chia's own lifetime she experienced a seasonal round that was the result of multiple, intersecting historical processes: generations of familial alliances through marriage, colonial displacements from ɬaʔamɪn sites such as Emmonds Beach and tiyskʷɑt (the location of the original mill town of Powell River), and the manufacture of "postage stamp" Indian reserves. Her paid work history, meanwhile, offers a picture of the challenges and changes facing Indigenous women in the mid-twentieth century: she was the first woman elected to council in her community,[97] earned a social work certificate from the University of British Columbia, co-operated with early RCMP initiatives on-reserve, and participated in addiction recovery programs for over twenty years. Earlier generations of scholars would hardly have seen these jobs as ɬaʔamɪn work. Barnett, for example, saw wage labour as evidence that the "old culture" was "practically dead."[98] But Chi-chia approached each of these jobs as an opportunity to practise and share the self-care that, in her words, is the "common thread" of ʔəms taʔaw. These jobs were as much a part of her life as a ɬaʔamɪn woman as raising children and preserving fish. To borrow the anthropologist Mario Blaser's conceptualization, we can see her simultaneous and mutually reinforcing commitments to live according to ʔəms taʔaw and to engage settler society as constituting her "life project."[99] Understanding Chi-chia's life as simultaneously ɬaʔamɪn *and* colonial demonstrates the interwoven nature of these influences on the production of ɬaʔamɪn ways and lives over time. And it underscores just how fallacious it is to attempt to segregate practices by labelling them "traditional" or "modern."

This perspective on tradition underscores an important point about historical change more broadly. Colonialism has been one particularly violent mechanism of change in recent ɬaʔamɪn history. But for the ɬaʔamɪn, change certainly did not originate with colonization. Without minimizing the trauma of colonialism, Indigenous scholars have challenged the pathologization of Indigenous peoples that results from overemphasis on "problems" and "loss."[100] Returning for a moment to Chi-chia's discussion of winter dances, for example, what would it mean if archaeological sources somehow proved this *was* previously a ɬaʔamɪn practice? Would that make her historically entrenched life experience as a ɬaʔamɪn woman any less "ɬaʔamɪn"? To which point in time do Indigenous peoples have to "return" in order to claim a tradition that colonial society recognizes as legitimately "Indian"? A hundred years ago? Longer? This is no abstract thought experiment, as anyone familiar with Canadian law and politics knows. Contemporary Aboriginal title cases hinge upon the ability of a First Nation to demonstrate cultural distinctiveness and exclusive control over territory at the moment that Britain asserted sovereignty. By effectively freezing culture and territory at that arbitrary moment in time, this standard denies Indigenous peoples the reality of historical change that characterizes all human societies. Reading or listening to Chi-chia's life as *history* means understanding it as a story of change over time, and accepting such change as a historical given, rather than a marker of decline from an idealized and static past. Doing so reorients us to questions about historical mechanisms of change – questions of agency and power, volition and coercion, intention and meaning, cause and effect. It is with such questions in mind that all three authors hope readers will attend to Chi-chia's words.

Living Indigenous Womanhood

Such questions are immediately and intimately relevant to conversations in the field of women's history, conversations that we three authors also hope this book will join. The gendered dimensions of colonialism's assault on Indigenous nations are multiple and complex. Since the early days of their arrival in North America, diverse European newcomers consistently identified Indigenous women as essential to the success of a wide range of colonial endeavours. From early missions through the fur trade to residential schools, the roles of

Indigenous girls and women – as daughters, mothers, providers, sexual partners, educators, and leaders – have endured multiple transformations.[101] As Cree-Métis scholar Kim Anderson writes, "One of the biggest targets of colonialism was the Indigenous family," and this inevitably and disproportionately affected women. Crucially, as Anderson points out, the attack on domestic roles and structures was a political assault on Indigenous societies, because – as for the Coast Salish – kinship and family were often crucial structures of governance.[102] Among the Nishnaabeg, for example, in the wonderful formulation of the Nishnaabeg writer, scholar, and activist Leanne Simpson, "Breastfeeding is the very first treaty."[103]

Yet, despite centuries of targeting Indigenous women and families in invasive and destructive ways – and despite declensionist tendencies in early scholarship – colonialism failed to have a totalizing impact on Indigenous women.[104] The chapters that follow demonstrate this many times over. Chi-chia's grandmother was a woman who remained the "boss" throughout her long marriage. She defied colonial attempts to eliminate her role as a transmitter of knowledge to her descendants. She hid Elsie from Indian agents, keeping her close so she could protect her and pass on ʔəms taʔaw. Chi-chia and her grandmother were each important breadwinners in their families – whether trading baskets door-to-door or in the wage labour force.[105] Moreover, the baskets Chi-chia discusses in detail are emblematic of the ongoing importance of women's material cultural production.[106] Chi-chia has herself followed a path akin to other Indigenous women leaders in her career choice of culturally grounded service work.[107] And not least, she has carried the knowledge and language passed on by her Elders and shared it in and beyond her community. This book is one example.

Through this practice of sharing, Chi-chia speaks to Indigenous women who have been working for and thinking through Indigenous resurgence. In her discussions of historical trauma, community service, healing, material culture, and language, Chi-chia addresses topics of central concern for many Indigenous women scholars and activists.[108] Moreover, she has much to offer women who are engaged in the process of "reconstructing Native womanhood," to use Kim Anderson's framing. In *Recognition of Being,* Anderson describes "a four-part process of Indigenous female identity development that includes resisting oppression, reclaiming Indigenous tradition and culture, incorporating traditional Indigenous ways into our modern lives, and acting on responsibilities inherent in our new-found identities."[109] Chi-chia speaks to each of these aspects in ways that are thoughtful, and often moving. Her words can serve both as a practical resource and as an inspiration.

Living and Listening for a Change

Of course, Indigenous resurgence is not a project exclusively for women, nor exclusively for Indigenous individuals.[110] An additional journey that we three authors hope this book takes in its lifetime is into the hands of all readers broadly interested in movements for resurgence, reconciliation, decolonization, antiracism, or social justice. Chi-chia offers the teachings here in published form at a moment when they can join an emergent literature on Indigenous epistemology, ontology, and story that is increasingly accessible not only to scholars but also to activists and community members. The particulars of ʔəms taʔaw are specific to the ɬaʔamɪn, as Chi-chia emphasizes, yet the principles of respect, gratitude, and holism are common to the teachings of many Indigenous peoples. Chi-chia respects differences among Indigenous peoples while recognizing these shared world views. The growing literature on tribally specific teachings can assist individuals, nations, and communities in laying the groundwork for their own paths toward what Leanne Simpson calls "re-creation, re-surgence, and a new emergence."[111] ʔəms taʔaw are helpful in this regard because, as Chi-chia explains, they are "the very essence of our well-being."

Chi-chia offers a profound example of the possibilities for living a life that is powerfully and dynamically inspired by ʔəms taʔaw. Chi-chia spent two years of her youth in a residential school. Such institutions were among the most destructive instruments of colonialism in Canada through their genocidal practice of breaking up families and destroying language.[112] Yet I have never heard Chi-chia use the widespread term "survivor" to describe herself. As she makes clear in Chapters 4 and 10, she certainly does *not* feel residential school was benign: her experiences there were terrible. But those terrible experiences did not shape her lifelong sense of self. This is, in part, additional evidence of colonialism's inability to effect the totalizing change it sought. Equally, if not more importantly, Chi-chia's resilience in the face of her residential school experiences is testament to the strength, versatility, relevance, and wisdom of the teachings. For Chi-chia, ʔəms taʔaw have always defined her self-identity, providing what she refers to as the common threads of respect, gratitude, and self-care that have sustained and guided her through the joys and traumas of her life.

She conveys these common threads here because she believes they can help others too. She knows from personal experience the power the teachings have to offer with respect to practices of self-care, grieving, and healing.

Grief in particular is a theme that runs through Chi-chia's narratives. From epidemic diseases to derogatory racist messages about "dirty Indians" to the loss of children – whether to residential school or through death (and often the two were connected) – the perspective she offers implies a need for a more substantive recognition of grief throughout the history of Indigenous engagements with colonialism. In this, she is hardly alone.[113] For meaningful healing, resurgence, reconciliation, or decolonization to occur, the intergenerational suffering of Indigenous peoples under colonialism must be more fully accounted for. Yet historical writing has only recently begun to incorporate grief and suffering into its analysis.[114] Chi-chia highlights the significance of this collective grief and suggests how ɬaʔamɪn teachings can be applied in today's context as tools for healing.

Crucially, ʔəms taʔaw are relevant not only in circumstances of grief or colonial trauma. ʔəms taʔaw offer a framework for well-being and for living a good life that can be applied under any circumstances. Chi-chia's message here is for Indigenous and non-Indigenous readers alike – for anyone who seeks a path to something like resurgence, reconciliation, or decolonization. All readers can be inspired by her generosity of spirit, her refusal of bitterness, and her empathy for others. These traits and the teachings that undergird them have transformative potential. Whether you, as readers, enact this potential in your own lives will depend a great deal on how each of you listens to Chi-chia's words. Chi-chia, Harmony, and I invite you to avoid concluding that reading/listening to Chi-chia's words puts you in her shoes. Instead, as you read/listen, please resist the temptation to jump to conclusions, fill in the blanks, or be certain that you understand too quickly. We invite you to see points of apparent tension or contradiction in Chi-chia's words not as things to be resolved or subsumed, but as possible openings onto new understandings. We invite you to approach this book not as a singular and finite act of knowledge acquisition – a "Eureka!" moment – but as an ongoing process of engagement and self-inquiry. This process of learning through story can yield transformational listening. Despite contemporary rhetoric about certainty, any meaningful process of reconciliation will necessarily involve something much closer to certainty's opposite – the opening up, rather than the closing down, of relationships, opportunities, and understandings – the uncertainty that inevitably accompanies a change in footing. This ongoing and open-ended approach to listening and learning is thus also an approach to relating to the world around us. This approach is very much in line with ʔəms taʔaw as told to Chi-chia by her Elders, and now told to all of us by Chi-chia: the history and teachings, written here as she remembers them.

NOTES

1 Linguistic orthography renders "Chi-chia" as "čičiyɛʔ," but because of Elsie's preference, this word constitutes an exception to our practice in this book of using a linguistic orthography for Sliammon words. An explanation of terms is warranted here. As Elsie explains in Chapter 1, "Sliammon" is an anglicization of the word "ɬaʔamun" in her mother tongue. The word "Sliammon" therefore appears throughout the following chapters as a direct quotation of her English speech. Following Elsie's stated preference, elsewhere in the book we have used the term "ɬaʔamɪn" wherever appropriate, and thus refer to "ɬaʔamɪn people," "ɬaʔamɪn history," and "ɬaʔamɪn practices." We use the term "Sliammon" to refer to the place today known in English as the Sliammon village and to the legally recognized entity the Sliammon First Nation. We have also followed local, colloquial practice and used the term "Sliammon language" because "ɬaʔamɪn" is not a term that would be applied to the language. The language itself has been referred to using various terms over time. For more details see Honoré Watanabe's "A Note on the Sliammon Language" at the beginning of this book.
2 On training to become a storyteller in another Coast Salish context, see Jo-ann Archibald, "Learning about Storywork from Stó:lō Elders," chap. 3 in *Indigenous Storywork: Educating the Heart, Mind, Body and Spirit* (Vancouver: UBC Press, 2008), 59-82.
3 For critical discussions of the deployment of the concept of "certainty" in relation to treaties and title in British Columbia, see Carole Blackburn, "Searching for Guarantees in the Midst of Uncertainty: Negotiating Aboriginal Rights and Title in British Columbia," *American Anthropologist* 107, 4 (2008): 586-96, and Andrew Woolford, *Between Justice and Certainty: Treaty Making in British Columbia* (Vancouver: UBC Press, 2005).
4 Paulette Regan, *Unsettling the Settler Within: Indian Residential Schools, Truth Telling, and Reconciliation in Canada* (Vancouver: UBC Press, 2010).
5 On settler allies, see ibid., 236. On the pitfalls of believing that we "already know what the woman is saying" in an oral history interview, see Kathryn Anderson and Dana C. Jack, "Learning to Listen: Interview Techniques and Analyses," in *The Oral History Reader*, 2nd ed., ed. Robert Perks and Alistair Thomson (New York: Routledge: 2006), 136.
6 See, for example, Marlene Brant Castellano, Linda Archibald, and Mike DeGagné, eds., *From Truth to Reconciliation: Transforming the Legacy of Residential Schools* (Ottawa: Aboriginal Healing Foundation, 2008); Gregory Younging, Jonathan Dewar, and Mike DeGagné, eds., *Response, Responsibility, and Renewal: Canada's*

Truth and Reconciliation Journey (Ottawa: Aboriginal Healing Foundation, 2009); and Ashok Mathur, Jonathan Dewar, and Mike DeGagné, eds., *Cultivating Canada: Reconciliation through the Lens of Cultural Diversity* (Ottawa: Aboriginal Healing Foundation, 2011). See also "Statement Gathering," Truth and Reconciliation Commission of Canada, accessed 25 April 2013, http://www.trc.ca/websites/trcinstitution/index.php?p=102.

7 Bain Attwood, "In the Age of Testimony: The Stolen Generations Narrative, 'Distance,' and Public History," *Public Culture* 20, 1 (2008): 75-95.

8 Regan, *Unsettling the Settler,* 16-17; Rauna Johanna Kuokkanen, *Reshaping the University: Responsibility, Indigenous Epistemes, and the Logic of the Gift* (Vancouver: UBC Press, 2007), 3, 7.

9 Julie Cruikshank, Angela Sidney, Kitty Smith, and Annie Ned, *Life Lived Like a Story: Life Stories of Three Yukon Native Elders* (Lincoln: University of Nebraska Press, 1990), 4.

10 See Kuokkanen, *Reshaping the University,* 76.

11 Attwood, "Age of Testimony," 92-95. For an extended exploration of this issue, see Victoria Freeman, *Distant Relations: How My Ancestors Colonized North America* (Toronto: McClelland and Stewart, 2000).

12 See Kuokkanen, *Reshaping the University,* 102, 103, 117.

13 Sophia Rosenfeld, "On Being Heard: A Case for Paying Attention to the Historical Ear," *American Historical Review* 16, 2 (2011): 328. On the politics of listening, see also Susan Bickford, *The Dissonance of Democracy: Listening, Conflict, and Citizenship* (Ithaca, NY: Cornell University Press, 1996).

14 For extended critical analysis of listening in relation to reconciliation, see Kuokkanen, "Knowing the 'Other' and 'Learning to Learn,'" chap 4 in *Reshaping the University,* 97-127; Regan, *Unsettling the Settler;* and Sophie McCall, *First Person Plural: Aboriginal Storytelling and the Ethics of Collaborative Authorship* (Vancouver: UBC Press, 2011).

15 Attwood, "Age of Testimony," 84, 86, 88. For a critique of Attwood on this issue, see Rosanne Kennedy, "Stolen Generations Testimony: Trauma, Historiography, and the Question of 'Truth,'" *Aboriginal History* 25 (2001): 116-31.

16 On the authority of Indigenous narrators, oral historians, and Elders, see Kennedy, "Stolen Generations Testimony," 507, 516; McCall, *First Person Plural,* 28, 32; Robin Jarvis Brownlie, "First Nations Perspectives and Historical Thinking in Canada," in *First Nations, First Thoughts: The Impact of Indigenous Thought in Canada,* ed. Annis May Timpson (Vancouver: UBC Press, 2009), 34; Annis May Timpson, "Introduction: Indigenous Thought in Canada," in Timpson, *First Nations, First Thoughts,* 1-3; and Bruce Miller, "Conclusions," chap. 6 in *Oral History on Trial: Recognizing Aboriginal Narratives in the Courts* (Vancouver: UBC Press, 2011), 163-75.

17 For an insightful critique of this tendency, see Kuokkanen, *Reshaping the University,* 82-85.

18 Attwood, "Age of Testimony," 76, 89-92.

19 Dorothy Kennedy and Randy Bouchard, *Sliammon Life, Sliammon Lands* (Vancouver: Talonbooks, 1983), 128.

20 See Chapter 1 for a story about one such instance.

21 Winona Wheeler, "Reflections on the Social Relations of Indigenous Oral Histories," in *Walking a Tightrope: Aboriginal People and Their Representations,*

ed. Ute Lischke and David T. McNab (Waterloo, ON: Wilfrid Laurier University Press, 2005), 194-98; Kuokkanen, *Reshaping the University*, esp. 102, 103. See also Dipesh Chakrabarty, *Provincializing Europe: Postcolonial Thought and Historical Difference* (Princeton: Princeton University Press, 2000).

22 Sarah Carter and Patricia A. McCormack, "Lifelines: Searching for Aboriginal Women of the Northwest and Borderlands," in *Recollecting: Lives of Aboriginal Women of the Canadian Northwest Borderlands*, ed. Sarah Carter and Patricia A. McCormack (Edmonton: Athabasca University Press, 2011), 13. See also Jean Barman, "Writing Women into the History of the North American Wests, One Woman at a Time," in *One Step over the Line: Toward a History of Women in the North American Wests*, ed. Elizabeth Jameson and Sheila McManus (Edmonton: University of Alberta Press, 2008), 99-127. For an early example of feminist approaches in this regard, see Personal Narratives Group, ed., *Interpreting Women's Lives: Feminist Theory and Personal Narratives* (Bloomington: Indiana University Press, 1989).

23 Paige Raibmon, *Authentic Indians: Episodes of Encounter from the Late-Nineteenth-Century Northwest Coast* (Durham, NC: Duke University Press, 2005), esp. chaps. 7-9; Paige Raibmon, "Naturalizing Power: Land and Sexual Violence along William Byrd's Dividing Line," in *Seeing Nature through Gender*, ed. Virginia Scharff (Lawrence: University of Kansas Press, 2003), 20-39; Paige Raibmon, "'A New Understanding of Things Indian': George Raley's Negotiation of the Residential School Experience," *BC Studies* 110 (1996): 69-96; Paige Raibmon, "In loco parentis: G.H. Raley and a Residential School Philosophy," *Journal of the Canadian Church Historical Society* 38, 4 (1996): 29-52.

24 McCall, *First Person Plural*, 16, 101, 122, 135, 136, 208, 209.

25 Kim Anderson, *Life Stages and Native Women: Memory, Teachings, and Story Medicine* (Winnipeg: University of Manitoba Press, 2011), 15; Cruikshank et al., *Life Lived*, 12; McCall, *First Person Plural*, 13. On the development of life history as an anthropological genre, see Regna Darnell, "The Challenge of Life Histories," chap. 6 in *Invisible Genealogies: A History of Americanist Anthropology* (Lincoln: University of Nebraska Press, 2001), 207-38.

26 McCall, *First Person Plural*, 205. See also McCall, "'Where Is the Voice Coming From?' Appropriations and Subversions of the 'Native' Voice," chap. 1 in *First Person Plural*, 17-42.

27 For analysis of these efforts, see ibid., 78, 206; and Michael Jacklin, "Critical Injuries: Collaborative Indigenous Life Writing and the Ethics of Criticism," *Life Writing* 1, 2 (2004): 47-69.

28 For an early example of feminist self-reflection on the ethics of life history research, see Daphne Patai, "Ethical Problems of Personal Narratives," *International Journal of Oral History* 8, 1 (1987): 5-27. For a rich and concise overview of the critical life history literature, see Leslie A. Robertson, *Standing Up with Ga'axsta'las: Jane Constance Cook and the Politics of Memory, Church, and Custom* (Vancouver: UBC Press, 2012), 479-80nn77-79. For examples of published life histories of Indigenous individuals, see the "Additional Readings" at the end of this book.

29 Carole Boyce Davies, "Collaboration and the Ordering Imperative in Life Story Production," in *De/colonizing the Subject: the Politics of Gender in Women's Autobiography*, ed. Sidonie Smith and Julia Watson (Minneapolis: University of Minnesota Press, 1992), 12-13 ; McCall, *First Person Plural*, 30.

30 Cruikshank et al., *Life Lived,* 16; McCall, *First Person Plural,* 7-8.
31 For a critique of literary scholars' failure to consider the agendas of Indigenous narrators, see Jacklin, "Critical Injuries." See also McCall, *First Person Plural,* 8-9, 35.
32 Theodore Rios and Kathleen M. Sands, *Telling a Good One: The Process of a Native American Collaborative Biography* (Lincoln: University of Nebraska Press, 2000).
33 Rigoberta Menchú, *I, Rigoberta Menchú: An Indian Woman in Guatemala,* ed. Elisabeth Burgos Debray, trans. Ann Wright (London: Verso, 1984). For examples of the subsequent commentaries and critiques, see Arturo Arias, ed., *The Rigoberta Menchú Controversy* (Minneapolis: University of Michigan Press, 2001); John Beverley, "The Margin at the Center: On Testimonio (Testimonial Narratives)," in Smith and Watson, *De/colonizing the Subject,* 91-114; John Beverley, *Testimonio: On the Politics of Truth* (Minneapolis: University of Michigan Press, 2004); Paul Gelles, "Testimonio, Ethnography and Processes of Authorship," *Anthropology News* 39, 3 (1998): 16-17; Greg Grandin, *Who Is Rigoberta Menchú?* (London: Verso, 2011); Jan Rus, issue coordinator, "If Truth Be Told: A Forum on David Stoll's *Rigoberta Menchú and the Story of All Poor Guatemalans*," special issue of *Latin American Perspectives* 26, 6 (1999); Daphne Patai, Joan Bamberger, Brian Haley, David Levine, and Luis Roniger, "Truth, Fact and Fiction in the Human Rights Community: Essays in Response to David Stoll's *Rigoberta Menchú and the Story of All Poor Guatemalans,*" *Human Rights Review* 1, 1 (1999): 78-112; David Stoll, *Rigoberta Menchú and the Story of All Poor Guatemalans,* expanded ed. (Boulder, CO: Westview Press, 2007; first published 1999); and Allen Webb and Stephen Benz, eds., *Teaching and Testimony: Rigoberta Menchú and the North American Classroom* (Albany: State University of New York Press, 1996).
34 Michele Grossman, "Out of the Salon and into the Streets: Contextualising Australian Indigenous Women's Writing," *Women's Writing* 5, 2 (1998): 182.
35 There are, of course, situations in which the narrator truly lacks the ability to speak for herself. See G. Thomas Couser, *Vulnerable Subjects: Ethics and Life Writing* (Ithaca, NY: Cornell University Press, 2004).
36 On the Indigenous use of life histories and narratives for healing, see also Anderson, *Life Stages,* 161-62; Archibald, "The Power of Stories to Educate the Heart," chap. 4 in *Indigenous Storywork,* 83-100; Susan Dion, *Braiding Histories: Learning from Aboriginal Peoples' Experiences and Perspectives* (Vancouver: UBC Press, 2008), 47-48; and Jo-Ann Episkenew, "Myth, Policy, and Health" and "Personal Stories," chaps. 1 and 3 in *Taking Back Our Spirits: Indigenous Literature, Public Policy, and Healing* (Winnipeg: University of Manitoba Press, 2009), 1-19, 69-108.
37 In what follows, I omit Janet's side of this conversation because of space constraints and because her interventions did not alter the direction of Chi-chia's train of thought. I also follow the practice of the anthropologist Leslie Robertson, who does not use block quotes for the words of her co-authors and collaborators. This typographical reflection of shared authority is related to the above discussion of informants versus authors. See Robertson, *Standing up with Ga'axsta'las.*
38 Sue Pielle is a daughter of Bill and Rose Mitchell, whom Elsie mentions several times, and who worked with anthropologists in the 1970s. Kennedy and Bouchard, *Sliammon Life,* 9-10. For another example of Elders' reluctance to talk about history, see Anderson, *Life Stages,* 20-21.

39 McCall, *First Person Plural,* 123. For related discussions of the difficulty of shar-
    ing Indigenous teachings in English, see Archibald, *Indigenous Storywork,* 75-76;
    and Margaret Elizabeth Kovach, *Indigenous Methodologies: Characteristics, Con-
    versations, and Contexts* (Toronto: University of Toronto Press, 2010), 59-61.
40 Cruikshank et al., *Life Lived,* 17; Harry Robinson, *Write It on Your Heart: The Epic
    World of an Okanagan Storyteller,* ed. and comp. Wendy Wickwire (Vancouver:
    Talonbooks, 1989), 15.
41 Bruce Granville Miller, "Introduction," in *Be of Good Mind: Essays on the Coast
    Salish,* ed. Bruce Granville Miller (Vancouver: UBC Press, 2007), 25.
42 On using the colonizer's language for healing colonial trauma, see Episkenew,
    Taking Back Our Spirits, 12.
43 The books I brought included the following, several of which Harmony had
    previously read: Agnes Alfred, *Paddling to Where I Stand: Agnes Alfred,
    Qʷiqʷasuʼtinux̌ʷ Noblewoman,* ed. Martine J. Reid, trans. Daisy Sewid-Smith
    (Vancouver: UBC Press, 2004); Margaret B. Blackman and Florence Edenshaw
    Davidson, *During My Time: Florence Edenshaw Davidson, A Haida Woman* (Seattle:
    University of Washington Press, 1982); Cruikshank et al., *Life Lived;* Earl
    Maquinna George, *Living on the Edge: Nuu-chah-nulth History from an Ahousaht
    Chief's Perspective* (Winlaw, BC: Sono Nis Press, 2003); Robinson, *Write It on
    Your Heart;* and Jean E. Speare, ed., *The Days of Augusta* (Vancouver: Douglas
    and McIntyre, 1973).
44 On turning oral words into written ones, see Michael Jacklin, "Making Paper
    Talk: Writing Indigenous Oral Life Narratives," *Ariel* 39, 1-2 (2008): 47-69; Nora
    Marks Dauenhauer and Richard Dauenhauer, "The Paradox of Talking on the
    Page: Some Aspects of the Tlingit and Haida Experience," in *Talking on the Page:
    Editing Aboriginal Oral Texts: Papers Given at the Thirty-second Annual Conference
    on Editorial Problems, University of Toronto, 14-16 November 1996,* ed. Laura J.
    Murray and Keren D. Rice (Toronto: University of Toronto Press, 1999), 3-42.
45 *Powell River Living,* July 2010, accessed 13 January 2012, http://www.prliving.
    ca/content/1007/index.html; *Powell River Living,* May 2008, accessed 13 January
    2012, http://www.prliving.ca/content/issue0805.html.
46 On the question of copyright when recording, preserving, and publishing oral
    histories, see Leslie McCartney, "Respecting First Nations Oral Histories: Copy-
    right Complexities and Archiving Aboriginal Stories," in Timpson, *First Nations,
    First Thoughts,* 87-89.
47 Michele Grossman, "Bad Aboriginal Writing: Editing, Aboriginality, Textuality,"
    Meanjin 3 (2001): 161-2; See also McCall, *First Person Plural,* 7, 30.
48 Grossman, "Bad Aboriginal Writing," 161.
49 Similarly, after making many hours of linguistic recordings in the Sliammon
    language, Chi-chia prefers not to do the time-consuming work necessary to
    transcribe and translate them.
50 Kathleen M. Sands, "Collaboration or Colonialism: Text and Process in Native
    American Women's Autobiographies," *Melus* 22, 4 (1997), 39-59; Dauenhauer
    and Dauenhauer, "Paradox of Talking"; Cruikshank et al., *Life Lived,* 16.
51 Miller, *Oral History on Trial,* 55.
52 For a sampling of the execution of tribally specific research methodologies, see
    Archibald, *Indigenous Storywork;* Kovach, *Indigenous Methodologies;* and Leanne

Simpson, *Dancing on Our Turtle's Back* (Winnipeg: Arbeiter Ring Publishing, 2011). On Indigenous methodologies more broadly, see Bagele Chilisa, *Indigenous Research Methodologies* (SAGE Publications: Los Angeles, 2012); Norman K. Denzin, Yvonna S. Lincoln, and Linda Tuhiwai Smith, *Handbook of Critical and Indigenous Methodologies* (SAGE Publications: Los Angeles, 2008); Linda Tuhiwai Smith, *Decolonizing Methodologies: Research and Indigenous Peoples* (London: Zed Books, 1999); and Shawn Wilson, *Research Is Ceremony: Indigenous Research Methods* (Black Point, NS: Fernwood Publishing, 2009).

53 On using life experience stories to share teachings, see Archibald, *Indigenous Storywork,* 112-14; Cruikshank et al., *Life Lived,* 165; and Kovach, *Indigenous Methodologies,* 95. For a wonderfully creative example, see John Borrows, *Drawing Out Law: A Spirit's Guide* (Toronto: University of Toronto Press, 2010).

54 Previously published legends have often appeared in children's versions for educational purposes: E. Tlesla Adams, *Mink and Granny* (Powell River, BC: Sliammon Band/School District No. 47, n.d.); *Mink and Cloud: Sliammon Indian Band Story* (Powell River: n.p., 1985); *Mink and Grey Bird: Sliammon Indian Band Story,* 2nd ed. (Cloverdale, BC: D.W. Friesen and Sons, n.d.); Hugh MacKenzie, *Pah* (Powell River, BC: Sliammon Native Council and School District #47, n.d.); R.E. Walz, *Mink and Whale: A Sliammon Legend* (Powell River, BC: Sliammon Indian Band, 1994). For a departure from this format, see Mary George, "The Seal: A Traditional Sliammon-Comox Story," in *Salish Myths and Legends: One People's Stories,* ed. M. Terry Thompson, Steven M. Egesdal, and Honoré Watanabe (Lincoln: University of Nebraska Press, 2008), 121-29; and Kennedy and Bouchard, "May the Waters Be Calm," chap. 10 in *Sliammon Life,* 93-108.

55 These materials were narrated and recorded in March 1996 and September 1997. They were subsequently transcribed and translated by Watanabe with the assistance of both Elsie and Marion Harry. Mrs. Harry is a lifelong friend of Elsie's and is mentioned in Chapter 4.

56 Susan Roy, *These Mysterious People: Shaping History and Archaeology in a Northwest Coast Community* (Montreal/Kingston: McGill-Queen's University Press, 2010), xiii.

57 On the ability of descendants to hear their Elders on the page, see also Julie Cruikshank, "The Social Life of Texts: Editing on the Page and in Performance," in Murray and Rice, *Talking on the Page,* 104.

58 The significant literature on the Coast Salish includes, for example, Pamela Amoss, *Coast Salish Spirit Dancing: The Survival of an Ancestral Religion* (Seattle: University of Washington Press, 1978); Archibald, *Indigenous Storywork;* Brad Asher, *Beyond the Reservation: Indians, Settlers, and the Law in Washington Territory, 1853-1889* (Norman: University of Oklahoma Press, 1999); Jean Barman, *Stanley Park's Secrets: The Forgotten Families of Whoi Whoi, Kanaka Ranch and Brockton Point* (Madeira Point, BC: Harbour Publishing, 2005); Homer G. Barnett, *The Coast Salish of British Columbia* (Eugene: University of Oregon Press, 1955); Crisca Bierwert, ed., *Lushootseed Texts: An Introduction to Puget Salish Narrative Aesthetics* (Lincoln: University of Nebraska Press, 1996); Crisca Bierwert, *Brushed by Cedar, Living by the River: Coast Salish Figures of Power* (Tucson: University of Arizona Press, 1999); Daniel L. Boxberger, *To Fish in Common: The Ethnohistory of Lummi Indian Salmon Fishing* (Lincoln: University of Nebraska Press, 1989);

Barbara Brotherton, ed., *S'abadeb, The Gifts: Pacific Coast Salish Art and Artists* (Seattle: University of Washington Press, 2008); Keith Thor Carlson, ed., *You Are Asked to Witness: The Stó:lō in Canada's Pacific Coast History* (Chilliwack, BC: Stó:lō Heritage Trust, 1996); Keith Thor Carlson, ed., *A Stó:lō–Coast Salish Historical Atlas* (Vancouver: Douglas and McIntyre, 2001); Keith Thor Carlson, *The Power of Place, The Problem of Time: Aboriginal Identity and Historical Consciousness in the Cauldron of Colonialism* (Toronto: University of Toronto Press, 2010); June Collins, *Valley of Spirits: The Upper Skagit Indians of Western Washington* (Seattle: University of Washington Press, 1974); Wilson Duff, *Upper Stalo Indians of the Fraser Valley* (Victoria: BC Provincial Museum, 1972); William W. Elmendorf, *Structure of Twana Culture* (New York: Garland Publishing, 1974); William W. Elmendorf, *Twana Narratives: Native Historical Accounts of a Coast Salish Culture* (Seattle: University of Washington Press, 1993); Alexandra Harmon, *Indians in the Making: Ethnic Relations and Indian Identities around Puget Sound* (Berkeley: University of California Press, 1998); Charles Hill-Tout, *The Salish People: The Local Contribution of Charles Hill-Tout*, vols. 1-4, ed. Ralph Maud (Vancouver: Talonbooks, 1978); Dorothy Kennedy, "Quantifying 'Two Sides of a Coin': A Statistical Examination of the Central Coast Salish Social Network," *BC Studies* 153 (2007): 3-34; Kennedy and Bouchard, *Sliammon Life;* J.E. Michael Kew, "Coast Salish Ceremonial Life: Status and Identity in a Modern Village" (PhD diss., University of Washington, 1970); J. Michael Kew and Bruce G. Miller, "Locating Aboriginal Governments in the Political Landscape," in *Seeking Sustainability in the Lower Fraser Basin*, ed. Michael Healey (Vancouver: Institute for Resources and the Environment, Westwater Research, 1999), 47-63; Claudia Lewis, *Indian Families of the Northwest Coast: The Impact of Change* (Chicago: University of Chicago Press, 1970); Michael Marker, "Indigenous Resistance and Racist Schooling on the Borders of Empires: Coast Salish Cultural Survival," *Paedagogica Historica* 45, 6 (2009): 757-72; Daniel P. Marshall, *Those Who Fell from the Sky: A History of the Cowichan Peoples* (Duncan, BC: Cultural and Education Centre, Cowichan Tribes, 1999); Bruce G. Miller, *The Problem of Justice: Tradition and Law in the Coast Salish World* (Lincoln: University of Nebraska Press, 2001); Miller, *Be of Good Mind;* Bruce G. Miller and Daniel L. Boxberger, "Creating Chiefdoms: the Puget Sound Case," *Ethnohistory* 41, 22 (1994): 257-93; Jay Miller, *Lushootseed Culture and the Shamanic Odyssey: An Anchored Radiance* (Lincoln: University of Nebraska Press, 1999); Kathleen Mooney, "The Effects of Rank and Wealth on Exchange Among the Coast Salish," *Ethnology* 17, 4 (1978): 391-406; Kathleen Mooney, "Social Distance and Exchange," *Ethnology* 15, 4 (1976): 323-46; Jeff Oliver, *Landscapes and Social Transformations on the Northwest Coast: Colonial Encounters in the Fraser Valley* (Tucson: University of Arizona Press, 2010); Roy, *These Mysterious People;* Susan Roy and Ruth Taylor, "We Were Real Skookum Women: The shíshálh Economy and the Logging Industry on the Pacific Northwest Coast," in *Indigenous Woman and Work: From Labor to Activism*, ed. Carol Williams (Urbana: University of Illinois Press, 2012), 104-19; Leona Marie Sparrow, "Work Histories of a Coast Salish Couple" (MA thesis, University of British Columbia, 1976); Wayne Prescott Suttles, *Coast Salish Essays* (Vancouver: Talonbooks, 1987); Brian Thom, "Disagreement-in-Principle: Negotiating the Right to Practice Coast Salish Culture in Treaty Talks on Vancouver Island, BC," *New Proposals: Journal of Marxism and Interdisciplinary*

Inquiry 2, 1 (2008): 23-30; Brian Thom, "The Paradox of Boundaries in Coast Salish Territories," *Cultural Geographies* 16, 2 (2009): 179-205; Brian Thom, "The Anathema of Aggregation: Towards 21st-Century Self-Government in the Coast Salish World," *Anthropologica* 52, 1 (2010): 33-48; Coll Thrush, *Native Seattle: Histories from the Crossing-Over Place* (Seattle: University of Washington Press, 2007); and Kenneth Tollefson, "The Snoqualmie: A Puget Sound Chiefdom," *Ethnology* 26, 2 (1987): 135-50.

59 Miller, "Introduction," 4, 12. This trend in Stó:lō scholarship has continued since 2007, much of it by graduate students under the supervision of Keith Carlson. See University of Saskatchewan, "Keith Carlson: Teaching and Supervision," accessed 26 July 2012, http://artsandscience.usask.ca/profile/KCarlson/teaching/.

60 For a historical review of literature on the Coast Salish, including a discussion of Boas's influence, see Daniel Boxberger, "The Not So Common," in Miller, *Be of Good Mind*, 65-68.

61 Some of the details of Boas's language documentation among the Island Comox suggest a possibility that he may have, in fact, worked with a ɬaʔamɪn informant while on Vancouver Island. However, these details may simply be a result of inconsistencies in Boas's use of phonetic symbols. I am grateful to Paul Kroeber and Honoré Watanabe for sharing these fascinating and insightful interpretations of the archival record on this point. Franz Boas, "Catloltq-English Vocabulary," Manuscript 711-b, National Anthropological Archives, Smithsonian Institution (hereafter cited as NAA); Franz Boas, "Caloltq Texts," Manuscript 719, NAA; Franz Boas, "Comox and Pentlatch Texts," Franz Boas Collection of Materials for American Linguistics (497.3 B63c, Section S2j.1), American Council of Learned Societies Committee on Native American Languages (hereafter cited as Committee), American Philosophical Society (hereafter cited as APS); Franz Boas, "Comox-Satlolk materials," Franz Boas Collection of Materials for American Linguistics (497.3 B63c, Section S2j.2), Committee, APS; Franz Boas, "Comparative Vocabularies of Eight Salishan Languages," Franz Boas Collection of Materials for American Linguistics (497.3 B63c, Section S.1), Committee, APS; Franz Boas, "Comox Vocabulary," Manuscript 350-c, NAA; Franz Boas, "Field Notes 1886 #2," Franz Boas Field Notebooks and Anthropometric Data (Box 3), APS; Franz Boas, "Field Notes 1886 #4," Franz Boas Field Notebooks and Anthropometric Data (Box 3), APS; Franz Boas, "Myths and Legends of the Çatloltq of Vancouver Island," *American Antiquarian and Oriental Journal* 10, 4 (July 1888): 201-11; Franz Boas, "Myths and Legends of the Çatloltq II," *American Antiquarian and Oriental Journal* 10, 6 (November 1888): 366-73; Franz Boas, "Salishan Vocabulary September, 1892," Manuscript 713, NAA.

62 On archival shaping of knowledge, see, for example, Antoinette Burton, ed., *Archive Stories: Facts, Fictions, and the Writing of History* (Durham, NC: Duke University Press, 2005), especially pt. 2.

63 See "A Note on the Sliammon Language" for further explanation of terms. The linguistics literature on this language is extensive. See, for example, Susan Blake, "Two Aspects of Sliammon Phonology Glide/Obstruent Alternation and Vowel Length" (MA thesis, University of British Columbia, 1992); Susan Blake, "Another Look at Passives in Sliammon (Salish)," *International Conference on Salish and Neighboring Languages* 32 (1997): 86-143; Susan Blake, "On the Distribution and

Representation of Schwa in Sliammon (Salish) Descriptive and Theoretical Perspectives" (PhD diss., University of British Columbia, 2000); John Davis, comp., "Sliammon," Survey of California and Other Indian Languages Audio Archive of Linguistic Fieldwork, Church House, BC, Canada, 1969-73, Linguistics Department, Survey Archives, Survey ID: Davis.001, Berkeley Language Centre, University of California, Berkeley; John Davis, "Pronominal Paradigms in Sliammon," *International Conference on Salish and Neighbouring Languages* 13 (1978): 208-36; John Davis, "The Passive in Sliammon," *Proceedings of the Sixth Annual Meeting of the Berkeley Linguistics Society* (1980): 278-86; Claude Hagège, *Le Comox Lhaamen de Colombie Britannique: Présentation d'une Langue Amérindienne* (Paris: Amerindia, 1981); Herbert R. Harris, "A Grammatical Sketch of Comox" (PhD diss., University of Kansas, 1981); Paul Kroeber, "Inceptive Reduplication in Comox and Interior Salishan," *International Journal of American Linguistics* 54, 2 (1988): 141-67; Edward Sapir, *Noun Reduplication in Comox, a Salish Language of Vancouver Island* (Ottawa: Government Printing Bureau, 1915); Jan Timmers, *Comox Stem List* (Leiden: n.p., 1978); Honoré Watanabe, "A Report on Sliammon (Mainland Comox) Phonology and Reduplication," in *Languages of the North Pacific Rim*, vol. 5, ed. Osahito Miyaoka (Sapporo: Hokkaido University Publications in Linguistics, 1994), 217-62; Honoré Watanabe, "A Report on Sliammon (Mainland Comox) Phonology and Reduplication" (MA thesis, Hokkaido University, 1994); Honoré Watanabe, "Sliammon (Mainland Comox) Transitive Constructions with -ʔəm, -ni, and -mi," *International Conference on Salish and Neighbouring Languages* 31 (1996): 327-38; Honoré Watanabe, "A Morphological Description of Sliammon, Mainland Comox Salish" (PhD diss., Kyoto University, 2000); Honoré Watanabe, *A Morphological Description of Sliammon, Mainland Comox Salish: With a Sketch of Syntax*, Endangered Languages of the Pacific Rim Publication Series A2-040 (Osaka: Osaka Gakuin University, Faculty of Informatics, 2003); Honoré Watanabe, "Clitics in the Sliammon Salish: Criteria for Their Formal Identification," *Asian and African Languages and Linguistics* 2 (2007): 115-30; and Honoré Watanabe, "A Look at 'Noun' and 'Verb' in Sliammon," in *A Festschrift for Thomas M. Hess on the Occasion of His Seventieth Birthday*, ed. David Beck (Bellingham, WA: Whatcom Museum Publications, 2010), 179-96.

64 Acculturation studies, a popular approach in mid-twentieth-century anthropology, cast "urban Indians" as ideal subjects of study. Accordingly, much Coast Salish research from that period deals with peoples near urban centres. This may have been a further factor that kept the ɬaʔamɪn beyond the view of scholars. On acculturation studies, see Boxberger, "The Not So Common," 69. One study using this acculturation paradigm does reference the ɬaʔamɪn: Edwin Lemert, "The Life and Death of an Indian State," *Human Organization* 13, 3 (1954): 23-27.

65 Barnett received his PhD from the University of California in 1938. Homer Barnett, "The Coast Salish of Canada," *American Anthropologist* 40, 1(1938): 118-41; Barnett, *Coast Salish;* University of British Columbia, Rare Books and Special Collections, H.G. Barnett Fonds, Box 1, Folder 6, Field notes: "Mainland Comox (Slaiäman, Klahuse, Homalco), 1936" (hereafter cited as Barnett field notes, folder 1-6). Suttles mentions the northern Coast Salish infrequently, and when he does, appears to rely on Barnett. Suttles, *Coast Salish Essays*, 172, 176, 177, 239.

66 Kennedy and Bouchard, *Sliammon Life;* see also Dorothy I.D. Kennedy and Randall T. Bouchard, "Northern Coast Salish," in *Handbook of North American Indians,* vol. 7, *Northwest Coast,* ed. Wayne Suttles (Washington: Smithsonian Institution, 1990), 441-52. Kennedy and Bouchard use the term "Sliammon" to refer collectively to the Sliammon, Klahoose, and Homalco peoples. Kennedy and Bouchard, *Sliammon Life,* 9.

67 The notes to the chapters that follow indicate where Elsie's subject matter intersects with the research of Barnett and Kennedy and Bouchard. Other relevant sources are listed in the "Additional Readings" at the end of this book.

68 Lyana Marie Patrick, "Storytelling in the Fourth World: Explorations in Meaning of Place and Tla'amin Resistance to Dispossession" (MA thesis, University of Victoria, 2004); Siemthlut Michelle Washington, "Bringing Traditional Teachings to Leadership," *American Indian Quarterly* 28, 3 and 4 (2004): 583-603; Jonathan Clapperton, "Desolate Viewscapes: Sliammon First Nation, Desolation Sound Marine Park and Environmental Narratives," *Environment and History* 18, 4 (2012): 529-59. Researchers interested in health, natural resources, education, and fisheries have also recently done work that relates to the ɬaʔamɪn. Jessica Ball and Pauline Janyst, "Enacting Research Ethics in Partnerships with Indigenous Communities in Canada: 'Do It in a Good Way,'" *Journal of Empirical Research on Human Research Ethics* 3, 2 (2008): 33-51; R. Collin and T. Hobby, "It's All about Relationships: First Nations and Non-Timber Resource Management in British Columbia," *BC Journal of Ecosystems and Management* 11, 1 and 2 (2010): 1-8; Christine Joanne Pearson, "First Nations Parent Involvement in the Public School System: The Personal Journey of a School Principal" (PhD diss., University of British Columbia, 2007); Clare Wiseman and Frank Gobas, "Balancing Risks in the Management of Contaminated First Nations Fisheries," *International Journal of Environmental Health Research* 12, 4 (2002): 331-42.

69 On the archaeological work at Sliammon, see Megan E. Caldwell, Dana Lepofsky, Georgia Combes, Michelle Washington, John R. Welch, and John R. Harper, "A Bird's Eye View of Northern Coast Salish Intertidal Resource Management Features, Southern British Columbia, Canada," *Journal of Island and Coastal Archaeology* 7, 2 (2012): 219-33; J.D. Jackley, D. Lepofsky, J.R. Welch, M. Caldwell, C. Springer, M. Ritchie, C. Rust, and M. Washington, "Tla'amin-SFU Archaeology Heritage Program 2009," *Midden* 41, 4 (2009): 5-7; Julia Jackley, "Weaving the Histories of Klehkwahnnohm: A Tla'amin Community in Southwest British Columbia" (MA thesis, Simon Fraser University, 2011); Sarah Johnson, "Combining Traditional Knowledge With Archaeological Investigation in Grace Harbour, Desolation Sound, B.C." (MA thesis, Simon Fraser University, 2010); Dana Lepofsky, "Everybody Loves Archaeology: Bridging Communities through Archaeological Research," *SAA Archaeological Record* 11, 5 (2011): 17-20; C. Springer, M. Caldwell, and N. Chalmer, "Houses, Settlements and the Intertidal: Simon Fraser University 2010 Field School in Tla'amin First Nation Territory," *Midden* 42, 4 (2010): 7-9; J.R. Welch, D. Lepofsky, G. Combes, M. Caldwell, and C. Rust, "Treasure Bearers: Personal Foundations For Effective Leadership In Northern Coast Salish Heritage Stewardship," *Heritage and Society* 4, 1 (2011): 83-114; and J.R. Welch, Dana Lepofsky, and Michelle Washington, "Assessing Collaboration with the Sliammon First Nation in a Community-Based Heritage Research and Stewardship Program," *Archaeological Review from Cambridge* 26,

2 (2011): 171-91. See also the website for the "Tla'amin and Simon Fraser University Heritage and Archaeology Project," Sliammon First Nation, accessed 25 April 2012, http://www.sliammonfirstnation.com/archaeology/.

70 The works of the Lushootseed elder Vi Hilbert and the Snuneymuxw Elder Ellen White are particularly noteworthy in this respect. See Ellen White, *Kwulasulwut: Stories from the Coast Salish* (Nanaimo, BC: Theytus Books, 1981); Ellen White, *Kwulasulwut II: More Salish Creation Stories* (Penticton, BC: Theytus Books, 1997); Ellen White, *Legends and Teachings of Xeel's, the Creator* (Vancouver: Pacific Educational Press, 2006); Vi Hilbert, *Haboo: Lushootseed Literature in English* (n.p.: Lushootseed Press, 1980); Vi Hilbert, *Ways of the Lushootseed People: Ceremonies and Traditions of the Northern Puget Sound Indians* (Seattle: United Indians of All Tribes Foundation, 1980); Vi Hilbert, ed. and trans., *Haboo: Native American Stories from Puget Sound* (Seattle: University of Washington Press, 1985); and Vi Hilbert, comp., *Lady Louse Lived There: ʔəsɫaɫil kʷsi bəsčad*, ed. Janet Yoder (n.p.: Lushootseed Press, 1996). See also Bierwert, *Lushootseed Texts.* I know of only three first-person life narratives of Coast Salish women. Two of these, also produced through the efforts of Vi Hilbert, are bilingual editions that include legends alongside life narratives: Susie Sampson Peter, *Aunt Susie Sampson Peter: The Wisdom of a Skagit Elder*, transcr. Vi Hilbert, trans. Vi Hilbert and Jay Miller, rec. Leon Metcalf (Seattle: Lushootseed Press, 1995); and Gram Ruth Sehome Shelton, *The Wisdom of a Tulalip Elder*, transcr. Vi Hilbert, trans. Vi Hilbert and Jay Miller, rec. Leon Metcalf (Seattle: Lushootseed Press, 1995). The third is Lee Maracle, *Bobbi Lee: Indian Rebel*, new ed., (Toronto: Women's Press, 1990; first published 1975).

71 Simon Baker and Verna J. Kirkness, *Khot-La-Cha: The Autobiography of Chief Simon Baker* (Vancouver: Douglas and McIntyre, 1994); Crisca Bierwert "'I Can Lift Her Up...': Fred Ewen's Narrative Complexity," in Miller, *Be of Good Mind*, 182-211; June M. Collins, "John Fornsby: The Personal Document of a Coast Salish Indian," in *Indians of the Urban Northwest*, ed. Marian Smith (New York: Columbia University Press, 1949), 287-341; Clayton Mack, *Grizzly Bears and White Guys: The Stories of Clayton Mack*, ed. Harvey Thommasen (Madeira Park, BC: Harbour Publishing, 1993); Clayton Mack, *Bella Coola Man: More Stories of Clayton Mack*, comp. and ed. Harvey Thommasen (Madeira Park, BC: Harbour Publishing, 1994); Henry Pennier, *Call Me Hank: A Stó:lō Man's Reflections on Logging, Living, and Growing Old*, 2nd ed., ed. Keith Carlson and Kristina Fagan (Toronto: University of Toronto Press, 2006; first published 1972). An important unpublished life narrative of a Coast Salish man is Paul Fetzer, "George Swanaset: Narrative of a Personal Document," Melville Jacobs Collection, University of Washington Manuscripts, accession 1693-71-13, box 112. Third-person biographies of Coast Salish men and women also exist: Robert H. Brown and John A. Ruby, *Esther Ross: Stillaguamish Champion* (Norman: Oklahoma University Press, 2001); Lawrence David Rygg, "The Continuation of Upper Class Snohomish Coast Salish Attitudes and Deportment as Seen through the Life History of a Snohomish Coast Salish Woman" (MA thesis, Western Washington State College, 1977); Trova Heffernan, *Where the Salmon Run: The Life and Legacy of Billy Frank Jr.* (Seattle: University of Washington Press, 2012).

72 Carter and McCormack, "Lifelines," 12.

73 Barnett, *Coast Salish,* 4-10, 59-70, 78-107,122-24.

74 Ibid., 67.

75 Suttles, *Coast Salish Essays,* 51-56.

76 Carlson, *Stó:lō–Coast Salish Atlas,* plate 10. See also Naxaxalhts'i, Albert (Sonny) McHalsie, "We Have to Take Care of Everything That Belongs to Us," in Miller, *Be of Good Mind,* 82-130.

77 Miller, "Introduction," 2-3. On the diffusion model of culture change, see Darnell, *Invisible Genealogies,* 47-51.

78 Roy, *These Mysterious People,* 55.

79 See note 58 above.

80 Barnett, *Coast Salish,* 9. Tommy Paul was from Saanich, Albert Westly was from Snuneymuxw, and George Mitchell was from Comox. Ibid., 5, 6, 7.

81 Emphasis in original. Barnett field notes, folder 1-6, 19. See also Barnett, *Coast Salish,* 89.

82 See, for example, Chapter 2. Kennedy and Bouchard describe a practice for welcoming the first spring (chinook) salmon. *Sliammon Life,* 26.

83 Emphasis in original. Barnett field notes, folder 1-6, 63.

84 Emphasis in original. Ibid., 68.

85 Emphasis in original. Ibid., 69.

86 Ibid. See also ibid., 67.

87 Emphasis in original. Ibid., 238-39.

88 Barnett, *Coast Salish,* 302.

89 Lemert, "Life and Death," 23.

90 Miller, "Introduction," 24-25.

91 For a historical timeline of ɬaʔamɪn history from the eighteenth century to the present, see Sliammon Treaty Society, "Timeline of Events of Sliammon Treaty Society," accessed 28 May 2013, http://sliammontreaty.com/who/historical -timeline.

92 This is essentially an inversion of an old-fashioned, Whiggish approach to history writing that simply reverses the positive and negative charges with respect to Indigenous history. That is, rather than change signalling progress, it signals decline.

93 For example, Alfred, *Paddling;* Blackman and Davidson, *During My Time;* Mourning Dove, *Mourning Dove: A Salishan Autobiography,* ed. Jay Miller (Lincoln: University of Nebraska Press, 1990); and Speare, *Days of Augusta.* For a critique of the tendency to position women as the "keepers of tradition," see Kim Anderson, "Affirmations of an Indigenous Feminist," in *Indigenous Women and Feminism: Politics, Activism, Culture,* ed. Cheryl Suzack, Shari M. Huhndorf, Jeanne Perreault, and Jean Barman (Vancouver: UBC Press, 2010), 87-88.

94 For an exception to this tendency, see Bridget Moran, *Stony Creek Woman: The Story of Mary John* (Vancouver: Arsenal Pulp Press, 1988). Autobiographies of Indigenous men seem more likely to include discussions of wage labour. For example, Harry Assu and Joy Inglis, *Assu of Cape Mudge: Recollections of a Coastal Indian Chief* (Vancouver: UBC Press, 1989); Baker and Kirkness, *Khot-La-Cha;* George, *Living on the Edge;* Charles James Nowell and Clellan S. Ford, *Smoke from Their Fires: The Life of a Kwakiutl Chief* (Hamden, CT: Archon Books, 1968; first published 1941); Pennier, *Call Me Hank;* Rios and Sands, *Telling a Good*

One; and James Sewid, *Guests Never Leave Hungry: The Autobiography of James Sewid, a Kwakiutl Indian,* ed. James P. Spradley (New Haven, CT: Yale University Press, 1969). For a biography that focuses explicitly on work, see Sparrow, "Work Histories." On Indigenous wage labour in British Columbia and beyond, see Rolf Knight, *Indians at Work: An Informal History of Native Labour in British Columbia, 1848-1930,* 2nd ed. (Vancouver: New Star Books, 1996; first published 1978); John Lutz, *Makùk: A New History of Aboriginal-White Relations* (Vancouver: UBC Press, 2008); Raibmon, *Authentic Indians;* Brian Hosmer and Colleen O'Neill, eds., *Native Pathways: American Indian Culture and Economic Development in the Twentieth Century* (Boulder: University Press of Colorado, 2004); and Williams, *Indigenous Women and Work.*

95   For extended consideration of historical change among another Coast Salish people, see Carlson, *Power of Place.*

96   My thanks to Dana Lepofsky for this perspective on herring.

97   Women could not serve on band councils until after the 1951 amendments to the Indian Act. Cora Voyageur, *Firekeepers of the Twenty-first Century: First Nations Women Chiefs* (Montreal/Kingston: McGill-Queen's University Press, 2008), 4-5.

98   Barnett, *Coast Salish,* 2.

99   Mario Blaser, "Life Projects: Indigenous Peoples' Agency and Development," in *In the Way of Development: Indigenous Peoples, Life Projects, and Globalization,* ed. Mario Blaser, Harvey A. Feit, and Glenn McRae (London: Zed Books, 2004), 26, 29, 31. See also the other contributions to that volume.

100 Gail Guthrie Valaskakis, Madeleine Dion Stout, and Eric Guimond, "Introduction," in *Restoring the Balance: First Nations Women, Community, and Culture,* ed. Gail Guthrie Valaskakis, Madeleine Dion Stout, and Eric Guimond (Winnipeg: University of Manitoba Press, 2009), 2; Anderson, *Life Stages,* 161-62.

101 See, for example, Karen Anderson, *Chain Her by One Foot: The Subjugation of Women in Seventeenth-Century New France* (New York: Routledge, 1991); Jean Barman, "Taming Aboriginal Sexuality: Gender, Power, and Race in British Columbia, 1850-1900," *BC Studies* 115/6 (1997): 237-66; Kathleen Brown, "The Anglo-Algonquian Gender Frontier," in *Negotiators of Change: Historical Perspectives on Native American Women,* ed. Nancy Shoemaker (New York: Routledge, 1995), 26-48; Jennifer Brown, *Strangers in Blood: Fur Trade Company Families in Indian Country* (Vancouver: UBC Press, 1980); Carol Devens, *Countering Colonization: Native American Women and Great Lakes Missions, 1630-1900* (Berkeley: University of California Press, 1992); Carol Devens, "If We Get the Girls, We Get the Race," *Journal of World History* 3, 2 (1992): 219-37; Jo-Anne Fiske, "Gender and the Paradox of Residential Education in Carrier Society," in *Women of the First Nations: Power, Wisdom, Strength,* ed. Christine Miller and Patricka Chuckryk (Winnipeg: University of Manitoba Press, 1996), 167-82; Allan Greer, *Mohawk Saint: Catherine Tekakwitha and the Jesuits* (New York: Oxford University Press, 2005); Eleanor Leacock, "Montagnais Women and the Jesuit Program for Colonization," in *Women and Colonization: Anthropological Perspectives,* ed. Mona Etienne and Eleanor Leacock (New York: Praeger, 1980), 25-41; Michael Harkin, "Engendering Discipline: Discourse and Counterdiscourse in the Methodist-Heiltsuk Dialogue," *Ethnohistory* 43, 4 (1996): 643-61; J.R. Miller, *Shingwauk's Vision: History of Native Residential Schools* (Toronto: University of Toronto Press, 1996); John S. Milloy, *A National Crime: The Canadian Government and the*

Residential School System, 1879-1986 (Winnipeg: University of Manitoba Press, 1999); Joan Sangster, "'She Is Hostile to Our Ways': First Nations Girls Sentenced to the Ontario Training School for Girls, 1933-1960," *Law and History Review* 20, 1 (2002): 59-96; Susan Sleeper-Smith, *Indian Women and French Men: Rethinking Cultural Encounter in the Great Lakes* (Amherst: University of Massachusetts Press, 2001); Sylvia Van Kirk, *Many Tender Ties: Women in Fur-Trade Society, 1670-1870* (Norman: University of Oklahoma Press, 1983).

102   Anderson, "Affirmations," 83, 86.

103   Simpson, *Dancing*, 106.

104   For a useful and concise summary of the trajectory of the historiography on Indigenous women, see Carter and McCormack, "Lifelines," 8-13.

105   On the economy of Coast Salish women in an earlier period, see Carol Williams, "Between Doorstep Barter Economy and Industrial Wages: Mobility and Adaptability of Coast Salish Female Laborers in Coastal British Columbia, 1858-1890," in *Native Being, Being Native: Identity and Difference: Proceedings of the Fifth Native American Symposium*, ed. Mark Spencer and Lucretia Scoufos (Durant: Southeastern Oklahoma State University, 2005), 16-27.

106   On Indigenous women and material culture, see Carter and McCormack, "Lifelines," 17-18.

107   On Indigenous women and leadership, see Rebecca Tsosie, "Native Women and Leadership: An Ethics of Culture and Relationship," in Suzack et al., *Indigenous Women and Feminism*, 29-42.

108   Valaskakis et al., "Introduction," 3-9.

109   Anderson, "Affirmations," 85. See also Kim Anderson, *A Recognition of Being: Reconstructing Native Womanhood* (Toronto: Sumach Press, 2000).

110   For thoughtful reflection and analysis of alliances between Indigenous and non-Indigenous people, see Lynne Davis, ed., *Alliances: Re/Envisioning Indigenous-non-Indigenous Relationships* (Toronto: University of Toronto Press, 2010).

111   Simpson, *Dancing*. See also Tsosie, "Native Women." Particularly noteworthy is the recent flourishing of scholarship that draws on Anishinabek/Anishinaabek/ Anishinaabeg/Nishnaabeg teachings, of which Simpson's work is one example. See also Kathleen E. Absolon, *Kaandossiwin: How We Come to Know* (Black Point, NS: Fernwood Publishing, 2011); Edward Benton-Banai, *The Mishomis Book: The Voice of the Ojibway* (Minneapolis: University of Minnesota Press, 2010); Borrows, *Drawing Out Law*; Jill Doerfler, Heidi Kiiwetinepinesiik Star, Niigaanwewidam James Sinclair, eds., *Centering Anishinaabeg Studies: Understanding the World through Stories* (Winnipeg: University of Manitoba Press, 2013); Niigonwedom James Sinclair, "Nindoodemag Bagijiganan: A History of Anishinaabeg Narrative" (PhD diss., University of British Columba, 2013).

112   The United Nations describes forced removal of children from a group as genocide. See *Convention on the Prevention and Punishment of the Crime of Genocide*, art. 2e, accessed 27 April 2013, http://treaties.un.org/doc/Publication/UNTS/ Volume%2078/volume-78-I-1021-English.pdf.

113   See, for example, Cynthia C. Wesley-Esquimaux, "Trauma to Resilience: Notes on Decolonization," in Valaskakis et al., *Restoring the Balance*, 23-25; and Cynthia C. Wesley-Esquimaux and Magdalena Smolewski, *Historic Trauma and Aboriginal Healing* (Ottawa: Aboriginal Healing Foundation, 2004), accessed 25 April 2013, http://www.ahf.ca/downloads/historic-trauma.pdf.

114 For two works that move in this direction, see Ned Blackhawk, *Violence over the Land: Indians and Empires in the Early American West* (Cambridge: Harvard University Press, 2006); and Michael McNally, *Ojibwe Singers: Hymns, Grief, and a Native Culture in Motion* (New York: Oxford University Press, 2000).

Where I Come From

1

The Territory and People

When we talk about territory in today's world, it's quite different than our lands and our territory from when I was a child. ʔəms giʲɛ, ʔəms naʔ giʲɛ – this is our land, this is our territory. Wherever people lived. And when I say "our" people, I include Klahoose and Homalco. Klahoose being the toʔqʷ qaymixʷ, and Homalco being ʔoʔp qaymixʷ. "toʔqʷ" being Squirrel Cove, "ʔoʔp" being Church House. The Church House people are the Homalco people. "tuwa št ʔoʔp" – "We're from Church House." "ʔoʔp qaymixʷ" – "We're Church House people." And the same as Klahoose – "We're toʔqʷ qaymixʷ." So those are the terms, the language that was used for describing people that lived in those areas. So. And prior to that, I would think that was just the name of the territory, and because our people were placed there after contact, they took on the name and it stuck, that we're the ʔoʔp or the toʔqʷ qaymixʷ. Or we're the ɬaʔamɪn qaymixʷ. And "ɬaʔamɪn" being Sliammon. But that's the name of the place, ɬaʔamɪn, that's where I live now. In English, it's "Sliammon" because they couldn't write or pronounce "ɬaʔamɪn." When I write my address down it's "Sliammon," otherwise I won't get my mail, right? So those are the changes that were made. But I think prior to that, from my understanding and from my own memories, that people travelled a lot, even after we were identified as three different people. But I've always felt that we are one people. paʔa št qaymixʷ – we're one people with Klahoose, Homalco, and the Church House people. Prior to that, the old people used to talk about how they worked together very effectively, the three communities. They were one people. They spoke the same dialect. They understood one another. So when we're looking at overlapping territories, you know, I find that difficult – of course it's overlapping! Because we've shared the land. We shared the territory. 'Cause we're one people.*

So it caused a lot of problems when the government decided to separate the people: "Okay, put boundaries here. That's where you people will live, and this is where you people will live." It's caused a lot of problems – it still does today. You know, we disagree on who owns what land and what territory. And I think that's what the treaty is about, to come to terms with that in their treaty work and their agreement with all three Bands, or all three groupings of people that shared the land at one time.† That we can still share the land. And we still are in close contact with the two other groups of people. There's a lot of intermarriages and so we became more of one group of people. And the same as Sechelt. Although we do not speak the same dialect as Sechelt, it's similar. It's close to ours, but a lot of their words I don't understand. Quite a few people came from Sechelt and transferred to Sliammon, I think way before Indian Affairs was in place. They were from Sechelt, and there's a lot of descendants today identifying those people were from Sechelt – nišɛ?ɬ. That's what we call Sechelt: "nišɛ?ɬ." That's their title in our language, the Sechelt people. And Squamish people that transferred to, or married into Sliammon – qʷʊχʷo?miš. That's what we call Squamish: "qʷʊχʷo?miš." So a lot of changes happen that way and people transferred, legally transferred through Indian Affairs to move – transfer to Sliammon or to Klahoose, or wherever they desire to transfer to, for whatever reason. So there were transfers that happened. But they were quite a few that transferred from, from Homalco to Sliammon, and some from Klahoose. If it was through marriage, then they had to legally transfer. If I was to marry a Homalco member, then I would automatically become Homalco in the early days. I don't know if it's still like that now. But if a man married a woman from another community, he had to legally transfer to her community if that's where they wanted to live.

---

* For lists, meanings, and maps of some Homalco, Klahoose, ɬaʔamɪn, and Island Comox place names, see Dorothy Kennedy and Randy Bouchard, *Sliammon Life, Sliammon Lands* (Vancouver: Talonbooks, 1983), 149-70. They explain their orthography, which differs from the one employed in this book, on pages 147-48.

† In August 2012, the Sliammon First Nation voted to approve a Final Agreement with Canada and British Columbia. The Klahoose and Homalco Indian Bands are each engaged in treaty negotiations of their own.

So all these things are governed by the Department of Indian Affairs, our membership. And, you know, speaking of membership, that's all so messed up! Because of the name changes – a lot of people had just one name when they were baptized as a young child, or as a young person. So it's really hard sometimes to trace a person's heritage, or their family line, because of the mess that the Department of Indian Affairs made through membership. Because a lot of children were not baptized until they were probably a teenager, but there was no record of their actual birthdate. And so the names got mixed up too, because "Oh, my dad's name was Joe, so now I'm Elsie Joe!" or whatever. That's an example. And "What was your dad's last name?" "I don't know." So when people went to apply for old age pension, in my time in social work, I kind of helped people through that, researching: "What was your dad's name?" "Well, he only had the one name." So that was really difficult. It's getting a little better now, because things are changing but – so there's not just the overlapping territories and the who owns what, it's who am I? Who am I as a person? It seems like you've got no identity. A true identity of who you are. Am I Klahoose? Am I Homalco? Am I from Comox? Or where did my dad come from? Those things were never questioned before the government stepped in to take over our lives. Everything was recognized. Everything was orderly. Everything was shared and controlled by our own leadership in the day. Our waǰman,* our hʌwhegus. "hʌwhegus" is our advisers in the community, the senior people in the community, like the Elders. Until Indian Affairs stepped in and we went from a hereditary Chief to elected Chief. And things really started to change from then on. Forgetting the old ways of doing things and going to your hegus in the community to – going to Indian Affairs now is giving us direction. Where to go and how to live and what to eat and what language to speak. So there's a lot of change in that, and not always for the good. And people were helpless to – they couldn't fight against the system. 'Cause it was total control of the government and the resources they put in place to help the government to change our lifestyle and where we live.

---

* Translation: watchmen. The position of watchman originated in the 1860s with the Roman Catholic Durieu system. According to Kennedy and Bouchard, Elsie's great-uncle maksɛma (Sandy Timothy) was one of the last watchmen in the community, and her great-grandfather Captain Timothy was the last church captain. Kennedy and Bouchard, *Sliammon Life,* 122. See also the "Additional Readings" at the end of this book.

Yeah, so when we talk about territories, I think it's really important to remember that, for me anyway, that I'm from the coast – I'm a Coast Salish person. But all Coast Salish people are not all the same. We're different. We all have our unique language, our dialect, from other Coast Salish people, like the West Coast people or the people from Saanich or the people from North Island or way up north, Kingcome Inlet and all of these other groupings of people. They all have their own dialect. Along the coast here, like, Campbell River people have a different dialect from us. So we're not all Coast Salish in how some people see us to be. I'm Coast Salish. But I'm a ɬaʔamɩn person. And it's unique that we are three groupings of people, Klahoose and Homalco, that speak the same dialect. And I think that's really important to know – 'cause I think to a person that doesn't know, or is a non-Native person, or is a visitor from elsewhere – that we do not all speak the same dialect 'cause we're brown! You know, "Oh yeah, that's an Indian person. They must be like this or like that, or they must speak this language." And we're not. We have different traditional practices, styles of practices. We use different tools in how we practise our traditional ways. Our spiritual kinds of ceremonies are different in how we do it where I come from, through the teachings of my ancestors, my grandparents especially. That we practise differently than other tribes or bands of people. Theirs is different, different style. But unique to them. And it's important to remember to respect all of the other practices and how they do it, the tools they use. The longhouse.* We don't have that in Sliammon. We never have. We never did. Ours was more the cleansing, the self-care, the taking care of yourself and getting your power, your spirit, by going off and living on your own off the land for as long as it takes. Might be six months you go off to prove yourself. And you do it alone. You bathe in the lake or in the river daily and you just live off the land. And you will eventually find your spirit – your spirit will come to you. You will get your strength, your power to be who you are. And that was very important. The women didn't do that. It was just the men that did that. Women have different rituals, different way of becoming a woman. When you became a woman, there were different ways or practices that acknowledged that you are now a woman. And you are taught by your Elders

---

* By "longhouse," Elsie means practices historically referred to by scholars as "spirit dances" or "winter dances." She is not saying that Sliammon people did not build or live in longhouses or big houses.

how to take care of yourself. That's your life-changing time. You're becoming a woman. You are an adult. You are now responsible in a bigger sense. By being clean. You're given duties to do, like house-keeping and different chores to do, because you're being taught now to be responsible. 'Cause women married very young in my grand-mother's time. My grandmother was I think about twelve when this marriage was arranged for her. Because she's now a woman. And they were together for about seventy years. Yeah, they were quite old when they died. So that was how the different sexes were guided by their parents, their grandparents, of their destiny in life and how to be a good person. It's like training to be an athlete. So we didn't go through the longhouse process. I know very little of how their practice is. But we don't do that. Ours is different from that territory, from those groups of people. The same for Homalco and Klahoose people – we were the different grouping of people in the way we practise. Yeah.

It was all shared. It was never, *ever* competition. But there were certain areas, by certain groups of people that stayed mainly in one particular area, or travelled in one particular area. Whereas, like for an example, Campbell River people or further up north, they didn't always come down this way. But the Sliammon people, Sechelt, Squirrel Cove, Klahoose people, and Homalco, they travelled more on the coast. But it was never in a disrespectful way. They would always go and talk to whomever the leadership in the community, or the "hɑys qɑymixʷ"* as we call it, you know, whoever is in charge. They didn't call them "Chief" back then. But it was like there was always someone that oversaw the other people in each community. And it was disrespectful to just go and help yourself to whatever is available there. Like if we went to Sechelt area, we'd have to go and get permission: "Oh yeah, that's okay." They would give you that okay: "Go ahead." 'Cause there was a lot of resources! And it wasn't restricted.

Well it was the hereditary system, right? That was our leadership. That was who oversaw the people, the community. It wasn't just one person lookin' after the community. It was the Elders, we called them "associates," *[laughs]* the hegus. hegus always had other people that helped them, or they consulted with, in how the community is run. If you didn't have a hɑys qɑymixʷ in your household, you always

---

* Translation: respected/knowledgeable person.

went to another household that has a hays qaymix[w] or knowledgeable
person, or experienced person in whatever it is you're dealing with.
Or a spiritual person. Those could be called "hegus" too because they
assist the people – they help the people. So when we talk about hegus
today, we see hegus as somebody with lots of money, they're wealthy.
You're hegus, you're rich. Different kind of richness in our ancestors'
way of thinking. hegus was you've got lots of knowledge and you share
that knowledge – you pass on that knowledge. So before Indian Affairs,
it wasn't overpowering the people, but it was sharing the knowledge,
sharing the wisdom, and be there as a support person to their family
and their communities. So every community had those people around.
That was very important to the people to have that person.

And all that changed when the election system came in. Chief Tom
– my great-uncle – he was the last hereditary Chief. And he had a
large family. And his father, his dad, who was my great-grandfather,
had a large family. So it didn't go anywhere else. It just stopped there
when Indian Affairs came in. And Charlie was the first elected Chief
in our community. Charlie Peters Williams was the first elected. He
was a very young man. And I don't remember the details of how that
happened or how many Council members there were at that particular
election. But because we were smaller membership then, we had less
elected Councillors. I think there was only three, two or three, and
the Chief. So that has really changed and it's not always for the better.
As the population grew then the elected leaders grew as well, so now
we're at nine elected leaders. And it's done in a real kind of a – it's
not constructive sometimes in how the election system is done.
Anybody could run, whether you know what you're doing or not. It
depends on who you know. So it's so different – the system just
abruptly changed! From that time on. That made this huge change in
our community – and as it grew, now it's really big. We're about a
thousand people now, with about six hundred, six hundred and fifty
maybe, living in our community. A lot have gone away from the community and living elsewhere, whether for jobs or school or they've
transferred out or whatever. So we still have the nine elected leadership. Although there's only over six hundred on reserve. So there's a
breakdown there too, because our people who are living away from
the community don't seem to have much of a say in what goes on
with our government of the day. And they quite often feel left out of
the loop because they don't have an input. But they can vote come
election, although they're not really involved in the running of the
community. And I don't think that's fair. I don't think that's fair to

people living away from home. They still come for a visit and that's still their home. That's where they were born. Their roots are there, their ancestors are there, and their parents or grandparents are there – relatives are there. But they're now sort of in a different category that they're kind of out on left field, you know, and I know they feel they're not included with decision making.

So I don't know if that's all going to change come treaty, when treaty's finalized. I'm not sure about that, what'll happen when we are now self-government – we're gonna have our self-government one day – and whether that's going to make things better. A lot of people are afraid of it. A lot of people are afraid of that change. It's so complex. The whole process is so complex. I'm sure the people that are working in treaty know in their discussions what's happening. But for people on the perimeters, or the people off-reserve or you're not involved daily in the process, it's really hard to understand. I know it is for me. You know, I'd have to hear and see daily what's happening. So – and I'm sure they're trying their very best – and when we come together for a meeting, for me anyway, I still find it hard to grasp where we're at. 'Cause it's just so much content in this whole process. And the whole argument about our territories and where we belong and where were we situated before land claims or treaty, you know? How can we prove we lived there? How can we prove that was part of your land? You know? And then they're asking questions: "Oh, go to the Elders." Talk to the Elders about – "How do you say 'constitution' in your language?" "How do you say–" um, what are all these big high words or strawberry words that the government uses? So in a way that's to define or to prove that we actually lived on this land and we have to translate – or people come to us for translation of big words like "constitution" and "governance" and "traditional territories." What does that mean? Why you asking me that? The Elders used to get really upset, you know, and they don't understand. We've always lived here. "Oh yeah, I lived there. I lived over there. My grandparents had a property over there. They had a house there." And on and on it goes. And then a year later someone else is asking you the same questions again! So you don't know where it's going! *[laughs]* Yeah.

I remember spending some time in Theodosia, at the very mouth of Theodosia where there used to be, I think, the last big house. It was a shared kind of an accommodation, and there was one over there at Harwood too, where the clam bed is, where we've gone digging cockles over there. There's a sandy beach there. So just above that, in the woods there, in the trees. There was one there that I remember.

It was probably ... forty feet, about. And probably twelve, fourteen feet wide? But it's made out of cedar planks. And with a hole on top to let the smoke escape. And a dirt floor. And all around the perimeter were the beds, like, the plank beds. So that was most times shared with families and guests, friends that come to stay. With a central fire in the middle. I guess that wasn't long ago, 'cause I remember seeing it there, the remains of it. And I've seen the one that was in Theodosia. But I imagine there was one wherever.

Last week I went with a group to Cochrane Bay area.* And they uncovered an area there where there was a house. Of, like, 8,200 years ago. And it's dug – it's like a big bowl in the ground. It's big! So they dug around there and found posts down there. The remnants of posts and flooring. And a midden – there's clamshells and that. And they estimated it was 8,200 years ago. Which does not surprise me. It only confirms for me that our people lived on the coast and lived off the land! And they lived off the clams, and people just lived everywhere in nature. I just felt when I was there, that this is where our ancestors were, from ever so long ago. You know, it doesn't surprise me that this has been found. There's proof everywhere that our people lived in all these different locations, all around the territory. Yeah. So what we're getting is a very small portion, I feel. Very, very small. You look at that little dot on the map of the land of the territory. That little piece of land there. That's an Indian reserve. And over here is another little piece. Our people mostly lived in the inlet because it's sheltered in the winter months, like Okeover Inlet and in Theodosia Inlet. 'Cause in Okeover there's a village site at the head. There's a river there. Okeover is "toχʷnač"; "toχʷnač" is the name of that place. And that means it's an inlet, it's a long inlet. "toχʷot" means to string out something, like if you string out a net or a rope. And that's the inlet: toχʷnač. "nač"† is the head. And Theodosia is the other inlet and our people lived there. So in the winter months that was a very safe place to be, because it's sheltered from the wind. So I'm not surprised they found all that there. 'Cause that's what I've always heard.

And I caught the tail end of that in growing up in that kind of environment, that everywhere we went as a child, "We'll stay here overnight. We'll camp here for a couple of nights." And so we'd be there, we'd haul blankets and our pots and pans, whatever our needs

---

* This refers to July 2010.
† Translation: end. Here, Elsie translates using the more common English geographical term "head," as in "head of the inlet."

were that we could carry in a canoe to travel from here to there, from this inlet to the next inlet, and we'd stay there, haul our stuff and just set up camp and be there for overnight or for several days, depending on what was happening around that area at that time. So, and that same thing applied to other people further up the coast here, like the Klahoose people. They had their places where they went, and they knew exactly where to go: "This cabin is there – that's where we'll stay." And these cabins were shared by people that travelled. And so they went in and they would light a fire and cook their meal, whatever they did. But every time, before they left they replenished the wood, the kindling, and left it just as they found it. That's how much respect there was. No one came around, vandalized these places. It was kept like that. It was simple, but it was shelter. So there were different places like that all over the coast, up to Toba Inlet. For us, we reached up there. We travelled up there. We didn't go up to Bute Inlet much. I remember once going up there. Maybe before that people travelled up there more, but that's Homalco's territory up there. Because I guess that's where they were when people came and said, "Okay, you can keep that as your reserve" or "We'll situate you there." And up to Toba Inlet and some people were living there. "Okay, now you're gonna stay there. We'll corral you in!" So no more of this wandering around all over the coast for us! "Okay, you're the Sliammon people. You stay here now! Don't you go beyond these borders!" In Sliammon where I live, right by Powell River, tiyskʷat, there's a river there, or there was a river there, way before my time that I remember. It was in the early 1900s that river was dammed when they decided to build a mill there. And our people lived on that site by the river. Our people always lived where there was a river, or creek, or where there's water. And so when they decided to put us on reserves, they took us from that area, took my great-grandparents from that area and placed them in Sliammon. There's a boundary there: "You are now the Sliammon Band." Well, I don't – I don't care for those titles they put on our people. We are ɬaʔamɪn qaymixʷ. We're people of the land. 'Cause our people travelled all over the land! They just didn't stay in this corral like a bunch of cattle.

So it happened gradually over time. It didn't happen overnight. I remember seventy years ago, or seventy-two years ago, in all that time there's been a lot of change. Like I was saying, I caught the tail end of it by remembering those two big houses, the longhouses – one was over at Harwood Island, on this side. And I'm sure there were others on this side of the island. Because our people stayed in different parts of that island over there: "Oh, this was so-and-so that lived there." Like, "Jimmy Williams lived there and his family," and "The Harry family lived over there on that side," and "Over on the far side was the Williams property." There was no fences. There was no borders. But they just – that was their favourite spot as a family to go there. No one said, "You can't go over there. You can't go there." It was open. And that's what they chose as their spot and that's where they would go. On Cortes Island, p'aq'ey?ajɩm, that's one of our reserves. But it's small. People lived there, and they lived in cabins as well. And nobody has lived there in a long time. But it still belongs to Sliammon, that particular parcel of land. And there were just cabins all over the place. And people that lived at Emmonds Beach had cabins there. Our people haven't lived there since it was given away! *[chuckles]* Yeah, it's a beautiful place. It's a beautiful place to go fishing outside of there. You know, it's sheltered and there's a creek going through there. That's where my auntie Katherine was born. They lived there. Yeah, there was quite a number of people that lived there, 'cause the fishing outside of there is good, and the land is nice. They had gardens and that. They still have gardens there! *[laughs]* Vegetable gardens, I think. Um-hmm. That's where a lot of our people were when the smallpox hit, was in Emmonds Beach. I'm sure there's a lot of remains there. I'm sure of that! Because people didn't get moved or, you know, there was not enough manpower to move people to somewhere else for burial. A lot of people were buried there. There were a lot of people that come down with the smallpox. And the rest of the people were looking after them, getting them water. Pretty soon they were getting sick. There was no one else to get water for them. People died on their way to the creek, going crawling to the creek to get water. So this is what my grandparents told me about. And that was a real sad time. There were hundreds of people that got wiped out. And that was one area that there was a large group of our people there. Yeah. So when they designated these lands out, people didn't have a say: "I want to keep that property! That's where our families lived. That's where our people died! That's where our people are buried." We're told, "You can't live here. It belongs to someone else now." In my heart I know that is our piece of land because my ancestors lived there. No consideration of that sort was given to our people. It was just, "We designate this land to you and, okay, you people stay there. We'll build a church there and you stay there." It's like – I don't know what to call it. Yeah. I think it was so unfair. So unfair how things were done.

So in the older times when I was much younger, I used to hear a lot of the people saying, "That used to be our property. My great-grandfather lived over there. That was his property, although it was never surveyed at the time or identified. It was not registered that that portion of land belonged to my great-grandfather." I know my grandparents always had this end of the community. And like, the Timothy family had this end of the community, about three houses before the church – it was where the Timothy family was situated, all the way up to over here. Yeah, so you know, the way people travelled, it was so easygoing. No restrictions. Just get on your boat and go there. Put up a sail – you will get there much quicker if the wind is blowing the right way. And living in Theodosia and in Okeover and Grace Harbour. It's like this fella phoning this morning. "What was the origin of that cabin in Grace Harbour?" he asked me this morning on the phone.* And I didn't quite understand: "What do you mean about 'origin of that cabin'? Who lived there first? My people have always lived there." "But is it correct to say that Chief Tom Timothy lived his last days there and died there?" "No!" *[laughs]* Yeah, he lived there most of his life, but I remember him here in Sliammon. He was our last hereditary Chief. That was my grandfather's brother. Yeah, and he lived here and he died here. But when he was younger, he always lived around the inlet. "q'aʔq'eyq'ay" is Grace Harbour. That's a small village site: q'aʔq'eyq'ay. The meaning of that is, it's like a place you go and stay. Camp. q'aʔq'eyq'ay is like – "q'aʔyem'" is to stay overnight. So that tells me that's what's behind that name. Same as maksɛma, Sandy, the other brother. He loved being around Okeover, toχʷnač. He loved being out here. He loved being out at Texada Island and other side of Harwood Island, and Mystery Reef and all those little reefs way out there. Yeah, he had cabins all over the place.

Theodosia was where my grandmother was born and raised. As well as her grandparents. That's where they always lived. And it was a beautiful village site there. It was the homestead of our people on my Granny Molly's side. Bob George† family lived up there, in Theodosia. And it was pretty much that family, Bob George family, that occupied Theo. And they had nice houses there. I recall about three houses there, like, permanent homes. They were not little cabins. They were really nice homes. And by the time I was probably twelve or so, or

---

* This refers to July 2010.
† Bob George was Elsie's maternal grandmother's (Granny Molly's) father.

ten maybe, going up there, they had pretty much depleted and were getting all rotted down. But that's where they lived was up there. I remember as a child going up there. The one that's further up the slough, on your right as you're going up, is where Granny Molly's house was. I don't know if that was her grandmother's house, prior to her, or her mother's house. But it was a fairly big house. It was a comfortable house. That's where I remember going up that slough and tying up and there was so much snow! And I guess being a child I thought it was really high. It was like a tunnel taking you to the house. Must've been pretty cold winter up there. It used to get really cold up there. And so, therefore, people would leave there in the winter until it thawed. And then they would go back again, and they would come back down here, 'cause Bob George had a home here too. So they travelled back and forth. It was quite convenient, you know. They travelled a lot. When we went to Cochrane Bay, we were going around, past Bliss Landing there. That's where people would take a shortcut if it was windy. If they wanted to go inside the inlet, then they would pull into Bliss Landing and they had a pass going over to the other side into the inlet. And they would pack their belongings, and sometimes pack their canoe over to the other side. And it's not an easy task. So they had ways and means of getting to where they're going, you know, come hell or high water. I was asking Henry Bob about that one time: "What is the name of Bliss Landing?" "Oh, qɛgišɛyɪn," he said. "Oh! How'd you know that?" He said, "Oh, that's where we used to qɛgiš" – you know, going over. Overland. To the other side. So they named it "qɛgišɛyɪn." And the other place is "qɛgɑyɪn." It's real narrow – it's closer to Theodosia. And if you come out of there, it's another shortcut. It's different from the one in Bliss Landing. So it's like a grassy kind of area, and it's so easy to walk over and you're onto the other side. You're into Theodosia area. And we used to live there, on the other side, when my grandparents had their cabin on the float.

Now we go up to toqʷanən,* there's overtaken by other people. You can't go to the beach and get clams. You can't go onto the beach and go onto the shore to go gather roots or whatever: "Get off there! This land is private property." So we're very restricted now and our territory that used to be our gathering grounds, my grandparents' gathering

---

* toqʷanən refers to a village at the head of the inlet named "Theodosia" by settlers.

grounds. Yeah, it's restricted. A lot of oyster leases through that area and Okeover Inlet and, yeah. So there's not much to get there anymore. They're trying to revive the river. The river was diverted to Powell Lake, I don't know how many years ago. That was quite a while ago. But there's been work done to get some of that water diverted back into toqʷanən River. I went up there and I was just horrified. I was just blown away. My nephew Lee George took me up there. He works for our hatchery. And I've heard about this diversion, and so one day I went with him way up the river, about four miles up. And it was nothing but, like, this huge slab of concrete or cement across the whole river way up there when they diverted the river. And men did that! You know? Human beings did that! They diverted the natural flow of the river where the salmon came up. So for a long time there were no salmon going up there, because they couldn't get up the river. So it was pretty sad, really sad. And they've totally ruined the land down below, where our reserve used to be.* There was a landslide, and I don't know how that happened, but there's debris – we walked down through a trail and couldn't go down any further because it was a mess there. Debris and rocks and tree stumps and everything. So it's really ruined there for people that want to go back and live there! You know, nobody had thought of the consequences: "If we do this, this is what's going to happen." They just went ahead and did it. Again, there's no consultation. "What is it going to do to that river that goes through that Indian reserve there?" It's a small place, but it had a lot of use for our people.

You know, we would've been a lot better off if we had choices. We were lucky to get that little piece in Sliammon, 'cause it's a nice location there. And we're getting crowded as it is now, 'cause the population's growing. But when I say we "got" the land, it was designated to us, but it's not our land. It still belongs to – who does is it belong to? The government, or the Queen or the – who? *[laughs]* Certainly not mine! I can't call it mine. My house is mine, but I can't claim the land to be mine. It belongs to the Queen. The Queen doesn't even know me! I have to send her copy of my book. *[laughs]* Yeah. So you're so restricted in what you can do on the land that you're sitting on, that's not really yours. It's sad. And when you die, you got to report

---

* Today this reserve (IR No. 4) is uninhabited. It was greatly damaged by the construction of the dam as well as by logging in the area. For more information, see the "Additional Readings" at the end of this book.

to the Department of Indian Affairs. Otherwise, they have to decide who's going to get your house, who's going to live in that house, who's going to live on that property. If I had a car and I willed it to one of my grandchildren or my children, I have to ask permission of Department of Indian Affairs. They are – what are they? Our guardians? Well, they don't do a good job of being guardians of the people, let alone the land. Our rights. I just don't understand that system. Yeah, I can't go to a lawyer and say, "Here's my will. You take care of this. I want to register this." Sure, I can do that, but Indian Affairs will counteract that and argue their point with the lawyer that I don't have the right to go and decide what happens to my property. Even through a lawyer. They have to have a hand in it. Make sure it doesn't get spent the wrong way and – ugh! *[laughs]* Oh my. So, those are just one of the things I think that – when we're talking about our rights, our territory, our right to make a decision – not everybody's helpless and can't make a decision. Sure, maybe some people need guidance and support, but not everybody's in that same boat. We're, like, lumped into that same boat that, "Oh you all don't know what you're doing and you don't know where to go and what to do and what to buy, how to spend your money." Like we're children! We're wards of the government. That's what it boils down to! So those rights of ours were taken away a long time ago, in my grandparents' time. Yeah.

The end of this month is their hundredth birthday in Powell River.[*] And there's a big write-up in *Powell River Living* magazine, celebrating this and celebrating that, and how Powell River originated, how it first started. And I'm thinking, we were here! We were already here. My ancestors were here for thousands of years. And this man comes along in his schooner or whatever, he came by: "Oh, what a drab place this is." It's like, didn't notice the Indians around. Maybe they were hiding – they were scared of the schooner. 'Cause that is part of the story too, that people would run and hide. They didn't know what that schooner was. They thought it was a floating island or whatever. They were afraid of it. It took them a while to warm up to them coming to shore. So maybe that's why this guy didn't see any Indians at the town – downtown Powell River there. 'Cause that was the village site. Powell River was the shortest river, right? And big salmon went up there, so people lived there. But this guy – that story is in that magazine, says that it was just a drab place, desolate, drab.

---

[*] This refers to July 2010.

Sliammon village waterfront in 2008. Elsie's residence is above the beach on the left-hand side of the photo. Photo courtesy of Davis McKenzie.

And then he went away and then someone else came along and saw the possibility of building the mill site there and damming the river. Not one word is mentioned about he seen some Indian people, or he seen living people! *[laughs]* And that kind of ticked me, you know? And I have mixed feelings about that. Now I'm asked to go and – to join in the celebration. And *[sighs]* so I have to really prepare myself for that, you know. The past is the past, I realize that. That's all happened way back when. And I've got a lot of good friends now in Powell River and, you know, we are part of the community. And so I have to work with that. I have to accept that. But just the way that, when stories are being written, the true story, the true history is never talked about, you know? That related to the story of that day, add a little piece about who lived here, that we actually were – not me, but my great-grandparents, my ancestors for thousands of years. It's never mentioned in there. And I think that has to be mentioned. So I'd like to have that mentioned in my book, *[laughs]* in case people didn't know! And I think a lot of people don't know that. They don't know that. The newcomers, the younger people – I'm sure the first people that came are all long gone. There's no one that will remember that day. That's a hundred years ago!

So people need to know how we became where we're at, how we were moved and – it's like being fenced in over there: "You're not allowed to come on this side of the fence." So seems like all our lives we've been fenced in somewhere. Going to residential school and you're in this institution and it's fenced in. You can't go outside the fence. There's no freedom to do what our people were used to, living and moving and going from place to place, and there were no boundaries, no restrictions as to where you can go. People would climb the highest mountain to go and hunt for mountain goat, wherever that may be. And they were very industrious and so self-reliant and survivors. And they knew how to survive and how to gather food and work together and be just – families helping families. And getting along with one another. And if you didn't get along, you were sat down and dealt with by the hegus in your community, by your leader, by the Elders, whomever they were. They were always there. There was always those designated people. It wasn't written somewhere in a book, or you had to fill out a form to do this, or whatever you had to do. People worked in harmony with one another. And I'm sure there were some that didn't, you know, abide by the rules, and they were dealt with accordingly.

Legends

A MAN TAKEN BY THE SEAL FAMILY[*]

So this story is about a man and the seal, or the man that was taken by the seal family. Years ago, our people went seal hunting. And the way they did that was there would be two of them that would go together. 'Cause the seal will sink as soon as you kill it, soon as you've shot it. It only stays afloat for just a few minutes, and then it'll sink. And this happened around Mink Island, just up the coast here. And the people used to say this is a true story. I used to hear it over and over when I was a young girl, about the man that was taken by the seal. Then they would point out this one area when we were travelling up and down the coast here. And we quite often went by Mink Island, and we actually lived in Mink Island for some time. And my grandparents used to talk about this: "This is where the man was taken by the seal." And it's real rock bluff, and there was always seals around there. Seemed to be always active and about.

So this one day these two men went seal hunting, and one of them stayed on the bluff. The one that's going to shoot the seal is on the bluff, and the other person is on the boat, but kind of hidden. So the man on the bluff shot a seal. And the plan is for the fellow on the boat to rush out right away so he could grab the seal before it sinks. And they were not far from the shore, but it's very deep in that area. So the guy on the bluff took a shot at the seal, hit his target. The fella on the boat started to paddle out very quickly. But at the same time, the man that had shot the seal dove into the water, and he started swimming out there towards the seal. And before he got there, the seal went under. And the man followed it. He dove under to retrieve

---

[*] For another version of this story, see Mary George, "The Seal: A Traditional Sliammon-Comox Story," in *Salish Myths and Legends: One People's Stories,* ed. M. Terry Thompson, Steven M. Egesdal, and Honoré Watanabe (Lincoln: University of Nebraska Press, 2008), 121-29.

the seal. And the fella on the boat just sat on the boat and waited for him to come back up, and he never came back up. He was gone. And he stayed and stayed and waited and – wondering what happened. And he knew something has gone wrong. So he waited for a while. All of a sudden *all* these seals came to the surface. They were just *all* over the place. They were splashing around and making all kinds of noise. And that was the end of that man. He never surfaced. So the story goes that the seal family took this man and kept him.

So for years later people used to see, on the beach at night – especially in Grace Harbour because our people lived in Grace Harbour – and at low tide, in the winter months, the seals would come onto the beach. And they could see that there was one seal that really resembled a person, a human being. But they couldn't catch him. They tried to catch him. They would go and lay in wait for the seals. They'd sneak down there at night and wait for the seals to come in. And sure enough the seals would come in and they're on the beach, and this one time this one man just really snuck up and ran and managed to grab a hold of this man, the seal man. And by now he'd started to grow a hide, like fur. But he was really slippery, and he fought against the person that caught him. He couldn't hang on to him. And he slipped away and dove back into the water. So for years, they used to say – when I was growing up, they would always talk about that – the man that was taken by the seal. And they say they see him sometimes come out of the water with the rest of the seals and bobbing around the water, and he looked more like a man than he did a seal. So that's how the story came about. And they swore it was a true story that this man was taken away, and now lives with the seals. So that's the end of that story. ☙

TWINS ARE GIFTED

This healer, him and his twin brother, they could really read each other so well, they could feel, they could sense what the other one was doing.[*] Because twins are very sensitive to each other. They share

---

[*] The healer, named Felix, resided at toqʷanən in Theodosia Inlet and therefore was known as "toqʷanən pɛlʉks." Another story about toqʷanən pɛlʉks and his healing work is shared in Chapter 7. The anthropologist Homer Barnett

the same feelings. And because people travelled and camped quite a lot, the other brother went over to the other side of Texada Island. They were fishin' out there and a storm came up. So they decided just to camp there, on the far side of Texada, decided just to stay put and wait out the storm. And they had been gone for a couple of nights, and the mother got really worried. She was becomin' very concerned – it's been two days, maybe three days, and he hasn't come back from his trip. There's him and this other man that had gone on this trip. So she said to her son, to Felix, said, "Why are you not worried about your brother? You should be doing something. He's been gone for several days and you should be worried. You should be concerned. You should find him – go and find him." "Oh," he says, "oh, I'll meditate on it." And he did. He went out to his fire, lit his fire and called upon the energy, the spirits around him, and reached out to his brother. Looked for him: "Where are you?" When he came out of his trance he said to his mother, "Oh, I found him. He's okay. He's camped way over there, outside of Texada Island, or that island over there. That's where he's at."

And when the brother came back home, he told *his* story of how his brother found him over there. He said while they were camped, he seen a lightning way at the point – point of, like, Blubber Bay end there. He seen a lightning there. It just flashed there and there was thunder. And then it came closer to where they were. And then it came *very* close to where they were. Three times that hit. And it was gone. So he said to his travelling companion, "That was my brother. He's looking for me. Now he's gone. He's found us." So that was his story when he came back.

And to me I don't doubt that that happened. That was the story that was always told in our family. So workin' with things, like, workin' with nature, that they were able to use the resources – that nature was the resources of the people. Whatever it was, the water, the lightning, the animals, the birds. *Everything's* connected. And in that particular case it was the lightning that found a way for them.

presents a discussion of twins that is generalized across the Coast Salish peoples, but it is clear that he acquired some of his information on the special way in which twins were regarded from his ɬaʔamɩn informant Chief Tom (Elsie's great-uncle). Homer G. Barnett, *The Coast Salish of British Columbia* (Eugene: University of Oregon Press, 1955), 135-36, 139-40.

So to me, that's a very special story. It doesn't happen if you are not a believer. And that's what we were always told: "You have to believe. You have to honour. You have to be serious. It's not a laughing matter. You do not belittle the work that the worker does, the healer does. Respect that healer. Honour what he does. Believe in it. Only then will good things happen. Or only then will you hear what is the truth." And these are proven facts as far as I'm concerned. That because people believed, and they went into it believing, and getting the answer they were looking for. They were rare. They were gifted people. They were very gifted people. Like in this incident with the two brothers. Because they were twins – our people have always believed that twins carry good energy. They are gifted. They come with gifts. So in this case, it was proven that they were gifted.

Child

2

Life with My Grandparents

Well, my name is Elsie Paul. My ancestral name is qaʔaχstales, a name that was handed down to me by my grandfather. That was the ancestral name of his mother. My grandfather's dad was Captain Timothy. His name was William, but everybody just called him Captain Timothy. I didn't even know his name for the longest time. I just knew of him as Captain Timothy. And he got that name by showing the explorers around the coast, the first explorers that came to our coast. And so he got nicknamed Captain Timothy. His parents did not want – that would be my great-great-grandparents – didn't want him to go and get lost and go away on that schooner he was on. They looked for him and at the same time they'd gone and picked a wife for him. In those days, trade was happening a lot between the different communities, like Sliammon would go to Campbell River and do some trading of goods or food and stuff. And so that's how they knew that family from Cape Mudge. So they really wanted their son to come back home. So after a couple attempts, they got him to come off the ship: "We want you to come home. We want you to settle down. We don't want you to get lost. And we want you to stay home, come home." So they brought him home and they told him, "We've got a wife picked for you. A nice family up in Cape Mudge." Cape Mudge is another First Nations community. So they brought him over there, and this woman was from a large family, and several girls in the family. And so the family all came out and they got together and gathered in this one place. And he seen these girls, and he said,

"What if I choose this other one?" Yeah, he chose to pick another one, other than the one they picked for him. It was funny, I guess. It was kind of bold of him, because you just didn't do – it would have been insulting to the one they had picked. But I guess he knew love when he spotted love, and there you go! There's no arguing around that. So they let him. They said, "Okay, you can take this one."

And that was Annie. Her name was Annie. And her ancestral name was qaʔaχstɑles. I carry that name now 'cause my grandfather said to me, "I want you to carry my mother's name." My other cousins carry that name too, as well. I barely remember her. My memory of her is as a real thin, small woman with a long dress. And she always wore a hat of some kind. But she was very thin, very lean. But I always remember in her bed, because she lived at my grandparents'. I guess her husband had passed away. I don't remember him at all. But she was living alone by then, quite an elderly woman. And she lived in a lean-to attached to my grandparents' home. And I remember sleeping in her bed. I loved her bed 'cause she had a feather-down mattress and feather-down quilt. All handmade from the ducks. All plucked and all the feathers saved over – how long would that be to save all those feathers? But that's what I remember most about that elderly woman, was sleeping in her bed and snuggled up to her. And her smoking her pipe! She had this pipe that would be just glowing in the dark. She'd be puffing and I just really liked the smell of that smoke from her pipe. Yeah. I don't remember if we had any conversation. But that part is vivid in my mind, being in her bed. Yeah, she was quite elderly then.[*]

Arranged marriages, to my recollection, would be my great-grandparents: Captain William Timothy that married a lady from Cape Mudge on Quadra Island. That's the first that I know within our family. And then my grandmother Molly and my grandfather lɑsɑ, Jim Timothy, that was an arranged marriage as well. And then later on would have been Aunt Agnes. There was arranged marriage to happen, but it didn't happen because she refused to go ahead with it. And this was already in the time of when we had the church here in the

---

[*] According to Chief Tom (Elsie's grandfather's brother), Captain Timothy and Annie (Elsie's great-grandparents and Chief Tom's parents) were healers. Homer G. Barnett, *The Coast Salish of British Columbia* (Eugene: University of Oregon Press, 1955), 235, 236; University of British Columbia, Rare Books and Special Collections, H.G. Barnett Fonds, Box 1, Folder 6, Field notes: "Mainland Comox (Slaiämɑn, Klahuse, Homalco), 1936," 234.

Captain William Timothy and his wife, qaʔaχstales (Annie Assu), Elsie's great-grandparents, in the early 1900s. Elsie's grandfather lasɑ (Jim Timothy) was the son of Captain Timothy and qaʔaχstales and gave the name of qaʔaχstales to Elsie. Photo courtesy of Elsie Paul.

community. And the church could see she was really unhappy about something, and got her by herself and questioned her, why she's looking sad or unhappy or teary. She was very upset. She didn't want to go through with this marriage. She didn't know the fella that was arranged between the two families. And so she told the priest, "This is not my idea. It's my parents' idea." And the priest went to my grandparents and said, "This is so wrong. You're forcing this girl to marry a man she doesn't want to marry. So the marriage is off." That marriage didn't go through. But my grandparents' marriage was arranged, and it went through, and they lived to be old, old people and I think they were married for something probably like seventy-five or close to eighty years, seventy-five I would think. He was quite a bit older than her, and she was quite elderly when she passed away. It's hard to determine age a long time ago, because births were not registered. So could be ten years off, you know, you don't know for sure. So they lived together all those years, and died within six months of each other. As did my great-grandparents – they lived together all their lives. And I know a lot of other families that have had that, arranged marriages that lived together a long, long time because they picked families that the parents or the grandparents figured were a good match. And most times it worked. And then for myself, I almost got into that, where a lady came to my grandmother, probably when I was about, I don't know, maybe fifteen-ish. And this lady came knocking on the door and just outright asked my grandmother, "I want my son to marry your granddaughter." And I was so afraid of that! I was really frightened, 'cause I didn't know that man at all! He was much older than I. So luckily my grandmother pondered for a minute or two or five, and said, "No, no, she's too young to get married. No, I don't think so." What a relief for me to hear that. Needless to say, this lady was very upset and slammed the door on her way out. She was not happy with my grandmother. Oh, I was really relieved. 'Cause arranged marriages happened at a very young age for most girls. You didn't have a choice. Didn't matter if the man was much older than you, but he's got prestige, he's got a boat, he's got a – whatever. He's already established and – so you didn't have choice as a young girl. 'Cause he's going to be a good provider for you and he's going to be a good husband. He comes from a good family. So that's how those marriages were arranged. And I don't know of any cases that didn't work. There were quite a few that I remember hearing about. That would be during my grandmother's and my great-grandparents' time. So I think it ended after my grandparents' time, like, during my mom's time. I don't recall it happening after that. 'Cause it was all arranged through the church then, you know, that people had to go see the priest and get some counselling and all that, and to get married you prepared through the church. Yeah, so that's pretty much the details of the arranged marriages that I know.

There was a dowry system. Whatever the man's family had to offer to the girl's family. It could be anything from blankets or other goods. Whatever they had in the day. Could be a canoe. Could be, I don't know – just goods, 'cause there wasn't an awful lot of money. There was no money, actually. But it was other goods that were offered. Canoe was a big thing. It was a big thing. 'Cause there were a lot of canoe builders, cedar canoe builders, back in the day. Everybody had a canoe. They had their own canoes. So if that was the intention, then whoever in that family would've prepared and built that canoe and offered it for dowry for the hand of this young woman, offered it to the family, her family.

Yeah. So that was a good, good match for Captain Timothy and the woman he was with all his life. Came here, moved from Quadra after the ceremony and just stayed here, never went back. They lived happily ever after and had many children, of which Chief Tom Timothy comes from. He was my grandfather's brother. And Sandy Timothy, another brother. And numerous sisters, siblings that went from Squirrel Cove to Homalco to Squamish. So they're spread out all over the place and so it's a very big tree that comes from that union. So I'm very honoured to carry that name. There aren't very many ancestral names left because all those names were taken away from our people, back at that time, you know, upon contact, and we were given Christian names, biblical names. So my grandparents lost their ancestral names. So in our culture it's very important, it's very necessary, to always acknowledge all your siblings and where they're from, and you'll hear it quite often at gatherings, how they acknowledge the different branches of the family and how they're connected. Yeah, it's very important to our people, the traditional way of life. Which I was accustomed to when I was growing up.

I grew up with my grandmother. She took me as a child, actually, a new baby when she took me. Because my parents – my mother and father were moving to Port Alberni. And they already had two very small children that was just a year and two years older than I. And as was the custom with our people, the grandmothers always helped with bringing children up. That was really important. No one questioned that. And when my grandmother took me as a new baby, she told my mother, "I'm gonna keep the baby. Your hands are full with these two small babies." And besides, my grandmother had lost her youngest daughter with that residential school experience that we all have heard and know about. She was about ten when she was taken away to residential school, in Sechelt. And she got very ill, very sick there, within a few months. And by the time they let my grandparents know – they went to pick her up by canoe to Sechelt. They got her home and she was so weak they had to pack her on and off the boat. And within a few days she had died. So her name was Elsie. So that's where I got my name from. My grandmother, when I was born, wanted me to be named Elsie after the daughter that she lost. So she raised me, I guess, as a replacement for the daughter she lost. And it's been good. For me it was very good. I thank her for that. So they took me. Kept me. And I stayed there the rest of my life with them – the rest of their life. I grew up with them and – treated me like I was their own. I was just an extension of their children. And a lot of the families were like that. A lot of grandparents took on grandchildren, especially if the mother was single or the spouse had passed away or whatever. They always just came together and took – whether they could afford it or not! They just accepted you into the family. So that's how I came to be with my grandparents was through their generous big heart. They raised other grandchildren. I don't think there was ever a time that they didn't have grandchildren around, some of us more permanent than others. Yeah, and they raised a bunch of kids – my grandparents had a large family. They had a lot of children together. A lot of them died, at a very young age. She had sixteen children, and out of the sixteen, six survived. So she had lost ten children throughout her life. Some at a very young age and some, you know, like the girl they lost through residential school, she was probably about ten or eleven when she got sick and died. But the rest were babies. They were very young babies, through one type of illness or another. And they died – she lost two children in one day. Got very sick and within a day two of her children died. These were just very young children yet. So that was most difficult for them as parents. So I guess that's why they took us in as grandchildren. I guess maybe in some ways we helped their loss in that way. Yeah.

My grandfather was easygoing. He was easygoing. He was a man of very few words. But he was busy. He was always busy doing something. And my grandmother was the boss. She was this short woman. Short and tubby – kind of chubby. And I always remember when she was upset about something, her legs were so short, like they barely touch the floor like that *[gesturing]*, and she'd stomp her feet. *[laughs]* And she would get really annoyed at him in later years 'cause he was quite deaf. He was really deaf. And so she would be jabbering away at him and it's like he's ignoring her. Maybe he was pretending to be deaf, I don't know! Yeah, she was a good woman, my grandmother. She was the boss of the house and controlled the house. She never laid a hand on me. She never struck me. Neither did my grandfather. So they were very loving and nurturing to me. So I was really lucky that way. I have good memories of them, real good memories. Yeah.

I DIDN'T HAVE A lot of opportunities to get into mischief when I was growing up. Sometimes I think I was always old. *[laughs]* 'Cause I grew up with old people, right? And you always had to behave. And you listen up when you're told something. And you didn't really have a chance to get into any mischief. I was always around with the older generation, and doing what they did. I wouldn't say there was no fun, because to me, it was just a way of life – what we did, what my grandparents did. I just went along with that. There were not an awful lot of girls my age when I was growing up. And I think because just being with my grandparents – and quite often we travelled in isolation from other families – just to be with my grandfather, for him to do what he had to do, like, he's logging – "handlogging," they called it. Or just when he needs to be near the fishing ground that he's fishing in. So it wasn't like a daily interaction with other young people. But from time to time we would get together, like my being around Sue Pielle and Liz, and our families were situated together. Then we had all the fun time of playing on the beach and going in the little canoe fishing, and that was at Harwood Island that I spent time with that family. But other than that a lot of it was spent almost like in isolation from other young people. So there was not a lot of that. But a lot of our fun and recreation was from the grandparents and grandfather making little toys, dugout canoes for the little boys to play with. And he made little ones – so that was a real treasure for the boys. They would go and play with the little canoes down the beach. Little handmade canoes. And for myself, as a young girl, a little girl, I remember my grandmother making little tiny dolls about the size of your little finger out of old rags and whatever she had. And they looked like little dolls, and oh! I treasured those! I had a *bunch* of them. I only had one doll that I remembered that was, like, a porcelain doll – like, had this porcelain head. And I thought that was really something. And later on I acquired more dolls. And my grandmother used to talk about how I always favoured the one that was the saddest-looking doll. *[laughs]* I don't know where she got these dolls from, but she picked it up. Maybe through trading. But I remember having a whole line of dolls *all* lined up, sitting propped against the wall. They're all sitting together. But I always favoured the saddest-looking one. *[laughs]* I don't know why! I would just play like they're a family. Put them in groups of families. And I guess we had the church then, and I laid it out like how we all sit when we go to church, *all* in rows and rows, and all facin' one way, and one side are the men over there. They're all facing the front, the altar area. And then have one up at the front that is the priest, right? Facing the people. My grandmother thought that was pretty funny that I created that. And I don't know how old I would have been then. I was probably around six years old. But that was because my grandmother would go to church and take me to church. So that was my little church group. All with little kerchiefs on their head. *[laughs]* You didn't go to church without your kerchief, in my grandmother's day. You had to have your head covered. Because if you didn't have a kerchief on your head, you were sent out of church. But that is the extent of the toys that I had. I didn't have a lot of toys. I didn't have any books, like, to read. Like, storybooks for children? We never had that. All I had was just storytelling. I was told in the language. And I guess that's pretty much the same as reading out of a book. But these were stories or legends and things like that, that was readily available for me. Yeah. So that was my kind of recreation. That was my kind of fun time.

   I lived there on the spit at Harwood Island where my grandfather had pulled up our houseboat there. And we lived there for that one summer. And that was really a fun time. Going out fishing. I used to do some fishing – just trolling. It wasn't a rod-and-reel kind of fishing, but it was just a fishing line. And that was a lot of fun. And that was the summer that I think I first really got to know Sue Pielle. And we were the same age. And her and I did a lot of fun things together. Just going out fishing and, you know, spending time with our parents, grandparents. So that was a lot of time, just being out in the boat and enjoying things in nature. Going out jiggin' for cod. Or going out clam diggin'. To me that was fun. That was my activity. It kept you busy. Kept you, you know – just occupied your time, so you didn't have time to be bored or – you were so tired by the end of the day that you went willingly to sleep. *[laughs]* Course we didn't have radio or TV or anything, so we made our own fun.

Another time I remember, my very early childhood, I guess, maybe I was probably about eleven, we were up in Salmon Bay that summer. Up in Brem River. And that's close to Toba – just close to Toba there. There were some houses up there. Yeah, it didn't belong to us, but uh, the people let us live in those houses. And so there were a lot of other people there. And I'm not sure what they were doing there, if they were logging. But we were there for a few months. And Bill Mitchell was there, and quite a number of other families were there. And so that's where we lived. It was quite remote, quite isolated. But that's where the living was at that particular time. And some of them are working for a small logging outfit, handloggers, real gyppo loggin' outfits. Now people can't do that anymore because everything is owned by big companies. Back then it was gyppo outfits. And being up there and, again, that was with Sue Pielle and her family and we'd play together and – oh gosh! I remember one incident. Sue and Liz and I got into mischief. And I don't know where we got this tobacco from, but we wanted to experiment smoking. So, we went *[laughs]* and we were hiding in the old boat that was pulled up on a beach. Old fish boat. So we went in there and we had this cigarette – I don't know if we rolled it, or if it was already rolled. It wasn't bought cigarettes. You had to roll it. So there we're sharing this one cigarette and I was getting green at the same time. And who should come along but Bill Mitchell? That's Sue Pielle and Liz's dad. And I got away just in time. I don't think we were in the boat. I think we were outside of the boat and hiding on the side. And I took off. I ran home. And I got home and there was Bill Mitchell getting after his girls, "You go on home! You're smoking and you're in trouble and –!" Oh, he was taking them home. *[laughs]* And I was already in the house and it was just right close by. And I was like, "Oh! Thank goodness I escaped that." So the girls didn't tell on me, but I *was* there. *[laughs]* Oh my gosh! That was my big mischief. But my two friends got into trouble. I'm sure they were dealt with! Grounded, I'm sure. Well that's one memory that sticks in my mind, oh my gosh! We got into mischief.

In Sliammon before we had plumbing into the homes, in the old homes, we had homes that first came from, I guess, the department. And we had to pack water. And we would go to the river and do our laundry. Like in the summer months especially. Made sure that all the heavy laundry, like the bedding and blankets, were washed. But we would also have a real good time swimming in a swimming hole. It's still there yet, and it was deep enough that we – bunch of us would go there and we'd take our bedding and wash it and help each other and wheel it home in this old wheelbarrow, and take it home and hang it over the rail or on the clothesline. But it was fun. We made fun. Like, we made our own fun by doing those things.

And my grandmother had a *big* orchard over there, close to the river. And that was my dad's mom. And she was really protective of her orchard. And a bunch of us kids would go and raid her orchard. *[laughs]* And she would come yellin' at us, "You kids get out of here! You're stealing my apples!" Oh, we'd be running out of there with apples we'd scooped up in our dress or our shirt and – *[laughs]* oh my! So those were our fun times, our mischief times. Yeah. You know, life was tough but we didn't have much for entertainment outside of doing work. But work became our entertainment and, you know, we didn't see the hard part of the work. It was what we all did. It was what was expected of us. Yeah.

MAYBE A HUNDRED YEARS ago or whatever, our people didn't celebrate Christmas per se. Like, there's no Christmas or Easter celebration, or Halloween and all these holidays that we see on the calendar – St. Patrick's Day and everything, you know. For us as First Nations people, I think every day was pretty much the same. It's the seasons that our people honoured and acknowledged. It wasn't, like, this is July the first or this is Labour Day or this is Canada Day – all these different holidays now that we have? But how we as a people celebrated was by celebrating different things that comes within the year, the seasons. That was our holidays. That was our festive time. So Christmas, I guess, and all these holidays, the New Year's holidays, is quite recent for us as a First Nations people. Sometimes I've been asked, "What did you used to get for Christmas? What did you get for a Christmas present?" Well, when I was growing up, we did celebrate Christmas, because we already had the church in place by that time. And I don't remember getting a lot of gifts. We might have got candy and things like that. Oranges, mandarin oranges. And the old people used to call them, or how I've heard it is they're called, "Jap oranges": "The Jap oranges have been brought in!" Everybody's excited about that. That's a *big thing*. It wasn't about any big fancy toys or anything. And it's just still very recent that my family has corrected me, you know? "Mom, that's not politically correct!" That just stuck in my head that that's how I always heard it from the old people, you know? "Jap oranges, oh boy!" Give you a treat, "Here is a Jap orange!" And me never thinking about how people might be offended by that. I just didn't think about it. Not until my one of my daughters corrected me and said, "Mom, that's not politically correct!" "Uh-oh." *[laughs]* And some of our elderly people still say that, so it's not meant to be offensive to anyone. Yeah. *Now* I *know* and I was, "uh-oh." Well when I was growing up, my memories of Christmas – it wasn't a turkey roasting in the oven. A lot of people got turkey. They went out and bought a turkey, but they cut it up and made turkey stew. And we'd go out visiting. Course, we didn't have a phone. And me and family members would go visiting door to door. We'd go visit, you know, an aunt and her family – or they come over. People were out and about and knockin' on doors and, "Come on in!" And by the time you've gotten to the other end of the village, you have eaten twenty times, 'cause everywhere you went there's turkey on the stove. It's just sittin' there, in the late afternoon, they're starting to cook it. And quite often in some homes, they had their turkey dinner at midnight. When they came home from church, after midnight mass, then some friends would come with them and then they would have a bowl of turkey soup. So that's how we brought in Christmas when I was young. One time I remember I was very young, we went to church – my grandparents and I. And my great-grandmother was still alive then. And she was in the house. But she was getting quite elderly and weak and was in bed. And my grandmother had a big pot of turkey stew on the stove for when we come out of church – then we'll have something to eat before we go to bed. And we came home – somebody had broke into the house while we were in church and this whole pot of soup or stew was dumped on the floor. There was soup *everywhere*. What a disaster that was! We never did find out who did that. Somebody was on the loose, I guess. And people made, like, a homemade cake right from scratch. And it was usually just, like, a big pan decorated with all this colourful little, um, they look like little beads. What do you call those? You sprinkle it on? Sprinkles! Yes, sprinkles. *[laughs]* So after you have your turkey soup, that's what you had for dessert. My mom used to make that all the time. She would make a *huge* cake and I think every household did the same thing. And of course Jap oranges. *[laughs]*

And New Year's, there would be a dance. We had a dance hall – a small one, which was behind our, um, where our church is now? It was in a small lot directly behind there. And it was a small building. And we used to have a fella that played the accordion come from Wildwood area. Think his name was George Zorzi. He was a brother to Carmella Toigo, who was a friend of mine. And they're one of the first families in the Wildwood area. And they were *very* good friends of ours. So her brother used to come out and play the accordion for a New Year's dance for our community. And there were no tables set up, of course, 'cause the place is small, and you know, there's benches all around the perimeters of the hall. And it was a grand old time! Ever since I was little I remember going and just sitting with the grandparents and – everybody went, the Elders and the younger people. That little place would be packed. And there's a big barrel of a stove – like, an old oil barrel of a stove that was cut down as a wood stove. That's what heated the building. And someone would bring a big kettle of tea. That's what we had. So when you left home, you took your teacup with you. And a bag, something, maybe it could be a pillowcase, because they're going to pass around the Jap oranges, or regular oranges and apples. You pass around the fruit. And there's sandwiches. They would make sandwiches. Some people make sandwiches and they got passed around as you're sitting on these benches, and they'd come passing it around in boxes. And you'd just grab a sandwich – they're all wrapped up – and you had your midnight snack there. Then someone would come with a kettle with tea, big kettle of tea. And you dig out your cup and they pour your tea for you. So that was our celebrations back then, and you went home with your bag of goodies and your pillowcase and had your fruits to take home.

There was dancing to the music. And then later on, some of our own people used to play music. They had guitar players, a drummer, accordion – we had three fellas I would say. They were all cousins, related. There was Moses Wilson, he played *beautiful* music. He played the accordion, but he could play the guitar as well. And his two cousins, Joe Harry and Stanley Harry, that played the accordion. And some relative of theirs, I think that was their uncle, who had come down from the Homalco reserve, and would come and play. And he would play those drums like nobody's business and these guys are playing the guitar and playing the accordion. Joe Harry was such a *great* player of the accordion. He was a small man, but he had this *huge* accordion and he just – going at it. And I just used to be so fascinated watching him. He was a *great*, great player. They were happy. They had so much fun playing. Nobody was getting paid, but they *sure* enjoyed playing. We *sure* enjoyed their music. My late husband used to play the guitar. He used to play the guitar with Moses Wilson. And they got along famously. Course they drank together and played the guitar. They'd be up all night playing the guitar. And it was, a lot of it was country and western music. And they just loved that. People loved that. They were always getting invited to go: "Bring your guitar," and "Want to hear some music." Years ago our guys never learned to play music from any instructor. They all just learned by ear. And we had quite a few in Homalco, guys that were beautiful musicians. And prior to them playing the guitar and drums and stuff like that, there was, like, a band. I don't know who taught them how to play the saxophone, trombone. There was some people that learn to play the piano. Some homes in Church House had pianos. And how they got them up there – they were *huge* things! And someone knew how to play the piano. But they used to have a marching band. And we also had a marching band in Sliammon and in Squirrel Cove. So they used to compete. These two other villages would come down to Sliammon and they'd march back and forth in front of the church, near the beachfront. And I barely remember that part, where they used to do that. My grandfather, apparently, was one of them that played an instrument. And for the life of me, I don't know who taught them or how they learned. I don't know where they got the instruments from. But it was there. They're beautiful brass. One of the old-timers that still used to play was Ambrose Wilson. He had a – I think it was a saxophone. He used to come visit our house and bring it with him and oh, he *really* knew how to play that thing. He really enjoyed play-ing it. And what other instrument was there? One of our guys, Bill Galligos, he was the Chief at one time, and he used to play the violin. Yeah. I don't know where that instrument would have gone, but I remember hearing him play that. So there was a lot of talent, music-wise, and they seemed to really thrive and enjoy it and play together. It would be summer months they would be doing the competition for their brass band.[*]

There used to be other types of competition, which was the race canoes. Every community had a race canoe. Klahoose and Homalco did. We had one. It was called *King of the Sea.* And Sechelt, Squamish, Cape Mudge, Comox, Musqueam, Campbell River. And they used to come to the front of our village, and they would race back and forth, competing. That was really something to see. I remember going to Cape Mudge and having it there as well. All the communities from

---

[*] Kennedy and Bouchard note that brass instruments were introduced by the Roman Catholic Church. Dorothy Kennedy and Randy Bouchard, *Sliammon Life, Sliammon Lands* (Vancouver: Talonbooks, 1983), 123. See also the "Additional Readings" at the end of this book.

up north had the same kind of sports. It's different now from the canoes they use on the canoe journey, 'cause these are deeper and bigger. They're meant for rougher waters. These race canoes were more for just competition. So that was really fun times. It involved a whole community, where people would just gather and down the beach and *cheer* them on and it was something to see. I don't think there was any prize or any trophy that went to a winner, but it was just, you won and everybody knew who won.*

Another competition they used to have was at one time there was this huge rock. It wasn't really overly big, but it was quite round with no grip to it. And they used to compete – it used to be always in front of the church, down at the lower end of the field? And men would go there and compete who could lift that rock and walk with it. There were very few of the men that were able to lift it. And one of the fellas that used to pick it up and walk with it was not a very large man. But it was very awkward – just you get your arms around it and pick it up and then walk with it. It's kind of slippery and kinda rounded. So they had a difficult time with it. And then that rock disappeared. I don't know what has happened to it! Someone took a walk with it, and didn't come back! *[laughs]* So that was the talk amongst the men, and who could walk with that. Who could go the furthest – or even lift it.

And another thing was this arm wrestling that they used to have. I don't know if men still do that, but that was something I seen a lot through my married life and watchin' my late husband arm wrestle and pull fingers with his logger friends and – "Why do you *do* this?" you know. But they would *go* at it. They would just *go* at it, arm wrestling and pulling fingers. Him and all his logger buddies. It was just a big competition, who's the strongest, I guess. *[laughs]* Yeah. So that was their sports.

I know for a short time I remember a game called lahal game. It's sometimes called bone game. I think it came from – like, the Duncan people still play it. It's *so* fun to watch. West Coast people play it still. And I think someone brought it here – that our people picked it up from going to pick hops in Sardis. Our people went down there for work. And got to know people that played those games in those fields, where they worked and they would have some recreation time, and

---

* Elsie states that there were usually about seven or eight people, including the skipper, in a race canoe.

Elsie posing with the Sliammon racing canoe *King of the Sea* in front of Sliammon village, circa 1940. Photo courtesy of Elsie Paul.

play this bone game and brought it home. So I used to see it, when I was quite young yet. It's two teams that play. And then of course all your supporters are chanting and egging you on. And that's a fun sport. So there was a lot of things that people did to entertain and enjoy the gatherings. Those were our kind of holidays, I think. That different seasons of the year, when people got together in the winter months, those were the kinds of things that people did.

WELL, I CAN TALK about how a day begins for me as a young child in my grandmother's house. She would get us up in the morning. It doesn't matter whether it was winter or summer, "It's getting daylight – you get up now." So we had long, busy days in the summer. It's time to get up. The people didn't sleep in. That was considered to be lazy and you're wasting time by laying around in bed. It's daylight. As a young girl you got up and you started doing things. Whether it was helping with the cooking, preparing for the day, workin' alongside with your mother, your grandmother – just be busy. Cleaning up, house cleaning, getting water. In my day as a child and especially where we lived on the coast, sometimes we lived in cabins and we had to pack water, you know. Gotta go to the creek and get water, heat the water up on the stove – wood stove – and do the laundry. My grandmother was very clean. She always insisted on a clean, tidy house. Soon as we were finished eating, "You do the dishes right now. Don't go and sit over there. Don't leave the dishes for later on. Do it right away." So that was done. "'Cause you're going to have to come back to it anyway," she used to say. "Why put it aside? It'll be there. So do it now." So I got into that habit of doing the dishes right away – right after a meal, get the dishes done, put away. Same as at night, you don't go to bed and leave your dirty dishes on the table, or untidy. You take care of those things, *then* you go to bed. Our lives were very scheduled, very structured. We had our day planned – or the day was planned for us. What are we going to do today, depending on what the season was. If it was summer, we go out, berry pickin'. There's a *lot* to do in the summer months. Right from around May till around end of September was gathering different kinds of berries and fruit, and preserving, putting stuff away, or going out root diggin'. So you learned how to do those things, because of your grandparents: "This is the time to go do that now." I never thought it was work. I never thought it was something that I was forced to do. It was just a way of life. I would just, "Okay. Today we're going to go do this," and off we'd go.

Days were very full. And it might have been repetitious, the things that you did. But nevertheless each day was full. It was meaningful. And still today, if I don't have anything constructive to do today, I feel, "What's wrong with this picture," you know? I feel like I should be doing something! And so my mind is still going, "I should be doing this. I know I should be doing this." And sometimes the body's not always co-operating: "I think I'll go and have a nap for a while." *[laughs]* My grandmother used to say, even in her old age, "If you're feeling sick, don't allow yourself just to lay there and wallow in it" – of course, she's speaking in the language, right? You know, if you allow yourself just to lay there, then you become just *lazy* and you were giving up on life? "Get up!" And, "It's difficult sometimes to get up in the morning." I guess this is when she was getting older – and I heard all the other old people talking like that too: "It's difficult to get up in the morning, but you have to make yourself get up! Get up and get moving!" Once you're up, it's like you've beat that – you've made that first step. And you'll feel better: next thing you know you're busy doing something. But if you're just gonna lay there and say, "Oh, I'm so tired! Oh, I'm achy, I'm this, I'm that," then you're giving in. And that's a no-no. You don't do that. You fight it. The old-timers, years ago, I used to see a lot of them, they were very, very independent. They were really up and moving, and self-reliant, and as old as some of them were, they were still able to get out. I'd see old people down the beach gathering wood for their fire with a cane. They're walking around with a cane. And I used to see an old lady always – every day in the summer, walkin' along the beach packing the big basket on her back and gathering wood, piling it for later use. With her cane she'd be walking along the beach gathering driftwood. She didn't go and expect someone – "Come cut my wood for me," or "Bring me wood." She was self-reliant! So a lot of the older people were very, very hard, where they were used to hard work. They were used to doing things for themselves. And that has become different now too, you know, that there's more resources – or more help for people that are getting on in age, and more services for people. In a way it's good. Our Elders need that service today. But it's there now, whereas it wasn't there before. But thinking back on how resourceful the older people were, the Elders, back in the day of my grandmother, they never sat down. They never said, "Come and do this for me," or "Do that for me." They did everything to the best of their ability. Hard work. There was a lot of hard work. But that was the lifestyle. It was the lifestyle, it was acceptable. It was good. Life is so precious that you utilize your every waking moment doing something constructive.

And I think today that it's pretty difficult to bring the two, the youth and the Elders, together, for the Elders to share with the youth the kind of lifestyle they had, and how hard it was for them growing up – or the expectations, maybe, from the Elders to the youth that "this was how I grew up, and it was hard. We worked hard. But we were resourceful." And to be saying that to the youth that have totally different outlook in life, sometimes I think can be hard on the youth? The children? It's like you're judging them and where they are today. And I think it's really important to just share your history and how you grew up and what times were like when you were growing up, and what times were like in my grandmother's time, and the stories that I hear about how things were in my great-grandparents' time. It was totally different lifestyle. And in order to honour the youth today, we need to just share that history with the young people, with our grandchildren, that this is how it was, and it's good for them to know all that. That's history. But not to condemn their lifestyle today. 'Cause it's totally different. It's a different world. But one thing that never changes is the respect for one another. Whether it was that lifestyle and how they lived, and where you came from – that's where you came from. That's your roots. That you respect that. That's history: "That was my great-grandparents!" And it's a good thing. It's important for them to know that history, our history, which was never really documented. There's nowhere that says, to show them, "This is how it was." But I think it's important for them to know. And those same kind of rules and guidelines needs to apply to young people. No matter what they do in life. That respect is the most important thing. That boundaries – other people's boundaries – to respect people no matter what colour or race or who they are in life. That first of all they're human beings. That they are just as important as you or anyone else. And that you treat them accordingly. To live in harmony with nature and every living thing. To be respectful to everything around you. To be always, I don't know, just to respect who you are as a person. But not to be boastful of who you are. It's be yourself, just do the best you can in life, and not to put yourself above anyone else: "Oh I'm better." Or to be judgmental to other people. That was our teachin'. That was the life. It's not so much teachin', but you lived it from the time you're little, to treat other people this way, to treat the animals this way, to treat life this way, to treat the universe this way.

WE LIVED QUITE A bit up on the coast. We lived in different places: we lived in Theodosia, we lived in Okeover, Grace Harbour, just in other places that our people travelled wherever the food gathering was at that particular time of the year. So we'd move around. We lived there, and moved to another location after two weeks, three weeks, a month. Or if you travelled, like, we would travel from here to say, Squirrel Cove, that some of our people are living there, and it was a day trip, just to get from here to there. And there were no fast boats to take you there, no water taxi. So you just put up your sail. If the wind was blowing that way, you were there in a few hours. And you always went with the weather, of course. You just pulled in and camped wherever there's a cabin. And that was a good thing with people years ago, they had little cabins along the coast. My grandfather and his brothers were all travellers. The cabins were made of rough cedar shakes. And the beds themselves, like, were homemade, but off the ground. And they were also cedar planks. So that's all you had. And your bedding of course. And so we didn't have beds and mattresses and all that kind of stuff 'cause you were moving quite a bit around. So you just had those plank beds. Wood stove in there.

My grandfather had this huge dugout canoe. He didn't make it, but he went and traded with another man way up in Bute Inlet. And we got up there – I went with him and my grandmother, and he made the trade. I don't know what the trade was, but we came back with this huge dugout canoe. And he used that a lot. Just going out fishing in front of the village, or travelling further up the coast. It was our vehicle. One person can manage it, but you had room for two people to row the boat, or you could put the sail if there's a breeze. So that made it a lot easier to go from one place quicker. And so you would just need one person at the stern to paddle, to keep going in the right direction, right? So that was a fun thing for me. And to hold the strings, the rope that controls how much wind is in the sail, and my granny used to show me, "You pull this one, that one" – there's two ropes that's attached to his homemade sail. And so it was fun. We were living at Harwood Island and we went over to Refuge Cove. My aunt was living in Refuge Cove and my grandmother wanted to go visit her. And there's a nice breeze that day, so off we went. We were there within a few hours, maybe three hours. It was a good little bit of wind took us there. Yeah. Stayed there till it was nice and calm and we just rowed back. Took our time. And that's just how people travelled. That's one of my fond memories. Travelling just with my grandmother, just the two of us.

My great-uncle, that was my grandfather's brother, used to row *everywhere* he went.* He would go fishing and row *all* over the place, all day long. That was his life. And we were in Okeover Inlet at the head of the inlet. There's a river that goes through there but in the fall time it's kind of fishy – I guess the fish are going up. So he would want to go and get some nice drinkin' water. So, "Oh, we'll go over there and bring the containers." So I go with him. And he would say, "Oh, it's not far. It's just over there around that point over there." So

---

* maksɛma, also known as Sandy Timothy.

Elsie and her younger cousin Stella standing against a floathouse built by their grandfather lɑsɑ (Jim Timothy). Photo taken in Deep Bay circa 1945. Photo courtesy of Elsie Paul.

I'm rowing, I'm helping him rowing, and then we'd get to that point and, "Oh, another – next point over." Next thing you know we've gone quite a little distance. So we'd fill up our containers and come back. And to him it was just the normal thing to do. And he would row over to Refuge Cove to get some goods, because there was a store there then. And he would row over there. Take him all day from the head of Okeover to go over there and then come back again. It's just about dark when he gets back. But that was all okay. Yeah.

My grandfather eventually built himself a house – a floathouse. So it was just a house, one-room house, but it was on a float. And the float was logs all tied together. And so we travelled on that quite a bit. He would tow it. He got a gas boat then, just a little putt-putt. He had a five Easthope motor on there. So he would tow it – on a good day, he would tow it. And he'd go to a bay, and that's where we'd be. And just anchor it and tie up to the beach where it's deep water, and they don't go dry there. So we lived like that. We went all summer to different places. And come back and one summer he had it pulled up over on Harwood there, where they pulled it up at the beach. So we were on dry land there, at Harwood.

THERE'S A BIG RIVER in Theodosia, which is toqʷanən, and so we went up there around early September and stay up there and wait for the fish to come in. The big dog salmon went up there that time of the year. So you had to be there, because that's the time to be there. And these dog salmon were huge. Otherwise known as chums. So that particular kind of salmon was used for just barbecuing pretty much, because they're really heavy, and if you hang them to dry, they come off, and they're too heavy. So that was its main use, was to barbecue it around the fire, and dry it. We used to dry them after they're barbecued, and you dry it right up. You put it in your smokehouse once it's barbecued, and you let the fire go on for, I don't know, a week to ten days you're smoking it, till it's dry. It's just as hard as a board. And then you store it like that, very dry. So when you went to eat it, you soak it. If you want to soften it, you soak it for a couple of days. And then you can warm it up, you know, over the fire, or cook it a bit. And you just had that with potatoes. It's entirely different flavour from just smoked salmon too. And most times they were just eaten fresh or made into soup or just barbecued and that's how we ate it. 'Cause they were huge! Were really double the size of the fish that went up to Okeover Arm.

And then moved to Okeover, where there's a smaller river. So the fish that went up there was dog salmon again, but they were smaller. But richer. And we had a house there, cabin. And my grandparents and other people, other relatives, lived there, right by the river, and would smoke those fish. And that was a different brand of fish, if you may, although it's still chum salmon. They would smoke it dry, real, real dry for toasting – that was used for toasting over the open fire. It was so good. Really rich and oily. The oils come right up the surface when you toast it. Whereas the ones that you get in Theo doesn't do that. So you prepare that differently than how you would prepare the fish from the other river. So people recognized that, the differences.

And then after that was done, we would move back to Sliammon. Probably in early November. The winters were mainly spent in Sliammon, because the snow and ice would be too much to handle up in Theodosia. And then we'd come over here, and this is a different texture of fish again. Although it's still the dog salmon! I know my grandmother – as well as all the other people of her generation – when the fish came here, they would honour the salmon. They would welcome the salmon. It was, like, a very exciting time: "The salmon have come in!" You know, they see the fish jumping. There's different signs they watch for when the fish come in. So everybody's in a buzz about "The salmon's come in." And they welcomed the salmon. The old-timers would go down the beach and welcome, raise their hands to the sea: "Come," you know, "You've come back!" So they welcomed the salmon in a good way. They just didn't go out in the water and scoop up the salmon. And none of it was ever wasted. None of this food was ever wasted. And it just really blows my mind when I see all the fish sometimes get wasted or people don't know how to do it anymore, how to prepare it the way we used to. And course we have the freezer now, when people utilize that or your canning jars, you will prepare your fish that way. Whereas people had totally different ways of preparing the salmon for preserving. They used it mostly for hanging and smoking in the smokehouse. It's just a different quality of fish. It's not as heavy. So they won't come off the racks and drop. So we'd be here in the winter months, around November. And my grandmother used to smoke *a lot* of fish from this river. My grandmother would dry a lot of fish. By the hundred and – course, we were there helping and other family members would help. And the men would go out and get the fish. The women would prepare the fish with the help of the men. It was a joint effort. And it was fun doing it and it was, I guess, social. And I don't remember it as being work. But it was necessary at the same time to do all those things.

She smoked fish until she died, and she died in – oh, she was in her eighties when she died. She died in her smokehouse. I was helping her hang her fish, and she was just doing a few that day. I think she was doing about six, maybe eight. But she had some already hanging in the smokehouse. So she was moving those around. You know, you have to always be moving, shuffling your fish around, just so that it's evenly smoked. So that's what she was doing. She was inside the smokehouse and moving her fish around. And I guess holding her arms up, working on her fish, hanging there and there. Racks. I thought I heard some thud or a noise, and I went to look and she was – she was gone. She had a heart attack. Massive heart attack. Yeah. So she died doing what she enjoyed doing. She enjoyed. And she was sooo tidy. Sooo clean with how she did her smoked fish. She used to get after us and she'd get after the guys if they went out to get the fish: "Make sure the boat is washed out! There's no sand in the boat!" And she looked after the salmon, that it didn't come in contact with sand. And pack it up, and she'd have a nice clean place to put it out by the smokehouse, and all lined with fern and all cordoned off. It looked like it's fenced in. And covered nice and clean. And they all had to be facing the same way. The fish had to be all facing the same way. You just didn't throw them any which way there. Had to be lined up just nicely. Just so that it's easy when she went to cut it, clean it. That she could just reach over and grab under the gill and pull it towards her. And the other reason was that when it's fresh and it's put into a container, if it's not sitting properly, then kind of rigor mortis sets in the fish. So they could be twisted or warped the next day when you wanted to clean them. So she wanted them to be laying flat. Just even. Evenly stacked. Yeah, and so she was really fussy about those things. And really took a lot of pains and how to do it properly, and get your fern ready, 'cause that's what you use for wiping the fish down is the ferns. So we'd go and gather all bundles of fern. And so the table's lined with fern. And so it's not slipping and – you know, the dog salmon's pretty slippery. It gets pretty slimy. So she would be working on her work table. It had to be covered with fresh fern. And she would be changing that all the time. And there's just a way that she did her fish that – it always turned out so nice! Well, I try to follow as much as possible all the things that – now we have other things, like burlap, we use, instead of the fern. But she used to say that the fern was the best, because before you hang it, you washed it, and you wipe it down with a fern. You take handfuls of fern. You've gotta crumple it together. And you wipe it down. You wash the face of it, like, the inside. You wipe it down. It has to go one way. And she used to say that it helped the texture of the flesh, 'cause it kind of scrapes it with a fern. So that's almost like there was a method to her madness! And then you flip it around and you gotta hold it now on this side, and you wipe it this way now. So lot of people nowadays don't use that. They just use the burlap, 'cause burlap is smoother. You don't get that nice shiny finish to it. So she was so particular about stuff like that.

And then you just go and put your sticks on and then hang it up, in the smokehouse. Usually it's three sticks. One at the upper end and you put it right into the flesh of the fish – flesh side – and onto the other. If you're not experienced in doing that, it'll always collapse. Your stick will go right through. So you have to kind of know just how to do it. And that's the part that I always say, "I will do that part! *[laughs]* Let me do that part. You can go and hang."[*] Yeah. After all that – and if you're not careful – 'cause you've got one stick that's bigger, that's going to sit on the rafters like that – if you put that too close to the edge of the butterflied fish, it'll rip, and there goes your fish. It's landed on the ground.

And always looking after the smoke, how big the smoke is, and they were constantly always looking after the fire. And moving all the fish around, reshuffling it every day. When I'm smoking salmon, I have to be up all hours of the night to keep that smoke going. So you have to be very diligent and you have to be there all the time. It's like looking after a new baby. It's a lot of work. People used to dry it totally dry, as hard as board, in order to store it in boxes and store it away. And then you toast it over the open fire. Or you could take it and put it in a tub of water, take it to the creek and let it sit there for a day or two. And it swells up again. Then you can boil it and cook it that way. You don't really have to boil it. It's already cooked, pretty much. But if you want – for easier eating, as part of your meal. But the jerky, you could sit by open campfire and toast it over the fire and that's so good! Same as that idea of toasting the herring. It becomes softer. Once it's heated and toasted a bit. As long as it was in a cool, dry place, it would last you all winter, you know – come springtime and it's pretty much used up by then. But the fish must be really dry, and then kept in a dry place. Otherwise, if it's not really dry then the mould will appear. Yeah. So it's a lot of work that goes into it. And you have to know what you're doing, right from when you get it from the water.

There's always meat left on the bone, so I fillet that, both sides. 'Cause you don't want to cut your fish right down to the bone. You have to leave some of the meat on the bone itself. Then you cut away that. And my grandmother would get about two fillets before you get

---

[*] Elsie is suggesting that the other person go hang the prepared fish in the smokehouse.

to the bone. That's how sharp her knife is.* And she'd have these – the kids call them neckties, but they're fillets. And I will put it in brine for a little while, and then I'll drape it over a rack. And then you gotta keep turning it otherwise it's gonna dry stiff with its own shape. So you gotta keep turning it – that's to keep it from getting sour, too. So after a couple of days you can take it and you can hang it. You can put it through sticks and hang it up. But you can pull the bones out of those fillets. The old people use their teeth. You just kind of bend it and the bones really show – they're sticking out. And it's hard to pick it because the flesh might come too. And I used to do that a lot. I think that's why my teeth are going on me. I used to just kind of hold on to it and bite on the bone that's sticking out, and it's just a whole row down the whole fillet. And you'd get a very sore lip just from touching against the little bones that are sticking out. But I used to see the old people. They would take it down and they'd have, like, a nice block of wood, and, like, a wooden hammer, and they'd pound it. People that are really working hard at it and want the real good quality. It's so soft. It's *really* soft. And my grandmother would soften it, and pound it, and roll it. And it was sooo good. It's dried – it's like jerky – but it's soft. It's almost like – it becomes like cloth because she really gave it a lot of her time. She'd be there every morning and working on it, and then she'd put it on a block of wood and pound it gently, soften it. And then she would hang it up with small sticks, and she'd make holes on the top ends of them. Then she'd hang it up. That was the best. I do that. Yeah. It's so good like that. You could take it and chomp away at it! *[laughs]*

When I do my fish now I will – after my fish is dry or semidry – I will cut it up and put it in jars, and use a pressure cooker to finish the process. And it just lasts forever. It's really quite tasty. You will have already put brine before you hung it. And you just use any – whatever brine. Could be just, your coarse salt or pickling salts. And brown sugar, if you like that. I never seen people using brown sugar, you know, they just did theirs plain. But through time that's changing. People using more brine.

The roe of the salmon was even used to dry. Yeah. We used to dry that. My grandparents dried that. You would take it out – they're still in the sac when you're cleaning your salmon and you get that. And

---

* For illustrations of cutting and hanging chum for smoke-drying, see Kennedy and Bouchard, *Sliammon Life*, 27-30.

then you dry it. You put it up on racks when you're drying your salmon. Once it firms up, then you can tie them up and hang them to dry. So they almost looked like the corn that's dried. You must have seen that corn that's still in the husk and peeled back and dried? They became really dry. They're hard. They looked like a – like a Oh Henry! bar! *[chuckles]* And they were crunchy. So in the springtime, when the new shoots would come out, like the wild salmonberry shoots, or the red cap berries – they have these nice shoots. They're really tender when they first come out. So we as kids used to go and gather those shoots. And then we would eat those. Peel them back and eat them and have a bite of the dried roe with it. It was quite a combination. So that, again, was a treat. It was a real treat. So that was specifically stored away just for that time of the year, in the springtime when you can have it with the shoots. Yeah. It's "paʔajɛ" in our language. paʔajɛ. "qeyχ" is the salmon roe. "šaʔmɛt" is dried. šaʔmɛt qeyχ. And it's smoked also. Yeah. And they had other uses for the salmon roe too, where it was put away in containers and it kind of fermented. Although I never really tried that myself. But there were some of the *old,* old people that used that, like, as a spread, on other foods. And they did that also with wild cranberries. Where they gathered cranberries in the swamps or wherever they were growing, and they would put it in containers and let it sit and kind of ferment. And that was used too. It's like all these different kinds of foods – combining it with other foods to enhance the flavour of other foods.

So they're well taken care of – and a lot of that is the teachin' to respect that salmon. You don't throw it about. You handle it with care. You look after it. You keep it clean. 'Cause that's your winter feed. It's food for your family. So you look after it – and I know my grandmother did. She – and other people, of her time, her age. When I see sometimes, young people, how they handle fish now, I just cringe! I just cringe. Because it's not how you handle the fish. Yeah. My grandmother tells a story about a beautiful chum salmon that's going up the river. You know, you have your female and your male, right? It's obvious, the male has big kind of a beak and big teeth. And the female has a smaller head, and usually you could tell too because it's plump and it's got the sac of eggs in there. And this one young person was just goofing about and bringin' the fish in and he kind of stepped on it and it made a squirting sound. It's like a fart sound. And he laughed, and he said, "Oh, the fish is farting!" And someone said to him, "You cannot make fun of fish like that. That's *really* disrespectful for you to talk like that." And that night, this young person had a dream. He woke up and he was in *such* pain to his side. He was in *such* pain. And he dreamt this beautiful young woman stabbed him with, like, a pitchfork – something very sharp. So anyway, that was his dream, his nightmare, that he got stabbed by this beautiful woman. And he woke up with *severe* pain. So his parents told him, "That's because you were making fun of that female fish. You know, that was once a human being. Or it's provided to you as a giver of life. It had the salmon eggs in there. And it gave its life for you. And for you to make fun of it and to step on it and you laughed at that sound that fish made. So this is what happens to you." It's like payback time, kind of a thing? So that's why you looked after whatever food was brought to you. You don't waste – don't treat it disrespectfully in any way, shape, or form. You protect it. It's precious stuff. So there's a lot of those kinds of beliefs and teachin's around animals and other life. But you don't make fun of them. That you are respectful.

It's not so much prayers, but it's how you handle it, how you receive it. A lot of it is by the hands: raised hands, like you would greet people, a visitor. That's what the old people used to do. You didn't have to say anything. You walk in the door and they would raise their hands to you. That's a gesture. That's a welcome. That's a show of kindness, you know – you're welcome to come in. So there's not an awful lot of words that need to be said. I think some communities, some other First Nations communities, actually do salmon ceremonies and things like that. But I know with us, it was more like how you treated – and the teachin' that comes with that. *You know* what you are not to do. You know how you should treat that salmon or that deer or whatever game is brought to you. All these things had a life, and now it's gonna give you a life. So you need to thank the Creator for that. You need to thank what's there in front of you. It might be just in your thoughts or your gestures, or how you look at that. How you look at the meal before you. Yeah. I got a kick out of my grandson Davis. He loves to help me clean fish when I get fish. We got a delivery of sockeye a few years ago and we were all out in the backyard and we got the hose going there, and we've got the tarp on the ground. We got all the fish laid out and so I'm cutting their heads, and I'm saving the heads. And I'm busy, whatever I was doing over there, and he's doing his thing, washing all the stuff. And he says, "Chi-chia, come look at this. Isn't this neat?" And I go look and he's got *all* the heads *all* lined up. They're all facing the same way, on this tarp. I said, "What are you doing?" He said, "I just think it's so neat. They're all facing the same way." I said, "Well you better not be making fun of the salmon heads." I said,

"It's not right if you doing that." *[laughs]* And he's just, like, "Oh."
[laughs]

Like when the herring came in – it used to be around February and
March, people are watching and ready and going down to the beach
and really looking for – "Is it out there?" The seagulls are out, so that
means they're here. And the word would get around. People are all
hyped up and visiting back and forth and down the beach and it's
almost like you're welcoming them: "Thank you for coming!" you
know, "Come on in!" And everybody just gets really busy and gets to
work at going out and getting the herring. One time my uncle and I
went out on this big canoe we had. And it was *so plentiful*! And we're
just scooping it out of the water with a scoop net? And we overfilled
the boat – or what should've been its capacity, I guess, we exceeded.
It was so much fun. But it was dark. It got dark and there were so
many boats out there already and some were just getting ready to go
out – we were heading back towards the shore. And I could feel the
water coming up to my knees in the boat. I said, "We're sinkin'! We're
going down!" *[laughs]* And my uncle was sayin' to me, "Don't you
scream! You're going to attract attention." *[laughs]* He was *embarrassed*! And we had just gotten close to the beach where there was –
probably was about three feet of water, and we're lucky it didn't
happen way out there where it's deep. We were just heading in and
we didn't quite make it, but we sunk and all the herring floated out
of the boat and they're pretty much, I guess, dead, or stunned from
being, you know, in the boat like this, and people were going by in a
canoe and it was very dark. "Look! Look at all the herring!" Like, they
started to drift out? "Look at all the herring! They're dead. They're
floating!" And we're going, "Oh." Being real quiet. *[laughs hard]*
We got little too greedy. Oh gosh. That's what happens when you get
greedy and you don't think about what you're doing.

Well, once you got the herring to shore you would just dry it whole.
When you take the guts out of it, the flesh, it's not as tender once it's
dried. So it seems to help to leave the insides in and then dry it. The
process is you thread it through the gill and out the mouth so they're
all hanging on a piece of, um, wood, if you will. And they're about,
maybe, four feet in length. So you maybe have, twenty, thirty herring
hangin'. And then you just hang it in the smokehouse and you have
a low fire going to smoke it dry. Or you could hang it out, if it's a
sunny day – you take them out and you air-dry them. But that time
of the year, usually, it's not very dry so you pretty much kept it in the
smokehouse. And had a little fire going. And it becomes really dry,

and then you store it away, in a dry place. So when it's time to eat it, you toast it over an open fire. It's like toasting marshmallows or wieners over an open fire – with a stick. And when it's toasted, it's really *tasty*, and then you rip it open then take out the backbone. So, it's quite tasty – you know, toasted smoke-flavoured. And I haven't done that in a long time, but we used to do it a lot.

"t'ɩšosəm" is another name of this place. It got called that because out here in the bay in front of the community, all the way to Scuttle Bay, when there used to be a herring spawn, every springtime, maybe 'round ending of February, March, we used to get the herring come in. And that was one of the foods that people used a lot of here, the herring and the herring eggs. The herring spawn. And this *whole* area would be just white. It's t'ɩšosəm – the water is "milky." That's why people started calling this place "t'ɩšosəm." Because of that. And we would go out and put cedar boughs in the water, around that time. People would start gathering their stuff and getting everything ready for – "We're gonna get spawn pretty soon." And so they knew where to go and grab the cedar right away – cedar branches, boughs. And they would just string out, tie the cedar boughs on it and anchor the top ends – anchored both ends of the string out there so that it's float-ing. It would have buoys on there, so it's kept up, away from the bottom of the ocean. So that it's not picking up the sand. So it's dan-gling in the water. The tip is down – the tip of the tree. Then the trees could be, like, four feet to six feet in height, like little Christmas trees? Then the herring will spawn on those branches. And then by the time they've spawned for a couple of days – you're lucky if you get a couple of days of good spawn – then you'll have fairly thick eggs on them. Or, might be even three days, maybe two to three days, and it will be quite thick. So then you pull it all in and pack it up and you drape it over your racks and to dry. You would probably have to have a tarp over it to keep it from the rain. And every day you gotta go and turn it and make sure you're moving it about, otherwise it gets sour. So you have to tend to it and it's *a lot* of work. It takes a long time. It takes maybe couple weeks or so if you have good breeze and it's under shelter – but it takes a lot of work and time for you because you really have to look after it.[*]

Once it's dried, it's very, very dry. And you can store it – it'll keep for a long, long time in the dry form still on the cedar boughs, or

---

[*] On catching and drying herring, see Kennedy and Bouchard, *Sliammon Life*, 31-32.

spruce boughs. It's kind of tasteless. When you make soup, you can make fish soup and when your soup is just about ready you can throw in a handful, and it's crunchy. And so, it's the flavour of the fish that is going to give that a flavour, right? You can put it into your cooking and it takes on the flavours of your other cooking ... although, you know, I'll eat it on its own. To remove the fish eggs from the branches, you peel it. Yeah, so the thicker it is, the easier it is to peel. It's like peeling an orange. There was always more than enough that you could go out and get the whole herring to dry as well. Yeah, so that was food that we dried and used some of it for trade to other communities, like to Cape Mudge people and Campbell River, Comox. They really liked our style of herring and eggs. So we'd go over there and they would trade us for what other foods they had too – barter system. Now we don't get herring anymore. It's all cleaned out. Several years ago, they opened seine fishing in this area. This whole area was lit up front of the village from Sliammon to Scuttle Bay and towards Powell River, over to Harwood. There was *all* kinds of seine boats out there. And they scooped the herring. We never did get herring after that.[*] The fisheries are saying it was not from that. That's got nothing to do with the herring not coming back to our area. It doesn't make sense, but ... we can't prove it was for that reason. But it happened from then on. You might see a little bit now and then, just the water starting to get milky, and then it's gone. It's nothing like it used to be.

But how some people from the North do it, like from Bella Bella, they use kelp, the wide kelp. And the herring will spawn on the kelp. So they take it kelp and all and they salt it. Then you can pull it out of the salt – the brine – and you wash the salt away, running it through the fresh water. And you can eat it with the kelp. You just cut it in little squares and you can stir-fry it – with garlic it's great! You can also peel it from the seaweed. If you don't want to eat the seaweed, you can peel it from the seaweed. Yeah. I got a little bit of it left that was given to me, a friend of Leslie Adams brings him some every year and then he shares it with the Elders: "I've got some herring eggs here! You want some? Come and get it!" *[laughs]* So he's one of the people that still loves the traditional foods that way and he shares it with us. Yeah, one time he dried herring. And he's got this, like a big verandah – porch. And that's where he hung his strings of herring.

---

[*] Elsie is referring here to two years of commercial herring fishing in 1983 and 1984, after which the herring disappeared.

'Cause it's sheltered and there's nice breeze through there. Well they were pretty much all dry and the neighbour's little boy seen it. And there's a tub of water, so the little boy decided to come and play with the herring. Pulled them down and put them in the water. He had a tub full of dried herring! *[laughs]*

I'd go out clam diggin' with my grandparents.[*] Whatever beach you were at, if you are at Harwood Island or anywhere where there's clam beds – and you know, clams are pretty heavy in the shell, so you would have a whole lot of clams. And so a fire is just built on the beach, big fire. There's lots of rocks, like the size of a watermelon or whatever, you know, that size. And those rocks are heated. A lot of hot fire going on. And when the rocks are thoroughly hot, hot, hot, then all of the debris would be pushed away, like the charred wood and that. And then the clams are dumped onto the hot rocks and then covered with whatever material you had on hand, whether it was, like, seaweed or anything that's going to help steam the clams. And then you cover it more solid with other kinds of branches that added flavour to it as well. And it would just steam and open up. So when they were all cooked and steamed, then you took it and you put it on – thread it onto ironwood material. You threaded it and then you baked it around the fire. You barbecued it around the fire. And then when that's done, then you take it home and you smoke it for as long as it took to get it really, really dry. You could eat it like that, or if you want to store it for later use, or trading, then you smoked it. 'Cause people didn't have freezers back then, so that was the only way to preserve it. But people really liked it. 'Cause it was so chewy and tasty. Or you could soak it and then eat it. Or just eat it as it is just in a dry form. That was one way of preserving butter clams and cockles. People were so good at braiding. Sometimes they used three sticks, and you put the body here *[gesturing]* and you weave it around this one and you put the other end of the clam this way, and then you start on the other side and go the other way. It was really pretty. It was like a nice braided rug. Three sticks. And you'd cook it by the fire. It's all, like, propped up by the fire.

We don't get clams in front of our community anymore because it's all contaminated. At one time, me and my grandfather would go down front of my place down the beach at the point there and dig clams for supper. Just enough for clam chowder. Now we go down

---

[*] On shellfish, see Kennedy and Bouchard, *Sliammon Life*, 33-36.

there and the little clams are so black and – it's not edible. So that's how people gathered food. The ocean was their fridge. You know, you want fresh fish, you're going to go out there and get a fresh fish. You want clams, you're going to go down the beach and dig clams. So everything was fresh.

A lot of the food was cooked in a pit. Like the clams or the deer, when you had a large amount to do, you did it in an open fire, like, steamed? Like, it's not barbecued but it's covered and cooked over hot rocks, so it steams and cooks under all this cover. So that's how you would do your seal meat, your deer meat, your clams. I guess if you had a lot of duck, that's how you would do it too. It's almost like a slow cooker. Once that part is done, you can smoke it in the smoke-house. And dry it. Everything was dried. Simply because, I guess, we didn't have the freezer and other ways.

A male deer, a big buck, is a θαραχ^{w}os. That's a *big* one. Yeah. But otherwise it's just qegaθ.[*] *Every* part of it. Every part of the deer was used, like, even the skin – the hide was used. My grandfather used to boil the head of the deer, and it was a delicacy, for him.[†] So, once every part of it was gone, he would end up with the head and he would scrape it, scrape all the fur off around the head. He would scorch it on the fire, open fire out there. Then he would scrape it some more. So once all the fur was scraped off and burnt off, then he would put it in a big pot and boil it for *hours,* just simmering. And I never did eat it myself. But he really enjoyed it, as did the other people of his generation. They found it to be a real delicacy. Yeah. But it was something I was never really attracted to. *[laughs]* Well, the fish head is different for me, you know, it's kind of the same idea but fish head to me is a real delicacy. And I still use it today, although my own children and grandchildren will not touch it. It's like, "Oh! What is that?" But I love it, you know, and I don't have it all the time. But when I have it I'll just really enjoy it. And quite often go sit with the Elders or invite a couple of Elders in – we'd have a meal. You know, just pick at it. It's something that's – really was used a lot. One of the Elders here in the community will freeze some. You know, she'll freeze a bunch or she'll cook it and then freeze it and then just pull it out when she's wishin' for a treat. *[laughs]*

Some of the men went hunting for mountain goats. And that's more up towards Bute, I guess. But I remember where my grandfather and

---

[*] Translation: deer.

[†] See also Kennedy and Bouchard, *Sliammon Life,* 38.

some of his relatives had gone, was up in Toba Inlet, going looking for mountain goats. And they have to go pretty far up to do that. It was only the very trained – the *very* fit men that went after the mountain goats. I've never, ever tried mountain goat. But the old-timers did. That was just something different, like the different texture I guess. And the wool was used for making things – clothing or whatever, or bedding. The hide was used for something else. And it had fat in it too that they rendered down and used. Just like the way they used the fat from the big deer. 'Cause I remember seeing that when the hunter would come home and it was a big buck and it would have a lot of fat in the stomach area of the deer. In this fine – it looked almost like a mesh net, and wrapped around I guess the stomach of the deer. So they would pull that out and dry it – hang it over something and dry it a bit. And the kids would be all excited about that. That was a real treat too. They'd take a little bit of that and wrap it around a stick and toast it over the fire. And it's like marshmallows! *[laughs]*

The duck was eaten by our people. Yeah, that's another thing I haven't tasted since I was a child, I think, was like a duck stew. They're pretty tough. But you simmer it for a long time. It's got very dark meat. But it was mostly used for soup, more of a soup type of a stew. And very plain again. Just the duck meat. Then you'd add in your potatoes and your onion, and season it with salt or pepper. And it was nice, because it had a smoked flavour too, because you burnt the feathers off it. Once you plucked all the feathers off, you did the same as what you did with the deer head. You scorched it over the open fire and scraped it and got rid of that fuzz on the duck. Then you cut it up, and course, you know, boil it. And so it had a little bit of a smoked flavour to it. Quite different. Yeah.

There's your berries of course. And that was special. It was a treat. The dried berries. It's like those roll-ups you see today. And there was no sugar added in those. They would just squish the berries and pour them on flat beds. They laid flat beds out, and just dried it in the sun. My grandmother did that to a lot of the berries: wild blackberries, salal berries, huckleberries, salmonberries. You used to get a lot of black caps. And they're *so* tasty! Like, they ripen up the same time as the wild blackberries. And that is really nice. Now we have these different blackberries that's all over our yard! I call them tame, but they grow all over the place around here now. We never used to have those. It got imported here from somewhere. It's good. You can extract the juice from that and make jelly – that's pretty much what I do with it. I remember my grandfather, he lived next door when we first built our house here, and that's, like, sixty years ago. And he actually planted the tame ones here. Someone had planted them over by the river – across the village here. And he went and got some and he planted a whole row and I thought, "Oh my goodness!" Now we've got it going, you know, I'm forever cutting it back, cutting it back every year. Now we find when there's been a fire somewhere, and the following year that's where you go and that's where the wild blackberries are growing. They really like that site that's been burnt out. Sometimes we lived over in Harwood Island, 'cause there's a lot of salal there. And we'd go there and just pick a whole lot in the fall time. That's a fall kind of berries – when they get ripe is around September, early September. And wild blackberries. Salmonberries was always plentiful over on Harwood. Yeah.

Across the other end of the village there, my dad, his mother had a large orchard there. They had a great big grape – not a vineyard, but they had this *big* house – he always had the biggest of everything! And so he had this big tool shed–woodshed combination. It was made out of tin. I don't know where he got that from. I think from the mill, when the mill was first being built. And I don't know if this was discarded, but they're great big slabs of, like, galvanized tin material. And he built this *biiig* big shed out of that. And then he grew the grape vines on one side of that. And it covered the total shed. And there was all kinds of green grapes there. And he had this huge orchard! He had apples and plums. We had loganberries and we just had this huge orchard – yeah, we had a lot of apples. And so did my grandparents. And they had a vegetable garden. They always had potatoes and carrots and turnips – mostly root vegetables. And, course, you know, they had the plums too, and apples. They had a lot of that up in toqʷanən. My grandparents had a big orchard up there. We used to go back there every summer and pick the plums – they're the Italian plums? Really nice plums. Then they let the cows run amok up there. There was a farmer up there that had cows. And they were just free range, and they went on to the reserve, and they did so much damage to the fruit trees that were there. So there's no longer anything like that up there. Course there's no one that's there now. But the reserve is still there. Maybe one day it'll come back to life, and people will want to go back up there and live. My grandmother used to always dry apples. My mother-in-law did that. She would have apples hanging all over the house, you know, on strings, drying it in the house. So everything was dried that way and preserved. Once it was dry, then you'd take just a bit of it and soak it and it comes to life! Or you could just eat it in the dry form.

I guess the people just did not eat a lot of greens. I just remember very plain diet when I was growing up. There was no things like we have today, salads and all this kind of stuff. Corn was used a lot when I was growing up. That was what my grandparents purchased or they grew, once they started doing some farming. Potatoes, corn, carrots, turnips – mostly root vegetables. That was something that was a new addition to the diet of two hundred years ago, I guess. As long as I've been around, we've always had potatoes. But prior to that, I never did see what they used for – like, as a substitute. They did have some kind of a root, bulby material, although I never saw it myself. That they would use, more like a turnip kind of a – I'm not sure what it was. And our people lived long lives, you know. My grandparents were very old when they died, as well as all the others that I remember as a child. People very old. They lived a long life. So I guess that was not really that important for them, to have all this, like, your different fruits and your vegetables. They lived on meat, clams just very plain, like I mentioned. Just potatoes and clams, potatoes and deer meat, potatoes and fish, potatoes and this, potatoes and that. So it was very plain. There was no additives.

And seal oil was used a lot. People would render down the seal fat and so the oil was used. Or bear grease. It was used for cooking. It was just used to enhance the food or add on to the food, to give it a different flavour. I know with the dried salmon, people today use different kinds of dips, to dip their fish or just put over the fish, however it's prepared. But people used, like, the seal oil or the bear grease to dip the fish in. Or put a little bit in the fish stew. So that changed the flavour of it. Bear grease, it's very bland. Actually, it's really good. Not long ago a friend of mine gave me a small package of it – almost like a pound, I guess. And it makes the best pastry. Um-hmm. Really white. Really white lard, like, kind of a texture? And it just makes *beautiful*, flaky pastry. It doesn't have any taste to it. No distinct taste to it. Like the seal oil, it took a lot of getting used to for me to be able to eat seal oil in the cooking. It's got a very strong flavour and very strong odour to it. If you're cooking it you pretty much had to cook it outside, because it really goes through the house and everything. So my granny used to cook it on the beach, and they'd have a fire on the beach. But they would take the fat off it. It's like, um, it's like pig, you know, pork. There's so much fat on the outer layer. Thick – about maybe an inch thick of the fat. And you'd trim all that off, and then you would cut it up and render it down. And that was the oil that was used for cooking. Yeah. It's an acquired taste. But again, there was no lard or oil in those days. We didn't have that. So my granny'd use that for cooking, like frying bread, or frying other kinds of foods. Like Mazola oil? Yeah, 'cause we didn't have Mazola oil back then, so that's what was used, like, for frying bread or frying meat or whatever. I did acquire a taste for it when I was young then. I was probably about, I don't know, thirteen, fourteen. But I remember we had to depend on that for cooking 'cause there was no lard and I guess that was during the war too. But prior to that, it was always used. Then the other commodities came in, like lard and oil, things like that that you could buy. But my grandparents still used the seal oil because they were accustomed to that. They were used to that. And I remember when the margarine first came out, it was in a plastic container. It was, like, in a pouch form. Thick plastic. And it was white. And you take it and you squeezed it and there's a little ball in there of food colouring, I guess that's what it was. It was orange in colour. So you squeezed it and you worked this pouch until you got the yellow margarine. Yeah. So that was quite the new thing, back then. Yeah, I remember that. And later on it came already yellow, right? Took the fun out of my life. *[laughs]*

I remember I was quite young, maybe I was around twelve or thereabouts. No one asked us if we wanted welfare, but somehow this box ended up on our doorstep. It was delivered through some outside organization. And all that was in this box was a big bag of beans and – oh gosh! I can't remember what was all in there – probably five pounds of sugar, ten pounds of flour, that kind of a thing. And baking powder. There's nothing really fancy. It was just staples. A lot of beans. There was always a big bag of beans and, yeah – white – always remember those. Little white beans? Still today, I don't eat it. I don't buy it. I think I just got all beaned out. I just didn't – not friendly with the beans! *[laughs]* And the other thing was oatmeal. We'd get that – oatmeal. No milk, just that. But my grandfather couldn't figure it out: "Why are they giving us this food?" 'Cause we never asked for it. Our people lived from food they gathered and worked for.

TRADING WAS A BIG part of our lives, in my grandparents' lives. Whether it be trading to non-Native people for other goods or for other food and goods, but also to other First Nations communities where they had different types of food to trade for our goods. So that was, I guess, part of our survival. And also appreciation for other peoples' goods or whatever they trade for. It's almost like a part of the social fabric. To go and visit with people and just visit and trade and build relationships. Because there was not an awful lot of money for trading. It was mostly in goods. Whereas in the older day, you know, years back, when they traded with other communities, such as going to Comox or to Campbell River, Cape Mudge, where they would trade mostly for other types of foods, traditional foods that they have there that we don't have. That would be, like, eulachon oil – that was quite popular up the coast.* Not so much in Sliammon, but the older people here did acquire a taste for it. And it's something they put in their fish soup, or dipped the dried fish in. It's almost like a dip. Now that is like gold to them. As it's so hard to get anymore. It doesn't come by as easily as it did, you know, fifty years ago. They say it's very difficult to get now. It's been depleted or – it's just not there anymore. But I don't miss it myself because it's never been one of my favourites! *[laughs]* And just other kinds of foods that they had, different types of foods. Or maybe they were more advanced and sometimes it was foods that they had purchased out of the store and that – like canned goods. You know, other types of foods or clothing or bedding or blankets. Whatever! They would bring dried herring, dried herring roe. That was very popular. Dried clams, which had been steamed open and dried, smoked – barbecued by the open fire, then dried. And it's very, very dry. So when you go to eat it, you have to soak it. Or if not, you can just take it if you're going on a trip and eat it – it's quite chewy. So you can chew on a clam for a good hour or whatever. And then they used to take these dried clams too, my grandparents, when we started going down to the States, or going to Chilliwack area. There used to be a hop field there. I don't know if it's still there. But my grandparents used to go there and pick hops for the hop season. And they would bring the dried clams and dried fish and dried herring. And they would sell it to the other people from other communities such as people coming from that area, the First Nations people from that area? And they have a different way of drying their salmon from up that way. They wind-dry it, whereas ours is smoke-dried. So there would be that trade. Or sometimes they just paid cash for the dried goods that our people brought there. So there was a lot of trading with foods. Dried berries was another commodity.

---

* Elsie notes that eulachon oil is used for cold medicine as well as for a condiment.

Dried berries, dried fruits. Any kind of fruit or berries that was harvested. Because there was no deep freeze – it was traditionally dried by sun. Just out in the sun. So, and that was easy to pack too, when you are travelling. You just took some of that along with you. Didn't take any room at all. So that was one of the things that was used for trading.

As we got to know other people, and shared with them and traded with them, of course they'd become familiar and get to know the other people that are there. They had a lot of friends up and down the coast. Sechelt, going down to Sechelt. Going up to Chilliwack. Going to the Island. So that's like your extended kind of family kinda thing. There was no such a thing as just your brother, your sister. Everyone was your cousins, or your ʔayiš. That's your relative. That's your brother, your sister, although they may not be in blood. You still refer to them as your ʔayiš. That's your relative.

Well, the trading just did not apply to foods. There were things like dugout canoes that not everybody was good at – making dugout canoes. So they would trade with whatever they can get – whether it's labour or someone to help build a house or whatever. And the payment would be in goods like that. Canoes were also looked at as something that was very highly regarded. It had a lot of uses. So if there's an arranged marriage, quite often what had happened would be the groom's family would give up a canoe to the young woman's family. So there's another trade. And I guess when then modern tools came about, like axe and that, it was very important as a tool, as something that was treasured. And our guns – when the guns came. That was also used for trading for other things.

So in later years going trading with non-Native people – and I remember my grandmother doing this – I used to go with her to sell baskets. She would make a basket or a couple of baskets, and I'd go with her. We'd walk. Just go door to door, and sell baskets. I always remember going down to – when we had to walk to Powell River, right? Before we had cars. And walking to Powell River with my grandparents, going down the hill. So that was our stop for refreshments at that restaurant, the Chinese restaurant in Shinglemill area. And it wasn't a big meal, but we'd stop and my grandparents would have coffee. They enjoyed a cup of coffee there, and a piece of pie. And they made good pie, apple pie and raisin pie. Yeah. And this elderly Chinese man would always come and – pretty sure he recognized us all by then – and he'd ask what we wanted: "Coffee?" And "Pie? Lacy pie?" He'd say, "Apple pie? Lacy pie?" *[laughs]* And my grandfather would always order "lacy" pie. He loved raisin pie.* *[laughs]* Yeah, and then we'd continue to walk – whatever our business was – to go into Powell River, which was small then. The mill site. Whether it was to go and sell fish or to sell baskets, my grandmother's baskets that she made and sold in the townsite. There's a lot of baskets out there. I hear about a lot of baskets – families today have a lot of beautiful baskets. And all the women in the community, that's what they did. Handwoven baskets from cedar material – cedar roots. My grandmother made beautiful, beautiful baskets. Big baskets. All different sizes and shapes, which took her, you know, days and months to make. And she got next to nothing for them once it's made and sold in the townsite. So I'm pretty sure those baskets have travelled all over the world to a lot of people that have left and gone to wherever they've moved to. So there was a lot of that here, and that was all part of, I guess, our livelihood. Going to Wildwood area once that was developed, selling baskets, selling fish – or trading with the people there for meat or chicken or vegetables, potatoes, whatever. Or just goods. I remember my granny coming to the Wildwood area – there's a farmer there. They used to call him the meat man. In our language it was "mɩjɛθ" man. So there would be a trade of things like beef, or eggs – just things like that from the farm. Or potatoes. Anything that was negotiable. So that was in later times that I remember, myself – walking from Sliammon to the Wildwood area and sometimes into the townsite to trade with baskets. My granny used to be really good at bartering. She didn't speak much English, but she knew what to ask for, whether it was men's clothes or men's shirts or blankets or whatever. And the lady of the house keep going back in the house – she'd bring back some more articles and, "Okay, okay, yeah. Okay." Next thing you know she'd have a pile of clothes and a little bit of money – maybe two dollars, maybe five dollars if she was lucky. I don't think she ever got ten dollars in cash. It was mostly clothing or other goods. So that's my memory of trading. And having to walk home – me carrying the goods, helping my grandmother pack this home. And then she would be back to making more baskets.

I'm surprised when I think back on it that they didn't restrict us from doing that. That we could go and sell baskets in town. Or do

---

* The humour of this story turns on the fact that neither man's mother tongue has an *r* sound; as a result, both men pronounced "raisin" similarly, to sound like "lacy."

Granny Molly *(right)* and one of her three sisters, Annie Blaney (Annie Blaney
was also Elsie's mother-in-law), sitting behind Molly and lasa's house in
Sliammon in the mid-1960s. Photo courtesy of Elsie Paul.

business with the town people. Because we were not allowed to be in
Powell River, unless we had business. So I guess that's business so it's
okay. You didn't go and hang out, or you weren't allowed to mingle
with the white people. Unless you had business. Yeah. Everything was
so segregated – you went to the Rodmay to eat, there's a certain area

to sit. You went down to the cafeteria, which used to cater to the mill workers. It's no longer there. But there's a designated area that you would go and sit. The corner's for Indian people. And we didn't eat out a lot. Like, we're so free today to go and, "Which is the best restaurant to go?" And you have your choice. You have your pick. Well, back in the day, as small as Powell River was, we didn't have that freedom. We didn't have the choice.

We've been able to get back some of the baskets. Some of 'em were returned to us. A lady who lived in Portland, Oregon, she was in her late eighties at the time – this was only around 1994. She was lookin' at that *Beautiful British Columbia* magazine. And she seen a picture of Mary George in that magazine. And Mary George had these baskets around her. And she said, "That's my basket!" Because she had a whole collection of baskets in her attic. She lived in this old, old house. *Biiig* house! And she lived alone. But her ex-husband's father was one of the first people in Powell River. And she didn't know that. And him, I guess, and his family bought baskets from our people here. That woulda been in the early 1900s. So when her and her husband split up, he took what he wanted, I guess, out of their home, and left these baskets up in the attic, which had belonged to his family way back. So she was, I guess, puttering about, and she came across these baskets. Then she didn't know where they belonged. She had no idea where these baskets came from. And so she'd been trying to, you know, find out. And she found out by this magazine. She was visiting this lady, and it was on her coffee table, and she went and she asked her where did this come from, and, "Oh, my friend lives in Powell River, sends me these magazines." "Oh my God!" She's so excited about it. So she got a hold of her friend in Powell River, which happens to be a friend of mine! Ah! And my friend Donna called me: "There's this lady that called from the States." And "A friend of hers down there has these baskets." So that's how the connection was made. Anyway, we connected up, and eventually Marlane and I went down and picked them up. She gave them back. Yeah, so it's waiting for our future museum or wherever it's going to be put. Oh! Talk about exquisite work. *It's just beautiful!* Some of those baskets are just *sooo* beautiful, *sooo* well made. The thought that went into it, the work that went into it. They didn't have a plan, they didn't have a pattern to follow. It was all inside their head. Just learning from their moms or their grandmothers. Way back then. *Sooo* detailed. Oh!

There's another lady that gave us some back as well. She lived out in the Ladner area. Denise and I – my niece, she was Chief then. And this woman got a hold of her, and wanted to return some baskets. And I think we got 'bout four baskets from her, four, five baskets from her. And those too are really nice, so they're with our collection. We got it stored up in Child Development Centre.

Yeah ... so it's really nice. You know, we advertised here in the community, in the newspaper, if anyone had any baskets. We had a couple more people that came forward and gave us their baskets. One time on Telemarket, the radio station, a lady was talking – this was quite a few years back when I was still workin' – and the lady came on and said, "I have a local Native basket for sale" or "baskets for sale." I went right away. I phoned her right away and I told her, "Hold on to those baskets," I said, "I want to see them." And she just lived two miles off the reserve here. So I went and looked and lo and behold, one of them is my grandmother's. I recognized it right away. It's what's called a picnic basket – yay big, with a handle and a lid. Nicely made. So I still have that. I bought it from her. I gave her forty dollars. She wanted more, and like my grandmother I bartered and I said, "You know, I'm sure," I said, "when you bought that basket off my grandmother," I said, "I don't know what you would have gave her. Two dollars? Five dollars?" And, you know, "I would just like to get it back. I know that's my grandmother's work." So she let me have it for forty dollars. *[laughs]*

Nowadays it's hard to find anyone to make baskets like they did, because the material we need is not there. We used to be able to go out and didn't have to go that far away. We used to go to Savary Island, Harwood Island, just to dig roots, cedar roots to make the baskets with. Now all the big cedar is gone. You can't find anything anymore that is good enough for those beautiful baskets. There's a lot of work, a lot of material, different kinds of material that's needed to weave the basket. So it was a lot of preparation time, a lot of prep time. And that was done through the summer, gathering up all those materials. So in wintertime when there wasn't anything else to do and the days were shorter, the women sat and weaved baskets. They'd sit together and – again it was like a social – so there was never really downtime. You didn't have time to just sit around, do nothing. You are always doing something.

WELL, I WAS ALWAYS with my grandparents. I always went with them, wherever they went. I just remember being with them and living that lifestyle and helping my grandfather with the work he was doing. In Deep Bay, when we lived in Deep Bay in our floathouse, we had to

Elsie sitting on
the beach in Deep
Bay, around the
summer of 1944.
Elsie and her
grandparents
spent a summer
on a floathouse
in Deep Bay.
Photo courtesy
of Elsie Paul.

go in the canoe and go on to – there was a creek running through
there. It was where we would go and get fresh water for drinking
water, or household-use water. We go fill up our containers with water
and bring them onto the float boat. Every day we had to go out and
get water. And my grandfather at that time had a trapline in that
area. And I sometimes went with him to check the traps. He was trapping for mink and otter and just things like that, 'cause they used to
buy the pelts, right? And so he would cure it. He would skin it and
with as little damage as possible to the fur, to the skin. So it would

look like it was just one solid piece with the head still on, and his little arms and that. Now I guess they don't do that anymore, otherwise you'd be in trouble with the – what do you call? – the animal activist people. But they used to, you know, buy, the government or whoever. He would ship them away once he got them all cured, and he would have it on a rack and curing it and scraped and cleaned. But they were really nice mink and otter. That's what he got out of the trapline. And there were traplines identified for different people. Like, that was his trapline, someone else had their trapline, maybe across the water, and so on like that. And that was a long time ago. There's no more trapping – I don't know if it was because there's a law that came in to be or whatever. So there's no trapping that I remember as I got older.

And he also had a dogfish line. A deep line. 'Cause Mink Island and Deep Bay are quite close together, maybe like from here to Texada, that far. So he always had his deep line out. And he would go and check that and he'd catch dogfish or other bottom fish. Like ling cod or red snapper, rock cod. So that would be for our own use. My granny would dry that and cure it in one form or another. But the dogfish was for – the liver was for sale. So he would cut them open out there, as it was being pulled into the boat already. So it's like you – this is your deep line, right? *[gesturing]* And the hooks are hanging off it, about four feet apart, maybe. So as you're pulling them over from one side of the boat and over the boat into the other side, that's how you were able to check your line and leave your line in the water. So you're pullin' it from one side of the boat into the other side and out. And you're baiting those hooks as you're going along. So you would get your dogfish and you slit open right now and take the – pull the liver out of it and put it in your big containers. I think they're about four-gallon containers. And so he would sell it. That was a way for him to make a little bit of money as well. They rendered it down, I think in Blubber Bay – there was a station there. So he would go there to bring the containers of dogfish liver, or if not he would go over to Comox. There was another station there where he would row across over there to bring it over there. That's what people did! They rowed *everywhere* they went.* I heard it was used for – they sent it off to whatever they needed it for during the war. I guess it's just to grease whatever, you know, but our people also used it for when they're cutting wood, they

---

* Elsie notes that rowing from Deep Bay or Mink Island to Blubber Bay took roughly six to eight hours.

grease the saw, like, the "Swede saw," they called them? Just things like that. Or for hauling logs down from the woods, from the forests. They would grease the logs or grease the skids, and that helped to bring the logs down to the water. Yeah, so it had a lot of uses.

And quite often I was the one to go and check the line. So it was every day that you went to check the line. And the traplines, quite often I went with him. I never went by myself to do that. But I quite often went out to the water and checked the dogfish line. Yeah. So it was quite a life, livin' in those two areas. And he'd be seal hunting as well. I guess the reason for that was to keep down the seal population. So he'd go seal hunting and just cut off the nose. And dry salt it. And he'd have a whole stack of them. Then he'd ship it away at Refuge Cove. And he'd get five dollars a nose. That was big money! Five dollars a nose. If he had ten of those, boy, that was big money. So that's how he made his living. By doing a little of this and a little of that. The rest was living off what you got off the land and the water.

I travelled a lot with them. My grandfather, he did handlogging, he fished and – not on a large scale, but just making a living off the land. He did dog fishing, gillnetting. In the summer, we would go up to Rivers Inlet where there was commercial fishing happening there. And so, he didn't have a gas boat the first time that I remember going up there. We would go on the steamship that used to go through here. Going up there was really difficult travellin', but that was how things were back then, where we got on the Union steamship and headed up there. And to be treated as third-class citizens, and riding down below where they keep the baggage in the boats. We would be all herded down there, all the Indian people coming on the boat. We're straight down there. And my grandmother would pack our food, enough to last us – I don't know if it was two-day journey or a little more than two days – to get up to Rivers Inlet. 'Cause it pulled into other ports. And other people would come on board and they would come into this holding area where we were kept. So we had our lunch down there, our meals down there, what my grandmother prepared, and I remember one thing she packed – I always remember that – were seagull eggs. We used to eat seagull eggs. And so I guess it was around May or – ending of May, I guess. 'Cause May is the time that the seagulls lay their eggs, out at Mitlenatch Island. So people used to always get excited about that. They'd go and gather these eggs. And so she'd hard-boil them. I remember it being in a big container. And that's what we had as one of the foods we would have at lunch. Mealtimes. They're big. They're really big. They're like extra-large eggs, but they're bigger than that, little bigger. They're grey and speckled. Just like – I was going to say robin eggs – quail eggs, you know. But they're so tiny. But these were huge. So, I liked them! There were different foods that we had that I had acquired a taste for them growing up, because it's what my grandparents ate. And a lot of it was dried. Dried deer meat. Dried clams. We used to dry clams. Lot of the foods that we ate was dried. 'Cause, of course, we didn't have coolers or refrigerators or freezers when I was a child. So everything was dried. Smoked salmon, dried and smoked clams. Anything, dried berries even. And just eat them dry. And of course, bread. Bannock. So my granny would bring along the bread, and the rest was all basically dried foods, or jams and things like that.

Yeah, 'cause we had to pack light too. 'Cause we'd know we were staying in a small place once we got there. So we only took what was really necessary. And we packed our belongings in those big galvanized tubs. You had to bring your dishes and all that. And a few little pots and pans. And your dishes. So that all ended up in the big galvanized tub. And we used that for our bath as well – in this tub. And our blankets were put into, like, big duffle bags or sometimes they're just tied in from the four corners, and you put all your bedding there and tie in the four corners, and away you go. But we didn't pack heavy, 'cause we'd only be there for about two months up there. Yeah. Well, that was quite an experience. Quite different for us to travel. Because there's no work here in the summer. And there was no welfare in those days. Our people didn't go and apply to collect welfare. That was so foreign to our people when it first started to come.

They were cannery homes there. They kind of jutted out from the shore. These were, like, bunkhouse-looking kind of homes. They were all in a row, and they kind of jutted out into the water. They're small homes. I can't remember if they were partitioned off in two rooms, or if it was just one room. No, it was partitioned. So that's where we lived while we were there.

And my grandmother worked in a cannery. So I would be at home with an elderly lady who was my grandmother's aunt. She was quite elderly. And so I was left in her care during the day. I wasn't old enough to work. Besides I had to look after my Patsy. *[chuckles]* Patsy was my little dog. I got Patsy as just a puppy, and I was so fond of her. And it was time to go up to Rivers Inlet. And I was quite young then – gosh, I don't know how old I was – maybe I was about seven or eight. And I had to sneak her on the steamboat under my shirt, 'cause she was just a puppy. I was so afraid they weren't going to let me take her, if anyone saw me taking her into the boat, steamboat. So I managed to get her – snuck her aboard. This elderly lady didn't care for my puppy: "Gets into everything! Leave it outside!" Oh, I didn't want to leave her outside! So it started to pour rain and I was so worried about my puppy. So I got out the door and I went and sat right up against the building and I was holding my puppy. I think I must have been crying, real sad, holding on to my dog. She came out and she looked, and she said, "Okay, get in here. You can bring her in, but make sure you hold on to her. She gets into everything." *[chuckles]* So me and my puppy are called back into the house and sitting there, I'm all soaking wet, so is my dog. *[laughs]* So while we're there, the puppy got bigger, and of course it grew. We were there for about four weeks, five weeks. And we came back home and they let me take her onto the steamboat. Managed to get her on. And we got back here in the community, and they used to kill the dogs here. The police would come and shoot the dogs when there got to be too many dogs in the community. So they were coming anyway to shoot all the dogs. And I couldn't convince anyone that, you know, "That's my dog. I look after my dog!" I had to go tie the dog myself to a post. And so the police wouldn't chase the dogs all over, we all had to have our dogs tied to a post down towards the beach. And the police would come and just shoot them off, pick them off – shoot them. Oh, I was so upset about my Patsy. I loved that dog! And I don't know who took care of the remains. Probably the parents or the grandparents took care of the remains. I don't know what happened after that. But they came and shot my dog. The things we had to endure. Yeah. Yeah, it's a wonder I'm still sane, if I am – I don't know. *[laughs]* Traumatized for life!

So we would go up there by steamship and my grandfather would rent a skiff up there. We used to see them going by here, towed by big seine boats from BC Packers, towing a whole lot of skiffs, all in a stream, maybe a dozen at a time – taking them up to the fishing grounds which was Rivers Inlet specifically where we went to. And so he would fish. And he was renting one of those fish boats. And they would have each just a small – enough for a net. And it had a like a little doggy house in the bow of the boat, enough for one person to sleep in there. But they would have to row while they're on fishing grounds, and pull by hand. They had a drum. There's the drum, but operated by hand. So when we would get to Rivers Inlet, then the men would then be towed out to the fishing grounds by the seine boat, by BC Packers. And then they would be left out there to put their nets out and fishing, then they would be towed back to the cannery to unload the fish and be towed out again. Yeah. Quite different now than what people use for going out fishing. High-powered.

And fish was plentiful then! Now, if there's an opening in Georgia Strait, people would have to be there, and they don't make that announcement until, like, the day before. And there's gonna be an opening in Georgia Strait for maybe an hour or two hours, whatever it is – really short window of opportunity. So you need a fast boat to get there right now and be waiting to put your net out soon as that pistol goes, you know. Everybody would set their net. Or it could be in the Fraser Valley, Fraser River. Then you gotta be going from Georgia Strait to back there, so you need fast boat, real sophisticated equipment, all the insurance and every kind of coverage there is and licence for your boat. So a lot of people have dropped off, dropped out of the fishing industry for that reason, 'cause it's just too costly to make your living that way anymore.

Quite a number of people got their really nice boats from when the Japanese people were, um, all gathered up – what do they call that? – interned, yeah. And they gave up their gillnet boats. The boats were taken away from them. Everything they owned! They just left with what was on their back. So I guess they had their mistreatment too. And to be confined in a camp somewhere. They didn't know why. How sad is that? And they were just innocent people. So their boats went on the market. And they were sold for next to nothing by BC Packers. So some of our guys here bought boats. They were like twin – they were sister ships, right? They were beautiful. They were called "Jap boats," right? Yeah, that's what they were called. Jap boats. Moses Wilson had one. Joe Harry. Several other people along the coast bought into gill boats. Yeah. They were really well maintained, really well built boats. They were, like, wood hulls. They were not fibreglass or anything. They were beautiful boats. Don't see any of them anymore.

There was a cannery there at Redonda. There was a processing cannery there – a fish cannery. I was about fifteen, I think, when I lived there. And I was working in the cannery then with my grandmother. There was quite a few people there. The same as when we lived at Rivers Inlet, same kind of setting. The cabins were, like, bunkhouse-type. They're all joined together, and jutting out into the water. And the toilets were way out, jutting out. So when it's low tide – it's sitting out there. Like, over the dry land. It was kind of a weird thing, you know. Nobody wanted to go to that bathroom when the tide was out. *[laughs]* Needless to say! 'Cause it's all part of this one building, right? And juts out. Yeah. So, anyway, that's where we were living when that earthquake happened. In 1945? – I think it was, or '48.* And that's where we were. All of a sudden the building started to shake. It was like, boom! Rumbling noise – and building's shaking. Thought for sure that a big steamship hit the processing plant, 'cause it was out into the water. Rumbling, just rumbling! Shaking. It was pretty scary. Everybody was just scrambling, trying to get out of there. It's a good thing the cannery didn't collapse. Everybody got outside, then it stopped. "What was that about?" Yeah. It was an earthquake. It was on a Sunday. We were working. On a Sunday. Yeah. And in the afternoon, same afternoon, we were given the day off. Everybody decided to go up to Church House. Gonna have some kind of sports day over there or fun day in Church House. And we all loaded up on this gillnet boat. Gillnet boats. And they loaded both of those boats with a lot of people. And off they went. Good thing I didn't go. I've never been good in the water. I would have been gone forever. So I decided just to stay home. I was really shook up from the earthquake. I just didn't really want to go in. I felt really sick. So off they went. And your grandpa was with that group of people that went. And they collided – the two boats were just kind of having fun – the skippers were having fun and they were going too close together. And this boat tipped the tail end of this boat and rolled over! With a load of people. And your grandfather – I guess he was laying on the bow. When the boat was rolling over, he just kind of climbed over like that and ended up on the bottom side of the boat. And your great-uncle was there. And there's a whole bunch of kids, young kids – three of them almost drowned, and your great-uncle saved them. He was just going down and he dove in and grabbed them by the hair and pulled them onto the boat. No one died. No one drowned. It was lucky. So they were picked up and your grandfather used to say, "All these women's shoes were floating!" It was when the new cork shoes came out. You know, the cork soles? And they were floating! He remembered that quite well. *[chuckles]* All these women were all dolled up, and young women all dolled up to go have fun in Church House.

As I got older, we ventured further to Seattle, Tacoma, Bainbridge Island, to go and pick strawberries there. And pick for a farmer there – hired our people to come and pick. So we'd be there for about four

---

* The earthquake occurred in 1946.

Elsie at Steveston in the late 1940s. Photo taken while working in the cannery alongside her grandparents. Photo courtesy of Elsie Paul.

weeks, five weeks, picking strawberries. And I must've been probably around fifteen at the time. And then go on to other farms that grow, like, currants or blackberries, raspberries. And then come back home after the summer's over. And I remember my granny bringing dried clams and it was very popular. She would trade with people from other First Nations that were there. These camps consisted mostly of First Nations people. And a lot of the people I know ended up just staying down there. They met their husbands down there and just stayed. Quite a few, I think – there were a couple from our area, couple or three, maybe. And they never came back, and they raised a family down there. So there is some – I don't know, Filipinos or Mexicans. Yeah. One lady went down there – quite a young person and raised a *large* family down there and is still down there. And so they not only trade food! *[laughs]*

Every summer there would be the farm boss from down in the States would come up and recruit pickers. And he would bring his bus and a – not a pickup truck but, like, a big farm truck that carried a lot of their farm stuff, you know, with, like, the fence around it, the back. Yeah. So our stuff was loaded onto that. Same idea as gettin' on the boat and going up north. We just took our big galvanized tub and loaded our dishes in there and our blankets, and pretty much that was it. Then we all rode on the bus. And stayed in, like, bunk-house type of homes down there, on the farm. I used to go with them. A number of times I went with my grandparents down there. And then later on, when I got married, in the fifties, and there's not an awful lot of jobs here. So we'd go down there too, to pick berries. It was hard work, picking berries. And you have a coupon, and it's punched for you every time you brought a crate of berries. A dollar a crate, you got, and there's twenty-four boxes in a crate. I did about ten crates a day. But you're out there, breaking daylight, you can go as early as you want. With the breaking daylight and I would go out there. When I was still with my grandparents, before I had children, my grandmother would get me up, "You get out there now it's day-light." And she would stay behind and she would prepare our meals for the day. She would cook what needed to be cooked for the rest of the day. And then I would pick and I would probably pick about two crates, early in the morning. And then I would go back to the cabin and have my breakfast. And then pack a little lunch and go back to the field and be there all day till five o'clock. So that's a pretty full day. That's, like, ten dollars, you know, you felt so good if your ticket was all punched in, like, all the way around. 'Cause they punched it in, punched holes in it. So that was ten dollars if you filled the ticket. Over the whole summer before I was married, and down there, we made a hundred and twenty dollars – was my profit for the whole summer. And that was outside of – you got advance, maybe ten-dollar advance. We were in Bainbridge Island. That's where the farm was, strawberry farm. And we'd go down, the boss would let us go down, probably on a Saturday afternoon – we'd get half a day off to go to the market in Seattle. So we'd catch a ferry and go to the market. And we'd go to the second-hand stores there and buy whatever it was we needed. Ten, fifteen dollars' worth of stuff, and you go back home. So, the end of the summer, felt pretty good to get that hundred and twenty dollars that I'd profited. And my late husband was there at the same time. That was before we were married and he was there with his family. And course him being a young guy then, and he's out – he's havin' more fun than picking, with him and his buddies. The end of the summer, he just broke even. He didn't have any money to go in his pocket after the summer season was over. And he used to tell me

Painting of *lasa* (Jim Timothy) and Molly Timothy, Elsie's grandparents, which currently hangs in Elsie's home. Commissioned in the 1990s and based on a photograph taken in the early 1970s. Photo courtesy of Elsie Paul.

how embarrassed he was that I was able to walk away with a hundred and twenty dollars – and here he had just broke even. He didn't have any profit whatsoever. Kibitzing about with his buddies, and went out and having drinks and not be able to pick every day, when he should be out pickin', you know. So we're only down there for about six weeks, and then we're back home. My grandfather didn't like to be away from the coast too long. He was always anxious to go down there, but he was always anxious to come back home. He wanted to come back home. He didn't want to go further on. Yeah, he really loved being on the water. Out to fishing. Around here, that's how we basically live. That was the lifestyle here, of our people.

Sliammon Narrative

nohotəm
(They Invited Them to a Feast)*

[hɛ́ ʔxʷ námʔos kʷ qáymixʷ sx̌ʷóx̌ʷoɬ]

hi	ʔ‿xʷ‿nam-ʔu-s	kʷ‿qaymixʷ	sx̌ʷux̌ʷuɬ
it's	CLF‿NOM‿similar-PAST-3POSS	DET‿Native.person	long.time.ago
it.is	how.they.were	Native.person	long.time.ago

'That is the way people were a long time ago.'

[ʔáʔayšɬàwʊm kʷut ʔú·kʼʷ čénʌs]

ʔa-ʔayš-ɬaw-əm‿kʷut	ʔuwkʼʷ	čanas
IMPF-exchange-food-MDL‿CLT	all	somewhere
exchanging.food	everywhere	

'Exchanging food everywhere.'

[ʔóšt mʌ́ʔmi:t tʌ qégʌθ]

ʔut‿št	maʔ-ʔəm-iyt	(ʔə‿) tə‿qigaθ
if‿1PL.INDC.SBJ	obtain-A.INTR-PERF	OBL‿DET‿deer
if‿we	get.something	the‿deer

'If we got a deer'

[há·hʌs ʔéʔamìš tə támtu·mìš]

hu-h-as	ʔiʔamiš	tə‿təm-tumiš
go-EPEN-3CNJ.SBJ	hunt	DET‿PL-man
they.would.go	hunt	the‿men

'when the men went hunting,'

[qʷúlʼ hɛwtùxʷʌs ʔi· ʔá:θatàs gʌ tə ʔú·kʼʷ gʌtʌs]

qʷəlʼ hiwt-əxʷ-as	ʔiy ʔaθ-a-t-as‿ga	tə‿ʔuwkʼʷ gət-as
come home-NTR-3ERG and	give-LV-CTR-3ERG‿MTG	DET‿all who-3CNJ.SBJ
come they.bring.home and	they.give.(it).out.to.them	the‿all someone

'They would bring it home and distribute it to everybody.'

---

* This text was recorded on 22 March 1996.

[ʔú·k'ʷ gʌt θoˑ χʌ́nχʌnatəm]

ʔuwk'ʷ	gət	θu	xən-xənat(-t)-əm
all	who	go	PL-give-CTR-PASS
all	who	go	they.are.given

'They gave it to everybody.'

[ʔáˑθɑˑtəm]

ʔaθ-a-t-əm
give-LV-CTR-PASS
they.are.given

'They gave it out.'

[tóχʷnexʷʌs ʔot tʌ́səm ʔot kʷxʷ máʔmiːt͡s tán' ʔaǰù ʔʌ kʷ náʔs qégʌθ]

təxʷ-n<i>xʷ-as ʔut	təs ˏsəm ʔut	kʷ ˏxʷ ˏma-ʔəm-iyt-s
know-NTR<STV>-3ERG ˏCLT	reach ˏFUT ˏCLT	DET ˏNOM ˏobtain-A.INTR-PERF-3POSS
they.know.it	it.will.reach.to	the.time.when.he.gets

tan' ˏʔaǰu	ʔə ˏkʷ ˏnaʔ-s	qigaθ
DEM ˏCLT	OBL ˏDET ˏpossess-3POSS	deer
that	it.is.his	deer

'People knew when it was time for them (the hunters) to go hunting for deer.'

[ʔi qʷúl'səm χʌ́natùwʊm ʔaǰù]

ʔiy	qʷəl' ˏsəm	xənat(-t)-uw-əm ˏʔaǰu
and	come ˏFUT	give-CTR-1PL.OBJ-PASS ˏCLT
and	come ˏthey.will	it.is.given.to.us

'And they would also give us their catch.'

[tʌ́gʌmùwəm səm qʷúl']

təg-ə-muw-əm ˏsəm	qʷəl'
return-EPEN-1PL.OBJ-PASS ˏFUT	come
it.is.returned.to.us ˏwill	come

'They would return the favour.'

[xʷáʔ čam'as ʔiˑ xʷúǰùmos št kʷ šin' kʷ táˑmʌs naˑ ʔéɬtən]

xʷaʔ	čəm'-as	ʔiy	xʷuǰ-um-us ˏšt	kʷ šin'
NEG	why-3CNJ.SBJ	and	sell-MDL-APPL ˏ1PL.INDC.SBJ	DET ˏDEM
not		and	sell.to.them ˏwe	that

kʷ ˏtam-as	naʔa	ʔiɬtən
DET ˏwhat-3CNJ.SBJ	FILLER	food
whatever	(umm)	food

'We never sold anything ... like food ... to anybody.'

[ɬʌ́χmot gʌ náˑməxʷ kʷán']

ɬəχ-mut	ga‿ nam'-axʷ	kʷan'
bad-very	if‿ similar-2SG.CNJ.SBJ	DEM
it.is.very.bad	if.you.act.like	that

'It is not a very good thing for you to do,'

[xʷúxʷuǰuməxʷ kʷ támʌs]

xʷu-xʷuǰ-um-axʷ	kʷ‿ tam-as
IMPF-sell-MDL-2SG.CNJ.SBJ	DET‿ what-3CNJ.SBJ
you.would.be.selling	whatever

'to sell things,'

[xʷúǰumos čxʷ θ ǰɛ́ʔaˑǰɛ]

xʷuǰ-um-us ‿čxʷ	θ‿ ǰaʔaǰa
sell-MDL-APPL ‿2SG.INDC.SBJ	2SG.POSS‿ relatives
sell.to.them ‿you	your‿ relatives

'to sell to your relatives,'

[xʷúǰumostʌxʷ (kʷ) θ táˑč̀ìːmɪxʷ]

xʷuǰ-um-us-t-axʷ	(kʷ‿) θ‿ tačiymixʷ
sell-MDL-APPL-CTR-2SG.CNJ.SBJ	DET‿ 2SG.POSS‿ people.of.same.origin
you.would.sell.to.them	your.people

'to sell to your people.'

[hóy tʌ θ θò· χʌ́nat]

huy	tə‿ θ‿ θu	χənat(-t)
only	DET‿ 2SG.POSS‿ go	give-CTR
it.is.just	that.you.go	give.them

'You should just go and give it to them.'

[yɛ́ɬʌ čxʷ θó kʷ háy's qáyəwmìxʷ táʔa]

yaɬ-a-t ‿čxʷ	θu	kʷ‿ hay's	qay<aw>mixʷ	taʔa
call-LV-CTR ‿2SG.INDC.SBJ	go	DET‿ respected	Native.person<PL>	DEM
call.him ‿you	go	the.respected	Native.people	over.there

'You should go and invite respected people'

[qʷúlʌs ʔɛ́ɬtən tʌ θ ʔayɛ́ʔ]

qʷəl-as	ʔiɬtən	tə‿ θ‿ ʔayaʔ
come-3CNJ.SBJ	food	DET‿ 2SG.POSS‿ house
they.would.come	eat	your.house

'to come and eat at your house,'

[gʌ máʔmi:tʌxʷ kʷ tám ʔéɬtənmòt]

ga‿maʔ-ʔəm-iyt-axʷ	kʷ‿tam	ʔiɬtən-mut
if‿obtain-A.INTR-PERF-2SG.CNJ.SBJ	DET‿what	food-very
if.you.have.gotten	whatever	traditional.food

'if you have caught some traditional food...'

[qégʌθ]

qigaθ
deer
deer

'deer...'

[ʔú·kʼʷ tàm títačùmìxʷ]

ʔuwkʼʷ	tam	titačumixʷ
all	what	animal
all	things	animal

'all different kinds of animals.'

[payéʔ χʷáχʷahaθàyʌʔmoɬ tᶿ čúʔjʋɬ]

payaʔ	χʷa-xʷah-a-θay-am'-uɬ	tᶿ‿čuj'-uɬ
always	IMPF-tell-LV-CTR+1SG.OBJ-PASS-PAST	1SG.POSS‿child-PAST
always	I.was.told	my.being.a.child.in.the.past

'They always told me when I was a child:'

[hó gʌ yéɬʌt ɬo·náʔa táʔa náθìyəm gʌ̀]

hu‿ga	yaɬ-a-t	ɬu‿naʔa	taʔa	na-θay-əm‿ga
go‿IMP	call-LV-CTR	DET‿FILLER	DEM	say-CTR+1SG.OBJ-PASS‿MTG
go	call.them	(umm)	over.there	I.was.told

'"You go and call so-and-so over there," they would say to me.'

[hó čxʷʋm yéɬat ɬo ʔánši:l hey' ɬo· maši:l]

hu‿čxʷəm	yaɬ-a-t	ɬu‿ʔanšiyl	hiy'	ɬu‿mašiyl
go‿2SG.INDC.SBJ+FUT	call-LV-CTR	DET‿Ansheel	and	DET‿Marshal
go‿you.will	call.them	with.others‿Ansheel	and	with.others‿Marshal

'"You will go and call Ansheel and Marshal and them.'

[ʔú·kʼʷ ɬo náʔa táʔa]

ʔuwkʼʷ	ɬu‿naʔa	taʔa
all	DET‿FILLER	DEM
all	(umm)	over.there

'All of them over there."'

[nán·agʌtəm gʌ̀]

nan-ag-a-t-əm ‿ga

name-PL-LV-CTR-PASS ‿MTG

they.are.being.named

'She was naming them off –'

[qáyəwmìxʷ nέʔ táʔa θóhε·nʌs]

qay<aw>mixʷ	niʔ	taʔa	θuhinas
Native.person<PL>	be.there	DEM	the.other.side.of.the.reserve
Native.people	there.is	over.there	the.other.side.of.the.reserve

'the people at that end (on the other side of the reserve).'

[qʷúl' səm tέʔε ná·natmèn]

qʷəl' ‿səm	tiʔi	nanatmin
come ‿FUT	here	supper
come ‿they.will	here	supper

'They would come over here for dinner.'

[ʔí:mot tᶿ qʷàyigən]

ʔəy-mut	tᶿ ‿qʷayigən
good-very	1SG.POSS‿ feel/think
very.good	my‿ feeling

'I was so happy.'

[χʷʌ́ č ʔʊt θo ǰíʎ ǰiʎ']

χʷət ‿č ‿ʔut		θu	ǰəʎ'-ǰəʎ'
extremely ‿1SG.INDC.SBJ ‿CLT		go	PL-run
extremely ‿I		go	run.around

'I was running around'

[táʔgʌm]

tag'-əm

tell-MDL

tell

'telling them (about the dinner).'

[yέyεɬʔʌms tᶿ číčiyεʔòɬ ʔiy tᶿ kʷúkʷpàʔoɬ qʷúlʌs ʔέɬεwtàn tə ms ʔayέʔ]

ya-yaɬ-ʔəm-s	tᶿ ‿čičiya-ʔuɬ	ʔiy
IMPF-call-A.INTR-3POSS	1SG.POSS‿ grandmother-PAST	and
they.are.calling	my‿ late.grandmother	and

tᶿˍkʷukʷpa-ʔuɬ		qʷəl-as	ʔiɬ<iw>tən	təˍmsˍʔayaʔ
1SG.POSSˍgrandfather-PAST		come-3CNJ.SBJ	food<PL>	DETˍ1PL.POSSˍhouse
myˍlate. grandfather		they.would.come	eat	ourˍhouse

'My grandmother and grandfather called to them (those on the other side of the reserve) to come eat at our house.'

[nóhotə̀m]
nuh-u-t-əm
gather.for.feast-LV-CTR-PASS
they.are.gathered.for.feast
'They invited them to a feast.'

[tʌ́s kʷxʷ hós ǰúʔ ʔiˑ naː χʌ́nˑačxʷ ʔʊt]

təs	kʷˍxʷˍhu-s	ǰuʔ	ʔiy	naʔa	xənat-tˍčxʷˍʔut
reach	DETˍNOMˍgo-3POSS	home	and	FILLER	give-CTRˍ2SG.INDC.SBJˍCLT
it.reaches	the.time.of.their.going	home	and	(umm)	give.themˍyou

'When it is time for them to go home, you should give them something'

[táˑmʌs nέʔʌs kʷʊ θ ʔʌ́xʷǰɪmen]

tam-as	niʔ-as	kʷəˍθˍʔəxʷǰəmin
what-3CNJ.SBJ	be.there-3CNJ.SBJ	DETˍ2SG.POSSˍleftover
whatever	if.there.is	yourˍleftover

'to take home if you have leftover food,'

[mʌ́ǰɛθ... táˑmʌs ǰɛ́nxʷ]

məǰaθ...	tam-as	ǰanxʷ
meat	what-3CNJ.SBJ	fish
meat	whatever	fish

'meat ... or fish.'

[χʌ́na čxʷ θó ʔot kʷínatʔèms hi: θò̀ˑ ǰúʔ]

xənat-tˍčxʷ	θuˍʔut	kʷinat-ʔ<i>m-s	hiy	θu	ǰuʔ
give-CTRˍ2SG.INDC.SBJ	goˍCLT	carry-A.INTR<STV>-3POSS	??	go	home
give.themˍyou	go	their.carrying		go	home

'You should give them something to take when they go home.'

[č'ɛ́hč'ɛha čxʷ kʷʊ s qʷúls k'ʷúθes]

č'ah-č'ah-a-tˍčxʷ	kʷəˍsˍqʷəl-s	k'ʷə(n)-θi-s
RDPL-pray-LV-CTRˍ2SG.INDC.SBJ	DETˍNOMˍcome-3POSS	see-CTR+2SG.OBJ-3ERG
thank.themˍyou	that.they.come	they.see.you

'Thank them for coming to see you,'

[qʷúl's ʔéɬtən q'á:t'ᵊèt ʔʌ nígi]

qʷəl'-s	ʔiɬtən	q'at'ᵊ-it	ʔə‿nəgi
come-3POSS	food	gather-STV	OBL‿2SG.INDP
their.gathering	eat	be.gathered	you

'and for coming to eat with you.'

[héhɛw ʔέʔa·jùsmotoɬ]

hihiw	ʔi-ʔajus-mut-uɬ
very	RDPL-enjoy-very-PAST
very.much	it.was.fun

'It used to be so much fun.'

[kʷíkʷà:nač gʌ tə́mtu·mɪš]

kʷi-kʷanač‿ga	təm-tumiš
PL-sit‿MTG	PL-man
they.are.sitting	men

'All the men would be sitting around,'

[tá:q'ʌm]

taq'-əm
talk.about-MDL
they.talk

'chatting away,'

[q'ʷáq'ʷθəm' kʷut yέʔyɛθotèt]

q'ʷaq'ʷθəm'‿kʷut	ya-y'a-θut-it
story‿CLT	IMPF-do-CTR+RFL-3PL.POSS
they.tell.stories	their.doing

'telling stories about whatever they were doing.'

[ʔi· nám' ʔot tə nʌ́gʌptì]

ʔiy	nam'‿ʔut	tə‿nəgəptiy
and	similar‿CLT	DET‿women
and	it.is.the.same	the‿women

'And it would be the same for the women:'

[ʔú·kʷ tà·m q'ʷáq'ʷθàʔmèt tán']

ʔuwkʷ	tam	q'ʷaq'ʷθam'-it	tan'
all	what	story-3PL.POSS	DEM
all	thing	their.telling.stories	that

'they would be talking about everything.'

[q'ʷáq'ʷθòstàwɬ]
q'ʷaq'ʷθus-t-awɬ
tell.story-CTR-RCP
they.tell.stories.to.each.other
'They would be telling stories to each other'

[níniǰi· kʷ čí·čùy']
niniǰi kʷ‿ čəy-čuy'
about DET‿ PL-child
about children
'about children.'

[táytàynòm gʌ kʷ čí·čùy']
taytay-nu-m ‿ga kʷ‿ čəy-čuy'
talk.about-NTR-PASS ‿MTG DET‿ PL-child
they.are.being.talked.about children
'They would be talking about children.'

[χʷɛ́t ʔot hóy yɛ́ʔyɛθotʔòwɪt]
χʷit ‿ʔut huy ya-y'a-θut-ʔuw-it
really ‿CLT only IMPF-do-CTR+RFL-PAST-3PL.POSS
really it.is.only what.they.were.used.to.be.doing
'That is all they did.'

[xʷúkʷt ʔʌ kʷ gʌt hóθosxʷùɬ kʷ ɬʌ́χ]
xʷukʷt ʔə‿ kʷ‿ gət huθu-sxʷ-uɬ kʷ‿ ɬəχ
NEG OBL‿ DET‿ who go-CAU-PAST DET‿ bad
none who bring.along bad
'Nobody was doing anything bad –'

[gʌ hóθostìgit kʷ šín' kʷ tá·m ɬʌ́χ qʷóʔo·qʷò]
ga‿ huθu-stəg-it kʷ‿ šin' kʷ‿ tam ɬəχ qʷuʔu-qʷu
if‿ go-CAU-PASS DET‿ DEM DET‿ what bad PL-drink
if‿ it.was.brought.along that what bad drinking
'bad as in drinking or bringing along bad stuff.'

[xʷúkʷtmòtoɬ]
xʷukʷt-mut-uɬ
NEG-very-PAST
there.was.really.none
'There was nothing like that.'

[páyɛ ʔot t'ᵊɑ·p'aw kʷut ʔúk'ʷ gʌ́tʌs p'ɑ́·p'ɛm]

paya?	ʔut	t'ᵊap'aw	ˍkʷut	ʔuwk'ʷ		gət-as	p'ap'im
always	ˍCLT	busy	ˍCLT	all		who-3CNJ.SBJ	work
always		busy		everybody			they.work

'Everybody was always busy working.'

[xʷaʔ čɛʔmʌs ʔiy θo t'ᵊɛt'ᵊɛyʔʌm kʷ tám nɑː]

xʷa?	čəm'-as	ʔiy	θu	t'ᵊi-t'ᵊiy-?əm	kʷ ˍtam	na?a
NEG	why-3CNJ.SBJ	and	go	IMPF-search-A.INTR	DET ˍwhat	FILLER
not		and	go	they.are.searching	something	(umm)

'They would not go looking for anything'

[xʷaʔ yʌ́q'ɛtʌs kʷ yέʔyɛθòts͡]

xʷa?	yəq'-it-as	kʷ ˍya-y'a-θut-s
NEG	use-STV-3CNJ.SBJ	DET ˍIMPF-do-CTR+RFL-3POSS
not	it.is.useful	their.doing

'that was not useful to them for what they were doing.'

3

Teachings on Learning

I n the winter months when the darkness came early and you'd sit
by the open fire or by the stove, and the grandparents or your
parents would tell stories – legends. And that was *so* entertaining.
And those legends always had a moral to the story. So that was your
classroom. I did not go to school, myself. I don't have formal education,
per se. I didn't go to university. I didn't go to college. I didn't go to
high school. My lesson in life was from my grandparents. So it's from
all those legends I heard as a child – those were the lessons I learned.
And you had to pay attention! When the story's being told. And if it's
told to you night after night, you never tired of listening to those stories. It was really interesting. And our language is an oral language?
It's not a written language. So a lot of it was paying attention to what
was told in the story. And then you were always asked at the end of
the story, "What did you learn from that?" And so it was a *real* good
teaching tool. You listened, you paid attention, and then the storyteller
would explain to you at the end of the story, "This is what you learned
from that story. If you're gonna live this kind of life, this is how you're
gonna end up. If you're gonna behave this way, these are the consequences." So all of those things just happened! You didn't get a quiz,
or you didn't do a written quiz. But it was just how much you absorbed
and you learned. It became a very personal thing? It's your life, it's
your way of life. It was not "You're going to be marked on how much
you learned," "You're gonna get eighty percent, a hundred percent,"
or whatever. Or "You didn't learn nothing!" *[laughs]*

And if you're told that over and over again, that legend or that story, and then you knew your way. You knew what is inappropriate and what is not? You knew what is appropriate and what is not appropriate, just by listening to those stories and legends, you know. They used examples and the favourite, or the one consistent person, I guess you might say, was the Mink. He was called "qayχ." But he was always the bad example. He was always the one getting into trouble because he did not heed warnings. He doesn't listen to his grandmother. He did not listen to advice. He was always going off in the wrong direction. He did his own thing. He did not pay attention. So from those stories you learn to really pay attention when someone is talkin'. You listened. "And what did you learn from that story?" Because in the end, he would always get into trouble of whatever it is he was doing. He got into trouble. And then he would – he would not learn a lesson from that? Never learned his lesson. He would always go off and do something else, and blame someone else for his past mistakes. So that's another lesson to be learned, that you don't blame other people for your mistakes, because look at what he did. He didn't learn. He just went on and carried on. But always blaming other people. And he'd carry on and go and make another mistake and do something else totally out of the ordinary. Caused a lot of havoc, they say, in his village. That's what they used to say. Caused *a lot* of havoc in his village. Caused a lot of heartache to many people, embarrassment. But he was pretty slick. He always got away and he was always one step ahead that people in the community wanted to deal with him, bring him in and sit him down. But he was very elusive, and he always got away. But he never had a good life. He did not have a fulfilling life. Because of all the stories we heard about him and his different adventures and the many different women in his life that he never learned to stay one place too long. I guess you might say the grass was always greener on the other side of the fence. And that was him. He didn't respect other people's boundaries.

So sometimes when I go to the schools here in town, I tell one story in particular about qayχ. Because I figured this one is a real good teachin' tool for the children? There's so many different things that you learn from this one particular story. And it's a good lesson. And this story was about this bird that lives in the river, always swimming up and down the river. And he's a little tiny bird that is really happy and always seems to be happy, always mindin' its own business and busy and dives under and catches tiny little fish or whatever feed from

the bottom. And he's just always busy going up and down. And qayχ
with his grandmother were camped by the river. He was always with
his grandmother. His grandmother was always trying to save him,
trying to correct him, but he would not listen. So they're camped by
the river – and he was lazy, he was very lazy, this qayχ, we called
him. But he was the Mink, so I'll just use the word "mink." Anyway,
he resented this little bird because he was lazy and this little bird was
so active, up and down, going up and down. So he told his grandmother, "That little bird thinks he's so smart! Who does he think he
is, anyway? I'm gonna challenge him to a fight. I won't have him
going prancin' around in front of me back and forth like this. He's
showing off!" In the meantime the bird was just minding his own
business, going up and down, up and down. His grandmother said
to him, "You must not do that. You leave him alone. He's minding
his own business. Why do you want to fight with him?" He says, "I'm
gonna call him over here to the beach and I'm going to show him
who's a better person." And, she says, "No! Please don't do that."
"No! I'm going to do it." He was really insistent he was going to do
this. So, bird goes by and he goes down to the beach, and he says,
"Hey you! You come here!" And the bird says, "Why, what do you
want?" He says, "How would you like to wrestle?" And the bird says,
"Why do you want to wrestle?" Says, "You're bigger than I am." And
he says, "Well, I'll show you. I can throw you around. You think you're
so good – you're showing off. You've been going back and forth here
for couple of days, and I'm going to show you I'm a better person than
you." So after a few attempts, the bird just ignored him, went by,
and finally, the second day, he's still at it, and he says, "Come on!
Come on! Come on!" And the bird says, "No!" So, finally the bird says
to him – 'cause he's telling him, "You're scared, aren't you? You're
scared!" – and the bird says, "Well, I'll tell you what. Tomorrow when
I come back up this way, if you still wanna fight, then we'll have it
out. But I don't see any reason for us to fight." qayχ says, "I just want
to prove I'm a better person than you." So the next time the bird came
around, he'd already told his grandmother, he cautioned his grandmother. They always had a campfire going with hot coals going on
the campfire there. And he told his grandmother, "I want you to be
ready. 'Cause when he's coming back again, we're gonna have it out.
For sure this time. So I want you to be ready. I want you to be ready
with a shovel full of hot coals. Be ready with that shovel. When I
knock him to the ground and pin him down, I want you to throw hot
ashes all over his face, just to further embarrass him." So the bird

came to shore finally, and reluctantly. So they went at it, they were rollin' around the ground, the dust flying. And the grandmother was there, and she *always* gave in to him. She spoiled him. She wanted him to be good, but she gave in to him. Many times, over and over. So she was there, against her better judgment, with this shovel full of hot ashes, ready to throw, as soon as her grandson was going to pin the other person on the ground. So she's there all ready, all ready, and finally, through all the dust, she sees one person on the ground and she goes and she throws the hot ash on the person that's on the ground. And the other person went running off into the water. And here it was her grandson. He got up, and he says, "What did you do that for? I told you to throw the ashes on Mr. Bird's face." "Well, you're the one that was on the ground," she says to him. "You're the one that was layin' on the ground. I didn't know it was you." And he says, "Waah, blah, blah." He was really mad. And so with that he did not learn his lesson! So just in that story itself, it teaches you, you know, first of all, mind your own business. Leave other people alone to do whatever they're doing. Don't bully people. Don't be a bully. Just because you're bigger, doesn't mean you're better. And you didn't listen to your grandmother when your grandmother was givin' you – you know, I talk about discipline and respect, respect other people, don't bother people. She always talked to him. He never listened. So he didn't learn his lesson even then. But there are those lessons to be learned in that particular story. And there's quite a few stories that are of that nature, that are for teaching the young kids. But that, I think, was one of our favourite as children, listening to that particular one. *[laughs]*

So it wasn't just the legends or the stories. It was by watchin' – watchin' your Elders, your grandparents, the adults in what they did. How they lived, how they gathered, how they fished, how they hunted, how women wove baskets, how they went and gathered roots. You didn't learn that out of a book. You learned by watchin'. You were always brought along.* So when the older women went root diggin', you went along – the children went along. So it was by watchin'. Because every step of the way, everything they did around root diggin' was really important to pay attention. Such as, first of all when you go to a cedar tree, which is where we got our cedar roots from, is to

---

* See also Dorothy Kennedy and Randy Bouchard, *Sliammon Life, Sliammon Lands* (Vancouver: Talonbooks, 1983), 45.

ask permission before you take the roots from that cedar. You just didn't go and dig around the tree without any thought or considera- tion for the life in the tree. 'Cause that's a living thing to our people. The cedar tree is a living thing. And it's gonna house you. It's going to give you the materials you need for basket weaving. It's going to give you material for building a house, the branches itself – so *every* part of the cedar was used for different things, such as making a rope or mats and cedar hats and just everything! There was bailers, and this comes from the inner bark of the cedar, or portion of it. So people didn't just go out and strip a whole tree. When you wanted just the bark for making bailers, you went out and you just took a strip, and that's what you used, the inner bark. Because you can only do this in the springtime and through the summer. So probably about August, it's the end of the season for doing that. 'Cause the tree's not going to give you its bark anymore, because it – bark becomes very tight. So you knew all this. This was talked about when you're out there: "This is the time we're going – we're preparing for this. We're going to go out and do this now, while the sap is running." And it was the same for the roots. Again, you offer prayers to the Creator and thank the Creator, that you're going to use this tree. So everything from the branches to the bark, the inner bark, and to the tree itself, the inside of the tree itself. And even the core of the tree is used for when you barbecue salmon or smoke salmon. You use that inner core to hold the fish open when you cut it open and you want to hang it. So you need little sticks to keep it open. Years ago, the clothing came from that tree, like, from the inner bark of the cedar was treated until it was so fine it was like cloth that people used to make garments. A cape or a skirt. That and other things, like hide for clothing. Which was way before my time, but I know the story behind it is that you treat in this way. You don't abuse it. Don't take any more than you need. It was always about that. And whatever remnants you have, you don't leave it laying here or there or whatever. You took care of it, and all your shavings, you gather that and you use it for something else, whether it's to start the fire – you just don't discard it and leave it laying about. So everything had its place. And that you took care of that.

And people never really overused. They would just move on and go and gather something else. And move on to something else. And by the time they came back around – it's like when you're out in the berry fields. You pick through the berry patch in a really thorough, you know, orderly manner. By the time you come back, the berries

are ripe again, new berries are ripe, and you pick and leave the semi-
ripe ones there, you don't take everything. You didn't take everything.
The same as when we went to dig roots to make baskets. You don't
dig all the roots around the tree. You just go and you get little bit,
what you're going to need from that tree. And use that as material
for your basket. And you go somewhere else.

So, you know, the ladies would go together. And sometimes the
men. My grandfather used to come and help my grandmother. 'Cause
it's hard work digging for those roots, so the men would help go and
dig the roots. But a lot of women just did it on their own too. They
all went as a group of women and did that. And as they're doing
all these things, it was explained to the children – the process, how
important it is to thank the tree, to thank the Creator for putting these
resources in front of us so that we could gather them and share the
resources with nature. So there was all that, almost like a ceremony
as you're entering into the forest, you thank Creator, thank the land.
So anyways, you go to dig. You find a nice patch where there's *big*
cedar trees, and these were first-growth cedar. And sometimes you
had to go deep into the woods to find what you're looking for. And
you say, "I'm gonna borrow some of your roots. Allow me to borrow
some of your roots." And those are the words you say, whatever words
comes to your mind: "This is what I need to make a basket." Well,
you would say, "čʼɛhčʼɛhaθɛ č." That's pretty much what you would
say. It's like humbling yourself and you honour the tree. And you raise
your hands. You always raise your hands to the tree and the Creator.
čʼɛhčʼɛhaθɛ č, which means, "I thank you, I honour you." So you use
those words, those gestures.

And you start from maybe about fifteen feet, twenty feet away from
the tree. Otherwise it'd be really hard, stiff – not pliable. And once
you get going, if you were in good ground – the ground has to be so
good and sandy soil. Or sometimes they prefer to dig where the
tree was up on the hill and it looked like coming down the hill would
be nice sandy soil, and that was really the best, 'cause the roots were
really straight. Otherwise if you're digging where it's rough grounds,
then you'll get gnarled roots and twisted and all that. So you had to
find the right place to dig. You can't go out and dig in the backyard.
[laughs] And you dug around the tree, and you just didn't dig in one
spot, but you went around the perimeters of the tree. So you gathered
those roots and you explained to the children that are around you
why you're doing this thing and what you need to avoid and don't
step over the roots as you're diggin'. Once the root is exposed, don't

step over it. 'Cause their belief was that if you stepped over the root it's going to get twisted, and so you really had to pay attention. You go around, if you have to go around the tree or go further away before you get to where you wanna go, but you don't ever step over the root that's exposed. So that's how important it was and how alive it was for our people. And you would just cut the roots to whatever size you wanted. But first, before you'd dig, the first little bits and pieces of roots – the real thin small little pieces that are just, like, attached to the root itself – you will take some of that and tie it around your wrists, tie it around your waist, or around your neck and it's like a necklace and they believed that brings the bigger roots to come along. It makes it easier. It's almost like the bigger roots follow the little roots and therefore you will have access to more roots by doing that. And you just don't take it and cut it and tie it around yourself. You just say, "You're gonna help me. You're gonna bring more roots to me." So that was really important part of the root diggin'.

So when you got those roots and you take them home and you split them right away.[*] You take the bark off it right away. Otherwise it'll stick and when it dries it'll be harder to strip. So you take them home and you do that. And it takes several days, several sittings to get it to where you – where it's usable for your basket? Because you split it one day, split all the roots you got into bigger pieces. Then another day you will sit down and you will fine down the roots. And the third time you go to handle it, you're going to make it really fine, and it becomes really soft and to the point that now you can use it to weave your basket. So there's a lengthy process to preparing the roots. So then you'll have your long roots, which could be as long as four feet – three to four feet long in length. And the shorter pieces, where maybe there was a knot or whatever and then you had to cut the knot away, you might have ones that are maybe just a foot long. But those are just as important. So when they are all bundled up, as we've seen in the pictures, then they're bundled nicely and they're put out to dry. They need to be dried, otherwise they'll get mouldy if they're damp. 'Cause your roots have to be damp, they have to be wet, actually, when you're working with them. So you always have water, a basin of water, and you soak your roots in there. So the short ones then are bundled as well as the long ones, and they could be folded in half and bundled that way. And the ladies would say, "Oh, this is the grandpa.

---

[*]   For illustrations of basket weaving, see ibid., 76-78.

Agnes McGee (Elsie's aunt and Granny Molly's daughter), Katherine Blaney, and Elsie at the Sliammon Elders Lodge in 1999, with cleaned and bundled cedar roots. Photo courtesy of Elsie Paul.

This is the long roots. And this is the dad, and this is the mom, and this is the children." And "Oh! These are the babies!" And the real short ones – so they didn't throw any of that away because every bit was important. So they would line it up, or hang them on the line to dry as bundled roots drying on the line. And they would just be so proud of it and just feel so good to see those roots hanging as their family, and "this family's come to us." So that's how important the roots were to our people.

So there are a lot of other parts to that material as well. Like, for the inner part of the basket weaving, the cedar strips – you would fall the smaller cedar and it's the inner part of the bark, not the core but the inner sap is what you use – that's part of the basket weaving too, part of the materials that goes into basket weaving. And then you gather your designs, which is the wild cherry bark. You go out and gather that and same process. You always ask the Creator, you should thank the Creator, thank the tree for allowing you to take these materials for your work. And the gathering of wild cherry bark is also during that time when the sap is running. That's the best time to go and gather it, otherwise it won't come off the tree. They were bundled and stored in a different way where they were laid out flat and put into kind of a rack – you'd tie it down flat. And then you could dye it to black from the red in its raw form, pretty much. They just put it in a container once they're all bundled up or racked up – they put it in a container, like a bucket or old rusty bucket or something that's going to change the colour. They would use, like, maple leaves, I guess, in the very old days when there was no, like, rusty iron or whatever. But in more recent times that I remember, they would use rusty material, like nails or whatever. Anything that would be rusty you just throw it in the water, and you let it sit from maybe three months to six months, and they're totally black. You just put it way out there and not touch it for three to six months. And you go and get it and wash it and scrape it and you've got your material. And once it's dyed then you can scrape it till it becomes shiny, shiny black or shiny red. And it lasts *forever* as you can see in some of the baskets that you know – they're still bright red although it was, like, sixty years ago, maybe a hundred years ago. You could still see the wild cherry bark in there. Though our people didn't use the colourful kinds of designs? I know that in the other areas where there's some kind of a reed they get out of swampy lands, I believe. And people dyed that to different colours, like pink or purple or blue, green. And your basket could be quite colourful. But in time they fade. They're not like the wild cherry bark. And I've seen my grandmother's work in some of those where she made – through trading got this material, the reed. And so she wasn't as satisfied with that: "Sure it's pretty, but it's not going to last as long." Yeah, so that's pretty much the material they used. So that's really important in gathering for these materials. So basically that cedar and the wild cherry bark is what was really the essential part of making baskets.

So the young people learned from watching their mothers or their grandmothers making baskets. They would give you smaller little roots and pieces just to get the feel of it, and you eventually learned. You learned from a very early age how to weave baskets. You didn't learn by picking a book and "This is how you do it." You learned by watching. That was like your classroom. When you were little and you were taught right away to sit and watch as your mother or your grandmother or the other grandmothers, they all used to sit together and weave

Baby baskets made by Molly Timothy (Granny Molly) in the early 1950s. The basket on the left was made for Jeannie, born to Elsie in 1954, and has been used for all of Elsie's children, grandchildren, and great-grandchildren since. The design on this basket is made with natural and dyed cherry bark. The basket on the right was made for a daughter of Agnes (Elsie's aunt), and the design is made with dyed reed. Photo courtesy of Davis McKenzie.

baskets. You were asked to come and sit and pay attention. They didn't exactly take your hands and guide your hands or show you. You watched. That's how you learn. So that's really important teaching. You have to really pay attention, and it just took all your undivided attention to learn how to do this, and if you didn't do it right, you had to take it apart and redo it. And it was enjoyable as well.

In the beginning it was for your own use. It was, like, if someone in the family was expecting a baby, the grandmothers would right away start to make a basket, a baby basket. And they would make a big basket for whatever the baby's going to need. It's like a little hamper kind of idea, for the diapers or whatever other needs the baby has. So they would get a baby basket. Which she will use for all her children. She is going to have, you know, two, three children or ten children. She's going to take care of that basket and use it like that, keep it in the family. And another basket or container for the baby's belongings. So there would be the two basket items that were very important for this young woman that's gonna have a baby. By the time the baby arrived, these baskets were ready. And they made big ones in those days. Big enough for the baby to be in until they're walking. And sometimes they made two: one for the newborn infant, until they're about three, four months old, then they were moved into the bigger basket. And so that's how they were used. Some of the baskets were *huge*! I remember my grandmother having this oval basket – it was huge! It was just a beautiful basket with a lid on it. Beautiful design. Probably, you know, a good part of the winter making a huge basket like that. But a baby basket, I think, once your material's all ready and it's there for you to use, then, like, a big baby basket might take you two or three weeks to make. And that was, like, sitting down every day and working on it.

And I still have a baby basket that my grandmother made for me for my daughter Jeannie. So I've had that for quite a number of years now – Jeannie's fifty-five, just about. So all my children from Jeannie down have been in that basket. Yeah. All my grandchildren, my children, and great-grandchildren have been in the basket. I treasure it. And it's had a lot of use and it's starting to wear a little bit, but it's more now for show? But its full use and purpose was that you put the baby in the basket, and used that basket until it's maybe about a year old, 'cause the baskets were fairly big – but now the young mothers don't. It's just more for show because we have a different method of travelling now. When you go in the car you gotta have seatbelts, you gotta have baby just buckled in, but in my day I used to travel in the car with my baby basket. There was no regulations then that said I couldn't do that, but nowadays you can't. So we just use it in the home and put the baby in there and take pictures – the new baby in his basket. And so those baskets are very special. And it kept them really protected and sheltered, because you kinda made a tent for it too: they're covered with a blanket so that they are not exposed to the elements, whether it's the sun or the rain and the wind. And they were very comfortable and cozy in there. You had a lace sort of material that you tied together like lacing up your shoes? So that's how they were snug in there. So I just love babies in the basket. I think they're so special! I've seen other styles of papoose baskets. Women carried them on their back. We didn't have that here. Ours was a different style altogether. The basket was just carried in your arms, not on your back. But when women carried their children on their back, they used a shawl. But that was when the child was older. So it was easier to pack the baby in the back with your shawl and kind of tying it around you, so freeing up your hands to do the work that you need to do. But mothers carried their babies everywhere they went, whether they were going out clam diggin' or they're going out root gatherin' or whether they're going picking berries or whether they were doing the laundry. Packing water! *[laughs]*

Yeah, so it's really important that the babies were always close to you. My grandmother used to say that when she would see the young mothers. I guess her day was very different. And, "Oh, it's not time for the baby to eat yet. The baby's crying, it's not time for it to eat." And she'd say, "Oh, the mother would look at that clock like the clock is the boss: 'You can't feed the baby yet.'" 'Cause we were always told in the hospital, every four hours is when you feed the baby. And oh, my grandmother used to get so annoyed at that. And my mother-in-law used to just get so annoyed: "When the baby cries that means it's hungry! You pick it up and you feed it! Never mind that clock! Forget about that clock!" How different things have become. *[laughs]* But I think they've gone the other way now. And I watch on TV, young mothers, and that you can pick up your baby and loving the baby, holding the baby – it's not going to spoil the baby, right? It needs comfort, it needs care, it needs to feel the mother close. Needs to be snuggled.

My grandmother was so fussy! When she made baby baskets, the papoose baskets? She made a lot of those in her life. And they're big. I've got one of those that she made. But she saved all the outer part of the cedar root, 'cause it's shinier. And long. And she picked her long ones, set them aside, and saved them: "That's gonna be for the next project. That'll be for another baby basket." So the finished product was really shiny, really, like, glossy? And she made sure that's the material she used for that. The whole basket has a sheen. So it was made with care and love. She had her own pattern. Other ladies that made baskets like that had their own design, their own pattern. And they were *so* meticulous. They were *so* fussy about their design. Each family had their own design. I always recognize my grand-mother's work when I see baskets elsewhere today. And other ladies' baskets: "Oh yeah, that was so-and-so's basket. That's so-and-so's basket." So they all had their own unique design. Very beautiful, beauti-ful work. Some people attempt to make baskets these days, the young people. But the material that we get when we go root digging is very short pieces and gnarled and crooked. It's not worth the effort. People quite often ask, "Can we get a class going?" 'cause they wanna learn how. It's frustrating because the material is just not there. It's not the lack of interest or wanting to do it. And pretty much everywhere you go you're restricted. You can't go dig roots here, you can't go dig roots there. Even if it looks good. People will say, "This is private property, you can't dig here." Yeah, it was very important work. It was a piece of art. The work that was put out was like artwork. Yeah, my aunt Agnes was really particular about her design, her measurements. And it was all in her head. It was not anything that was drawn out on paper or a diagram she followed. But she made it up herself in her head, how her design would look. And the little basket that's sitting in our church here in Sliammon – she was asked if she would make a basket for the church. So she did and the design is really beautiful. It looks like the centre design is the chalice. And the two on the sides are like the little wine and water containers. So it's really nice to see that, you see it when you go to the church and there's Agnes's work, and she put so much care, so much thought into creating that basket without a diagram to follow. But she counted her roots. *Every* little strip where she would count from one end of the basket to the other corner, and she would count, count, count, count back. And if she was one off, she would take it apart and she would go at it again. And I would say to her, "It's not gonna be that noticeable!" She'd say, "Oh, I'll know!" She would say, "I'll know." Yeah. So she was very – in just how she built up her basket. It's going to be straight up and down. It's not gonna start to get bigger at the top – much bigger at the top than at the bottom where she started. 'Cause if you're not an experienced basket weaver, that will happen – it'll kinda spread out at the top. So if you want your basket straight up and down, then you have to be really careful. So it's a *real* work of art. It's a real work of art. And over the years of basket weaving I guess you become a master at what you're doing. Yeah.

You know, I've been cleaning roots I've had in my house for quite a while. I just haven't had time to work on it. And I wanted to fine it down. So for the past three weeks, I've been sittin' my every spare moment and handling the roots and cutting it down – making it really fine so that I'm able to get to that stage where I will, hopefully, weave a basket. But the more I worked on those roots, it really got me in touch with my ancestors, my grandparents, and by doing this it was such a good feeling. It wasn't a chore. I sat there, hour after hour, workin' on the roots and during all this time I'm rememberin' all the teachings and it was very enjoyable! Very, very enjoyable. It was just like getting in touch with the past again. So a lot of the teachin's are by watching.

And it was the same thing for the boys. They went out with the guys and went with their dad fishing, or their grandfather. Or just go gather wood, go hunting. You know, helping fishing, gathering. Helping make fish traps or whatever and going out fishing with the men. Building a boat. Because our transportation was with boats, and it was dugout canoes. So we had quite a few men that built dugouts. Beautiful, beautiful dugouts! And so the boys watched by following the men. They were taught that way, on how to do it exactly right. And I don't think there are too many around anymore that can teach the young. Because the cedar, again, is really, really hard to get. The canoes that we see today, the ones they do use for canoe journeys and stuff like that, that are narrower and longer, whereas with our transportation kind of boats that we had, canoes, was wider and not as long as those canoes. If it was wide enough and long enough, you'd end up with this beautiful boat. Like my grandfather did. He didn't make that boat, but he traded with a relative up in Bute Inlet. I remember travelling up there when I was about thirteen, I think. And oh, I don't remember how we got there. But he went up there to get that boat. It was quite big. And it must've been a big, big cedar tree that was carved. But there's a real craft to that, how to steam it and how it will expand as you're steamin' it. 'Cause if you end up with a boat that's narrow, it's gonna be tippy. So there was a way that they would put the hot rocks in there and put water into the boat and they covered it and let it steam – so they kept putting the wedge in there. And making beautiful oars, beautiful paddles. Yeah. It was necessity to learn. Just down the beach, just front of the reserve, I used to see people building boats there. Yeah. Jimmy Harry, his brother Dan Harry, they were both builders. Yeah, Bill Mitchell was a beautiful boat builder. His work was a work of art. And there were others that, you know, did beautiful work, before my time. Chief Tom Timothy was a boat builder. There was a whole bunch of them. I don't know how many years it's been since anyone made a boat. Probably Bill Mitchell was the last to make a boat. Yeah. Not just anyone can make it. You have to have watched and learned and developed the technique, and very time-consuming.

And going back to adolescence and young boys and girls, what they must do to build up their strength. How to be strong and how to be a survivor. And all of those things were taught. And that's what was pounded into young people: "You can't do that because you're at a critical time," to a young boy. "Your voice is just changing, you're becoming a man. So you don't do these foolish things. That's going to become a lifelong habit. Now is the time to be learning a man's way of life. You've become a man and you're gonna be a hunter, you're gonna be this and that, you're gonna be a provider." And it was the same for a woman, a young girl. There are certain things you learned how to do that's teaching you life skills and survival. So those things are *very*, very important. That you don't lay around and sleep: "It's getting daylight, it's time to get up." You go to bed when it gets dark and, you know, it's "Nighttime is for sleeping and daytime is for working." Young men were, right from puberty, brought to the river for morning baths and brushin' and cleansin' themselves. Cleansin' their minds – not just their body but their minds. To focus on what do you want in life. It's like opening the doors. It's like thinking about what you're gonna do today. Not only today but your future. How are you going to be strong? How are you going to toughen yourself up, to be able to go out there and be a provider? Whereas if you're laying back in your bed by a cozy fire, you're never ever going to find your strength.

Well, the boys were – at that time, puberty and their voice changed, right away they were pulled aside pretty much and taught to do certain things, or going to the river and bathing in the river and changing your eating habit if they had bad eating habits.[*] Give up certain foods. They were not allowed to eat the bone marrow of the deer because that's greasy, right? And it's really delicious if you boil the deer down and you break the bone and you can dig in there and get the marrow out. And it's quite delicious. So the boys were not allowed to have that, because when they go hunting or climbing on cliffs or mountains, they'll be slipping all the time, they'll be falling. Yeah, so that was a no-no. You don't have that. You will be unbalanced. You're not going to be able to climb a steep hill without slipping and sliding.

So there was all those different things that, you know – taught to be with the men and going hunting with the men and men taking them in tow and making sure they're watching, they're learning how to hunt and fish and things like that. And bathing in the river – and brushing, cleansing themselves with cedar boughs or hemlock – qʷowʔay. That helps you to be – that's for power, right? I think that's pretty much what they used on the boys was that hemlock branches. It's different from cedar. That's more for men and for power and strength. Whereas the cedar is just pretty much for cleansing. It's more spiritual, spiritual purposes. Yeah. Brushing off any negative or evil spirits around you, you use the cedar branches. But the hemlock was more to give you strength. And men use that. I think it's a

---

[*] On puberty of ɫaʔamɪn boys, see ibid., 47-51.

little rougher. It's got kind of piny needles on it. And yeah. And going for runs. They made you run. You're at that time in your life where you become what you strive to be. Like running a great distance. And you'll always be like that then. So in other words, it's training time. Time to train and become strong in mind and in body. In mind 'cause you're bathing in the river and brushing yourself with those boughs. And watching your diet and be guided, going out and seeing how it's done by the older men. And you prayed to the Creator while you're in the river to help you on your journey through the forest, while you're out hunting. The same as when you went fishing. And they were told, you know, "You can't be noisy. Don't be talking. You know, the deer will know you're coming." And there's certain signs to watch for. 'Cause if your spirit was not all there, you were not healthy, there would always be some bird or animal or owl – always ahead of you. They're walking or they're going ahead of you. You'll see them from this tree to the other tree and it's like they're warning the other animals to keep away so you can't reach them. It's almost like they're protecting the animal life. And that tells you you're not healthy. You're not in a good place yourself. So you would have to go and really take care of yourself and focus on your own well-being. Because you had to be healthy and appreciate the hunting expedition, and be feeling good about that. 'Cause it wasn't just you pick up your gun or your weapon and go out there without thought and preparation.

And teachin' the boys how to look after themselves and fasting before they go on a hunt. "You don't go out hunting with a full stomach," they used to tell them, "'cause the Creator knows you're not hungry." So those were important teachin's for the boys. And you don't go around and you tell people, "Oh, I'm going hunting." As you're preparing to go, you just go away quietly. If you're going by yourself or you're going with another person, you don't broadcast it. 'Cause right away the message is out there: you're going hunting. The animal people know that you're coming. So just keep quiet. Just do what you need to do and go. And it was not a good thing to be boastful. The boys were always told not to be boastful or braggin' about their kill, or bringing the deer home or the salmon, whatever it may be. Different kinds of foods. You don't boast or brag about that. You have to be humble, because you would give the salmon or whomever – whether it be salmon or deer or mountain goat or whatever. They had life. They're giving up their life for you. So that's nothing to brag about. You just need to be thankful for all of that. And the men were always, like, they would say, "Thank you, Creator," once they caught a deer. "Thank you, Creator. Thank you for giving me this." Or thank the deer family for sacrificing one of their own so that you may live. So it was not handled in a disrespectful way. Everything had to be really handled in a good way. And you didn't just throw the other parts you're not able to take home, like the guts of the deer. You buried it. You dug a hole and you buried the guts of the deer. And what you brought home, you used it all. You didn't waste it. You shared it. You dried it – you preserved it that way for your winter use, or future use. So people did not waste.

And the girls also had their teaching, but it was a bit of a different teaching. It was more preparing the food and watchin' how it's prepared, and smoking salmon and smoking deer meat. Drying deer meat and drying clams and all of those things that you really had to watch carefully and learn how to do that. And storing food. And it was shameful to be lazy. If you're lazy, then people will laugh at you and make fun of you, and if you're not resourceful, then you're labelled as being lazy. So everybody had to be busy. They had to be out there doing whatever was required for the day. But with the girls, it was about being – "Oh, be quiet, you're not a child no more. You're a young girl, you're a young lady. So don't draw attention to yourself. Don't draw attention especially to the opposite sex. You are now a young woman." You're to be protected and be always with the ladies in the community, whether that's your parents or other women. So, again, the same thing. You went with them when they went berry pickin' or they went root diggin', or sitting down with them and making the baskets and this grooming that was a common practice. When a young girl got her first period, she's now a young woman. Eyebrows were plucked. And other facial hairs were cleared and plucked away. Didn't have tweezers, but they used ash – fine, fine ash from the fireplace. And they would just rub that around and then it's easier to grab a hold of the hair and pluck it with your fingertips. So there was all that grooming. So you didn't have facial hair, like any extra around your hairline. Especially over your ears or side of your face. There's fuzz there, you rub some of that on, you pluck it and – I see I need to do that. *[laughs]**

---

* According to Homer Barnett, historically, both men and women plucked their eyebrows using tweezers made of corrugated hemlock called "haklómatin." University of British Columbia, Rare Books and Special Collections, H.G. Barnett Fonds, Box 1, Folder 6, Field notes: "Mainland Comox (Slaiämɑn, Klahuse, Homalco), 1936," 53.

And again we were taught to be getting up early. To be clean. To be always bathed and keep yourself clean. They were quite adamant about that. The mothers or whoever's coaching you. 'Cause you don't want to be smelly. You want to smell nice and clean and be clean. And again, your diet. You are restricted to eating certain things. You didn't eat overly much. You're just taught to eat small portions. So it's a critical time for you. You could either become an obsessive eater, a big eater, or have a control on your eating. Good practice at that time in your life. It's a changing – it's puberty. You're changing from that too. So there's certain times in your life when it's life-altering, it's changing, and the same as when you lost someone and you're grieving – and that's a powerful time as well. And that's another time for discipline. That you've lost someone close to you. So puberty and that time in your life when you're going through grief. You can put that to good use. So it's a matter of self-discipline and good practice.

So those were all part of the teachings and it was really, really important. So when we talk about the legends, such as Mink and the Wolf, and Mink and the Cloud, the Mink and – all the different things he married – the teachings were all in there. That he was lazy, he was unsettled, that he was very impulsive and never listened to his grandmother that was always forever trying to correct him. He was stubborn and set in his own ways. But look at the consequences. How he always ended up on a losing end, because he never listened. So those stories that were told, that was discipline in a nutshell in each of these stories, each of these legends: "What did you learn from that? What did the Mink – " or the "qayχ" as we call him – "What happened? Was that right what he did by marrying the cloud? By marrying the barnacle? Or marrying the salal bush? Or marrying the pitch?" It's not compatible to any of these things. So this tells you, you've got to think before you act. Think before you do something. If the Elders tell you you're making a mistake, you have to listen, pay attention. Look at what happens. So there's always that reference made to qayχ. Look at what happened to him in this case! Look at what happened to him when the whale swallowed him because he made fun of the whale. He says, "Oh, you baldheaded, shiny-headed whale!" And even though this was just in his thoughts, the whale can read his mind. And the whale came along to his boat and swallowed him, boat and all. So this teaches you, you must respect all living things. The whale senses you, can read your mind, be respectful to the whale. And same as *all* other living creatures. You actually raise your hands to them when you see them. You respect all these things. Because you're good to all these things, then they'll be good to you.

People always took that time to give thanks. Never take things for granted. You always give thanks. Stop and think – give thanks for what you have. And don't complain. Be humble. And we were taught a lot of that: be humble. Don't show off. Don't boast. Don't be like this. And you were reprimanded very quickly if you didn't keep in that manner: "You come here and you sit down." And kids listened. It's so different now. Attitudes have changed, and it's totally different. I try to keep it alive. I know some people my age keep it alive and I think my own family are really good about, I think, doing things that way that I think I've brought down. My grandmother's teachings, and lot of people her age, that taught – lived! Not so much teach, but lived. And you followed that example. It was not about teaching. And so sometimes I have a hard time with that when I hear people say, "I'm gonna teach you about this!" Our people did not teach, per se. Wasn't a lot of lecture, but it was a lot of examples. A lot of legends and stories were talked about in the evenings, before you went to bed. Quite often, more times than not, we didn't just go to bed without some kind of little story told. Or little legend. And that was your classroom: 'bout, what's the moral of the story. And you had to stop and think. The moral of the story is, you do this or do that, this may just happen. And so it was done in a way that it was not structured. You didn't sit down at this particular time and, "Okay! Now we're going to do this!" You know? It just came together. And after dinner, after cleanup, we – just, I guess, like turning on the TV, and you're gonna watch TV. We didn't have those things, but we had something that I thought was really valuable. Really valuable.

Other Elders would come into our home, come for a visit. Or they're staying, spending a few days there with us. And you'd listen to them talking. Sharing stories about their hunting or their fishing, or just their travels or the boat they're making. The women talking about their berry picking and preserving food. Yeah. Our society was busy. A lot of learning. A lot of learning from example. I never tired of listening to legends and stories with my grandparents and other Elders, friends of my grandparents, other family members that would sit and – just exchanged – not telling so much to the children, or not directly addressing the children in their storytellin', but they just talk about, "Oh, remember this story?" And blah, blah ... and they would go on and on about the different legends and stories and reminiscing, and you were exposed to that. You were part of that family unit. You are there in the circle, in the company of your Elders. The children were there, they listened attentively. You were disciplined in a way that was good. You sat with the Elders in a good way. You were embraced. You were included. You were not, "Go off to your room!" Unless they had something very specific that they didn't want the children to hear, then you were separated then from that kind of discussion where it was inappropriate for children to hear. But generally it was always bringin' the children together to listen to conversations with the Elders. That was all part of the teachin' to be respectful: "When people are talking, you listen. You don't interrupt. When the adults are talkin', you listen. Don't be rude. Don't get up and walk out of the room. We're goin' visiting at so-and-so's house. When we get there, you sit next to me. Don't be running around." That's teachin' you boundaries in life. When you go to someone else's house, you don't go and explore and touch things. You got no right to do that. So children were taught that at a very young age: "You do not go and touch things that don't belong to you. You be respectful to that house, to those people that live in the house. You don't go and interrupt when people are talkin'. You're gonna sit next to me." So when we went somewhere, we always had to be close to our parent or grandparents. And that was so important to be taught at a very young age to respect other people's property and other people's boundary. Respect. Respect is always talked about. It was always there. Inappropriate actions were not acceptable. But it was not taught in a harsh way. If you hear it every day, then it becomes your policy in life! *[laughs]* I guess that's our teachin'. It's not written, but it's there. It's understood. That's how you behave. Respect. Don't touch anything that doesn't belong to you. Don't take anything that doesn't belong to you. And be respectful. And don't impose yourself on other people. Don't be a nuisance. It's a form of discipline at a very young age.

Our people always had their own justice system in place. And their own government. Our people governed themselves. They took care of one another. And when someone fell on the wayside, or did something to disgrace himself or the families around him, especially his family, or to have imposed any kind of hardship on someone else, or embarrass someone else, whether it was by words or action, you were made to go and apologize. By the watchman on the reserve. Or just your own family members, like your father, your grandfather, your uncle – whomever is the head of your family – would take you and you'd have to go and apologize. You would go to that other family and apologize and offer to do something to pay back what you did or offer to do some kind of work for that family. So you may have to go and cut wood for them, gather wood for them, to say, "I'm sorry for what I did." That was justice system in the simplest form. But so *very* important. You didn't just, "Oh well." You know? "So what if I kicked his door in or I embarrassed him by my words or whatever." It was taken care of. And it was done co-operatively with an offender, whatever he may have done. It was very strong. It was very necessary to do that. With no question! So anything, whether it was a big or a small kind of offence, it was taken care of right now. You just didn't walk away from your responsibility as an individual. As a child. I always remember my cousin Rose,* she passed away last year, and her memories of her grandfather Chief Tom Timothy. That was my grandfather's brother. When he was Chief, this is, like, later years. I remember Chief Tom. And this one woman was quite angry at the Chief for something or another, and she was very demanding. And she went over to him and was just very angry. And he was sitting there and she went over and she hit him with her cane. This is an elderly lady. She hit him with her cane or she hit him on his leg or whatever she did. And his daughter happened to be sitting next to him. And she got very upset and she got after the lady, and she said, "How dare you treat my father this way?" And he told his daughter, "You be quiet." So when they got home, he said to his daughter, "You know, daughter, you had no business to intervene. You had no business to open your mouth. That lady wasn't addressing you, she was addressing me. She was speaking to me. She was angry at me about something. And besides, she's an elderly person. Tomorrow, I want you to go over there and go and clean up her house. That's my apology to that lady. Because you intervened in the process." So he sent his daughters over with some goods: "Take some of this food over and you tell that lady you're sorry that you opened your mouth at that meeting. You had no business to do that." So they had to go over there, her and another sister of hers, and they had to go and clean her house and bring her this food and apologize. And that's a very strong statement. Very strong – it's a direction he's given his own daughters about respecting people. Although people may come on to you in an angry way, you don't necessarily have to get angry back at them and be insulting. That's a

---

* Rose Louie, mentioned several times throughout this book, passed away in 2006.

no-no. So he carried that into his later years. He was very elderly when he passed away.

So those were very important teachin's. And that carried right from childhood, from children. I remember my grandmother and the other Elders saying, "When you go somewhere, you mind your own children. Don't let them get into other people's belongings. Don't let them run around and be silly when you're out visiting. Or interrupting – you teach your children right from a very young age, that they must behave and be respectful. Not to take things that don't belong to them. Don't touch things that don't belong to you. Respect other people's property and belongings. And you teach them at that young age, so when they grow up, they will carry that." That's when you start teaching your children, when they're little. Don't wait until they're teenagers or twelve years old or fifteen to change their behaviour and the way they do things – going to be too late then. And I was seeing more and more of that in my grown-up years, when I was working, around me, I see it with kids being out at night and where is the parental supervision? Why are the kids out at that time of the night? 'Cause I always remember the Elders sayin', "If you're out there and something breaks, someone's window breaks or some damage happens, and if someone should come to me and question me – 'Where was your child last night?' – I cannot defend you if you were not at home. You have to go and face those people, 'cause you were not here. So I could say, 'Yeah, he was home or she was home.' I can then protect you. So if you've been out and you're mixed up with other kids or whatever, then you're going to have to answer to whatever comes up that is a problem out there." So that's quite a lot different today – I can't help but reflect on that and to think about that when I hear so much vandalism, so much damage, so much going on – the nightlife for young people. Not only young people, but older people! And no one's doing anything. The law can't do anything unless you're caught red-handed. If you're charged with something, you're going to get yourself a high-paid lawyer and they're going to get you out of it. Whereas in the old system your people dealt with those matters. You had to sit with a family you offended. You had to sit in a circle, and you apologized, and you each had something to say. Say you're sorry. You admit to what you're done. And the people that you victimized have a right to say whatever they have to say. And you resolve that by forgiveness, shaking hands and making amends. And all that style is gone. We've tried to bring back that old style of a justice system and resolutions and alternative justice into our community, and we've dealt with some success with some of those cases. You know, minor offences? That we can sit with the victim and the offender and their families and discuss and be able to avoid having to go to court, avoid having to get a lawyer. Just to admit that you did what you did and come to some resolution that's workable for both families. And it works! It still can work, if you don't want to go to face the court. But quite often you find now, "Who's going to prove it? Someone going to prove I did that?" Well, to me that is so *wrong*. It's *so* wrong. "Prove that I did it!" Yeah. Be big enough to apologize and admit that you did wrong. It's learning to be responsible. Be responsible for your own actions. And if you learn that as a young child, then it's the way your life is going to be. Otherwise, you're taught to get away with things when you're little. I used to hear the old people talking about young parenting: "Make sure that you're both on the same page with parenting, you and your spouse." So there is good parenting, very good parenting in our ancestors' times. And sometimes it's the grandparents that discipline the children. Quite often it was. "You go see your grandmother. She'll tell you!" kind of a thing. "You go and talk to your grandmother about this," or "You go talk to your grandfather about this!" So you carry an important role in life as a grandparent! That you have to be firm and you have to be the one that reads the riot act to these children. Not in a nasty way, but to pull that child and sit 'em down and talk to that child. It works! It does work. It's worthwhile when you see your grandchildren doing well. And to see the respect that they have. You may think that they're not listening, they're not being respectful, but it gets back to me: "Oh, what am I gonna tell my chi-chia?" you know, when they've done something they shouldn't be doing. Or "Oh, I hope Chi-chia doesn't find out about this!" Or they're threatened, their mother will tell them, "Oh, I'm gonna tell your chi-chia on ya!" *[laughs]* But I'm not mean!

So what is so different today in how things are dealt with – it's totally different, you know. Get into trouble, get a lawyer. Say, "I didn't do that. I never did that. Try to prove I did that." So that's one of the big, big changes – I really don't agree with that kind of change. That people have learned the system too well, that you can just go and get a lawyer. You can steal, you can rob, you can steal off your neighbours and be abusive to people – "Try and prove I did that. You can't prove it." That's a change that I just really don't like to see. I see other change that I agree with, 'cause we go with the flow. I believe in education. I believe in taking care of your children and loving your children and to be self-reliant. To me that's so important, to be independent and be self-reliant and not to depend on free things like "Gimme, gimme, gimme! Give me more!" I think that's so wrong. It just goes against the grain of where we should be as a people. What our ancestors were, what my great-grandparents were. They never went anywhere and asked for – it was a disgrace! That's why they trained you from a young boy how to be a hunter, how to be a provider: "You're old enough to get married, you're going to look after your wife and family. You're going to learn how to hunt and fish and take care." The same as the woman in the family: "You're old enough to get married, you're gonna learn how to make baskets. You're gonna learn to do this, you're gonna learn to gather, you're gonna learn to be responsible and look after children." And that was always in the guidance of their parents, their mothers, their fathers. And the parents were always there to embrace the grandchildren. The grandparents were there. And they helped in a good way, and a volunteer way. I knew a lot of grandmothers that did that. My grandmother did that. And embraced her grandchildren and helped. There's never any question of payment, monetary payment. You didn't have the outside world come and, you know, assess you, and "Are you able to do this?" and "How many rooms do you have in this house?" and "How many bathrooms do you have?" and "Who all lives here?" and on and on and on it goes. And that's the foster system. That our children that had come from residential school, institutions, and now going to foster system, and you're still being controlled like that. Different kind of control than how our people controlled their lives and helped look after children.

Now I find that a lot of young parents today that have serious problems with drugs or alcohol and dependency use the Elders in a totally different way than what it was in the past: "I'll drop the children off at Grandma's or Auntie's or whoever," while they go out partying. That's totally not acceptable to me. I'm just not favourable to that. And I think my family know that. I love my grandchildren, but I'm not going to babysit if they're sitting in the bar. Forget it! You know? I'll help with the grandchildren if they're doing something constructive out there. And they know that, and they've learned that. It's like I will not help them when they're doing wrong. I just don't agree with that. It goes without saying. I really don't have to say it. It just happens that way. So it just really makes me sad when I see grandmothers, grandparents, being abused by the grandchildren or their children. They get old age pension and their children are there, the grandchildren are there, 'cause it's pension time. Oh boy! That's

Elder abuse. We talk about that a lot with our programs. How do we get people to respect the Elders, to respect the grandmothers and not to abuse them and use them and abuse them. They say, "Oh yeah, that's how grandmothers always did. They always took care of the grandchildren." No, it's kind of a little bit warped. Yeah.

But there are good changes that I totally agree with. The good things that a lot of our young people have. The education system – becoming self-reliant in that way. Get a good education, using the tools we have today, 'cause we can't go back to how things were in our past, in our history. 'Cause, like, I for an example didn't have a lot of education through the school system. And I want education for my children. I want them to be self-reliant. I want them to have that freedom to do whatever it takes to get to their level of education they need. And I promote that. I encourage that. Whereas when I was growing up, my grandparents didn't like the idea of me going away to school. A lot of the older people didn't agree with young women going to school, because it takes them away from their duties and their chores and being around family. So it was discouraged. A lot of the grandparents discouraged – and the parents – discouraged children going to school. 'Cause, "What you gonna get out of reading a book?" That was like laziness to be sitting reading a book. And I had that same message from my grandmother. She figured all I need is to learn how to weave a basket or to gather berries or go root digging, whatever it was that she was doing, and I was always there helping her. So that's a totally different kind of education or training, learning from your parents, your grandparents. Now you go outside of the home to learn all this other stuff that we need to learn today in order to be successful in this world. So I support that. I really do support that. And a lot of our young people – although they've lost a lot of the teachings from the Elders and the traditional values and practices. A lot of our young people have lost that, because they're into other things. So I'm sorry to see that happen, that there is the loss of the language, the culture and traditional practices. So I find that it's a balancing act. I know some of my grandchildren are interested in the culture and our traditional values and practices, and I do my very best to share what I have with them. And some young people grew up without grandparents, and some without parents that were lost to the system. And they're the ones that are really missing out on the traditional practices and values. So I just feel it's a fine line in how we as Elders need to acknowledge the young people and to recognize the good path if they're on a good path, a good education. And to support that. Because I know that they'll never go back to the way I was raised and how I lived, and how I travelled and how I didn't go to school. So I think it's really important to acknowledge the young people, as long as you know they're on a good path. And it's really difficult when they fall to the wayside and it seems like they're searching for identity, 'cause they're not sure who they are. They're caught between a rock and a hard place. We're telling them, "You must practise your culture, you must learn how to do this and that." Yet then they go to school and they're told something different: "This is what you need to learn." So I think there's a lot of confusion sometimes with the young people about, "I'm told I'm a First Nations person, I'm an Indian, so therefore I should live a cultural style of life and practise my culture, my language." And what do you do? How do you choose what you want to be? Unless you had a lot of support around you to help you make those choices and to support you. So to me it's really important to acknowledge young people for where they're at and what they're doing, but to always remind them of their heritage and where their ancestors came from and how their ancestors lived. I think that's the message I'm trying to put out there, is that your identity is so important, whether you're a First Nations person or whether you're other! Whether you're from another part of the world, whether you're German or you're Chinese or whatever! It's different combinations now, people today. And they need to be proud of their heritage and their identity, and acknowledge their identity, because that's just how the world is. We're no longer all pure blood, like, as First Nations. There's a lot of mixture today. We're kind of in this melting pot. And we need to accept that and feel good about that. At the same time not forgetting your heritage, not forgetting where did my grandmother come from, where did my great-grandmother come from. I think that's really important. And I just want to kind of stress that in the book. Put it in a simple way that young people can maybe pick it up and read it. And that's okay. You know, it's confusing a lot of times with people and identity, 'cause in one hand someone's telling them right from a very young age, "Oh, you're dirty Indian, you're a dumb Indian. You're a lazy Indian," and we're telling them as grandparents, "Be proud of yourself. You're First Nations."

I know with my children that they're very important to me. They are my life. When I think back on raisin' my seven children – nine children, I had nine children in total, and I've lost two – but thinking back on the days when they were very little, I really don't have any memories of real hard times lookin' after my children, raisin' my children. Or maybe I erased it from my mind. But it's so different today. People that have maybe one child, two children, say that it's so much work. But I think with families in my time, and my grandparents' time, they raised *huge* families: ten children, fourteen children. Some of the people, women had sixteen children. So, you know, they managed – they raise the children in a very simple way. That it wasn't really stressful or unmanageable, because there were always other people around to help you. Your aunties or your grandmother was always there to assist you along the way. So it's quite a lot different today. But one thing my granny always used to advise me, when my kids were little, "Don't be impatient with your children. One day they will be your best friends. When they grow up they will be your best friends. They will be there for you if no one else is there for you. Your children will be your friends." And I often think back on that because my children are my best friends. They all have their own personalities – they all are different in their own ways. But every one of them is very special. They bring so much to my life. Not only that, the grandchildren that I have from my children – very special. So I don't have any regrets at all about having raised a large family through the hard times, 'cause I really don't remember the hard times. I guess it's like being pregnant and going through childbirth, you know: it's tough, it's hard work, but it's worth it in the end because your children are very special. I do a lot of things with my family now. I see them most every day, 'cause we all live in the same community, pretty much. But I see them a lot. We have family dinners either at my place or at one of my daughters' places or my sons' places. And if we don't see each other for a week, that's too long. 'Cause I see them just about every day or – one of them. So I have very close connection with my family. And with my grandchildren, I'm very proud of my grandchildren. They're very special. They all have busy lives, and some of them have gone away from the community after graduation, after they've gone to university – they're out there in the larger world and doing things and being resourceful and leading very constructive lives. I'm so very proud of that that I don't worry about them.

When I was growing up my grandmother used to – I guess that was just the way it was with the people back when I was a child, you didn't want your child to stray from home. You kept your children close to the community. And it was really difficult for my grandmother, always saying, "You can't go away! You're gonna stay," and that drive was there that wanted to see you carry on the tradition, the lifestyle. You were gonna stay in your community and you were gonna carry on like your grandparents did. Do the things that they did. Gathering and lookin' after children and just that kind of lifestyle was the teachin' my grandmother was brought up with, was how she wanted me to be. So it was very painful for her to see young people go away, 'cause you wanted to be together, she wanted us to be together. So for me it hurts when I see my grandchildren leave home and go off on their own, but I have to think on, you know, it's a changing world and the young people have to get out there. That's where they're going to make their living, because I believe that the lifestyle that I grew up with is not gonna be the same for my grandchildren. They're going to have a different lifestyle. Their way of earning an income is *a lot* different. Their job takes them wherever they're going to go in life, and I'm thankful for that, that they've got that confidence and that ability, and that drive to work and to be adventurous. But I still appreciate the fact that they are very interested in our culture. And I'm really pleased with that. I know they're very respectful of our teachings. I guess, along the way, I guess they have picked it up that it's important just to look after the things around them and to be careful, and to respect all things that the Creator gave us. To me that's what's really important and I've always stressed that to them.

Legends

MINK AND CLOUD

Today I'm going to tell some legends, stories about qαyχ – he was the Mink in the animal kingdom. But to us in the legends he was known as qαyχ, the trickster, the one that was always getting into trouble. He was always doing things that was not acceptable, or not appropriate. And he had many wives. He was always attracted to others that were not suitable to him. So when he would see someone that caught his eye, who was beautiful and very pretty, or just sounded good, or just, you know, anything that attracted his attention, he wanted to marry that person right away, or that thing right away. And first of all I will start with the Cloud. One day he was lookin' up there, beautiful sunny day, but there were huge clouds, just white – just like cotton, huge balls of cotton up in the sky. And he was so attracted to that, and he said, "Oh, Cloud! You are so beautiful. I just love you." And, "Oh, I want to go up there! I really want to be up there with you." And Cloud says, "Oh, for goodness' sakes. I don't think so. Why would you want to be with me? Why do you wanna get married to me when you are so different? You are a little animal. You belong on the ground, and I'm up here in the sky." And he said, "Oh, that's not a problem. I can get up there. It's not a problem. I can live up there with you." So after a lot of persuading the Cloud – and he was very persistent, very, very persistent – Cloud says, "What will you do, then? When we break apart. The breeze will come and we, as clouds, separate, we move." And he says, "Oh, I will jump from one cloud to the other. I will manage. Don't worry about that. I will manage." He had an answer for everything. So he got up there. You know, he's *so* happy. He's just there laying on his back, floatin' around. Just loved it. He was on cloud nine. So before too long, a breeze came. The Cloud started to separate and drift apart. And there was qαyχ, who's jumping from one to the other. Then he'd jump to the next one. And on and on he went. Finally, there was nowhere else to jump. And he fell. Fell down to the earth, fell to the ground.

So he was knocked out. He was unconscious for a long time. About two days he was laying there, totally unconscious. And kids used to follow him around. The children used to follow him. They were fascinated by him. They just were always in awe of what qayχ was about, and the things he can do and get away with and – so he was a very poor example, poor role model for children that watched him and followed him. And they came upon his body, he's laying there. He'd been dead for quite some time. The children thought, "Oh my gosh! Look at him! Look at qayχ, he's dead. He's got maggots all over." And at that, qayχ jumped up! Opened his eyes. He's spitting and sputtering and says to the children, "You go away, children! You don't have to be followin' me around all the time. I was just having a little nap here. So go away! Go home!" So off qayχ went. He wasn't about to admit that what he had done, fallen out of the sky after marrying Cloud. And that didn't work out, of course, because Cloud and Mink are too different to have a union like that. ☙

MINK AND SALAL

So then he goes off lookin' for another. And the next thing he sees is the Salal. The Salal bush. Beautiful Salal bush! They're *so* green and *huge* bushes. The beautiful berries on there. And he comes upon Salal bush, and he says, "Oh my goodness! Oh, you're so pretty, Salal. Oh, you're beautiful. Oh! I'd like to be with you." And Salal says, "Oh, go away. What are you doing here? Just go away. We're not a match." qayχ says, "Oh, I can live your life, and I'll be happy with you. I wanna be with you." And Salal says, "I don't think so." And this went on, but again, qayχ won in the end, 'cause he was so persistent. Salal says to him, "You know, every time you put your arms around me, I will be rustling, and that's not going to be very good." And qayχ says, "Oh, that's not a problem. That's not a problem. It'll be good. We'll be happy." So he gets together with the Salal, and sure enough, every time he'd go and give her a hug or embrace her, she would rustle, rustle, rustle. And he got pretty tired of that pretty quick. And he says to Salal, "Oh, this is not working. I'm just going to go on my way. 'Cause every time I embrace you, you're rustle, rustle, rustle," he says. So that was another failed adventure for him. ☙

MINK AND EAGLE

So he carries on, he goes along. And he sees Eagle. And the Eagle's *so* beautiful. Beautiful bird up there, up in the tree, and up in the nest. And qayχ sees this and he says, "Oh my, Eagle! You are *so* beautiful. Oh, I wanna be with you. Can I come up there and be with you?" And Eagle says, "I don't think so. You live down there on the ground, and I'm up here. No, I don't think so." So again he persisted. "Well, you know," Eagle says, "if you come up here and you're livin' up here in my nest, you have to hunt. You have to work." And qayχ was pretty lazy. He was always sloughing off and avoiding work, not wanting to do anything. He just liked to lay around and take advantage of other people and other things. But he wanted so much to be an eagle. Finally she said, "Okay then." So he scampered up there, up into the nest. And he was up there – he was so happy. He could see the water, the ocean. And he couldn't fly, of course. So all he can do is sit in the nest and watch what Eagle was doing. And she'd fly away and go and catch a fish or some other little animal for a feed for her – food for the nest. And Eagle says to qayχ, "Well at least you can make noise or holler the way I do, or sing." That beautiful sound that eagles make when they're up in the nest. So he makes that attempt. Every time the Eagle would make that beautiful sound, can hear it for miles. And she would go, "Kaneeeeek!" And qayχ would go, "Kaneeeeek!" Oh! He was happy to do that. So it didn't sound as good as the Eagle, but he was making an attempt. And every time the Eagle would make that beautiful sound, she would just lean over the nest, bent forward. And qayχ was doing that. He would lean over. Then he leaned over a little too far, and again he fell, fell out of that nest, ended up on the ground. Again, he's knocked out. He's laying there on the ground. He's unconscious for a couple of days. Again the children come along, 'cause they're always watchin' for him, lookin' for him. They find him: "Oh, look at him! He's dead. He's dead again." Oh, he woke up. He got after the children and he said, "You children go away! You're always followin' me around. Just leave me alone. Go home!" He was very embarrassed, but he wasn't going to tell the children what happened to him. So off the children went, and off qayχ went again. He's on his way, in search of another partner. ❧

MINK AND PITCH

So as he goes along, he finds Pitch. Beautiful Pitch. A hot summer day, it's a *beautiful* day. And he sees this fir tree, and the Pitch is just oozing and kind of running down the tree, and it's really pretty and golden colour. And he goes up to it and says, "Oh! You're beautiful. Beautiful!" He says, "Oh, I love you." Says, "Can we be together? Can you and I get together and be a pair? Be a couple?" And Pitch says, "Oh, don't be ridiculous. Go away! I don't think so." "Why? Why can't we be together? I love you." And Pitch says, "No, I don't think so. For one thing, when I go to bed at night, when I sleep, I will sweat. And if you're layin' beside me, you'll get stuck to the bed." And what they had for a bed was cedar planking. So finally he talked her into it. So he told her, "I'll just toss and turn. I'll toss and turn all night long. And I'm not going to fall asleep, 'cause I know if I fall asleep I'll be stuck to the planks." So he was all right the first night. He was tossing and turning and just kept moving. The second and third night, he was totally exhausted, lack of sleep. Finally, he fell into a *deep*, deep sleep. And sure enough, the Pitch was melting and sweating in her sleep. And qayχ woke up in the morning and he was stuck to the bed. He was stuck to the plank. Planks on the bed right across his back, 'cause he had been laying flat on his back. And the board was right across his back. So, after trying to get up for quite some time, he could not get upright. He couldn't stand up. Finally, he was able to stand up and get moving, thinking, "What am I going to do? How am I going to get this plank off my back?" Totally stuck to it. So he's walkin' along. He's holding the plank just in case someone's watching him, and he doesn't want to be embarrassed. He's so afraid that the kids or someone's going to see him being stuck to this plank. So he's walking along, pretending to be just out for a walk carrying a plank. He's gonna go look for two trees that are together enough that he can run through and it'll pry the plank off his back. And he's walking along there and the children, of course, they come along: "Where you going, qayχ? Where you going? What you doing with that plank? What's that plank for?" And qayχ says, "Oh, this is a plank I'm taking way over there – I'm gonna use it for something. I'm gonna build something. So you get going! Move on! Quit following me around. Go away!" So off he goes. He's lookin' for two trees close together. Finally he finds two trees that are close enough that he thinks he can take a dash through the middle, and that will pry that plank off his back. Which he did. *Several* attempts. He would just bounce right back and land on his back again. He would try to get up, and finally he would get up, and several, several attempts before he finally pried the plank off his back. So that was another experience for him. That didn't work out for him. He still didn't learn his lesson. It was the end of that relationship for him and the Pitch. ❧

MINK AND GRIZZLY

So he carries on, goes to look for something else, someone else. And so he came across the Grizzly Bear. The Grizzly Bear was – we all know Grizzly, how big they are. Grizzly Bear had a child, a Little Grizzly. So qayχ happens upon the Grizzly's camp or home. And, "Oh, she's beautiful! With her beautiful fur. It's just shining. She's got beautiful hide, and almost, like, golden brown." And he's just fascinated. He says, "Oh! You're so *beautiful*. Look at you! Because your fur – look at your hair. You're just so beautiful." Grizzly Bear was a very ambitious person who always gathered food, stored food for winter. And this is what she was doing. She had a big smokehouse and she had *all* this fish, all this salmon smoking and drying in her smokehouse. So, qayχ is there, sizing up everything, looking at all the food, and she was pretty stingy. She said, "Just go away! Just go away." Nope. Oh, he wanted to be with her. Begged her to marry him: "Let me stay with you." And qayχ had a younger brother. He had a little brother that was following him around. "I'll help you," qayχ says to Grizzly, "I'll help you. I'll gather wood for you. I will keep the fire going. I will help you with drying the fish and gathering." So finally Grizzly agreed to let him move in. So him and his brother moved in.

But pretty soon, he became lazy. He wasn't holding up his end. He wasn't helping. He much preferred to just lay around and just not do anything to earn his keep. So Grizzly said, "That's it! I'm not feeding you. You wanna lay around here and live off me and eat my food? You're not having any of this food. You're not going to share any of my food." And qayχ says, "Oh! I'm so hungry. Me and my brother are so hungry." He's just beggin' for some food. "No," she said. "I'm not going to feed you. You're lazy." So he talks to his little brother and he says, "Let's see what we can do to get a hold of some of that salmon. Let's think of a way. Let's devise a plan here." So they talked. "Let's go down the beach. Let's go way down the beach over there and we'll holler and say there's a buyer going by that just went by on a canoe. They wanna buy some dried salmon. They wanna trade." Sure enough, they go down the beach and Grizzly hears qayχ hollering out there. And Grizzly got curious and she goes and looks. "What are you hollering about, down there?" "Oh, there was a boat that went by here, that went around the point over there. They're very interested in buying some dried salmon. And they're askin' me to bring some around the point over there." Grizzly was suspicious, and she had to think for a while about this. Then she decided, might as well. They may have some goods to trade. So, a couple of bundles, she got all this ready and helped him put it on the canoe and off they went.

And they were gone for quite some time – hours. Then she started to worry: "What's keeping them so long? They've been gone for quite a while. Might as well go look for them. See what happened." So she walks the beach, and she goes around the point and, sure enough, she comes across some bones – fish bones and fish skin. And she's standing there lookin' at all this and she says, "Uh-oh, the poor thing must have been very hungry." And she's feeling a little sympathetic. And she carried on. So she goes around another area of beach and she finds some more skin, fish skin and bone. And by now she's getting pretty irate with him. He's eating all this fish and she's getting suspicious. She carries on at a faster pace. She starts walking. In the next little bay she comes to, there they were. Both of them sleeping in this canoe. They were just so full and content and having a nap. All this fish skin and fish bone around them. And qayχ was sleeping on one end of the boat, and his brother's on the other end of the boat. So she's *so* angry. Grizzly is *so* angry. She just runs down to the boat, and the first one she got a hold of was qayχ's brother. He was just a young, young man. She grabbed him and she ripped his head off. She was just mad. And qayχ woke up, and being the little thing that qayχ was, he was able to sneak between the Grizzly's two legs and get off the boat, and jump off the boat. She was trying to reach him and grab a hold of him. But he slipped out of her grasp, and off he went, running towards the trees, the beach, and the forest. Grizzly was on a chase after him, but she couldn't catch up to him. He was hiding.

So he finally lost her and went walking some more. He's crying. He's *so* upset. He's *so* sad that his brother was killed. And he's thinking, "Oh, I wanna die too. My brother is dead. I wanna die." So he's walking along there and he's cryin', he's moaning, and he comes to this tree – big tree. And he says, "Oh, I wish this tree would just fall on me and kill me. That'll end my misery. I'm grieving so for my brother," talking to the tree. Stood there and he's talking to the tree: "Fall on me, Tree. Fall on me! I wanna die." And he's chanting, singing to the tree and he's going, "Fall, Tree! Fall on me!" Sure enough, the tree falls. Comes falling right over him and he manages to – split-second – jump out of the way. He didn't want to die after all. So he carries on, he crawls under this big tree and carries on his trip.

He goes into the deep forest, and he walks for quite some time. And he comes across a creek, a small little river stream. And he sees all this trout, little fish in the river. And he thinks, "Well, I guess I'd better settle here. I'll just stay here." So for once, he's independent. Builds himself a home there. Builds himself a smokehouse. He fishes for trout, and he hangs the trout to dry. He's well established there in his little domain. One day the Little Grizzly comes walking along. And Little Grizzly says, "Oh, qayχ! This is where you are." He says, "My mom's been lookin' for you." "Oh! How is your mom doing, by the way?" he says to Little Grizzly. "Oh! She's fine." "Oh. Well, look at all my food! Look at all the dried trout I've got up." And the Little Grizzly was looking, and he was just really impressed. "Why don't you go and call your mom? Go and invite her. Tell her I am inviting her to come out for a feed of trout." The Little Grizzly went running, looking for his mom. Got home, told his mother, "qayχ's really got a lot of trout. He's got *a lot* of food. It's got a nice place *way* up in the forest by a creek up there. Inviting you to come! Come for a feed, come for a feast." So she grudgingly went. "What is he up to? He must be up to something." But she was so tempted by all this dried trout.

In the meantime, qayχ decides, "How am I going to do this?" He wants revenge. So he gets some bones – fish bones or deer bones – anything that he can sharpen, really fine, like needles. And he stuck them in the trout and he had a big pile there, and stuck the ones at the bottom with all these sharp objects. And he had a heaping pile there. And Grizzly arrives. "Oh, I'm so glad you came," qayχ says. "I'm so glad you came. Look at all this food! It's all for you. Have some!" And she's looking at it, and she's suspicious. What's wrong with this? It's not like qayχ to feed anyone. And in the back of her mind, she's really suspicious. He's up to no good. So she tries. She samples this very cautiously. She's eating some of this trout. And everything was okay. It was okay. She ate some more. Pretty soon she starts taking big mouthfuls. Next thing you know, she's got something caught in her throat as she goes *[cough]* – clearin' her throat. And qayχ says,

"Oh, be careful! *Be* careful. You know, these little fish are bony. Got lots of bones in it. Be careful." So she's cautious again. Starts eating a few more pieces. Well, lo and behold, she swallows a piece that's got a big piece of bone in it. And it gets stuck in her throat. And she's coughing and she's trying to cough it out and she couldn't. Pretty soon there's blood coming out of her mouth and she knew then that qɑyχ had tricked her and put bones in this food. So she knew, she wanted to get her hands on him. And right away he's jumping around. He was really pleased with what he'd done. And she reaches for him, and she's trying to grab him, and he's jumping here, and he's jumping there. And she's thrashing all over the place. And pretty soon she's bleeding heavily. And she couldn't get a hold of him. And in the meantime, he's laughing. He thought that was really quite the thing that he did – got his revenge. And he killed the Grizzly. The Grizzly died. So that was qɑyχ and his revenge. Killed the big Grizzly. So that's the end of that one. ☙

4

Residential School

A lot of changes came about especially with our people that have went away to residential school. That's where everything started to fall apart. Because prior to that there was continuity within families. That it was very functional and everyone had a role in life, in the home. Everyone knew what their role was and without telling them what their role was! It just happened naturally and automatically. And then when children were taken away to the residential schools, that really broke down the family system. I know it sounds like a broken song, but that's just the way it is. That's how I see it. My mother went away to the residential school. She was taken at a very young age, and she went off to residential school. I guess she may be the first generation to go in our community. She was sixteen when she left there. And she had a hard life. My grandparents found that really hard to adjust to, that breakdown in the family structure. It wasn't just her. There was a lot of other people her age. And she went off and had her family and – it was difficult for her. It was really difficult. Whereas if things flowed the way they normally should have I don't think we would've had that breakdown in the family system. Though, when she went off with my dad and I ended up with my grandparents, we did continue on that, you know, some continuity there with them. With the teaching, the culture, the practices. So I was able to hold on to that. My mom lost a lot of that. Because what she was taught was totally different with residential school. Totally different. She was a good person. But she taught with a heavy hand and a real structured – and very disciplined in a different way. And she was meticulous. The house had to be orderly and that was an order. She just made sure you did your job and it was totally a different teaching, her expectations of how a house should be run: "When you finish that, I want you to do that! When that's finished, you do that!" and just being bossy, real bossy. Yeah, just totally different. And it happened in a lot of places, a lot of homes. There's total breakdown in the loss of the language, the loss of the culture. Course, you know, they were not allowed, in the residential school, to even talk about those things, the kinds of things that you lived with. You go into the residential school, you lost all that which was so normal – everyday practice. "No, you can't do that. No, you can't share with your brother. You can't talk to your brother who's on the boys' side of the building. No, you don't look that way, the boys are over there." Or you're so regimented and controlled, you're like little robots. I feel that's where things changed, to the way they are now. Everything you did was, you know, something found wrong with what you did. You didn't get praises, you didn't get strokes, you didn't get compliments. You were just ordered to do this, that, and the other.

Yeah, it's a real shock. It's a real shock to the parents. It was hard on the grandparents. I know my grandparents, when their youngest one went off to the residential school, they didn't want her to go, but they pretty much were told. The law was brought in. If you don't send your children away to the residential school, then you may be – you know, jail term. So you had to allow your children to go. And their youngest daughter went there, whom I was named after, she even got sick there and died there. And – well, she didn't die there, but by the time they got the message that she was sick, they went over to Sechelt to pick her up, and she was only home for a few days and she died. Nobody told them what she died from. My grandmother said she died of a broken heart. She died of loneliness. 'Cause this was so foreign to her. She was only about nine, ten years old when she was brought there. She didn't know English or, you know, she never went to school. So it was a real shock for her. For me, when I went there it was a shock for me, but I'd already had a bit of exposure. So I'm sure it was worse for my mother. I'm sure it was worse for my aunt – in their time, when they went there.

And just the total different lifestyle, different foods, and just missing your family. And it's a harsh, very harsh environment. And not understanding why, "Why are things like this? Why can't I speak to my cousin who's on the boys' side?" I can't wave at them. I can't say hello to them. We were segregated. And you go to church together: they march you into church, you look straight ahead, you don't look over there or wave or smile. If you did, you got whacked on the head. So you went there like little tin soldiers, and they sat over there, and we sat over there. Straight ahead. No looking, smiling, waving, anything.

So if people are bitter today, that's why. If they're bitter and angry about what's happened in the past and – being that the culture'd been taken away. You don't speak your tongue. You don't speak your language. You don't worship the eagles or, you know, what we were taught! What we grew up with! That you have respect for all living things. And you have respect for Mother Earth and in the way we prayed or gave thanks to what we have. It was done in a different way – our way. Using cedar boughs for cleansing, and other First Nations people use different things, like sage and whatever else they use. But us on the coast here, we've always used the cedar boughs for cleansing. And that's no longer the case. When you went off to residential school if you were caught even believing that, you were punished. You were punished to just forget about all that. It's taken away from you.

A lot of people tried to hide their children. I know my grandparents did. And they would be away from here. They'd go away from this community, in the summer. I guess once the Sechelt Residential School was filled to capacity, then that was it for the year. Then there was a day school that was built here, the first day school that was built in our community. That was a one-room little school. So I went there. It was hit and miss for me. I just would go there when we're here in the community, for maybe month, two months, and then we're off again. Until I was probably about nine or ten – I was ten I guess – and I went off to the residential school. I was made to go, pretty much. My grandparents really didn't want me to go. They were just so upset. Because they had named me after the girl they lost – that she died after she'd been in the residential school and got sick and died shortly after. So they were very protective and didn't want that to happen again. So I was there two years and came back home, and then pretty much after that, we were always up on the coast, and they didn't bother me again. So that was the end of my school years, when I was about eleven years old. I didn't go to school again after that. Well, sometimes I wish that I had better education, schooling, 'cause things interest me and I'm limited. But I value what I learned from my grandparents as well. To me that's very valuable. That's something I'll never pick up in any school. So to me, that's very precious to me. And so, if I had a choice, I would not change anything in what type of teaching I had – or schooling I had.

Well, I guess for myself, going to Sechelt Residential School was, it was very difficult, because I'd never been away from my grandparents and my community. So it was really new for me to be finally caught and made to go away to residential school. And I was there two years. I don't know what happened in my mind at first. I always thought when I was younger that I was there one year – or whenever I thought about the length of time that I was there – but it was actually two years. According to the records I was there two years.* So that was, I guess, from ten to twelve years of age, in that area, or nine or ten years of age.

It was not a fun place to be. You're homesick. You're lonely. You don't know many of the people. And you're not allowed to speak your language. The lifestyle is so totally different than what you're used to. It's almost, I guess, like being in jail. You're in the institution – basically that's what it is. You're put in an institution. And I knew very few kids when I first went there. I got to know some of the girls later on, as time went on. But having arrived there first of all, my first day or first night that I was there, and sitting down having supper, to eat something totally foreign to me – I was a fussy eater when I was a child. I was a real plain eater. And to have this stuff which I thought was just real disgusting-looking dish in front of me, I was looking at it and wondering, "What is this?" And the young girl next to me whispered to me and said, "You'd better eat it all. You'd better eat it. You'll be punished if you don't." And I was thinking, "How am I going to eat this?" I just really didn't like what I saw in front of me. It was some kind of a stew or soup – but it must've been pork soup, because I recognized the rind in there, like, the fat. And the skin is still on there and it had some fur attached to it still. And I guess what they used to do when they slaughtered the pigs there, they would just scrape the fur off it. And so the skin is still on there. And a lot of fat on that part of the meat. And I just didn't want to touch it. I didn't want to eat it, and I just sat there and looked at it and I don't know what I did with it! I don't know if I ate it or not. But I always remember that, that horrible-looking pig skin with fur on it. On my dish. And a real thin soup – it wasn't soup, but it wasn't a lot of vegetables or anything in there. It was just that and, I guess, some potatoes and thickened with whatever, flour, I guess. And still today, I don't know

---

* Elsie learned this from her claim made through the Indian Residential Schools Settlement Agreement. This agreement was implemented in 2007.

what I did with that. It was going through my mind to throw it on the floor, but the girl next to me was warning me, "Don't – you have to eat it. You have to eat it!" So that was really hard. And then there was a custard. I never saw custard before in my life. I don't know what kind of custard it was. But when you force someone to eat something they've never tasted – and to me that wasn't in my diet. It was foreign to me. And I had to eat that. I had to eat this custard. So that was just one part of it that it was really distasteful about the whole thing.

A lot of the kids that were there were lonely, and so very lonely and homesick. And a lot of them were younger than I. Some of them were coming there at five years, six years of age – first time away from their parents. And it was really sad to hear them crying at night and wetting their bed 'cause they were so scared. And having to walk around with a sheet on their heads the next day and parade around in front of the kids 'cause they're wetting their bed. It's most humiliating for them. So just having witnessed all that, and I think back, why did they do that? Why did they do that to children? It was all about scaring the devil out of you at a very young age: seven, eight, nine years of age. You're a sinner right from the get-go. Your parents are sinners: "You've gotta pray for them. Remember them in your prayers. They're sinners!" was the message. How does that make you feel as a child, about your parents, your beloved parents? Your grandparents, they're sinners? They're going to go to hell if you don't pray for them. So that was really difficult – difficult thing to wrap your little mind around that.

And just the strict, strict rules and regulations of, you know, your clothes are taken away that you're familiar – you're given a uniform to wear, two sets of uniform that you wore. Which was, like, a tunic and a white blouse, and black or navy stockings, like hose. And everything was numbered. Your number was put on. The bigger girls did that. So when a new person came in, their clothes was sized and numbered. And my number was eighteen. And I hadn't thought of that for a long, long time. But I guess it was always in the back of my mind. Then one day we were just talking about that not long ago and someone said, "What was your number in school?" I said, "Eighteen." So after, seventy years later, I remember that was my number. So therefore you were called by that number. They didn't use your name: "Eighteen, come here! Eighteen, go do this! Eighteen, it's your turn to go do this." So I wasn't a person anymore, I was a number. I was like a prisoner. All of us were like prisoners with numbers. It's a wonder they didn't tattoo that on your forehead or on your lip. That's how cruel it was! You're not even human. It's bad enough that you have a number from the Department of Indian Affairs. You go to that institution, you got a number. I don't know where else they do that. So all your clothes were marked and numbered with that so there's no mix-up of – so that's all you had was these very few things. Your clothes were put away until you left the school. And quite often some of your clothes were getting a little small by the time you came home, by Christmastime.

I was lucky to come home at Christmas, but some kids didn't. Sometimes they couldn't even come home for Christmas if their parents couldn't afford to bring them home. So some kids were there from September till June. And that's a long time for a child that had never been away. It was very limited as to visitation rights when you went to visit: you didn't go and take your child out of the residential school for the day. You can come and visit for an hour or whatever it was, couple hours. Just sit and visit and that was it. You couldn't go out with them and go and be with your parent for the weekend. A lot of kids didn't get a visit, further up north, where it was harder for them to go for a visit, in the winter months especially. So some of the kids just didn't get visitors, and some of them that were maybe orphaned and didn't really have the family just stayed – grew up in the residential school, pretty much. So I feel those were the ones that really lost the language. And just lost the way of our own people. It was taken away from them.

So I always remember one of the girls that came in, that was my friend Marion. She was from Homalco. She was only five years old. And to hear her crying and being really lonely and missing home. So I became the big sister that looked after her. They always paired up the kids – the senior girl would look after a junior girl. So she became my little sister, kind of thing. And looked after her. So I'm in the big dorm, and she's in the small dorm. So we had two big dorms that separated the age groups. So I'd get up – first thing you do when you get up in the morning is make sure you go and get the child that's in your care. And I was only ten. And get her up and help her to the washroom, make her bed for her, plus make my own bed. Those were the duties that was designated to you as a ten-year-old: "These are your duties. You're gonna look after this child, this newcomer. You'll get her up in the morning and you'll take her and bathe her or comb her hair, dress her." You were limited really quickly, how much time you had. You had to make sure you were up and doing those things really quickly. And comb her hair, and we get all ready and start the day. She's still around. She's a friend of mine. Yeah, and she grew up there pretty much. Her mom passed away. And she's a wonderful lady. But she's maintained the language, which is really beautiful.[*]

It was so regimented and so strict, and you had to be on time. You had to be punctual. In the morning when the sister came and woke you up from a dead sleep, it was like, "clap clap" – clap your hands. It was like *[claps loudly]* – that loud! Really loud. Right away, you jumped out – rolled out of bed onto your knees on the floor. Right now! And you prayed. Then you made your bed. Then you went about looking after your care, then yourself. And you're lined up – it was so regimented that you didn't dare step out of line. You're like little soldiers. So it was every time you turned around, no matter what you did, you – you didn't play. You didn't talk to the other kids, 'cause you're busy. You're not allowed to just have a conversation with other kids. So you get up and you do what you have to do. You line up, you pray again, and you go down to mass. Then you come out of mass, you go to the dining room for breakfast, then you pray again. You finish your breakfast, which was a porridge – it was always porridge. I didn't mind the porridge. That was okay for me. And we leave that dining room and it's prayer again before you walk out of that room. Then you go outside for a little while, a short recess – not recess, but break outside in the yard. Fenced-in yard. And you only have a short time there, and then you go to class. And you enter the classroom, you pray again. You leave the classroom, you pray again. You do something else, you pray. We must have prayed, I don't know how many times – every time you turned around. That was the rule, that was the law in that place. And then you were given duties, chores. The boys had chores to do, working outside. So it really wasn't a learning institution. It was more like a labour camp. There was very little time for classroom. Might be two hours in the morning, and the afternoon, maybe an hour, hour and a half. The rest of the time was work. We all had our designated chores. And then they would switch around. They'd switch you with another girl, 'cause we're divided – the whole building is divided in half. And I'm in the girls' section, and the boys are on the other side, and the chapel sits in between the two sides to this institution. So we're quite separated from the boys. So even if you looked over to the boys' side of the chapel, you got a

---

[*] Marion Harry, who has worked extensively with linguist Honoré Watanabe, including on the Sliammon language narratives included in this book.

whack in the head, 'cause you don't dare look at the boys. Still today, I find that our people, when they go to church, the women go to one side and the men go to one side in the building, 'cause that's how it was when they were growing up. It's very recent that I see people, like, a couple will sit together with their children. That was just how it was supposed to be then. The women on one side, the boys on one side. So those things kind of get really ingrained in your mind: that's how it's supposed to be. That's the law. That's the rule.

And I had kitchen duties sometimes. I was tall, tall for my age. And I remember one time, washing dishes. You're supposed to stand straight like a good soldier when you wash dishes. And I guess I relaxed a bit and I had my one knee just kind of, you know, bent, and just standing on one knee straight and the other one is kind of bent or bit slouched, I guess. Next thing you know, I got a stick whacked across the back of my legs: "You stand straight when you're doing the dishes! You're slouching. You're lazy! A sign of laziness!" It's almost like you were a little tin soldier. You didn't show emotion. No one showed you love. No one embraced you. It was just always that fear of getting hit for something they deemed to be wrong. So that was really difficult. And the boys got the same kind of treatment. I don't know if the boys got it worse than the girls, but they did outside work, cleaning the building on the outside and yard work and working in the garden or working in the barn. But I remember hearing my late husband tellin' me about how they would stash apples within their clothes 'cause they were always hungry. We were always hungry! And they would get punished if they were ever caught with an apple in their pocket. You're not allowed to do that. And it was totally different diet for the kids than it was for our caregivers. If you happened to work in the dining room of our caregivers, everything is set in white linen and napkins and placemats and silverware and good food. Butter, real butter. The butter that I churned for hours by hand. Never tasted butter. It was for someone else. So there was a rule for, you know – there was restrictions for all of us as children. We were treated like little servants. That's how I saw it.

But when I think of it, it's like, maybe my time was a lot easier than my mom's time there. 'Cause it was starting to get easier as time went by from what I gather. I heard old, old people talking about their time in the residential school. It was tough, so tough. And I think that's when there was a lot of abuse – sexual abuse, physical abuse, not to mention mental and emotional abuse. So I was just lucky that I didn't get those kinds of abuses. But I always had to be on guard that I'm going to get hit with that ruler or a book in the back of my head, 'cause I couldn't do my math. It was called arithmetic then. I was stuck for an answer in my arithmetic and I got whacked in the back of the head with a thick arithmetic book. Boy, that sure hurts. You know? And not to mention embarrassment. You get whacked in the head in front of your peers in the classroom – that you're stupid. So those were just some of the things that I encountered in the residential school. And just watching the other kids being – it was almost like a bunch of jailbirds fighting over crumbs. Sometimes some kids were lucky that their parents didn't live that far away, and a parent would come and drop off a bag of whatever, oranges or apples, some goodies in a bag. And the rest of us would be drooling over someone that got something from home. Some kids were in a worse position that they didn't ever get anything 'cause they came from so far away. And there was a lady that lived down the reserve there in Sechelt who had family – it was from our family too, from this community. It was my grandfather's sister that lived down there, married to a Sechelt guy. And she used to take pity on us, and she used to bring us bread. She used to bring us bannock. Oh! That was a highlight. It was so good. But you can't hang around at the fence. Like if she were to come outside the fence, you don't go there. If you're ever caught near the fence or talking to anyone outside the fence, you're punished. So the whole thing about being cut off from family, from the rest of the human race. Like you're captive there. And some people will say, you know, it really disturbs me when I hear people in denial of how kids were treated and, "Why don't people just leave it alone? Why don't people just let it go," and "That was a long time ago." Well, you don't know if you haven't ever been there. You've got no understanding, no compassion. Just because you weren't there and you didn't experience it, doesn't mean that it didn't happen. So that really disturbs me – and I've heard it a number of times from different people, including non-Native people. And when I say "people," I mean our own people. I've heard from different people say that: "Why don't they just get over it? They're always using the residential school as an excuse for bad behaviour." Well! It's not a choice to make. It's something real that happened to you! Lucky for you if that didn't happen to you. So you know? I guess I could be real bitter if I want to be, if I allow it to be. 'Cause that's how some people are today. They're very bitter about it. And I can't say I blame them. It was tough.

It was really hard on the boys, like my late husband. They used to have him – had some kind of little work for him, his designated chore.

And he used to clean this one room, where there's a cupboard there with goodies. And he's telling me about it some years after we were married. And he laughed about it. He laughed about it then. But it must've been terrible for him then. He's cleaning this room – there's this cupboard full of goodies, like, when sometimes you have money sent to you from home, then you can go there and buy a chocolate bar or whatever, little goodies. So in his duties as a cleaning person in there, he was telling me that he got into the gumballs or something really hard, like jawbreakers. And he didn't know how he was going to get out of this room, but he really wanted to take more than just one. So he put in his mouth, the two jawbreakers. And then the supervisor came and said to him, "Are you done? Are you done your job?" And he's going, "Yep," noddin' his head. He wouldn't open his mouth. "What's wrong with you? You lost your tongue?" Shake his head. And the supervisor actually came to him, poked him on both sides of his cheeks, and these jawbreakers flew out of his mouth. So he was punished severely for that. He lost his job. He lost his designated chore – that was a privilege to work there. Yeah.

And some of the old-timers must have had it so much worse, too. 'Cause my late husband was about the same age as one of our old-timers that's still here today. And he too talked about them running away from the residential school. In the middle of winter they wanted to come home so badly for Christmas that they decided to run away. And they launched a little canoe. They snuck out of the school, and they went to Forbes Bay, across the inlet, over to the other side. And they launched a canoe there, a little boat. And there were three boys. Went down, they travelled – I don't know how far they travelled, but it was dark. It was nighttime. And it got really, really cold, and in that area, if you keep going as to where they were planning to go, there was rapids there. There's big rapids – what is the rapids called there, in, not Gibsons, but Egmont – Skookumchuck. That's where they would've had to go. And as young boys, I don't know how old they were, if they were around thirteen or fourteen, thereabouts. And they got scared. So they pulled ashore, and they thought they'll wait till daylight and carry on. But it was so cold. It was December. So they pull the canoe up and they flipped it over and they got underneath the canoe and they stayed huddled there for quite a while, and just shivering cold. And they decided, "Better go back. We'll never make it. We'll never make it – and if we go through the rapids then we're going to be finished!" So they went back. They tried to get back before it got daylight. So they got the canoe back, and they were just sneaking into the building when they were discovered. Boy, they were strapped! Over and over again for two weeks. Strapped on their butt and on their hands. They had to stand there and get the strap on each hand ten times with a thick strap, and ten times on the other hand. Every day for two weeks. And I didn't only hear that from this man that tells me that story. I've heard it from other Elders, other elderly men that had gone through that. And even the girls got that kind of strapping, that punishment. So it was really, really harsh punishment. It wasn't like, "Oh, you're homesick, okay. We'll let you find a way to get you home." "How dare you run away? We're trying to civilize you and smarten you up, and – be appreciative." You know, "You run away! You're a big sinner. You're gonna go to hell for sure!" So that's an awful lot to put on a child – any child! So my husband carried that burden for years. All the strapping that was done to him in punishment in the school. As did so many other hundreds of kids, hundreds of boys.

Yeah, it wasn't a fun place to be. And it's so unfair! Especially to very young kids. Five and six years of age, to be taken from a parent, taken from a community, taken from a place that's home and familiar with everything. And to be taken to a foreign place, for what reason? And I'm not just blaming the Catholic Church. They were all like that! The other churches that were put into place in the communities were all like that. Why? Why were they mean? But, to me, I'm thankful that I was only there for two years, where I was still able to maintain my language and my culture. And when I came home – I was probably twelve then, the last year that I was there, that they didn't get me to go back. 'Cause we kind of went back into hiding again, that time of the year. And they actually put people in jail for holding their children back, for hiding. So it's a lucky thing my grandparents didn't end up in jail. I guess once they had the capacity that was all fine: "That's enough, we're not gonna go chase after this particular kid." Yeah, so it was not a good place to be. And I think it's really unfair – for my own experience, to be expected to go to confession and confess – confess what? 'Cause we weren't doing anything wrong. "What did you think about?" It's like you were quizzed and questioned: "Did you think about the boys? Did you have bad thoughts about boys?" And all the leading questions, and what do you say? You're afraid of punishment. So you'd say, "Yes. Yes." "Okay, I absolve you from your sins." Give you a blessing, go away, next Saturday you're there again, confessing to the same thing again. "How many times did you think of the boys? How many times did you think badly of someone?" I never thought badly of anyone or – let alone think of the boys. At that age, I didn't have an interest in the boys, that we never saw except in church! Yeah. It was terrible. So they're creating things so they can absolve you: "There. Your sins are forgiven." That may sound harsh of me when it comes to our church and the teachings of the church. I have respect for my own church here. I try to combine my teachings, my own spirituality, and my own values in life to the teachings of the church. And I'm not going to go through life carrying bitter feelings and unforgiving feelings. These people are long dead now, pretty much, that – the supervisors when I was in school. So I have to let that go and go on with my life. I have to be more forgiving, and maybe not so much forgiving but I need to let it go, 'cause it's not going to do me any good to carry it all my life. So. But every now and then I think about it. And especially since I've been working in the healing program areas. And I hear other Elders talk about their experiences in the residential school. And a lot of it is so much worse than my own experience, and I feel thankful that I didn't go through as much as what these Elders have gone through. I have no doubt in my mind they are telling the truth. So I'm just glad that it no longer has to be that way. But there's a lot of healing to be done with a lot of our people – not just talking about our community, but other First Nations communities that have – we've all experienced this, right across Canada and probably elsewhere. It's a history I don't ever want to see repeated. They wouldn't dare do that today. Nobody would dare do that today. You don't do that to children and to families, break families apart. And that's what happened. It was a deliberate act of the government. So I don't just blame these churches, but it's the government that put these institutions in place.

Our people became pulled into that kind of teaching – instead of loving and supporting and nurturing children, after the teachings that came down, the new teachings, it was more punishing: "You'll be punished if you don't behave yourself." Whereas in history, our people didn't punish children like that. But as time went on, the people that went to residential school before my time picked up those kinds of punishing kinds of techniques and strapping and never telling their children they loved them. And I've listened to some stories of some Elders saying, "I never told my children that I loved them, 'cause nobody loved me when I was growing up. I blamed my parents for sending me away when I was just a child, no more than five or six.

And I blamed and hated my parents for sending me away to residential school." That's the child's mind, right? You're rejected from your parents. "Why did my parents send me here? Don't they love me?" You hear so much of that in the healing circles that I attend. And coming out of that system feeling unloved and full of anger and hate towards their parents. So what happens to them? They become that hateful parent. They have children and they never show love to their children: "If you don't behave, here's the strap. You're gonna get the strap." So there's our history. That's the learned behaviour. So things are changin' and not fast enough for my liking. But you can't rush change because people will change at their pace. Some people will never change. I feel it's so sad, what has happened to our people. That their lives were shattered. The culture was taken, the language was taken from them. Grandparents robbed of their children, their grandchildren. What it must have been like! When I think of my grandchildren that I love dearly, and my great-grandchildren, what would I do if they – what would their parents do? What would you do if your little girl is five years old and somebody snatches that child away and you don't see that child for ten months? For no good reason.

So that's pretty much my spiel on residential school, my take on it, my own personal experience and what my husband went through there. He was hurting. He was a hurting man. I don't know what ever happened to him other than being strapped. He never talked about anything else. And he was a hurting person. He didn't know how to express himself in a good way. And I used to get after him about the lack of trust. "You don't trust people." You know, you're being raised in that kind of a situation, who are you going to trust? Because he never trusted me. He always thought, when I travel in my job or whatever, he was suspicious. He would be checking on me wherever I'm going. And he didn't like that I was out there doing whatever I was doing. So he was very injured. And then he became an alcoholic, a very serious alcoholic. But he refused to open up to go and talk to someone: "I'm not gonna go talk to a stranger. You say I got an alcohol problem. You drive me to drinkin'!" *[laughs]* Yeah, it's a no-win situation. I cared for him dearly. I married him because I loved him, and we were young and in love. And had all these kids together – but he was very insecure. Very, very insecure. And there's no trust in him to trust anyone. And he picked up that punishment thing: "If you don't behave yourself you're gonna get the strap." He used to have a strap hanging in our house. And it was a strap, like, a whip kind of a strap. And he always had it hanging there. And when the kids were fussing or misbehaving, "You see that strap!" he would say. Although he never used it. Never took it off that nail that's hanging on the wall. But he used to threaten the kids: "If you don't behave, that's what you're going to get." He learned that from the residential school. So even that in itself, to threaten your child, "You're gonna get that strap!" – that's really harsh on a child. Yeah. I see in some of our pictures that we have, that strap is hanging on the wall. It just always was there, and nobody would touch it. A reminder. And actually people did strap their kids, which in the past they'd never done. People disciplined their children in a kind way, like the way you are with your child. You discipline your child with loving care. You explain things to your child. And to be taken from that environment and put in an institution where there's nothing but punishment and threats and punishment and more threats. So to me, that's very damaging – very damaging to people. Yeah. So. That's it.

So that's my take on the residential school system. That they just did a good job of robbing us of our culture. I was fortunate that I was able to maintain my language, and I'm thankful for that, that I remember stories, I remember legends, I remember the teachings. Thank goodness for that. Because if I'd been there any longer, then things might have been different. And it was for a lot of other people my age that just totally lost the language 'cause they were not allowed to use the language. We have people in this community that have never spoke the language. So there's no justification as far as I'm concerned. No amount of money. Now the government has turned around and said, "We're going to compensate people." They say, "Oh, we apologize, and we'll give you ten thousand dollars."* Well, for people that are so injured and so broken and that are living on the streets or they've become alcoholics or they've become so destitute. They've lost the teachings, they've lost the language, they've lost the culture. And to be handed this kind of money. It's like giving them poison. It's

---

* Elsie is referring here to the Indian Residential Schools Settlement Agreement, which included among its provisions a "common experience payment" for former residential school students. For more information see "Indian and Residential Schools Settlement – Official Court Website," accessed 30 April 2013, http://www.residentialschoolsettlement.ca/english.html; and Aboriginal and Northern Development Canada, "Frequently Asked Questions," accessed 18 July 2012, http://www.aadnc-aandc.gc.ca/eng/1100100015798. In 2008, the Prime Minister of Canada made a Statement of Apology to former residential school students. See "Statement of Apology," accessed 15 October 2013, http://www.aadnc-aandc.gc.ca/eng/1100100015644/1100100015649.

like giving someone poison. I know a lot of people have drank themselves to death, simply by getting that money. I said right at the beginning – and that's when I was still working in social work, when it was first introduced to our community – this is possibly what's going to happen. Sure, it's fine to open up wounds, but who's gonna be there to heal those wounds, you know? Once you open the wounds, these people: "Talk about residential school. Talk about your treatment there." And there's nobody – you have no support. We don't have enough support in our communities! To look after people that are being reminded of what it was like in the residential schools. To reopen those wounds, to open those memories: "That's what happened to me." You're more or less forced to talk about what happened to you. So to give them money, what happens? A lot of them drank themselves to death. Not so much in this community, but I've heard in other communities, especially people that have been living on the streets. All those people are victims already of the residential school system. The government system. And then to be given money – they either got killed, mugged, or just died of alcohol poisoning. So they became victims again. Victims of abuse of the system, of their fellow man or other people that were needy, or other people that wanna use other people for their own gain. So they became victims all over again. That part just irritates me, 'cause I said right at the beginning, where the money should go is into healing, into training of psychologists or psychiatrists or counsellors to counsel people. At least some of that money should go there. And to be just given the money – it's gone in two weeks. You know? They're no better off. Some, I'm not saying for everyone. There are some that have put whatever money they got to good use. And that's good. They're able to furnish their homes or do whatever. Get themselves out of big debt. But that still does not take care of the old injuries and the old hurts. No one is sitting there to talk to them about counselling, therapy. There's no support. 'Cause to me money is just another injustice. To me no amount of money is going to right the wrong. Yeah. It's not that I begrudge people of receiving money. But just the way it was handled, I really didn't like that. And whenever I brought it up in any meeting, it was like, "Well, people are entitled to decide for themselves what they want to do with their money. And what they want to do with their settlement. It's entirely up to the individual." And I agree with that: it's up to them. But there should have been some dollars separated or identified for counselling and therapy.

And the government apologized and they've made money available, and a lot of the people that were most severely affected were, like, our parents, the older generation that have gone on, that *never ever* was compensated for the hurt that they suffered. For the loss of their children. And their grandchildren. They *never, ever* were acknowledged and nobody ever apologized to them. So they were the ones that were just as severely hurt and traumatized by the loss of grandchildren and children. The communities were all of a sudden silent and quiet: no children around, no children running around. All the children got taken away, and that in itself is a *big* loss. So I wasn't a hundred percent agreeable to how it was done – how the apology came down. And it's hard to blame any one individual or any government or church or any other organization, the Department of Indian Affairs – and they all put their heads together and they did this. They were all in it together. So it's like you're fighting a faceless kind of a bureaucracy. There's no one there to talk to. The buck is passed back and forth and on and on it goes. It wasn't the government's fault. It wasn't the church's fault. It wasn't anyone's fault. Whose fault is it? Somebody had to think up and put this together. And it wasn't just the Catholic Church. It was other churches as well that were in existence back in the day. And how they were all of one mind: "This is how we're going to take the Indian out of the Indian," right? "And transform them – civilize them, and take the laziness out of them, and take the culture away from them. 'Cause what people are doing is not right. They're not adhering to the law of the day."

And when I say that, I think about the teachin' of the old people. How our people lived and they were very civilized. They had all the tools. They had all the teachin's. Their lifestyle, their self-government – our communities were well-organized. Our people were taught things: how to look after yourself, how to take care of your children, how to respect nature, how to respect your neighbours. Treat other people as you would have them treat you. Turn the other cheek. All of those kinds of things! Not to take on other people's issues and become bitter about other people's issues. And I think, if I can compare that to the Ten Commandments, the Ten Commandments say, "Thou shalt not this. Thou shalt not that," and all of those "Thou shalts." And I'm thinking, we had all these things in place already. It was only done differently in that it was, you know, "This is how you treat other people. This is how you look after the resources. This is how you look after the environment. This is how you look after your community.

This is how you look after your children. This is how you respect the Elders." All those teachin's were in place.

So I don't agree with that whole idea of "Oh, we'll teach them": "We'll teach them how to live a good clean life by taking away their children. And we'll teach them another culture. We'll teach them to speak English – and forbid them to even speak their own language." Our kids didn't know anything about English when the first scoop happened! And those children were totally lost! And some of them being little five-year-olds, right from five years of age, who were taken away to be taught English and to be taught how to live, how to pray, and how to speak, how to behave. Eat different kinds of food that they were not used to – just taking away their parents from them. So they were total captives. They were put in an institution. So that's where it starts, way back. 'Cause the grandparents were very lonely and the parents were very lonely when they were taken away, when the children were taken away. And at the same time, alcohol was introduced to our people. You know, "Here's something that'll make you happy," right? Yeah, make you happy all right! And people just had no life left in them. So what's the point? Yeah, and they were told what to do and if you don't listen, you get sent to jail. You become a criminal, 'cause you don't want to let your children go away to residential school.

So now when they talk about compensation, what happens to all of those older people that never heard of the word "compensation"? That never lived to see that. They went to their graves carrying that hurt, that pain of loss, and lookin' at their children, grandchildren, that don't know how to speak the language, that don't know how to do traditional things and preserve food the way they'd once taught their children. All that self-respect and respect for others was destroyed. So today we're trying to teach young people, "Be respectful," you know, "Respect your Elders," and it's uphill. It's hard to start teachin' people to respect grandparents that were never there for them. A lot of the kids that went to residential school felt abandoned by their parents: "Why did my parents send me to this place? They wanted to get rid of me." They come out of there very resentful to their parents, to their grandparents. And it's quite a sad story. It's going to take a long time for our young people to come to terms with what has happened in history. If it ever does. So again, I go back to counselling, I go back to therapy, I go back to healing. And money doesn't heal. Money is just money. It's your culture that's rich. It's not about money, it's culture that we lost. So how can we get compensated for our culture? How can we get back things that it's really hard to give back to our children? When a lot of the parents went through residential school and they lost it. Some of the grandparents today went to residential school. So how can they teach the language? How can they teach the children today about culture? When it was lost to them. So that's pretty much it – so much for residential school compensation and apology!

And, finally, not long ago here, the Pope made some kind of – how did he put it? That he feels for, or some such thing like that, because there was a group of First Nations Chiefs that went to visit with him. And that was the best that we got out of that, was that he felt for the people. It was not an apology, it was he felt sad or some such. I can't remember what his wording was, but he felt bad about what happened. So no one wants to own up to loss of culture. No one wants to own up to – and you quite often hear remarks made about, you know, "Well, where would you have been had the white man not taught you these different things? Where would you people be?" You know, "You wouldn't be still living off the land. You can't go back and live the way your ancestors did." Well, I don't know the answer to that. I don't know what the answer to that is. If there had been no contact – contact did happen. We can't change that. But it's how it happened. It's how we were treated. That's what matters. That's what hurt the people, to have something forced upon you. And that'll never work. Force your ideas onto someone else, force your culture on someone else, instead of respecting and acknowledging other people's culture.

And yet at the same time, the government isolated the people. Took away the lands and put people on reserves: "You stay there. You are not to go beyond this line. You are not to go into the white community. You are not to go into these stores or restaurants or pubs or whatever." So there's a whole history on that that is devastating. And some people are very bitter about it and I don't blame them. I don't blame them at all. I think it's going to take years of dealing with it, dealing with the hurt, the anger, the loss, the loss of culture, the loss of language. It's like building again. Building – it's like the fire we were talking about. Our community was devastated by fire.* Well, you can compare that to the change in how our system was changed for us: it was destruction. Our people were wiped out. There was thousands of people on the coast here before contact. Our people suffered. They

---

* The fire occurred in 1918.

got diseases they never have before. Not only did our people suffer with the loss of our children going to residential schools, there's institutions built for our people – segregated TB hospitals. Our people contracted TB and hospitals were built for them. They were in there for years. They were under quarantine. And then have children apprehended, because people didn't know how to parent children anymore. They lost that so-natural teachin': how to nurture your children, how to love your children. People that came out of the residential schools learned a new way. How to control people, your children. That is with a strap or just – just, you know, cruel. *[emotional]* People lost that ability to love and nurture. And telling your children you love them and giving them hugs and – 'cause nobody gave you those hugs when you were in residential school. You didn't know how to give what you didn't get. A lot of our people went through that. I'm not only talking about my people here, but I'm talking about First Nations people across our country, across Indian country. Many people suffered. So it's a real concern when we talk about Elders these days that have lost the practice, that've lost the language. And there's quite a lot of our Elders now that don't speak the language, that had been taken away to residential schools themselves. And they desire to learn the language now. So it's like starting over. It's like being reborn and struggling to overcome the stigma of being, "You're Indian. You're worthless. You are –" all kinds of names, labels put on our people. That is so cruel. So terrible. It's really hard to see the culture being lost, and the language – to lose the speakers. There's a few people in their sixties, maybe their fifties. It's dwindling. People in their sixties, some of them still remember the language, but not as fluid and not as rich and full-bodied as what I remember. Because a lot of the language as it's spoken is around the different activities that you do, the different seasons of the year, what you are doing that time of the year, the tools you used, what you gathered, where you travelled. All of those things is all wrapped in the language. So I always say that the language is our culture. The culture is our language. It's all blended together. And all of the things that I remember growing up that our people did is all gone. We're trying our best to carry on the language. And it's almost like you're hopping around on one leg. You're unbalanced. Because what is the talk about? When the young people don't remember a lot of the activities, a lot of the things that went along with what you're talkin' about. And that's as close as I can come to comparing, or to, you know, when I talk about the things we did, my grandchildren don't understand what I'm talking about. And they're lookin' at me kind of puzzled and, "Really?" It's so different for them.

So in saying that, to me, where our future is going with our children, I support that. I support education. I recognize and appreciate education. It's very important. The tools that our children need for the future. To get by, to survive in this world. But at the same time, I stress the importance of remembering who you are, where you came from, and our culture and how rich that was. Just to get rid of the stigma of you were lazy, you were no good, you were worthless. You were dirty, you're this, you're that or the other. So our people are survivors. They came from a rich culture. It's not that we're gonna go back there and want to live the way my ancestors lived. But to look at that and say, "I'm from a rich culture. Our people were here first in this country, on this coast. Our people survived." And just so that young people in the future know that we have a history, that we were once a proud Nation. That our people survived, they were resourceful, they were ambitious, they were hard workers, they were good providers to their families. They've got nothing to be ashamed of. What shame has been put upon our people has been our culture stolen from us. The language stolen from us. That our Nation was destroyed by someone else that came along and made it their business, made it their choice to abuse and destroy our people. And because our people survived so much in the past, I'm comforted that in the future our children will survive. New generations will survive and look back and be proud of who they were, two, three hundred years ago: "It's my history. That's our ancestors." Not to be ashamed of themselves. To be strong.

Legend

---

t'əl

(THE WILD MAN OF THE WOODS)

This story is about the "t'əl," as we call him in our language. He's the man of the woods, wild man of the woods. When we were children we were always warned about being outside or travelling or going far from the house: "You stay close to the house! Children, stay close to the house! Don't be wandering off, there's t'əl out there. He's gonna grab you. This is what happens." So we were always afraid when we were children of this big bad man from the woods. And he would come out at night, they'd tell us. He would come looking for children in the community. Be lookin' for children 'cause he ate children. So he'd be lookin' around, and if you're out there and it's after dark, it's getting dusk, the t'əl's gonna grab you. t'əl's got this huge basket – carries on his back. And his basket is woven with snakes, huge snakes. And that t'əl's gonna grab you and toss you in his basket. And he'll run back up into the woods, and he's gonna roast you by his big fire there, and he's gonna eat you. And you'd be just t'əl's supper. And sometimes if there were a lot of kids out and about, he just might fill up his basket with children and run back up into the woods. So he would have several children, more than he could eat at one sitting. So he would melt some pitch and stick the children on these stumps to hold them there until it was their time to be eaten. So sometimes he would have several children around. He didn't kill them. He just saved them for a later meal. So we were so afraid of t'əl as children. When we were kids, they would say, "t'əl's peering in that window. He's lookin' through the window. He's lookin' from the bush and he's watchin' for you." So we were very scared! And I carried that on myself to my children, when they were little, my older children, about the t'əl, and how it's gonna come and get you and – if the child is having a tantrum or fussing or whatever, for nothing, all you need do is knock on the wood or whatever, "Uh-oh. There's t'əl at the door!" Oh! Right away you have a real good kid on your hands here. You know, "Okay!

Okay! Yeah. I'll be good." So that was real frightening – I don't know if that would be acceptable today to scare your children like that. But it worked! It worked.

So anyway, the story goes on with t'əl up in the woods. He kidnaps a woman, a young woman, for his wife. Takes her up there. And half of the time he's got her glued to the stump or whatever so she wouldn't run away. So one day she's out and about with all these children that are being held captive there. And she says to the children, "We have to get out of here. We need to escape. Let's figure out something here. What are we going to do?" So they decided on the plan. She went and got some kind of a paint or whatever – colour. And she applied that to her face and it was like makeup. She got all made up. And t'əl comes back from his expedition and he says to her, "Boy, you're pretty today. Ooh, what's that you got on your face?" And she says, "Oh! You like it? It's makeup. Oh, I'm glad you like it. Would you like me to apply some to your face?" And he says, "Oh yeah! That sounds good." So she had melted this pitch and would use this on him if she can fool him into thinking this is makeup, like what she's wearing. So he agrees, he wants some of that makeup. So she takes some of this stuff, this goop, and she applied it to his eyes, his eyelids. And she said, "Now you have to stand near the fire. It'll work better if it's warm. You go stand next to that fire." So he's standing there and pretty soon the pitch is melting and glues his eyes shut. And he couldn't see anything. His eyes are glued shut and he's groping around there, trying to find his way. In the meantime all these children that are ready, they had this *long* pole, and they *ran* at him with this *long* pole and they shoved him in the fire. He fell into this big fire and he burned. So all the ashes went up – sparks, ashes. Downwind in the evening all this comes down to the community. So today, they tell us that's what the little mosquitoes are, or the no-see-ums. They're the ashes from the t'əl.

Mother

5

Teachings for Moms

My grandfather used to make predictions about how things were going to become – worldwide! It wasn't just my grandfather too, that predicted that. It was their time, their age – you know, his friends, all the other Elders back then. Whatever they heard or wherever they heard these things from – and my grandmother talked a lot about that too, as well as the other old-timers of that time. That you may think you have it good now – that was part of their teaching too, for appreciation of things we have, the food we get, the resources that are out there, that we can just go out and get salmon. "You think it's always going to be there? The cod that you go out and get. You think it's always going to be there? Or the clams? It's not always gonna be there." They knew that! Or the deer or anything you go hunting for. "It's not always going to be there. It'll be gone. It'll be depleted. There's gonna be things happening. There's going to be disasters happening." I don't know where they heard that from. I really don't. Or how they knew that. "One day, people will be flyin' in space." How did they know that? They used to always talk about that, and how did they know that? I don't know why didn't I question that: "How do you know that, Grandpa?" They would just go on talking about things like that. And new babies being born – there'll be deformed babies. There'll be problems with new babies born. Maybe they were thinking about – maybe they were predicting – maybe that's what the alcohol or the drugs has done to our people. Although it wasn't there then, like, alcohol or drugs. But you see today a lot of problems resulting from drinking or drugging when you're carrying a baby. That wasn't ever mentioned that's what would happen. But all they said was there'll be problems with babies, they'll be born deformed, they'll be born with handicap. So I don't know if that all ties in with when a woman was pregnant, how carefully she was guarded or cautioned or warned about the things you eat, the things you look at. 'Cause that was prevention of – you know, if you want a healthy baby, this is how you're gonna look after yourself as a pregnant woman. You're not gonna go out there and be cutting fish or butchering fish or doing things that might cause your baby to be deformed. You don't go out and gut a salmon and, you know, just looking at unpleasant things. 'Cause your baby might take on that and will look like that. That was their belief. They really believed in that! It's so hard when you're trying to translate that into English. They'd say "ɬəχ θ kʷʷənɛt, ɬəχ θ kʷʷənɛt tan'. ɬəχmot hɛw. t'at'matəm səm θ čuy'."* They'd say, "Your baby is going to copy that." You're lookin' at something ugly or something distasteful or something that's deformed or whatever it may be. Or things you eat. You were forbidden from eating fish head, which we love as Indian people. We love our fish head. Well, if you are pregnant, you don't touch fish head – baby might be born looking something like a fish head. All those kinds of foods you were cautioned against eating. Cutting things. If you wanted a baby boy, you shouldn't be handling a knife or some sharp objects. You know, you want a boy! That was kind of old wives' tales, now, when you think about that. But they had their own predictions, their own beliefs and their own teachings about how to look after yourself as a pregnant woman, and the things to be aware of. How to look after yourself, and how to look after the baby when it comes, and how to look after the afterbirth and all of those things. And the baby's belly button. And how different it is today when you have a baby, and of course there wasn't the hospital then. And that baby's belly button was – it pretty much rotted off the baby. You didn't put alcohol on it or anything to dry it up. And I always remember babies being just wrapped with, like, a wide belt, a little wide belt to protect that belly button – so if it falls off, it might cause the baby to bleed, right? To bleed to death. So they protected it and it stayed there and rotted off. They used to even go out and get barnacles down the beach and break a barnacle and just take

---

* Translation: It's bad that you're looking at it, it's bad that you're looking at that. It's very bad. Your child will copy it.

the inside of the barnacle and apply it to the baby's belly button so it would rot much quicker. And boy, did that ever smell! You had one smelly baby there for a while. *[laughs]* Yeah, so all of those different teachings that they truly believed in – the work they were doing and how they lived and how they treated and how they, you know, the different remedies that was there. And it worked. It worked for them. You know, how the new baby girl is, the ears are pierced right away as a newborn. You didn't wait, and little girls gotta have earrings, so right away the ears are pierced by the midwife. Yeah.

There's so many teachings and so many beliefs – but that's one thing that I always wonder about now. Or is it from when they first started to listen to the radio? There were very few people that had a radio. My grandfather had a radio that only he listened to, because it was operated by battery – big battery, about that big. *[gesturing]* About a foot long, foot and a half long, and about six inches high. And he would attach that and listen to it, and he's deaf as can be. None of us could hear, but he'd be right there with his ear to the radio listening to the news. And he'd – news is over, unplug it, put it away. So he'd tell us about the war, what's going on – must've been the Second World War. "Oh! There's war happening! Fighting." Oh, he'd be real sad about it: "Maybe one day it'll come here," used to say. He was quite concerned about that. He would tell us what was said, what was in the news, right? So I don't know if that's where they got their predictions from. That there'll be famine. There'll be famine – they were so sure of that. There'll be nothing to eat. And even new babies will be hungry, 'cause the mother is going to be dying of starvation. However did they come to that conclusion at that time? That's, like, seventy years ago, when I was probably about seven, eight years old. And I would hear them talkin' about that. That women will be smoking and that women will be wearing slacks. That was a no-no, 'cause all the women back then wore long dresses. So all these things. Women will be – you know, they frowned upon dancing. Women didn't dance. Yeah, the clicky heels represents, like, the devil's hoofs. Yeah. Yeah, so all those things they would – maybe it was just a way to scare us as young people! *[laughs]* I don't know. "No babe, you can't go dancin' around." Yeah. So old people had a lot of wisdom. They could see into the future and figure things out – so they always had a treasure full of information. A treasure chest full of information that they doled out whenever necessary. Whenever they thought it was needed, they'd tell you what's right and what's wrong. That was your guide and they were your guide in life. And we really believed! We listened to those kinds of warnings. But they knew: "At one time there was a flood. And then the next thing is going to be famine. Famine – there'll be famine, there'll be fire." I don't know where they got that from. Yeah. There was nothing written somewhere that, you know, predicted that. Maybe Nostradamus. Maybe they met Nostradamus! *[laughs]*

They would say, "ɬəχ tə θ kʷənɛt tan'. ɬəχ. t'at'matəm səm kʷə θ čuy'."* "Don't be looking at that! That's ugly. You're baby's going to copy that. Baby's going to look like that!" So you didn't dare look at things that were not pleasant. So you had to think pleasant thoughts. You had to think of good things in order to have a healthy baby. You thought good things. Not to be looking at things that were yucky – otherwise your baby might take that on. And that's why too, as a pregnant woman, you didn't look at a dead body if someone died in your community or your family. Pregnant women were not allowed to go and look at the dead person in the casket, 'cause your baby might take on that look when it's born. And that's why if you did go and look at – could be your brother, could be your father, your mother, someone you're really close to and you want to say your final good-byes – then you go and you can do that, but someone is always there to look after you. And then wipe the face of the body in the casket. Very lightly with white cloth or something, or maybe cedar. And you take that and you put it away. And when the baby's first born, you take that out and you wipe the baby's face with it. Then you will go and burn that with some food offering, so that you're taking from the baby what might have transpired from the dead body. 'Cause it could take the spirit of the baby too, so it might be unhealthy when it's born. It might be unhealthy all its life. Because they've done that, while they're still in the womb and the mother has exposed them to the dead person. So you gotta do your cleansing. And the baby, when it's born, you do your cleansing again. Then you thank the spirit of the dead person. You make a little offering so everything's now okay. Those things were really important practices, and people still do it today. I see other people wearing the blanket around their middle – that's to protect the baby. I've seen women here do that. But I've never seen it when I was growing up. All I seen was using the cedar, or have pinned to you or tucked in your pocket and that's to protect the spirit of the baby you're carrying. That you're not exposed or that it's not being drawn into the spirit world. So there's ways and means to protect a pregnant woman at times like that.

---

* Translation: It's bad that you're looking at that. It's bad. Your child will copy it.

Or even clams, like, you couldn't eat clams when you're pregnant because that's gonna cause your baby to clench its jaws all the time. The clam will – when you touch it if it's partially open, you touch it and then just clamps down really hard. And when the baby is born that it could happen with the baby, it's gonna have this clenched jaw. Yeah. So pregnant women were not allowed to eat clams.* Or fish heads. [chuckles] Or wild raspberries, you know, t'υqʷom? Little red berries. They're so small and thin. There's no body to it, but it's so tasty. If you go looking and you'll find that and just really small berries. And you will find that on a baby, a red spot, like a red berry. And so you kept away from that. If you're pregnant you don't touch that berry, 'cause that's going to end up on the baby. Yeah. And you see quite a few people that have that berry on their skin. It could be anywhere on their body, but if it ends up on their face it's quite noticeable. I don't know what causes that. There must be an explanation why babies get that. Or a black mark on their body. So you had to be really careful and selective of what kind of berries or fruits you ate, or whatever foods you ate.

Course we always had the baby in the basket. And babies stayed in the basket till sometimes they're a year old. It was their naptime: you tied them up in a basket and they went to sleep. And when you're travelling they're in the basket, but you just be careful which way you turn them, one way or the other, so that shapes their head. Tilting one way and then the other, just to keep the head shape so it's not flat-headed – it was your responsibility to make sure. And when a new baby is born, they used to get, like, bear paws. 'Cause they used to get bear, bears were a source of food. So they always saved the bear's paws. They would take the bear paws and take the baby's hand and rub the baby's hand on the bear paws. So it means they're going to be really fast when they go pick berries. [laughs] And they would also – when a baby's really new, you take their little finger and you wet their little finger. And then you go like that to the eyebrow [gesturing] with the baby's own fingers. And that's gonna shape their eyebrows. They'll have really nice eyebrows when they grow up. Yeah. That was a common practice. Or they would take bear oil – bear grease – and the roots of, like, honeysuckle for an example, 'cause they were so kind of curling and climbing. Mix the two together and apply it to their head. That way they have really nice soft, kind of wavy hair. [laughs] Had nothing to do with genetics!

---

* Elsie also notes that eating clams when pregnant could cause your baby to spit.

And caring for the baby, like I was saying. You know, medicines. When a baby had thrush. And how you use the snail to clear the thrush in the baby's mouth when a baby gets thrush, which used to always happen. The baby's mouth gets really sore, it's like big canker sores, and the best remedy they had for that was going way out in the bush and – not just your garden snails close around here, but you go up in the dense woods and look for a snail. A nice clean one that's away from where people are living. And you would get that and – of course you would do your little ritual, your little ceremony, and you invite the snail to come with you, 'cause you need its healing medicine. And so you would take it home, and you hold it by the head, like that *[gesturing]* – hold it by its head. And you put the rest of it in the baby's mouth and you just kind of go around its mouth, like that. Well, you know, the snail has all that slime on it, and so that gets left in the baby's mouth. And so you take that snail right away, and you take it back to where you got it from. You don't just put it outside, you take it back. You č'ɛhč'ɛhɑθɛ č – thank it, thank that snail family. "Thank you" – "č'ɛhč'ɛhɑθɛ č," we say. You take it way back. And you get something bright, like a little something bright, twine or something, and you tie it around its neck or just wrap it around its head area. And snails don't have necks, do they? Just around the head area. And then you put it back. That's its reward: q'ɑgɑt čxʷ.* You reward it. You put it right back where you got it from. You say, "Thank you." And you go back home. And that's a real good medicine for thrush on a baby. I would imagine it would work for anything else, or for adults for that matter. But I just know that was used with babies, to take care of their thrush. Yeah! People will go, "Oh!" when you tell people about it, but it was commonly used. It's a really important medicine. And again, it's not about just getting a snail, there always was an offering or appreciation or a little ceremony, a little prayer thank you. You know. And maybe that's what helped, I don't know.

Another medicine that was always used was the oil of ratfish. And we used to get a lot around here, I remember the old people used to put their net out certain time of the year. And sometimes you'd get a whole bunch of them on the net. And they're little – they almost look like herrings. They're that size. They're very silver. It's not edible. People don't eat it here. But now and then, it used to come in abundance. But I haven't heard of anyone getting them for several years

---

* Translation: You pay him.

now. I guess they're no longer coming. But that was good, good medicine. Sometimes they'd just wash up on the beach. And so you take that and you'd gut them. And you'd take the little liver. Of course when they're that small, the liver is very tiny. So you take that and you render it. You put in a pan and you render it down over a low heat and over a long period of time. And you get this purest of oil from the liver of that fish. And you will put it in a container and keep it. It had many purposes. It had a lot of uses for it. It was especially used for babies when they're colicky, I guess, or fussy. And you rub it on them and warm your hands and put some of that oil and you massage the baby with that. It's real powerful. And they used that as well on pregnant women, like when pregnant women are getting really heavy and you got backache, you're tired, your achy muscles. And another woman would come and give you that massage, whether it's your grandmother, your mother, or whoever – midwife. And massage you and rub you all across your back and your belly with that oil. It's very relaxing. So that was a very important medicine for pregnant women and for, you know, baby that needed a massage. Massaging was really, really important to our people. They did a lot of it.[*] When a baby was irritable, you just massage it ever so gently. Its legs, its arms – using that oil – its belly. And you'd be amazed. The baby just goes right to sleep after you're done. When you're not feeling well, as an adult, or in children – the old people used to say the centre of your being is right there [gestures] in your – where your ribs come together, right in there – your diaphragm. And when you feel it pumping there, when you're sick it's really pumping fast like that – hard. After a massage, you bring everything to there – from your legs, from your hips, your back – everything you pull forward, from your shoulders down. They massage your back first, pushing everything to the front. Then you lay on your back and everything gets pulled to the front. So everything you bring there, and you put your hand there and that heavy throbbing would just settle down, calm down. It's so calming. It's so relaxing. So you do the same thing to a baby when it's fussing. You start massaging its back and its little body and bring everything to that point. And that's so calming for the baby when it's irritable. They used that a lot. I think it's the human touch, right? The human touch. The warmth, the gentleness. 'Cause you don't see

---

[*] On massaging, see Dorothy Kennedy and Randy Bouchard, *Sliammon Life, Sliammon Lands* (Vancouver: Talonbooks, 1983), 52.

a lot of that anymore. Just grown-ups. Couple women massaging each other. Now when you need a massage, you go to a massage therapist and pay big bucks just to get that treatment. Whereas it was always there. The women massaged other family members. It was hands-on. It's wonderful. Yeah. I've gone up to the preschool here and showed the moms and that how to massage a baby when it's irritable and they really enjoyed that. *[chuckles]* Ratfish – kʷumɑ. Yeah. It's called "kʷumɑ." I don't know if that's with a *k* or a *c*. kʷumɑ! *[laughs]* Between the eyes and the forehead was a little thing that stuck out. And it was quite abrasive, the little bump there. It was sticking – more kind of like the little – oh, what do you call those things that go on your skin like that? – like a tag. But it was really abrasive to the touch. And that's where its power is. That's why it heals things. That's why it's medicine. Because that's where the power comes from. Yeah. So it was highly respected and highly regarded. It was really important. And the oil was so clear! And it takes a lot of liver – their little liver – to get a little bottle of this. But it was so plentiful. It seemed like they just came on the beach to die. We haven't seen any of that for-ever! Yeah, 'cause people used to always put their nets out and it'd be just hanging there, or washed up on the beach. It only came certain time of the year. And people would just go and gather it for that purpose. And just for the oil. Yeah. kʷumɑ.

Everything was around, like the baby basket, right? When you wrapped the baby and you put it in a baby basket, that you don't put a big diaper on the baby, 'cause that keeps their legs kind of spread, or their hips. So rather than put a big diaper on the baby, you just kind of wrap its legs together. And otherwise, if you use that big diaper on a baby, when it starts to walk it'll be bowlegged. One time there was a man living in this community, and he was quite bowlegged when he was a little boy. Moms always used to use that for an example, "See that man, they must've put a big diaper on him!" *[laughs]* But he straightened out after a while. His legs were quite fine later on in life. Yeah, so that was the important teaching too – and the thing with eyebrows like I mentioned. That was really important. To shape the eyebrows of the baby with their own little finger. Using their little spit from their mouth and shaping the eyebrows. It really worked. Obviously no one shaped mine for me! *[laughs hard]*

When Stella was born, my cousin Stella, my grandmother pierced her ears right away. And I knew she was going to do it, and I wanted to take off. I wanted to make myself scarce. "You come back here!

You're gonna have to hold this baby," and I'm, "Aghhh!" *[laughs]* – didn't want to do it. "It's not gonna hurt her. It's the time to do it when they're newborn. They don't feel much pain." Oh gosh! Just a needle and a thread. Those little ears were so tiny. And put something hard at the back of the ear and just pull the needle through. And the baby cries, but it's over real quick. Yeah. I don't want to do that again. But all new babies were done that way. I guess in the old days – my grandmother used to talk about was they used pitch from the fir tree. You know, if you take a splinter off of the fir tree and it's got pitch on it. Just a tiny splinter, that's what they would use, 'cause they didn't have the thread or the needle, right? So they would have a tiny little piece of that. And they would just poke it through and leave it in there till it healed. Yeah. That was way before my time. I just heard about it – I never saw that.

My kids – I never had their ears pierced, except for your mom. And of course my mother-in-law, she said, "You should've had her ears pierced when she was newborn!" So one time we had left her with her, left Jeannie – she was probably about four or five years old then. And I don't know where we went, if we just went to town or whatever. We came back and she had these little threads in her ear, like, just sewing thread. She had pierced her ears. And they used – when kids were older or anyone that wanted to get their ears pierced, they would use ice to freeze it, freeze your lobe with ice. And so that way you don't feel the needle, right? Could have frostbite, but you didn't feel the needle. *[chuckles]* So I don't know if that's what she did, but anyway after a couple of days Jeannie was fussing and fussing, crying, and pretty soon she started to develop a couple of lumps behind each ear here. And oh, she was so fussy! I took her to the doctor because I was really worried, 'cause – size of a marble behind each ear. The doctor removed those strings and, "Who did this?" and "Why did they do this?" and "This is infection!" Oh, my husband was so mad at his mother. He was so upset! "I've got a good notion to come and poke your ear with a needle!" *[laughs]* Oh my goodness! Some ear piercing, I'm tellin' you. Yeah. Not even sterilizing the needle or the thread. I don't know if she used ice. Yeah. I think she just about got her ears pierced!

They had midwives. It'd be the grandmother or the aunt or a midwife in the community would attend the birth. And quite often a woman went out and had the baby by herself. A lot of it was alone – that's just how it was. You don't call attention to yourself when you go into labour. You always had your little bundle ready, which you're gonna wrap the baby in. A little knife or whatever to cut the cord. And you just take your bundle when you know you're close to your time. You don't tell your family that you're in labour. You go, leave the house, and you go and have your baby quietly. Could be in the woodshed. My grandmother said even cold winter months women would go out to the woodshed and have her baby. Because it was just how they did it. That way the birth of the baby happens much quicker than if you lay there and you be pampered and have the whole household know you're in labour. Don't tell anyone you're in labour, otherwise it'll prolong your labour. Our women, I guess, were very tough. Very, very tough. It was a very private thing. It was private. It was special. But when the baby came and the family acknowledged and recognized the baby, then everybody fusses over the baby and then you're really taken care of by the rest of the family. You get your pampering then. But before you had the baby, during your pregnancy, as a pregnant woman, you were always told, "Don't pamper yourself. Go on about your business. You don't lay around because you're pregnant and put your feet up. You just go on with life. Don't think you're going to get away from doing work 'cause you're pregnant. And if you lay around and pamper yourself, then your birth is going to be harder. It's going to be a tougher birth, prolong the birth." So I guess that's exercise, right? You work, you go clam digging, you go pick berries, you walk long distance, and you just carry on. You don't take to your bed. *[laughs]*

We had a lady that was a healer and she lived up in Klahoose.* And she was also a relative in my family. She was on my grandfather's side of the family. And many people went to her for healing. She had, like, hands-on, just touching very lightly. I guess that would be your energy healing today. And she helped many people. And when my grandmother lost her youngest child, she was quite late in her life, and she wanted another baby. So she went to talk to that lady and she really wanted a little boy. She went to talk to that lady and that lady worked on her and prayed on her and hands-on with her and whatever she did. But it was a lot of hands-on, a lot of it was on the head, touching the head very lightly. But anyway, my grandmother got pregnant with her last child. And when she knew she was pregnant, she went back and told the lady in Squirrel Cove that she was pregnant and

---

* Kennedy and Bouchard write that "Indian doctors were usually men." Ibid., 85.

everything was fine. And that lady told her, "When you have your baby, when your time comes to have the baby, you stay at home. Have your baby at home." By then, the hospital was already here in Powell River – that old hospital? – and women were just starting to go into the hospital to have babies. All the babies were born at home prior to that. And she told my grandmother, "Whatever happens, don't go to the hospital. Don't go to a doctor. You have your baby at home." And I *remember* when my grandmother went into labour. I was really a small child. But I knew there's a lot of commotion going on in the house. Different women were coming and going. I heard my grandmother. She was moaning. She was having a difficult time. And this went on through the night and the next morning, next day. I remember her being taken out of the house. They took her to the hospital. When she delivered the baby, finally, it was a *big* baby boy. He's a big boy. And they kept the baby in the room at that time with the mother. I know they do again now, but for a while they were not. But they kept the baby in its little crib, across the room. And my grandmother was *so* very weak but she couldn't get up to attend to the baby. The baby was *cryin'* and crying. And she knew the baby was having some kind of stress. And she could not get up to go to the baby. And she called for the nurse and the nurses were busy and finally after a long time, the nurse came. She could hear the baby was getting weaker, the cry was getting weaker. The nurse went over, picked up the baby from the crib, "Oh, must be just wet, we'll change him." And she put the baby on top of the bed at the foot of the bed, and when she opened up the blanket, the baby was just bleeding. There was so much loss of blood. And the nurse just covered up the baby really quick and took off out the door. And when she looked at the foot of her bed, she said the bedding was all bloody. So I don't know what happened. *[emotional]* Those are horrendous things to happen. What a horrendous thing. But she lost her baby. Nothing ever came of it. There's no questions to be asked. I guess it was meant to be. 'Cause this doctor already told her, this healer, that if you went to the hospital, this is what's going to happen. So I guess she just took that as "I was told." But could have been other things, you know? I don't think it needed to happen, but who's to say? It happened. So that was just another example of treatment. *[pause – still emotional]* Course, medicine was different then too. Maybe no one was at fault. Who's to say? Yeah. Yeah, so that was probably about seventy years ago. There's a man that lives in our community that was born the same day. And my grandmother was always reminded about the boy she lost because this other lady was sharing the same room as her, a younger woman – young mother. And she had this boy. He's still with us. So my grandmother was well in age when she had that baby, up in age.

And, yeah, a lot of women had their babies at home. Just the mother or the aunt, whoever, with the midwife. Yeah, so Stella was born there. That was in October. Stella's birthday's in October, October the nineteenth. We lived in Mink Island. My grandfather towed the houseboat there – or our floathouse, I should say – and anchored it there. And that's where my niece was born. I call her my niece. Actually, she's my cousin. 'Cause my grandmother took her as well. Her name is Stella. And my aunt Agnes had her. She was quite young yet, and my grandmother kept the baby. So that was like my little baby sister. And she was born there in Mink Island. I was ten years old then, 'cause I know that Stella is ten years younger than I am. So when I count back, that's how old I was. I was ten years old. And her getting her ears pierced by Granny Molly right now real quick. Oh, it was the worst experience of my life to see that happen to see this little newborn baby, getting their ears pierced. Yeah. And my grandmother telling my grandfather, take the afterbirth and take it to the woods and bury it really deep so the animals don't get at it. But I didn't know that. In my inexperienced ears, I guess I heard her telling him, "Go and bury this, dig a deep hole and bury this." And she said it in a real – like it was real serious. It's not like, "Go bury that over there," kind of thing. It was like, "Take care of it, take good care of it. Handle it with care." And they did. They had a lot of respect for that part of the birth. The afterbirth was just as important as the baby. You took good care of it and handled it with care. But what I remember hearing was "Take this and bury it. Take good care of it." So, wrapped it up. My grandfather went off and buried it somewhere. So when Stella got older, and well, she was a few months old and she was fussing and crying a lot, and I used to babysit for her and have her in a papoose basket and rocking her in a swing over the bed. And my arms would get really tired, always bouncing her, and soon as I'd stop she'd be screaming again. And finally one day I just said to my grandmother, I said, "You should have buried this one instead of the other." *[laughs]* I guess in my child's mind I thought that was a baby! Oh, my grandmother never forgot that. She thought that was so hilarious.

That was very important, to look after the belly button. Years ago, the poor little things, they used to rot off, right? And I never did that to my own children, 'cause all of my children were born in the hospital

and I went with what the hospital advised me to do. But my grandmother used to talk about that, that's how they took care of it. So
once that belly button fell off, then you leave it exposed and dry it.
Then you make sure it's nice and dry and you wrap it up in a nice
clean cloth or paper, whatever. And you put it away. You could put
it in a container, airtight container. Then you go and bury it wherever
your home was, wherever your main house was, your property. And
you would bury it in a very deep and safe place. That way your child
will always go back there. That's where the root is. That's where the
roots will be. So that was very important. And I've done that with my
own children. I buried their belly buttons on my property. I still believe in that. And another reason they used to tell you to do that – is
to keep track of that belly button – was so that your child is not
searching all the time for something and never finding it 'cause they're
looking for their belly button. They're more grounded when you bury
that belly button. So then when little kids started to walk and get into
things and into the cupboards and pulling out everything, Granny
used to say, "Oh! Lookin' for the belly button. What did you do with
that child's belly button? They're searching for it." *[laughs]* Yeah.
Always searchin'. So that's the teachin' behind that. That was very
important. And I still believe that. They have a home to come to. And
I think that – I know my family, my children, my grandchildren always
come to my place. They come and when we have a big family dinner,
they want to have it at my place. And they all gather there. And to
me that's the belly button at work! *[laughs]*

There's so many things that people would say was not, um, "Oh,
that's just a superstition." But I think every culture has their own
superstition, right? Their own beliefs and stories. I know that some
people – that if you want to choose the sex of your child, you want a
boy child or you want a baby girl – people used to go up towards Toba
Inlet.* And up on the rocks, on the bluffs there – I've never seen it!
– but I know that the old people used to talk about that. If you want
a boy child, there's a waterfall there that looks like it's a penis, or it
looks like a male figure. You go and you get some water from that,
and that's what you drink. You're guaranteed to have a male baby.
And then there's another place not far from that, it's like a female
parts. And you go get water from there and you're guaranteed to have

---

* On this and other related practices regarding pregnancy, see ibid., 43-44.

a female baby. They truly, truly believed in that. I've never gone there
and I never seen it. But the old-timers believed in that. From Sliammon,
from Klahoose, from Homalco – people on the coast. That was their,
um, what would you call it? Their clinic? *[laughs]* You know for sure
you're gonna have a girl! Or you're gonna have a boy! Well, nowadays,
you go and you get what you call that? Ultrasound – and they tell
you, right now, "Oh, it's a boy. Oh, it's a girl." *[laughs]* Oh dear. Yeah.
I don't know if it worked every time, to tell you the truth. Who's to
say? And if you want a boy, you don't handle things like a knife or
scissors or sharp objects, 'cause it's like that you're going to cut away
the little part, right? Um-hmm. So you're quite selective in what you
did and who's gonna cut the fish or who's gonna, you know, do things
that might affect the baby. So you were always cautioned by that.
That was so important. Just a lot of different things. Those kinds of
teachin's that people really believed in. Never questioned it. They just
didn't question it. That's just what you were told and that's how you
lived. Yeah.

Legend

THE YOUNG GIRL AND ELEVEN PUPPIES

I'm gonna tell the story about the young girl and eleven puppies. This story has been told many times by different people, and maybe each time it's got a different twist to it, or a different interpretation. But the way I've heard it is how I will tell it. Some will believe that our origin is from the dog family, which is an interpretation of sorts. But the way I understand it, when it was told to us as children, was that it's a lesson to be learned. It was like a teaching tool, that we pay attention to the story, and what's the moral to the story. So this is how the story goes.

There was this young girl, young teenage girl. And she was always told by her mother, her grandmother, "Stay away from the boys. Don't be hanging out with the boys. Stay away. You don't want to get in trouble. We don't want you to get in trouble by hanging out with the boys. That's not acceptable." And she did. She stayed away from the boys. But there was this one boy in particular that she's watchin' – watchin' him. And he's chewing gum. And she sees him chewing gum. And the gum in those days was the pitch from the fir tree. So he's chewing gum and she's really wishing for some of that gum: "Oh, I'd like to get some of that gum." So she says to her little brother, "Would you please go over there and ask that young boy over there, that young man, for a piece of his gum?" And so the little boy runs over there, speaks to the young man: "My sister would like a piece of your gum. Would you give her a piece?" So he thought for a moment and then he said, "Well, go back and tell your sister that I'll give her a piece of my gum only if she swallows her saliva." So the little guy went back, told his sister. "Oh sure, that's not a problem," she said. "I will swallow my saliva." So he goes back, okay, gives her a piece of his gum. And from that the young girl got pregnant. And they were living in a small community. All the family members, all living in a small community. And when she started to show, her pregnancy started to show, people knew she was pregnant. So that was really not accept-able. She's a young girl, she doesn't have a husband, and here she is pregnant. So it was really not accepted at all. They had a meeting with the leaders in the community and family members, and they decided to abandon her. So everyone packed up to leave the com-munity. They moved camp. And it was decided to leave her there to fend for herself.

But she had a grandmother that cared a lot for her. And Grandmother felt very sad, very upset that they were leaving her behind. But they also had a little puppy in the family, and Grandmother decided to leave that puppy with the young girl. So of course, they all pack up to leave and along comes Raven. He was such a trickster and always out to do damage, or to hurt people or – he was doing the ultimate disgrace to this young girl that has disgraced the community. So he went dowsing the fires, campfires all over the community. Dowsed the campfires with water. And Grandmother took a hot coal, or ember. She had this big clamshell, and she put a hot ember into this clamshell. In the meantime, the young girl was out picking berries. She'd gone out that morning gathering. And before they left camp, the grand-mother said to the puppy, "You lead her to this hot ember. I will hide it over here, and you should go and show her when she comes back." So off they went and they just all left and the young girl came from her gathering. And the little puppy was all excited and running around in circles and barking and, you know, kept running to this one area. Everything was out. There's no smoke, no fire to be seen. So she finally followed the puppy to this area. And sure enough there was a hot ember there, she could see a bit of smoke. So that's how she got her fire started. She started a fire and she stayed there. She had no choice but to stay there. And she survived. She would go gathering. She lived off shellfish and other – she knew how to survive. It was a real struggle for her.

So the day finally came that she had her babies, which turned out to be eleven puppies. They were born, and they were eleven puppies. And she was really, really sad. Couldn't figure it out – why did this happen? "Why did I give birth to eleven puppies here?" They're ten male and one female. But she had no choice but to look after and care for these puppies and feed them. And the grandmother would come now and again to visit her, and she seen what was going on, what had happened. And she would talk and visit with her. And as time went on again, she would go down the beach in the winter months, 'cause the tide is out during the night. She would light a torch and go down the beach to dig clams. So she's way down the beach and she hears all this commotion going on in the house. There's chanting, there's singing, there's just a whole lot of noise – there's drumming – and she doesn't know what is going on. She picks up her torch and she walks up to the house. When she's getting close to the house, all of a sudden all this commotion would stop and it's all quiet and silent. She would walk into the house and they'd be all sleeping. They're all huddled together by the fire. And she doesn't know what is going on. Then another night she would go down again to dig more clams for their food, and the same thing would happen again. Her house just seemed to come alive and there's a lot of noise and celebration going on. So the third time that this happened, she thought, "I'm going to sneak up on the house and see what is going on." So she left her torch beside a big huge rock, big boulder. And she stuck around to the shaded area and she snuck up to her house. And what she found when she got close to the door was the young girl sitting outside the door. She was the watch. She was watching out for her mother, and she would be the one to let the others know someone was coming. So when she came up, she snuck up and she got into the building really quick and all the dancing was going on, this celebration, this chant-ing and drumming. And she came into the building – here were all her sons. They were men, they were not puppies anymore. They were men. And they were dancing and they were naked and they were just dancing around the fire and having a good time and happy. And their hide was all piled in a neat pile. She ran over there and she grabbed all this fur, the pile of hide, and she threw it onto the fire. And the little girl managed to get a small piece of it and she stuck it on her hand. So all her life she had this little fur patch on her hand. So they lost their hide and they became men.

They were pretty much grown by now – they were young men. And she said to them, "Okay. We have to do something. We've gone through a lot of difficult times because of our situation here. We've been disgraced by our community. We've been abandoned by our community. You are young men now. You need to train, you need to learn survival. We need to get our identity back with our community. We need to prove ourselves. *You* need to prove yourselves, that you are strong men. So you all pick what you wanna be, whoever wants to be the hunter, who wants to be the fisherman, who wants to do one thing or another. What are you going to do? What are you gonna hunt for? Each one of you has to make that decision so we can prove ourselves, you can prove yourselves to be real men. Hunters and fishermen. And then when all that is done, we're going to ask our people, our community to come together and we'll have a nohom." "nohom" means a feast. "We'll give a feast to our people." So they all sat around very silent thinking about this. Finally one says, "Okay. I will be the fisherman." The other one says, "I will go and hunt for deer." One says, "I will go hunt for mountain goat." All eleven of them picked their choice of what they were going to do, go after, what they're going to do to bring food into the family. And the young girl says, "I am going to be the one that prepares the food at home and preserves the food and I will look after the home." So all this decided, this is what they did. They all had their designated area or their choice of what they're going to do to bring food into the home. So off they went. And the grandmother would come and visit, and so she was updated on what was happening, but she didn't tell her community about all this. It was kept quiet.

So after all was said and done, it was finally time to invite the community to come for a feast. So they did this. Grandmother went home and told her community what has happened. So they were invited on a certain day to come. They arrived and *all* this food was laid out on the beach. It was on a *long* log, a long big log laying on the beach. Driftwood. And there was your prime mountain goat, your prime deer, whatever – all kinds of food, all lined up. And the very end of the line was a dogfish, which people didn't really eat. It's the lowest grade of fish. So who's there first but Raven? He's so excited! He's so happy. He's gonna get a good feed, and he's the first one in line, jumping around, hopping around: "Oh, is this mine?" And he starts right at the top of the line, "Is this mine? Is this mine?" And they would tell him, "No! That's not yours. No, that's not yours." All the way down the line. When he got to the end of the line and they told him, "That's yours. The dogfish is yours." So that's a lesson to the Raven. He's the trickster. He was always there to make sure other people suffered the consequences – which he deemed to be their consequences – of their actions.

And so that's what happened with them. They became people. They became self-reliant through a lot of hard work and a lot of mending their lives. The young girl had learned her lesson the hard way. But she survived because of her determination to uplift herself and to prove to her community that she could change her life. And she could become a good person and prove to her community by giving a feast, a nohom, and become respectable again. So that's that story. ❧

6

Married Life

I met your grandfather in Orford Bay, pretty much the first time that I met him. I was quite young then. I was probably about sixteen. And that's when my grandfather went there to go and purchase a canoe – that huge canoe that he had. So that's where the person was that sold him that canoe. And that's a long way to go. And you know I don't remember how he got that canoe back here. We went by a gas boat, and I think he towed it back here, that's how it went. But it was a huge dugout canoe. Anyway, my mother-in-law was living there. They lived there quite a lot up in Orford Bay. And he was really shy and so was I, you know – I had no intention of getting to know him at all. So we left there. That's the first time we met. And he used to go, "I knew from that day on you were going to be my wife." That's what he said. And he was so shy that he had this brooch, wherever he got it from, and pinned it on my jacket. And it wasn't till I got home that I realized there's this brooch on my jacket. No note, nothing! Yeah. So it wasn't until I met him again – that was in Redonda, when we worked in the cannery there. And they were there too, his mother was working there. A lot of other people were working there. And still we didn't really get to know each other, but at that time he told me he was the one that pinned the brooch on my jacket. Yeah. So I guess we were just sizing each other up. Two strangers! *[laughs]* So, anyway after that he transferred here to Sliammon because up until then he was a Homalco member registered to the Homalco Band. This was his mother, 'cause she had originally married a man

Elsie and William on the steps of the Sliammon Sacred Heart Church on their wedding day – 11 December 1950. Photo courtesy of Elsie Paul.

Elsie and her first-born, Glen, in 1950. Photo courtesy of Elsie Paul.

from Homalco. So they moved here and that's when we started seeing each other. And got married at eighteen. I was eighteen and he was nineteen when we got married. And we'd already had our first baby by then. And my oldest son was nine months. So we got acquainted rather quickly after he transferred here. Yeah, it wasn't an arranged marriage. Our parents really didn't become involved. And he was working up in – oh, what's the name of that outfit? – Daniels River. Daniels River, logging. That's where he was working. He'd be up there during the week and come back down for a weekend.

So right away, after we were married, we built a house. First we were at my granny's house, which was just two doors from my place.

Then we had a schoolteacher here – Mrs. Lacey was her name. And
her husband was a carpenter before he came here. He was quite on
in age by then, and he helped build – the department supplied us with
two thousand dollars to build a house. And you had to build it yourself,
so that was just for the lumber. So that man, the schoolteacher's husband, helped my husband build the house. It was just a shell of a
house. There was no inside plumbing. There's no running water. It
was called a two room and a path. *[chuckles]* Yeah, in those days we
just had outhouses around here. Yeah, it was kind of a real patch-up
job, 'cause it didn't have, like, plywood or anything or Gyproc on the
walls. So we got a piece here and there, so it was all like patchwork.
And painted the floor, the kitchen area. Wanted it to be fancy, so I
dabbed red paint all over it with a sponge. It looked pretty good! So
that was the only room and our bedroom. The rest of the house was
a shell. It was just two-by-fours. But it was for future to build – finish
it. So we had blankets or whatever to keep the heat in that part of the
house, 'cause we only had – our stove was a wood cookstove. That's
all that would fit in the area we were living in. And he was back and
forth to work. And we bought that stove for twenty-five dollars at a
second-hand store. I used to row over to Harwood a lot. I used to go
gather wood there. I would take the axe, and I would gather wood
and – you know, wood washes up there on the beach, and blocks of
wood and bark and stuff – and I'd gather that, load up the boat and
row home with it.* So there's a lot of physical labour with the women.
There's no washing machines and dryers. Everything was all hard
labour. But we didn't see it as that then. Nowadays it's so different,
very different. So now we have a stove and, you know, we're on our
way, and nice floor. *[chuckles]* Yeah, and he used to get up really
early, 'cause the crummy would pick them up to go – he was back
and forth to camp. Every day he'd go and come back at night. So he
got a bright idea and he gathered some creosote down the beach.
There was a creosote log, I guess, down the beach. Chipped away at
it and brought a handful of it home. Just so he could start the fire
going early in the morning. Well, lo and behold! That stove was just
dancing it was so hot. It was red-hot! It got overly hot. Oh my Lord!

---

* Elsie says that the fir bark at Harwood was especially suited for burning in
  wood stoves, because it took a long time to burn. "Conversation: Mary George
  and Elsie Paul," audio recorded by Honoré Watanabe, transcribed with Marion
  Harry, draft of 17 August 2010, copy in possession of authors.

Elsie and William's first home in Sliammon, built in 1951. The home was originally built on a two-thousand-dollar budget, with additions and improvements made in subsequent years. Photo courtesy of Elsie Paul.

I thought we were going to burn the house down. Eventually it burned out, and talk about smoke all over and creosote smell. It was terrible. So after all that, my beautiful stove – inside the wood box was all bent, and the iron or the grates were bent. You could hardly light it, and we had to change the grates in there. It got so overheated. What an experience!

So gradually did more things and started fixing the other rooms. But it was a long time before we had our bathroom in there, and running water. And my brother-in-law George was somewhat of a carpenter in his time too. He built the cupboards in that house. And then we got running water, of which we installed ourselves, the piping and that. So now we had to have a septic field, a septic tank. So my brother-in-law and I kind of put our heads together and we got that going, dug two big holes in the yard back here. And one where the initial flow goes and then it seeps to the next big tank – it's not a tank, but it's lined with heavy lumber, which we gathered at Harwood. We would go to Harwood and walk the beaches, go beachcombing. If there were those big logs – I think they're like two-by-twelves – and tow that across. That's what we lined our septic tank with. And we got that going, that was nice. Then we had that little addition that we put our bathroom in the back of the house. It was like a little addition, but it had no insulation, and the pipes froze in the winter. So there I am, I think I was probably about nine months pregnant with

Sharon and I'm under that small space which is yay high *[gesturing]* – it's probably about two and a half feet high. And I'm under there with a blowtorch of all things, trying to thaw out the pipes! I don't know how I got this blowtorch going! But I guess I knew how to light it. And it's a good thing I didn't burn the house down, 'cause the pipes were frozen and I'm under there and my big belly and I was really big! *[laughs]* 'Cause Sharon was born in November, right? So that took care of that. So I lived in that house until thirty-two years ago when these homes were barged in here.* These homes were from an army base in Ladner. And the Band at that time because of shortage of housing in the community – one government to the other, kind of a swap for a dollar – Department of Indian Affairs bought these homes to be sent up here. And all it's going to cost you is the shipping, or the transporting the homes. And they were already old homes then. They must've been about – close to forty years old. But they were solid, but everything else was breaking down. I guess didn't know that then. So we were asked, do we want a bigger house than what we had? So I agreed and my husband was really reluctant. He didn't want – "What's wrong with this house? There's nothing wrong with this house. I built this house." He was really stubborn about it. But we went ahead and we got the house. So it was barged up, set in place, and the old house was still a few feet away in front of this house. And he refused to move. He stayed in that house. Oh, he was such a stubborn man! So dinnertime would come and I would have to make a plate for him and bring it to him. He refused to come and eat in this house. *[laughs]* It took him quite a while for him to move in. Yeah, and then we had that house towed away to the back and we had it as a storage shed for quite a while. No, the addition to it. We kept that as storage shed. Then the rest of that building got moved to the other end of the village for some other family occupied it, smaller family.

But it's a wonder how we managed to live in that house. There was a narrow stairs that went up to the attic, and that's where my kids slept. No fire escape, nothing. And we had wood stoves. We later had an oil heater in the living room of that house. And then my brother-in-law fell asleep on the couch and burnt the couch and the house was full of smoke. I guess the kids smelled it upstairs. A wonder they woke up! Came banging on our bedroom door and, "Smoke in the house!" That couch, we dragged it – I did – I went outside, and we

---

* Elsie was speaking here in July 2010.

still had outside plumbing then. There was an outside tap. And it was summer. And I grabbed this galvanized tub that was there with water, brought it in and doused the – 'cause as soon as you opened the door, the couch just went up in flames like that. So that was a real close call for us. He fell asleep with a cigarette in his hand and that's what happened. So that was pretty scary times. We were always living so dangerously.

Like travelling in the car – whenever we went somewhere, we always had a rickety old car. I got to be a *real* expert at changing tires. Almost every time I went to town I had a flat tire and I'd just jack it up, put on the spare and take the other one in, get it repaired and – I don't know how many times – *many* times I changed the tire. I got to be really good at it, I'll say. *[laughs]* And me and my half a dozen kids – and seven kids travelling, no seatbelts. I had a station wagon loaded with kids all the time. And my late husband was a smoker. He was a heavy smoker, and he smoked in the car when we were travelling with a carload of kids. Never get away with that today. But back then, nobody thought anything about the harmful effects of smoking in – anywhere! This one time, talkin' about my old car, heading over to the ferry to send kids off on the ferry. They were going away on a school trip. And I got pulled over. There was a road check. That's when first the seatbelt regulations came in. And they were enforcing that and I'd never ever had any use or saw the use for seatbelts. And lo and behold! I got pulled over. Didn't know what I was being pulled over for. And this one auxiliary officer came up to me and, "How many people are in here?" and "How many seatbelts do you have?" So he counted heads: "You've got too many. This is going against the new regulations. You gotta have seatbelts for every person in the car." I said, "That is *so* unfair!" I said, "You know how many children I have? When I go to town I take my children to town with me." "Well that's too bad. You're just going to have to leave some of your children at home. You can only take –" whatever it was, five or six, 'cause we had the station wagon. *Oh!* I tried to put up an argument, but he wasn't hearing any of it. So I was really upset with him! I was upset with the law. *[laughs]* Oh my gosh. Yeah. That was quite the thing. And him smoking like a smokestack in the car. Everybody getting sick over second-hand smoke. Yeah. So that was life. It's a wonder we all survived. *[laughs]*

WE HAD A LOT of game. My husband went out hunting. We always had deer, so I learned how to skin the deer and butcher the deer. And

Elsie seated in living room of her and her husband's first home in
1955. Photo courtesy of Elsie Paul.

by now I've learned to can and use jars and that. So I always had
jarred deer meats. And that was our main diet, and clams and fish.
Pretty much. So all we had to buy was vegetables. And we were dealing with the store, the Toigos' store then. We would charge up grocer-
ies. And every payday the cheque went there, and it would clean up
the bill. And then start charging again till next payday. So we're just
living from one paycheque to the next. Peter Toigo was a young man

then.[*] He was probably eighteen, nineteen, and he worked there as a meat cutter. His parents owned the store, and they became really good friends of ours, really good friends of mine through the years. We're still friends. And so we charged there. That's where we bought our first TV, black-and-white TV. We were the first one in the community to get a TV. That was quite the thing, black-and-white. Yeah, and we got our first couch from there. He knew someone, I guess, or they knew someone that had a couch. So we bought our first couch set there. We were progressing pretty good.

My husband taught me how to use a rifle. He taught me how to aim and where to put the sight. And I guess I got pretty good at it. So we were living in Lang Bay area. And that was just before Sharon was born. We were living there 'cause he was working at a camp close to that site in Lang Bay. So we lived there I think probably a couple of months. So it was fall time – it was around when the apples are on the tree and that. And so I guess that's what attracts the grouse, and they're on the apple tree. I look and I see grouse there. And I thought, "Hmmm," got the gun out and aimed at the grouse and it fell to the ground and the rest are still there! Think there was three or four I shot out of that tree. It's funny they wouldn't fly away. They just stayed there. So that night we had grouse for dinner. Oh, it's so good! Plucked them, and it was so fresh and really tasty. Yeah, my husband didn't believe that I shot that grouse: "Where did you get this from?" "Oh, they were on the tree, over there."

And I shot a deer out here. It was low tide like that, and the deer came swimming in. I could see it coming. And I don't know where it was coming from. And I know that if you shoot a deer or kill a deer after it's been swimming a long ways, the flesh is really awful. They're so tired, I guess, from swimming. So the meat is not very good. It's kind of mushy. It comes kind of soft – different texture altogether.[†] So I don't know what I was thinking, and I went down there with my rifle, went right up close. When got close to the beach where it could reach the ground I guess, the bottom, and it just stood there and it wouldn't move anymore. It must've been so tired. So that was a terrible experience. And I just went there without thinking and started

---

[*] Peter Toigo became a well known British Columbia businessman.

[†] On the texture of deer meat, see Dorothy Kennedy and Randy Bouchard, *Sliammon Life, Sliammon Lands* (Vancouver: Talonbooks, 1983), 37.

shooting at this deer. It's just standing there. And I don't know how many times I shot at it, but I think I was missing it or whatever. Maybe I was too nervous. And I must've hit it. And I could see some blood coming down. And I thought, "Oh no!" And I'm having second thoughts. I shouldn't kill this deer. Like, it's lookin' at me. It's got huge eyes. And I'm not far from it. Oh dear! So I shot again and finally it collapsed. And by then my grandfather was coming down – came down to see me. Oh dear, you know. And he was really scared. He was afraid of the game warden, and rightfully so. My goodness! So we went out and dragged it out of the water and here the deer was very pregnant. Oh my gosh! And so he cut it open and it wasn't just one little baby deer. There were two. The deer had twins and, oh! It was such a terrible thing. So he quickly dug into the ground and buried it with lots of rocks – covered it up. I think it would've been really serious if we had been caught, and he probably would've gone to jail. So we manage to get the deer up here and cleaned and skinned it and by then, it's the end of the day and we left it outside in a tub of water. And that night the dogs must've came and got into it and I wasn't sorry, 'cause I wasn't going to eat that deer anyway. So it was all for nothing. The dogs had it. But that was a really awful experience for me. I think I had nightmares from it for a long time. I didn't realize it was pregnant. And lost the fawns in the process. There were little spots on them already.

WE PRETTY MUCH lived here. And only travel we did was the very first year of our marriage. We lived with the McGees up near Deep Bay area, 'cause he was logging with Smith McGee for a few months. So we went to live there. It was a really old cabin that we were living in. They were handlogging. And one day they were leaving to go off to the site where they were going to go and work today, and they got down to the boat and they looked up and there was smoke under the house. And they ran up and here something had caught on fire below the house – I don't know how that happened or how the drum stove was sitting. Caused a fire. So another close call for us. We got out of there, got the fire out. So that was quite a scare. Quite an experience. So that was just for a short time – that's when we came back here and built the house, and by the time Sharon was born, then we were living in the house and we became pretty much settled – such as it was. Yeah.

And after I had the next baby, which was Jane – she was thirteen months younger than Sharon – that's when we went down to the States to go and pick berries because there were no jobs around here. So people often went away, either to the hop fields or the berry fields in the States. People went different directions. They went to the different farms. The first farm we went to when we went up there that time was – it was just this cabin that was overgrown with bush. And it had no windows. It had nothing but straw on the bed. I think it was a wood bed, with straw on there! So that's where we ended up, when I was married and had the three children. In Sumner. So we stayed there, and we moved from there to the Hatch farm, which was just couple miles down the road. And the living conditions there was a little bit better. It had windows and – so you're really roughin' it. It was harsh. It was pretty hard life. We went down there just, you know, to survive through the summer. We left in June, early June, and uh, didn't come back till September, around 1954, '55.

And my baby got sick down there. She was seven months old. Her name was Jane. She was *beautiful* baby. A *really*, really healthy, happy baby. And then in just a matter of five days being sick, she passed away. And I never did find out what kind of illness she got. I blame it on the water – I blame it on the environment we were in, because the cabins we were living in was close to the fields and there was a lot of flies, a lot of fertilizers from the fields that we worked on. 'Cause I took her with me in her baby buggy out into the raspberry fields and blackberry fields, 'cause there were the bushes, tall, and she was protected in the shade in the buggy. She was such a beautiful baby. Really good baby, happy. She never fussed. And then just before we were finished blackberry pickin', we were in Sumner, just outside of Tacoma, and she got sick and she was sick for three days. And she wasn't takin' her milk. She wasn't takin' the bottle at all. But she was very quiet. She slept a lot. So being an inexperienced mother, I guess I was, and young – just didn't realize how serious dehydration can be for children, for adults. Because she wasn't taking any fluids at all. I knew she was sick, but she wasn't fussin', she wasn't cryin'. So the third day she was sick I brought her to the doctor and – there's a hospital in Tacoma that I brought her to. And I was told – after waiting there from ten in the morning till two in the afternoon – finally the doctor came and called us in, looked at her, and examined her quickly, said, "You just need to change her formula. Just put her on skim milk." And he said to me, "Why don't you Canadian Indians stay in Canada where you belong?" He said, "This hospital is not for Canadian people." So that was a real jolt for me. I just went there, I guess, blindly and out of concern. And it was like he scolded me and told me, "Go home – go back to Canada." I guess he had his point, but, you know, we didn't have medical coverage in those days, especially down in the States. So, brought her home. He said, "If she's not better in two days, bring her back." So she wasn't better the second day, and I brought her back to that same place. And the doctor – again we had to wait from about ten in the morning till mid-afternoon before he came around and looked at her, and by then, she had lost a lot of weight – body weight. She was really limp and, you know, just really tired. But it was so strange how she never fussed. She never, ever put up a fuss. But she would throw up whenever she tried to take her milk. She had diarrhea, but it really wasn't, um – it was very different. It was like curdled milk going through her. So they said, "Oh, we'll keep her in overnight for observation." So they kept her, went home. And about five o'clock the next morning there's a police officer at our door, 'cause we didn't have phones. And said, "Your baby passed away last night in the hospital. Three o'clock." So that was a real shock. *[emotional]*

So we went to the hospital. We went to talk with the doctors. And I was told at the hospital that she just took a turn for the worse during the night. And they were *never*, ever able to tell me what she died from. They insisted on doing an autopsy, because she had been in the hospital for less than twenty-four hours when she passed away. They insisted – it was the law to do an autopsy, which I was so opposed to having that done. But, because it was the law, we had to give our consent to get that done. So that took up all that day, the next day. It was into the third day before they released her. And they said we could take her home if we want, take her back to Canada. They provided – nicely covered – for the little casket. A tiny casket. And she just fit into it – she just fit nicely in it. But they said for all the examination, test they did, they could not find what caused her death. *[emotional]* And I've often wondered, you know, it's so unfinished for me. *[emotional]* We packed our belongin's. We had this rickety old car that my husband bought down there, I think for sixty-five dollars of our berry-pickin' money, just for us to get around in. And we left most of our stuff there because we couldn't fit everything into the car. And we brought her home in the trunk of that little rickety old car we had. And I had my oldest child, Glen, and Sharon, the second child, she was going on to two years of age. She was almost two, and Glen was four, and Jane was seven months old.

And this lady – I don't know where she came from, but there's a lady, and I don't – for the life of me I don't know her name – it was almost like I was in a dark place. But she helped me and she was there.

She prayed for me. And I don't know if she was a minister or a social worker or – I have *no* idea. I just remember her being there with her hands on my shoulders and saying some words, prayer words, and – so I took that beautiful basket that my baby had been in, and I gave it to her. I said, "Thank you for all your help." I turned that basket over to her. And she was saying, "Are you sure? Are you sure you want to do this? This is a *beautiful* basket." I said, "I'm sure." I've regretted it, that I parted with that basket. But at the time, that seemed like the thing to do.

So we headed back to Vancouver. My brother-in-law was with us. Stan was with us. And we headed back to Vancouver and we got into Vancouver late at night. I don't know how late it was. Maybe it was around ten or eleven. And we didn't know where we were gonna go. We had *very* little money. And this steamboat used to come from Vancouver to Powell River at that time. And we just figured, we'll see where we go when we get to Vancouver, how we're going to make that connection. So we were driving down on Powell Street and not knowing where to go. We were going to look for a hotel. And who should be walkin' on the street but a friend from Klahoose – he lived in Klahoose at that time – Bill Mitchell. And Bill Mitchell was a kind of a person who was always helping people. He was always there to give you advice or guide you or – very traditional person. Always, if you didn't have the answer for something, or you needed something done, or question about anything, "Just go ask Bill Mitchell!" and that was how we were, how everybody was towards Bill Mitchell. He was never too busy to help anyone. I said, "That's Bill Mitchell! Lookit, Bill Mitchell is walking on the street!" He was strutting along there. And we pulled over and told him what happened. "Yeah," he said, "I just went to the corner store and picked up something." He said, "Mom's in the hotel" – he always called his wife "Mom" – "Mom's in the hotel, just down the street here." So we told him what happened, you know, we had this little casket in the trunk and we were just go-ing to keep it in the trunk overnight. And he said, "No, you cannot do that." He said, "You must not do that." He said, "I know the funeral home," he said. He told me, "You go stay with Mom," he said to me and, "Take your kids and go stay with Mom. I'll go with Willie and Stan. We'll go up to the funeral home." So he did that. He was like, you know, guardian angel, as far as I was concerned. He was there when we had nowhere to turn. So they took care of that, and the next morning, he said, "I'll go with you guys." He said, "We'll go to the Indian Affairs office and see if they will help." He said, "They have to help." He was quite familiar with the different programs. Which we didn't have many, but he was a Chief for many years in Squirrel Cove, so he knew his way around.

So they went early in the morning, and by then we had gotten a room. It was one of those cheap hotels down towards the waterfront there. So I was in bed and I had the two children with me. They were napping, and I had a nap. I woke up – I was facing the window. And at that time these windows used to open if you'd just lift it, it would open. Quite easily. And my little girl, I woke up and she was sitting on that windowsill. And we're three storeys high. Oh my goodness! I was almost frozen, you know? She was looking down below on the street watchin' the cars. I just kind of snuck up on her and I grabbed her. I just grabbed her and pulled her onto the bed because the bed was right up against the window. And that's how she got up on the ledge. So I just about lost her, because if she had toppled over – not even two years old yet. I don't know if that window was open or if she was able to push it up. Oh, it was *so* scary. After I got her on the bed, and I just sobbed and I cried and I was *so* upset. I just was so overcome. So that was a very rough time for us. I believe it was the following day that we were able to board the boat that used to come up to Powell River and used to go up north. So Bill Mitchell helped take care of those things and we got on our way. And they were coming back on the same boat with us. And I was telling Mrs. Mitchell what happened that morning, early in the morning when my little girl was sittin' on the window ledge. And she said, "You know," she said, "that's the reason why you need to *really* keep your children close to you. When you lose someone in your family, chances are something just may happen. When you lose someone, you're very vulnerable. So you have to be very careful and cautious, and always be careful of your surroundings." And I really believed that, I still believe that till today, that we are weakened when we're in the dark. That our energy level is down, that we're not able to function and we're not as aware. And that's so important, to be so aware. And that teachin' still stands today. When we lose someone in our community within a family, we tell parents, children, siblings, "Keep your children close to you. Don't let them go far. Hold on to them. Because they could be – their spirit can be taken."

So that was our bad luck – our rough journey down there to the States. And from then on, I've never ever gone back there. It was a thing for our people to do. They used to go down there every summer, just to make a living for a few weeks maybe, from six weeks to three months – maybe longer if they went further into Yakima. Pick fruit there, apples and whatever. And the pay was not much. There wasn't much money to be made in the berry fields. So it was just struggle, just always struggling for, you know, how we were going to survive and get back home. But we managed. We got back home. We managed to bring our baby home for burial. She was buried in our cemetery. So that was a real difficult time for us.

After we lost the baby there. And it was fall time. And my mother-in-law lived in Okeover, it's one of the village sites, and she was living there at the time, smoking salmon. So I ended up going there because my husband had to return to Vancouver and take that ratty old car back across the line, because we had no way of keeping it, 'cause we were told we have to take it back there. We only paid about eighty-five dollars for that car to begin with down in the States. So him and his brother returned that car. They were gone for – I don't know – a couple weeks or a month they were gone. I guess they found some work along the way. So he came back and that's where we were living, in the head of Okeover, 'cause I was helping my mother-in-law smoke salmon. And it was just a small cabin – quite a small cabin. So I really experienced sleeping on cedar planks for a bed. *[laughs]* Yeah, and it was hard living down there, you know, 'cause you're nowhere near a store. You don't have a vehicle. And we lived with my great-uncle, Sandy Timothy. maksɛma. And he was used to livin' the hard life. Very humble life. And the only time we got anything from the store is he would row all the way from the head of Okeover to Refuge Cove. There was a store there. He would go and get just the bare essentials, like flour and sugar and whatever.

Ever since then we never went back – we never went back to the States. We pretty much stayed here. And my husband went loggin' and that's pretty much what he did in his life was working, logging. He would go away, like, a couple months at a time to Minstrel Island, north end of Vancouver Island – there's a big logging company there. And him and quite a few of the other guys. Our guys were good loggers. That was what they knew what to do. And off they would go and be gone for a month, two months. And come back and – yeah. That's the only work he had. He worked at the mill for a short time. He tried out the mill, but he couldn't adjust to the shift work and working at night and trying to sleep during the day when you got a house full of kids. *[laughs]* It was hard to get sleep during the day. So I think he lasted six months there and that was it. He decided to go back to logging.

But not everybody was logging. There was fishermen. They had their own boats, and they were able to go out commercial fishing. But most of them were loggers. The older men were just hunting and fishing for food and things like that. Like they were the home guards, I guess – but there wasn't a lot of income. I think that's when they first started, people first start turn to welfare because there was just no other way to survive. Course the welfare system was introduced by then. And fill out a form and then you get – they called it "relief." Our people called it "relief." That's what it was called. So much for a family, used to be – get the basic necessities. First it was goods, when I was young. That's when it first started. And just box of goods delivered to your door. And then later on, the Indian agent would come from Vancouver or the social worker for the Indian Affairs would fly in to Powell River and be here for the day. And if you wanted to make an appointment, you went there and filled out a form and was interviewed. So that was quite degrading. I don't think anyone chooses to be on welfare. I know at first for our people it was something that was very different. Now people demand it today. People have really adapted and have adapted to that kind of a handout. And I myself, you know, it's so degrading. To have to go and fill out – give people your history, why you need welfare.

And for quite a while there, when my kids were little, that's when we had decided to leave in the summer and we went down the States and picked berries, and I would just leave the reserve and go up – my aunt lived in Squirrel Cove. And go there and just kind of live off the land and not have to worry about going without, 'cause the closer you are to the land, the more readily available food was. So we could've survived. My husband had an old boat, and he would go fishing all day, and come home with a couple of fish and that – we still survived on that.

And I had a great-uncle who was a brother to my grandfather.[*] And he was so nice to us. He was so good to us. He'd go fishing. He loved to fish. He *aaalways* fished! He didn't have children of his own. And he would come home and he'd always bring me fish or clams or whatever. And if he went to the store, and by now he's a pensioner, I don't know how much pension he was getting, but the kids still remember – my older children still remember him. Whatever he could afford, he was

---

[*] Elsie is referring here to maksɛma, also known as Sandy Timothy.

Elsie with her children in the living room of her home, in 1962. *Left to right:* Walter, Sharon, Ann, Elsie, Cathy, Jeannie. Photo courtesy of Elsie Paul.

a generous man. He was very close to me and my family. And to Rose Louie. Rose Louie was my cousin, right? And he would go there and if he had fish to spare after he'd been out fishing all day, he would bring me a fish and he would go and give Rose Louie a fish, or he'd go and give her clams and he'd say to Rose, "Oh, give some to your sister." He seen us as sisters. All my cousins, they were – in those days, your cousins were your sisters. He would say "ʔayiš." "naʔs ʔəms ʔayiš tɛʔɛ." "This is for your sister." "ʔayiš" is a sister or a cousin. Or even a very close friend, you know, that becomes your sister, like, my sister. Yeah, so he always referred to us as that: "Your ʔayiš. This cod is for your ʔayiš," or "This clams is for your ʔayiš." Rose always remembered that. Yeah. So then if he managed to sell a fish, and he got a few dollars for fish, he would go to the store and buy treats. And he always came home with this popcorn in there – like the little satchel kind of a container. When you opened, there's a little prize in there, and the popcorn was pink. And all the kids would get one, you know. That was so exciting for the kids! They thought that was the best thing that ever happened. *[chuckles]* That was a big treat for him, to buy my children this popcorn. And now and then, he would buy us a bag of flour, 'cause times were really tough and there was no work during the summer months. So he would buy us some flour, just to help us out. He was a generous man. So he was like a real saviour. He was always good to us. Yeah, that's how he made his living, you know, he fished, and he just loved being out on the water.

And yeah, it was pretty tough, just to survive. It was tougher than I remember my childhood was. We lived without a lot of those things that by then we were getting used to, you know, having things that we never really had when we were little, when we were growing up. And yet it was quite acceptable – that was okay, that's how it was. We didn't have fancy things, we didn't have extras, but we always had enough. We always had enough. So by the time my children started going to school and – having to provide for them, it was hard to. So I picked up odd jobs myself when my husband was not working. Or if it was a hot summer and the woods shut down, so I had to supplement our family income by – I worked as a chambermaid, I worked as an oyster shucker, and doing stuff like that just to help bring in added income to our family. We don't have as much as we used to. Here we used to just go out there, down to the low water in front of the community here, down to the point. My grandfather went there and dug clams, just enough for supper. Just bring home a little bucket and that's for supper, that's for clam chowder. Now you can't go down there, because it's all contaminated from the mill. We could always go out here, there's a reef out there. I used to go and jig cod there. I would go there, jig cod and get a couple, and bring it home and that's our food for the next coupla days. Just so much that has changed. Sometimes I think it's for the better, but the more things people have, the more that people want. Life is not simple anymore. So I don't know if it's better or if it's worse. I know we can't go back to the way things were, 'cause the young people of today just don't know that kind of lifestyle, or the resources are getting depleted and we can't go there anymore. Yeah, it's a total different world now.

Yeah, life is not always easy raising a family, when I was raising my children. I really didn't have a formal education, because school was a hit and miss for me when I was growing. My grandparents didn't approve of me going to residential school. So we were always away from the main reserve, just so that we don't get sent away to residential school. So a lot of the families took their children away from the community. Around August, you just stayed away. So once the capacity was, you know – once they met their quota, I guess, the rest of us were not made to go. Until the following year. Then they would do another scoop. So I went to school whenever I could, in the day school. It was just maybe a month in the winter. Maybe a few weeks, then we're going again, travelling. So I didn't really have a formal education. I guess my next job now as a married woman, and I already had children then, was working at the oyster plant in Okeover. And that was hard, hard work. And my children were quite young then. And so the older ones babysat the younger ones, or sometimes it was my other relatives: my grandmother, my mother-in-law. Yeah, that was really hard work. And I was lucky to make seven dollars for the day. That's a dollar a gallon of oysters shucked. And these gallon containers had to be just overflowing. You don't stop till it's overflowing. So that was a dollar. Then you had your expenses. You had to buy your gloves, your apron, your knife and – yeah, so it was hard work. Oh God! I'd come home and I'd have to soak my arm in warm water because my whole arm was achin' up to my shoulder. It's not an easy job when you're not experienced in shucking oysters.

I worked at Walnut Lodge. There used to be a Walnut Lodge in the townsite there in Powell River, across the old court building. It was a rooming house for mill workers. So I would – on weekends, that was only on weekends, but we really needed the money, so again, the older children looked after the younger ones. And I went to work for this couple there. Their name was Mr. and Mrs. McCullough. They were from Wildwood area and they ran that boarding house. It was all men's rooming house. So they're all gone to work and I'm there cleaning all the rooms and making the beds and the usual housework on the weekends. And I was making about seventeen dollars a day. That was pretty good money. So every two weeks I got a cheque for about thirty-four dollars for two weekends of work. And that was quite a bit of money. So I guess that led me to applying for work at the old hospital.

And then from there I got a job at the hospital in housekeeping. And that was a lot easier than my two other jobs, my previous jobs. Housekeeping is – it was steady work. It was steady work for me. I worked for about five years there. Yeah, there weren't many women working there from here. Actually, Marion Harry worked there for some time too. After I was working there, she worked there for a while. Yeah, that was, like, shift work. Sometimes I went to work in the evenings till eleven o'clock at night. And that was good. I did okay there. I learned how to really clean house and scrub till everything was shining. So from there, I quit work for a while there because I got pregnant and I had to stop, take maternity leave. Then I went back again. And I was there working till 1972. But that kept us going.

And then when the Sliammon Band took over their own administration of the social services department, I was asked to fill that role,
simply because I was fluent in the language. And that I knew pretty
much all the people that live in the community. I didn't have any
training, but I was told, "You got the ability, you can do it. Just follow the policy." So I left my job at the hospital and took on that job.
I had two weeks' training. This wonderful man that used to work for
Department of Indian Affairs would come up and show me the forms
to use. And I had a crash course in how to take an application for
income assistance. I had a crash course in how to encourage people
to look for work, to go out on a job search. Took a crash course in
children that were at risk and who had to live with other family
members. All of those things. The binder was very thick in policies
and procedures. We had two binders. And here I am, without any
formal training or education, and to take on that work was very chal-
lenging. So two weeks is all I got, for training. And after that I was
on my own.

My husband was a logger. He was away a lot. That was his life,
was logging. And he worked hard. And he played hard. Like a lot of
loggers that I know of, he enjoyed going out and socializin' with his
logger friends. So he was not there all the time. There were times he
went away up north loggin' for two months, three months. Come home
and be home for a couple of months, and then go off somewhere else.
But when he was home, he was ... he was, I don't know how to put
it, you know – he had a weakness for alcohol. And that's – didn't do
him any good, health-wise. He died when he was forty-five of heart
failure. And my youngest child was thirteen. And the next one was
fourteen. And I had one graduating that year. And by then I was
working for our administration at the Sliammon Band Office.

WELL, MY MOTHER-IN-LAW used to make home brew, right? But her
brew was made out of all kinds of things. Anything that was available,
like raisins or rice or oranges or – anything that's going to ferment.
Threw into a big blue bucket, I remember that so well. And sugar and
yeast. It'd be just bubbling – smelled terrible. This was even before,
you know, we were allowed to have liquor. People found ways and
means of making their own brew, but it was so gross! So some people
used that – what are those berries? – t'ᶿɛwq'. We called "t'ᶿɛwq'" in
our language. They're red berries, looks like a cluster of grapes or
something. You see them getting ripe now, they're red – really red,
and they're in clusters. Some people use that for, to throw into the

brew as well. I think some people call it "poison berries." A lot of people wouldn't touch it: they say it's poison. But people ate it. My grandfather ate that too. Not so much as a dessert, but he said, "It doesn't taste very good, but it's good for you." You'd have some in a dish, and they steam it down, and then all those little tiny berries fall off. So you don't have to cook it in a lot of water. Just a bit of water in the bottom of a big pot. In – we'd have a big pile of it – in a big container of it, it melts down to nothing. So you shake it all off and those little branches that they're on, you shake it and you'll get, like, a bowl full. So my granny used to preserve that, put it in jars, 'cause it's good medicine. Or sometimes they'd add the wild blackberries into it so it gave it a different flavour. But you can't eat too much of it because you'd get diarrhea. So I guess in that way it was medicine – it was good for that purpose. But people made brew with that, too. I don't remember if my mother-in-law used that particular kind of berries, but she used everything else in her brew. And she always had a big pot of brew going, which was so gross. Then it's strained – all that stuff is strained, like, with an old pillowcase or something like that. All the pieces then are separated from the liquid. It was yucky looking! [chuckles] And actually people got high on that. And my granny started making that too. Learned from my mother-in-law. Then they started to make it with the malt. They were sold in the stores, malt extract. So that was a better quality of brew. So that was more like beer.

And that's what I used when I made – to surprise my husband who was away in camp up in Egmont. And he would be there until Christmas. I thought, "I'll do this. I have enough time to do this, 'cause it might take maybe six weeks it'll become really clear." Six weeks to two months, I guess, 'cause he was up there in around October, November. Yeah, late October he went there. So I thought I would surprise him and make this, following the directions ever so carefully. I thought I'll give it to him after Christmas. Not before Christmas, but it would be part of his Christmas gift. So I was really diligent and just followed the directions. And it turned out really nice, it was becoming really clear. You siphon it to another container, then you skim it. So I was quite proud of the fact that it was so clear. So when it was time to bottle it, I put it in, like, half-gallon jugs and a couple of one-gallon jugs. I didn't put them in beer bottles. They were in these jugs. So I had it up in the attic of my old house. So the police came around close to Christmas. Christmas night, I guess it was, Christmas Eve. People were in church, I guess, that night and somebody took advantage of that situation and broke into a house in the community, while the people were out of the home. And so they stole this very valuable wild blackberry preserve. It's really hard to get that, 'cause the little black-berries are so tiny and they're so tasty when they're in the wild. So this lady had a couple cases of that, and the thieves took off with it. So the police came. It wasn't a search warrant that they came with to search a house. No search warrant. And they just went door to door to door throughout the community, lookin' for the culprit. So I heard about this and I was so scared. Someone was mentioning, "They're coming this way now. They're coming this way." That's when we still lived in the old house. So I had to divulge my secret. And my husband and his friend Charlie were in the house. So I told him, I said, "Police are coming this way and I have to tell you this right now. They're searching the houses." I would have gone to jail, for goodness' sakes, for making home brew. So I said, "There's some homemade beer up-stairs I was going to give to you later, before New Year's." Boy, were they ever shocked – pleasant surprise. So they went upstairs, 'cause I had it up in the attic. I could hear them rattling around down there and they're coming down the stairs with all these jugs and went out the side door and it was all bush back here then behind the house. There were no houses back there. That other street there was not there then. It was just brush. Off they went into the bushes with these jugs of beer. And lo and behold! Two police officers come through that trail and knock on the door. Go to the door, pretend I don't know what's going on. They told me what their business was and they're looking for some house got broken into and they didn't ask to come and search in the house at all. I just talked to them at the door. And in the meantime could hear clanging and crashing through the bushes back there. And, "What is that up there? What was all that racket up there?" "Hmmm," I said, "probably kids playing." So they were gone. For several days they sat up in the woods and drank the beer. Invited all their other friends – and they tell me it was really strong beer. *[laughs]* They were gone until all the beer was gone. Yeah, that was quite the thing when people made brew. Learned to like alcohol. Yeah. It's funny how when something is forbidden you want it. It's a chal-lenge. Robbing the liquor store and making your own brew and going into the liquor store when you're not allowed to be there. Just a chal-lenge, I guess – when you're young you challenge things.

Yeah, and I think I told that story of him and Alec Louie, his buddy Alec Louie. They were caught with a bottle of whiskey at Rose Louie's. Yeah, anyway we were over visiting Rose and Alec, and they were

Elsie and William during the Christmas season in the early 1960s. Photo courtesy of Elsie Paul.

logging buddies. They were always talking logging talk and that. So I'm sittin' in the main living room with Rose, and we're visiting, and Alec and my husband were sitting off in a room – there was a bedroom there, and they were – they're sitting there talking and visiting. Next thing you know, a police officer comes through the door. And there was just a curtain on the door. There was no door, just a curtain to cover the doorway. So hearing the police come in, I guess they put their bottle on the windowsill – window ledge – in that little room. And the lights are on, of course it's dark. Yeah, "What's going on in here?" That's how he used to be. The police would just walk in: "What are you guys up to?" And it's like you're scolded or, you know, rough – it's not anything like "Oh, how are you today?" kind of thing. You know? "I was just passing through, checking to see if you're okay." No, it was "What are you up to?" and "Where's your husband?" Right away Alec came out of the bedroom and, "Oh, officers." And by then he's kind of jagged already. In the meantime they had put that bottle on the ledge, and there's a curtain. So officer went there, I guess looked around, didn't see any bottle there or anything. So left and went out through the kitchen and around the house, and there was, like, a walkway going down by the house. I guess when you looked like that at that window, you seen this bottle on the ledge. Comes back in, goes stomping into that bedroom, grabs that bottle, and walks out with it. So of course Alec and my husband were really upset by – they took away their bottle of whiskey. Followed the police officers outside and they're jabbering away like a couple of magpies. They're, "You can't do that to us," and "That's our right. We paid a lot of money for that bottle!" and blah, blah, blah. Officer just ignored them and went in his vehicle. So they kind of went around the vehicle – Alec's on one side and Dad's on the other side and they're nattering at the officer from both windows in the police car. "You can't do this to us. We've got our rights," Alec was saying. "I was in the Army. I served in the war." And what did he say he was? He was – oh! "I was in the 47th brigade," he said. *[laughs]* I don't know if he knew what that meant. And the officer was standing there and I'm over on one side. I'm telling my husband, "Come with me, let's go home." In the meantime the officer had spilled that whiskey right on the road by the vehicle – upended the bottle, spilled all that whiskey out. And he said, "Now you go home." He was telling that to us, like, me and my husband were standing there. I wasn't drinking at all myself, but I was telling him, "Let's go. Let's go home before you get arrested. Let's go!" Oh, they were nattering at the police officer. Finally the police officer just left. Left him there and – yeah, they were very disgruntled about their whiskey being poured out of the bottle and onto the road. So it was just always like a "catch me if you can" – hide and seek and always hiding from the law over nothing.

And one time we were at his other friend's place, which was at Charlie and Bessie's, Charlie Peters. And it was a beautiful day like this, and they're sitting outside on the grass close to the house. And this police car came whipping up the driveway off the main highway, 'cause they lived up on the highway. Officer pulls in. And just went up to him, and Charlie got up and he ran and he went down the bank. It was a steep bank there. He went tumbling down the bank. He was running away from the police. And of course my husband, being stubborn, wanted to argue. He was sitting there and he, "We're not doing anything wrong. We're just here visiting." And officer went, looked over the bank, and Charlie's way down there. There's a lot of bush down there. It didn't bother him. He just left him: "Okay, you. You're coming with me." And he didn't want to go. He's digging his heels in. So I'm helping the officer – help put him in the car. I said, "Come on,"

I said, "you go with the officer." 'Cause I was worried they would beat him or really rough him up. So I'm helping the officer! "Get in a police car – go, go!" *[laughs]* Oh my gosh. Just for nothing. You're sitting there, minding your own business. But I guess you're breaking the law. *[chuckles]*

One time we were at my mother-in-law's place. So next door to her was Moses Wilson's house and Agnes. And we all got together there and everybody was drinking and I don't know if it was some special occasion. And there were drinks around. And Chuck Pielle was what we called "non-status," right? At that time we had non-status people. So he could go in the liquor store and purchased liquor. So he was the provider. He was the one that could get the liquor for the rest of the buddies. So we were there and it was a late, late night. It was summer. And we were still there. It was starting to break daylight, and I don't know what we were doing. So, and someone from another party down the road was coming up the road and there was some kind of ruckus and somebody's yelling and fighting – they were fighting, arguing. And so-and-so came to the door: "You call the police! You call the police," you know, for this incident that was happening out there. Another party altogether. And Chuck Pielle digs in his pocket – there was no phones then on the reserve, but there was a payphone up on the highway at the logging road there. Yeah, that's where the payphone was. And it was a dime to put a call in. So Chuck Pielle digs in his pocket, comes out – "Here, you go call!" he says to this complainant that was at the door. Gives him a dime, and lo and behold! He went up there and called police. So what do we do now? We're all in this house and we're all, you know – we're having a good time until that point. Well, the police is coming. And we had the outhouses. And we *[laughs]* – and my husband and a couple of the other guys took off and through the bush they ran away. So that left the women there. And Chuck Pielle didn't run away, 'cause he's the one that was living there at that house at that time. And *[laughs]* by then it's quite light outside. So anyway, what am I going to do? I don't know why I'm running away. So I ran away and I went behind the outhouse and I'm standing there up against the building hiding. And my sister ran into the outhouse and she was hiding in there. The police officer came: "You get out of there!" *[laughs]* And then he comes – I'm hoping he's not going to come behind the building. He comes around the building and, "And you. Get over here." *[laughs]* So we all gather behind the house, and Chuck Pielle is there, and there's a block of wood there, and there's an axe. And Chuck says to the police officer – he was our mouthpiece, and he says, "I don't know what you officers are doing. What are you doing here? You know, we're not doing anything wrong. We're just having a visit" and blah blah blah. And the officer said, "There was a complaint that there was something going on." He couldn't find any liquor in the house. I don't know why there was no liquor there at that time, in the morning. But anyway, Chuck Pielle being a real smarty-pants, he says to the officer, "Well, you need a reason to come down here." He said, "Put your foot on this block of wood, and I could chop it off with this axe. Then you'll have a good reason." *[laughs]* And I thought, "Oh my God, he's going to get –" They didn't arrest him. They left him alone. The police officers left, and in the meantime our husbands had taken off for the bushes and left us – we could have been the ones to get hauled away for nothing. *[laughs]* Those were the good old days. *[chuckles]*

Oh yeah, my husband was an alcoholic. And it got worse as years went on. After he quit logging – and, you know, he lost his job because of his drinking, and the more he drank, his job possibilities got less and less. But he became really a heavy alcoholic. And that was really hard. That was really a difficult thing to live with. He could go days and go missing for days, just out drinking somewhere. So that was really tough to live with an alcoholic. It was hard. You just never know when he's coming home or when he's not going to come home – so you can't get a good sleep wondering, where is he? All on account of alcohol. Things a person would not normally do happens when they're impaired or intoxicated. Yeah. A lot of things happen. Not to mention the damage to your health. That's how it ended up with him, was just drank too much and shortened his life that much – developed real serious heart problems. And in the end his heart just gave out on him at the young age of forty-five. He was only forty-five. Yeah. I guess that was no surprise, 'cause his doctor had warned him. That he's, you know, he's gotta quit drinking. Being the stubborn man he was, he never listened. Didn't want to go for counselling or treatment or anything. Of course, there wasn't that much available then too. Yeah. But for two years he quit drinking. I believe that's when he was first diagnosed. But he never told me that. He quit drinking and that was so nice. But it was like holding my breath all the time, wondering when it's going to happen again. And he's really busy around the place and he did so much around the place, just cleaning the property and put the lawn in – and we were here already in this house then – he'd be out there raking and raking and raking. And did the shrubs down there. He planted those shrubs and before that he had flowers planted there. It was so beautiful. He placed those big rocks on the slope and planted flowers – that kept him really busy. He was really happy doing all that. And then he planted the shrubs and those shrubs overtook the flower garden he had there. But he put in a real nice lawn. It was a lot of work to clear this property, 'cause this became a garbage dump to the teacherage that was next door. They tossed all their garbage on the other side of the fence before we built our first house, before we built the house there. It wasn't a yard then, it was an empty lot. So when we built the house here, we had a lot of clearing to do and get rid of all the medicine bottles that used to come – medicines used to come in big containers, glass containers. That was the cough syrup and the liniment and the iodine – didn't have a lot of other medicines except those. And so when the jug is empty, they just tossed the bottles over the fence and into the brush next door. So there was a lot of garbage. So we took a lot of garbage out of here before that house was built. So once we got this house, he was cleaning and raking and levelling the place. There was still bits and pieces of garbage in the ground. Yeah, they sure left a lot of – and rusty cans and all kinds of garbage – my property was a garbage dump for quite a while. *[laughs]*

My late husband was a very nice-looking man. Yeah, he looked – he looked Italian. He was dark – dark hair, really black, pitch-black hair. When he was young he was very handsome, with this prominent nose, and he was a very handsome man. And he lived up the coast then, this was before we were married. And they would come down from Homalco, come to Lund, 'cause that's where the beer parlour was. And his buddies would send him to go and purchase beer. They would come to purchase cases of beer, 'cause he's the only one that could get into the pub. He passed as something else other than being a First Nations person. 'Cause at that time, even the men were not allowed in the pub, or to purchase or to have possession of alcohol. So he would go up and buy for his friends cases and cases of beer and then off they'd go. So after the pubs were opened for the First Nations, people were allowed now to go in, and he went in and the bartender discovered who he was all this time. I wouldn't be surprised if he ribbed the bartender, "Ha ha ha!" you know, kind of thing. And that bartender was so angry. Threatened to kick him out of the bar for deceiving him. And that bartender never forgot he was angry at him from then on. *[laughs]* He got fooled and he didn't like that at all.

And when they allowed men to go in the beer parlours, when they opened that up – and it was the men who were allowed to go into the pub, not the women. So my husband would go in with his logger

William, just prior to his marriage to Elsie, in the late 1940s in Sliammon village. Photo courtesy of Elsie Paul.

friends and sit there by the hour. That was fine for him. Then after some time, I don't know how many years later, they opened it up for women. So they opened it up for women and you were only allowed to go in from eleven o'clock in the morning till three o'clock in the afternoon. And then, that was it! "You go home now. Time's up for you!" So at the Rodmay Hotel, in the pub, there was a men's side and a women's side. So the women had to sit in the women's side, and the men across the way in the men's side. But at the Westview Hotel, I guess they were more forgiving, because I remember going in there to pick up my husband. I always remember going there and visiting my husband who was sitting there. I'd gone shopping and thought, "Well, I'll go pick him up now." It's about around two-ish, and finished my shopping, went to pick him up. So I sat down with him and had a beer. And beer is in front of me and there were quite a few Indian ladies there and quite a few of our people there. So I had a beer and – these were tiny little glasses at that time, really small. They were ten cents a glass for beer. And so I sat down and had a beer. And three o'clock came, the signal goes off, you know: "Time to leave" and "You gotta go now." I always remember this one lady. Yeah, 'cause this happened on more than one occasion that I saw. She was always really watchful. I guess she was the watchdog of the pub there, and watchin', make sure that all these Indian women left the bar at three o'clock! So anyway, I sat there, 'cause they said, "Okay" – and they'd announce this – "Indian women have to leave!" So I just sat there, and I guess I was just feeling rebellious and just sat there. Sitting with my husband and his friends. I wasn't going to move. I just let them come over and ask me to move. We're supposed to know, just by looking at that time, that's what our limit is. And I seen this woman get up and she went over to the bar, and she was just standing there, looking and counting, making sure everybody's out, like she was the boss in the bar. Like, she was just a old bar rag, as far as I was concerned. She goes over, and she's pointing right at me, telling the bartender, you know, "There's one more Indian woman left over there," you know, "We'd better tell her to leave. It's after three!" The bartender did not come up to me, but that was enough. I just – it just leaves such a bitter taste in your mouth, to be singled out and, "Get going!" So I never went. It was just too degrading to be asked to leave. That was the law! That was the law that was imposed. Yeah. But who wants to drink beer early in the day? Maybe you might have a beer at three o'clock in the afternoon if you're busy – you're workin' in the yard or you're sweatin' up a storm or whatever – you might enjoy a glass of beer. But you're not going to go there at eleven and drink till three o'clock and be asked to leave! That was the most *ridiculous* thing! That was *really awful*!*

---

* Elsie is referring here to the late 1950s and early 1960s. See also the "Additional Readings" at the end of this book.

IF YOU DIDN'T ADHERE to those laws and regulations, people were picked up. And the police had a right to pick them up and put them in jail. That little jailhouse in the townsite used to be always full of our people on the weekends. When they were – it was okay now for them to go to a pub, so you drink all you want there, the men did, and when you left there if you were staggering, you ended up in the jail. And it got to the point where it would be quite full and they even put women in there with the men. Yeah. So it was really bad that the police could come patrolling through the reserve several times a night. And if your lights are on, they come right to the door: "Why are your lights on?" In those days it wasn't even electricity. It was, like, a gas lamp or a coal-oil lantern. Come knock on the door, check what you're up to, why you're up that time of the night. So you can't be up late at night without causing the police to be suspicious. There was no street lights. There was nothing. So quite often people, when they started and if they wanted to party or socialize, cover the windows with heavy blanket and – so that the police don't come and check. A bunch of fugitives. *[laughs]* They'd come right in and look around. If there was any booze, they had the right to take any liquor that's around the house if there's any. Yeah. Woke up and the police were standing by the bed. We were both in bed, like, my husband and I were sleeping. And I don't know how he came in, if the door had been left unlocked, but there were two police officers with a flashlight shining in our face and wake up to that. It's quite startling. *[laughs]* I don't know what they were doing, if they were looking for someone else. I can't remember what their excuse was. Yeah. It's weird. So thank goodness it's not like that anymore. They had more right then, you know, never givin' people an opportunity to defend themselves. If you're found guilty, you're guilty – in their eyes, right?

Yeah, white people were not allowed to come onto the reserve. If you did, it had to be something important you were down there for. That you had some kind of business with some individual. If you were down there after five o'clock, the police would be chasing you outta there. That was the law. Dirt road at the time. Yeah. So there was one young fella that used to come and visit his cousin who lived on the reserve – my uncle was his cousin. And his mother married a man in the Wildwood area, and she was established there. She married this Italian fellow and he had children with her, but this man was from her former marriage. So that wasn't his son, but he watched over him and forbid him to go onto the reserve. If he didn't come back from visiting his grandmother on the reserve, he would phone the police and have the police go and track him down, because he's not allowed to be there. And quite often they used to – him and my uncle would talk about it and how he would get away when the police came lookin' for him. And the safest place that worked for him to hide was at the cemetery. Because the police would come with their big flashlights lookin' around for him, and people would be scared to hide him, so he used to hide on his own. And the safest place for him was up at the cemetery. He would lay flat on the ground and the police would go by with their flashlight, big flashlight. Yeah. He was like a *fugitive*! He can't go and visit his grandmother on reserve? His relatives? That's how *bad* it was. That's how *crazy* it was! It was *ridiculous*! Can't imagine who created these laws. Who made up these laws?

I never had a friend, a non-Native friend. I couldn't invite anyone to come to our home, because we were just totally different world. We were worlds apart. And if we went to town, it was to shop. There was one cafeteria in town, in the townsite just above the mill site there, that we would go, and there was a designated area for Native people. That's where you went and sat. You didn't sit with other people. You went and sat over there – it's in a delegated area for Indians. And then, going to the movies, that would've been in the later forties, mid-forties, that you couldn't sit with non-Native people. We'd walk to town to go see a movie, at the Patricia Theatre. And we didn't have cars then. I remember going to the movies with my grandparents, and I was just a little child, where I remember being packed on my uncle's shoulders and – we would go as a family. And walking home at night after the movies. There's a designated area for our people, which was upstairs at the balcony. And if that balcony was full, if it happened to be a good cowboy and Indians show, you know! We enjoyed that. Cowboys and Indians! *[laughs]* Our young guys were always the cowboys. Oh dear, that is the truth. That's a fact! *[laughs]* The young guys, the young boys, yeah. They were the cowboys. They'd say, "Yeah, go get 'em, cowboy! Kill 'em! Shoot 'em!" That's how naive we were! *[laughs]* Oh boy. But you know, we'd walk all the way there, which is what? About four miles. And sometimes we didn't get in – we'd walk back again. Walk home. But that section below, down in the main area. And there'd be lots of seats there. No! You weren't allowed to go there. So that was, you know, that history of discrimination and racism. So it was really difficult to – it was a difficult life, that you couldn't do anything. You didn't have the freedom to go to the movies and to go wherever, unless you're told. Unless you're given permission! "We've built the school now, your children can come here, but please don't dirty this building!" This just makes me so angry when I think of that. "And you can come to this theatre, but you sit upstairs. You can come to this restaurant, but you sit over there!" It's like we're dirty or we're – I don't know. We just didn't fit in.

THEY MOVED OUR CHILDREN over to town, to the Assumption School. That was where our children went up to grade six, I believe, seven. And then one day we were just told, "Your children are going to be going to school now at Assumption." We were *never, ever* consulted by the Department of Indian Affairs if we had a choice to go to another elementary school. We were never consulted, we were just told. We didn't even know. We weren't informed, "This building is going to be for your children." The building went up and when it was ready, our children were just automatically expected to go there. Because Indian Affairs had put some dollars into it, so that our children would go to that private school. Yeah. In Westview, at Assumption. So starting with Jeannie, she went to Assumption and all her younger siblings went there. And yeah, it was really like a shock for the younger children? To just be all bussed off one day. I sent my little five-year-old, Cathy, she was five years old at the time, thinking she was going to kindergarten. And then, end of the day she came home with a note: "There's no room for her at Assumption." You know, class was all filled. So, okay. So I went to James Thomson and enrolled her there. There was no problem. There were four other children of Cathy's age that did the same – their parents took them to James Thomson, and they were accepted there. So after about two weeks, I heard from the priest at that time. Came out to, um, questioned, "Why is your daughter going to James Thomson? Why is she going to public school?" I said, "Well, I was informed that Assumption's kindergarten was filled." "Oh. Well, I'll have to go back and talk –" you know, the priest over there, he was not happy because they felt that our children, being Catholic, should go to Assumption School. So he came back and he said, "There's room after all. You can send your little girl over there." But he said, "I need to give her a test first." And I said, "Oh well, she should be at home soon." I didn't know what kind of test he had to give her. So when Cathy walked in, he said, "Oh, come here, I wanna ask you these questions. Ask you this." He said, "How many fingers do I have here?" – holds out his hand – "How many fingers do I have here?" So she counted, "One, two, three, four, five," and then the other hand, counted to ten. "Oh! Well, you're pretty smart."

He was impressed, so, "I think we can get her in. We can get her into the school." So he went off, came back few days later. "Yeah, I talked to Father Collins and he said it's okay." He said something to the fact that Father Collins just assumed that a five-year-old Native child was not as smart as a non-Native child at five. I was so disturbed by that. I was so disturbed by that. I just did not appreciate that at all. So he tells me they'll take her and the other children that were now registered at James Thomson. So I told him, "She's doing really well. She's been there three weeks now, at the public school, and I'm not going to move her. I want her to stay there, she's doing well." Oh, he wasn't happy with that. He went back, talked to his superior. Talked to the boss. Oh. He came back and still tried to get her to go. I said, "No, I'm gonna leave her there." So she stayed on there, along with all her other little friends that she started with.

Then we started hearing things from Assumption – our children were not happy. There was a lot of racist remarks being made. Not only from my children was I hearing this, but from the other parents telling me that their children came home upset because of, "This is a brand-new building. We don't want it dirtied up. We don't want it messy. We don't want this place to be dirty like the reserve. You pick up after yourself!" and "Don't bounce that ball against the building! We don't want a dirty-looking building like you have on the reserve!" Just comments like that. And lining them up – all the Indian children, line up over here, and they would get a lecture. So that didn't sit well. I was really upset with that. I felt that was really, really harsh. So I wrote a letter. I wrote a letter to the archbishop of the day and complained about, "This should be a safe place for kids to go. It's Catholic church – Catholic school – and therefore it should be encompassing all children. I feel there's discrimination here. Racist remarks being made. Not only from my children do I hear this, I hear it from other people's children." So the archbishop forwarded my letter back to the pastor here in town, who was very upset by this letter. So he sent this younger priest out to talk to me: "Why did you write this letter? That's very, very damaging. That's very demeaning. This is a man of God. And you're writing these kinds of things about him?" He says, "We want to ask you to retract your letter. We would like you to write a letter to the bishop and make an apology, that you were misinformed or something to that effect." And I said, "I'm not going to do that." I said, "I've been told by my children. They're not lying. They're upset. And other parents have told me what's been going on with their children." So he came back to me again, askin' me again, would I write that letter. Because I've damaged this person's reputation. I said, "Well, I'll tell you what. I will call the parents and the children." I said, "We'll organize a meeting, and you and your supervisor come to this meeting. We'll all sit down and have a meeting." And I said, "We'll get to the bottom of this and see who's lying." And he said, "Well–" "At his convenience," I said to him. "We'll have a meeting at his convenience. Let me know when he can come. The parents are willing to get together on this." Well, he went away. Nothing came of it. He never came back. So I was not on good terms after that with that – back then.

And they've always been *really* good to my children at James Thomson. My grandchildren have gone there now, and they're treated well. Treated like any of the other children that are there. So that was really an unfortunate.circumstances, events around that time for my children, 'cause I felt they got a taste of discrimination. At that day and age! When I experienced that when I was growing up as a child, and nobody stood up for me – nobody stood up for us as children. We just had to accept: it's okay, it's the way life is. We were perceived to be different. We are Indians. We are not equal to the non-Indians. We learned that very young. We were segregated. No matter where we went, if we came into Powell River, you had to have a reason to go – a specific reason. You just didn't go walk around on the streets of Powell River! If you went to a restaurant – there was a restaurant in the townsite there down below the old Rodmay Hotel, and that was a cafeteria there. And there was one section designated just for Indian people. You didn't go and sit anywhere else but to that area. And that's when I was young. That was probably when I was thirteen, fourteen. And we just took it, you know? It was like, that was the law! So that was something I didn't want my children to have to face that – to live with something like that. You know, you eventually smarten up and say, "Okay, we don't need to be treated like that."

Cliff is my youngest – youngest son. And Cliff was always really smart as a child. He had his own mind. He had his own personality, and he always challenged things and he was not a passive child. Right from when he was in kindergarten, the day I brought him to school at James Thomson, started on that day that he rebelled. So he did well in school. He's really – he's quite smart. But in his marks he didn't do well because he always had his own way of doing things. His way. So he gets into high school, he gets to Brooks, and he figured he had all the answers to everything. So whenever the teacher asked

Paul family photo taken inside Elsie's current residence in Sliammon, on Elsie and William's twenty-sixth anniversary, 11 December 1976), five months prior to William's passing. *Standing, from left:* Glen, Cliff, Jeannie, Ann, Cathy, Walter. *Seated, from left:* Elsie, Bryce, William, Marlane. Photo courtesy of Elsie Paul.

a question, he's the first one to have his hand up: "I've got the answer to that." First they had him in the front row. They eventually moved him to the back of the class because the other kids are not getting a chance to put their hand up, 'cause Clifford wanted to be the one to answer all these questions. So they put him in the back, and he's still, just kept on doing that. He just – determined he knew everything. So one day I had a parent-teacher conference, and the teacher said there was a real problem: "Your son doesn't give the other kids a chance to answer. He wants to be the one to answer all the questions. Any question put out there, he knows it all." So he says, looks at me and he says, "Mrs. Paul," you know, "'cause most Indian children are not forward like that. They're really shy and they don't offer to speak or answer questions, but," he said, "your son is really different. Are you sure you didn't bring home the wrong baby out of the hospital?" he said to me. I think he meant it as a joke, but I didn't think it was funny at all. "Are you sure you brought home the right baby? 'Cause Indian children are not like that." *[laughs]* Oh dear. I think I was stunned. I was just stunned, and when I got home I was getting more angry and thinking, "How dare he ask that?" You know? How dare he? Even if just jokingly said. I don't think a teacher would ever ask that kind of a question today. You know, it's like – no. That's a no-no. His perception or his belief, or a predetermined mind of a teacher. What an Indian child is like compared to a non-Native child.

QUITE A FEW OF our kids at that time that finished grade eight in the school system went away for grade nine in a boarding school. Living with families. And so Sharon went to live with this family. And they were a nice family: they were good to her. She was seventeen when she was living there, sixteen, seventeen. And she met other kids through the school system and kids from Musqueam. Her best friend, girlfriend, was from Musqueam. And they had gone on a trip to Mission to visit other friends there this weekend and got into a car accident, so she was killed down there. She didn't come home for the holidays, it was a long-weekend holiday. Both her and her girlfriend were killed in that car accident. So that was really hard. It was really, really difficult. 'Cause we blamed each other for a long time after that, my husband and I. And I was blaming him, I – so angry: "It's all because of your drinking that our daughter didn't come home. She doesn't like to be around you when you're drinking." So we blamed each other and he would just tell me, just to "Leave me alone. I don't know why you're blaming me!" kind of thing. So that was a difficult period. It was terrible. And then I think it was two years later that I just finally kind of, I don't know, realized, "What am I doing? Why am I blaming him? He wasn't there. It was an accident." So I apologized to him and told him, "I'm sorry. Let's just leave it be." So I eventually found peace that way. Rather than being always angry and bitter about that accident. I'm sure he was hurting just as much as I was. And yeah, I thought – that's what people do sometimes, lash out and find someone to blame. And I've done that, been there. I done that. Yeah.

We were still in the old house then, our old house. And there used to be a trail that went through here – my grandparents' house was there. We never told him. Nobody thought to tell him or explain to him, because by then my grandfather had had a stroke and he was really sick in hospital for quite some time. He was kind of in a coma for a long time, you know, for several days – several weeks, maybe it was couple of weeks. He was in a real coma state. He was just, you know, right out of it. So it did something to him that he wasn't communicating after that with people. He couldn't talk. He would just look, and he was so deaf too. He was really deaf. So after that illness with him, his stroke – I don't know if it was a stroke, because he was okay, like, he didn't have any paralysis or anything. So anyway, we just took it he's deaf, he can't talk. So he wasn't really included in our conversations and that. So when Sharon died no one explained to him or told him about Sharon. And when we brought her home, we brought her to our house for the wake, to spend the night there. And we had a lot of people in the house and my granny was there and a lot of the relatives were there, were sitting at this wake. And he came. He walked through the door. He knew. It was the strangest thing. So he was quite aware of what was happening around him. He came in through the – and everybody just kind of gasped, you know like. And he died, um – that was in April, and he died in May, ending of May. His body was okay. I mean he was walking. It's just that he wasn't functioning, like, for instance he would get up at night and turn on the lights and strip his bed, then make his bed, get back into bed without turning the lights off. And my granny used to get really upset with him. And she'd have to get up and go turn off the light. And he would do this two, three times a night, where he would strip the bed, make the bed, get in bed. So I guess we all just thought, well, he's lost it, you know. He's not functioning. He doesn't understand anything. But he did. And he came through the door and went directly to the casket. And he stood there and spent time there. We were all shocked. We were so shocked. How did he get here? Who told him? How does he know? You know. Yeah. That was – *[emotional]*

Because he was so deaf, you know, that my granny would be kind of stomping around 'cause she was the boss of the house. She was the decision maker and he always went along with her orders. Whatever she wanted he would do without complaining, but I guess deep down he resented that she always bossed him around. And when he'd have a few drinks he'd come to me and says, "I'm ped up." He'd say, "I'm ped up. Ped up wit' the old woman," he'd say. He was fed up with that old woman. *[laughs]* And then, with her, she would complain. "I'm gonna leave the old man," she said. "I'm goin' to California." Oh, I don't think she knew where California was, but I guess she thought that sounded like a good place to go. How she was going to get there, I don't know. So they both had their minds going about, you know, they're disgruntled with each other over silly things. Because she's bossy, and because he's deaf and doesn't hear her and doesn't carry out her orders, so therefore she's annoyed at him and lets him know and he at the same time takes all this and – but it hurts, I guess, to be yelled at and ordered around. So he'd say, "I'm ped up," meaning he's fed up. But he couldn't say, "fed up." He'd say, "ped up." *[laughs]*

He was such a neat man. He was really organized and really – they had that opportunity to go down the States in their later years, to go pick berries for the summer. So I went down there the first time when I was probably about sixteen then, that summer, went down there to pick berries with them. Yeah. And they worked hard. I worked hard. We all worked hard. But long before we were leaving, he'd be boarding up the house. It's like, two, three days he's packing up, getting things stashed away, put away stuff, and 'cause nobody's gonna be home, so he would actually board up the house – he'd board the windows. And Granny Molly would be so annoyed: "Why is he doing that? We're not leaving for another day and it's dark in here, boarding up the windows." *[laughs]* Oh dear! And then we'd be only be there for – you know, it's not quite over yet, the strawberry picking. He didn't want to go any further than that. He would want to come home: "It's time to go home now." They'd be rushing to come back home, 'cause there's other things he wanted to be doing here. Five weeks in the strawberry fields was enough for him – time to go back home. He's quite determined to do that. He got into a very serious logging accident when he was – that must have been the first trip we went to the States to pick berries, just my granny and I, 'cause my grandfather was still handlogging yet. And I was much younger then. So that wasn't my first trip, when my grandfather used to come with us. We went once before that, and he stayed behind because he was handlogging. So as he felled this tree, I guess – and they used to work close to the beaches and that. Fall trees and they would slide it right into the ocean, and if they had to strip the bark so it's easier to slide the fallen timber into the ocean, that's what they did. So I can't remember who he was working with, but the sapling – something happened. And hit him right across the face – a big branch or something, yeah – and broke his jaw. He had a serious accident. So they got him into the hospital. We got message somehow. We came back home and went to see him in the hospital. He was in the hospital about a month. And his jaw was just broken. It was all wired together real crude, but he had just an opening for a straw, so that's all he was taking was fluids. Yeah, that was quite a serious accident with him. Yeah. And he was really hallucinating. He was saying that he was seeing people that are long gone and dead, and we thought he was gonna die for sure. He lost so much weight and medicine wasn't as good then and the care wasn't as good. Or technology wasn't as good. So it took him a while to recover and heal from his broken jaw. But we thought he was a goner at that time, 'cause he was seeing people around in the room. They're there visiting him – nobody's there.

That happens a lot when people are really ill. That's why I guess our people truly believe in the spirits of the people that have gone before, that they come back and they're there, especially if you're really, really sick. They appear in your room. And the doctor would say, "That's because of medication. They're hallucinating." Well, that's been happening a long, long time. Before the doctors. Before there was pain medicine. Before there was these drugs that make you hallucinate. And our people truly believe that, that the spirits will gather when a person is dying or close to death or seriously sick. The spirits are there in the room. And the old spiritual people, the people that had that power to see what other people can't see, and they'd actually recognize these spirits in the room, their ancestors, their dead relatives that have gone. And they're there. So to me, my belief is that is so true. That's why people bring cedar with them to the hospital or talk to the spirits: "Leave. Don't be here. Just go." And people that did, like, those prayers and that support to the family or person that's dying – there were always people that had that power to be able to see the spirits – would be there. And you heard about it a lot. You heard about it a lot. Yeah, it's so powerful. So they put cedar in there to protect, 'cause it's almost like they're there to take you away. And the relatives or whoever would be there to take care of that, to protect the patient. If they're in the hospital or if they're dying at home, which is what happened years ago with people dying at home. That the spirits are already gathered, they're there. That's so powerful. I've heard other First Nations talking about that as well. Same thing! I don't know these people. I don't know their history, but to hear them talk about these things, it's the same kind of experience. Yeah, so to me it's the truth. I can't argue that. And I don't think anybody should argue that. You know, I've witnessed it. I've seen it in times that our people – "Oh, so-and-so is sittin' over there." "Oh, my grandfather or my whoever is sittin' over there or came to see me today." Yeah, oh yeah. You kind of have to go along with it, 'cause they're so sick and dying. But these ancestors are already there to take them on their journey. I think that is so powerful. It's a good way. It's a good way for them to – you know they're going to a good place if their ancestors or their dead relatives are there. They've come to take him or her.

So I think that maybe that's the reason my grandfather knew what was going on with my daughter that passed away. He knew, he had that sense to know although he was deaf and not able to communicate with anyone. Yet he knew. And he died a month later. He wasn't healthy then, but he was still able to get around in the house. By that point he never really left the house. He was always pretty much in the house. But yet he had that strength and that energy to walk through the trail in the dark and come to my house. How did he know that Sharon passed away? 'Cause he was really close to my children. And maybe it's that spirit. Maybe Sharon's spirit went to him, you know, to say goodbye to him. How did he know? He was quite disabled by then because of his hearing problem and his lack of communication. There was no communication. And yet he came to the door, came to see her. I think it's the spirits that brought him. Maybe her spirit. Or someone invited him to come. So he knew. So I really believe that. How else does he know? Nobody really ever talked to him because he was so in his own world. Yeah. So he died a month after that and so he was already preparing to go on his own journey. It was already his time. So I think to me that's a message that just reaffirms my belief in the spirit world, that somebody came to tell – he got the message. Yeah. So. I believe that.

MY GRANDPARENTS HAD a long life together, those two. They did. They did. They had a long life together. They had many children together, many grandchildren. Yeah, many tragedies in their lives. They still stuck together. Yeah. Hardships, but to them it really wasn't hardships. They always managed. They – we were never really hungry, yet the meals we had were really plain. But that was good. It was okay. They always made lots of sɑplin – fried bread and oven bread. Always had jam. She used to always have a lot of jam. Yeah, every night the ritual was tea and bread and jam before bedtime. Before bedtime, oh, "tihaуɛ št gɑ, ho štəm ƛəč't." "We're going to have tea and we'll go to bed." That's the way it was with the old people. They always had to have that snack of tea and, you know, jam, bread.

Well, my grandmother had this really nice, fairly big-size stewing pot. I don't where she got it from. It was probably through her trading days. It was her favourite pot. She used it for making many things, from making deer meat stew or fish heads or anything like that. More like a huge casserole dish. You could either put in the oven or use it just on top of the stove. But gee, as long as I can remember, she had that pot for a long time. And I used to always admire it and really liked her pot. And one day I was in her kitchen and it was on the stove, and I said, "Granny Molly, I really like your pot." "Yeah," she said, "you've told me that before." "Yeah," I said, "I really like it." "Oh," she said, "you'll get it when I die. You'll take it when I die." "Oh, okay." Never thinking the next day she was going to die. Yeah, and that was fish season, right? Just smoking fish. And I don't know what she was boiling on that particular day. But it was on the cookstove – wood cooking stove was what she had – and it was sitting there simmering away. I said, "Yeah, sure. I'd love that pot." Just kind of jokingly said, "Oh sure. I can wait." So the next day I'm with her and she's doing her usual thing, checking the smokehouse and hanging up a few more fish. I think we only had about seven or nine fish to hang up that day. And she was checking what was in the smokehouse and kind of moving things around so that it's getting equal smoking time. And so I'm outside the smokehouse and next thing I heard this thud – she collapsed in the smokehouse. She had a massive heart attack. She died right on the spot. So that was a real tragedy. So I can't remember how soon after they took her away, and that pot was still at the back of the stove. So I took that pot right away, because my uncle used to always take things of Granny's and go and pawn them or whatever. Wasn't for his own use, but he used to really take advantage of Granny's stuff and Granny's generosity. So I took that pot. I put it away. And lo and behold! I don't know how much longer it was, maybe it was couple of weeks or three weeks later. And by then my uncle had taken a lot of her stuff from the house. But he knew the pot was gone. He realized the pot wasn't anywhere, and he was asking, "Where did that pot go?" Real gruff. And no one knew. I was the only one that knew that I had the pot. So I put it away. I didn't use it for the longest time. I just put it away. I had permission from my granny to take it, so that to me was okay. I did not feel guilty, not one bit guilty about that pot to be in my possession. So now I'm the holder of the pot. *The* pot, as my daughters would say. So my daughters are now debating about the pot. Yeah. "Who's gonna get the pot?" Yeah, they're jokingly kidding each other about the pot. They're all of the same mind. *[laughs]* And Jeannie says, "I'm the oldest. I get the pot." And Marlane pipes up and she's, "I'm the youngest, I get the pot." And Ann pipes up and she says, "I'm the best cook. I get the pot." Leave Cathy out of this. She doesn't know how to cook anyway! Cathy said, "Well, I don't know what'll happen to the pot. Maybe you will have to pull straws. Or maybe you'll just have to learn to share it. You can borrow it off from each other." And I think that's one way to settle it: you all have access to the pot. Since they all live here in the community anyway. But that's a special pot. It makes the best stew. And it's not real heavy cast iron. It's a little lighter. I guess it's more like aluminum, but heavy, heavy aluminum. And it's just the right size for big family meals. So that's the story of that pot. He died in June. And she died on November the eleventh, 'cause it was on Remembrance Day. So I always remember the anniversary of her death was on Remembrance Day. It's hard to forget that. Yeah.

Sliammon Narrative

qʷʋl č'ɛ tawθɛm kʷut tamʌs
(They [Spirits] Just Came and Told You Something)*

[ʔʎ́xti:stomayɛ̀ʔmoɬ sx̣ʷóx̣ʷoɬ]

ʔəx̣tiy-stu-may-am'-uɬ	sx̣ʷux̣ʷuɬ
similar-CAU-1SG.OBJ-PASS-PAST	long.time.ago
similar.thing.happened.to.me	long.time.ago

'It happened to me a long time ago.'

[na: hɛ́ɬʔʌnaʔa qɛ́qtɛ̀ tᵊmáʔnaʔoɬ na:]

naʔa	hiɬ	ʔə‿naʔa	qiqtiʔ	tᵊ‿man'a-ʔuɬ	naʔa
FILLER	it's	CLF‿FILLER	youngest.child	1SG.POSS‿child-PAST	FILLER
(umm)	it.is	(umm)	youngest.child	my.deceased.child	(umm)

'It was, uh ... my youngest child.'

[hɛ́ɬʔʌxʷ čɛ́ɬayɛs tᵊtígixʷʌɬ]

hiɬ	ʔə‿xʷ‿čaɬ-aya-s	tᵊ‿təgixʷaɬ
it's	CLF‿NOM‿three-person-3POSS	1SG.POSS‿children
it.is	when.there.are.three.people	my‿children

'I had three children at the time.'

[qʷʋ́lčɩn ʔʎ́xti:]

qʷəl‿čən	ʔəx̣tiy
come‿1SG.INDC.SBJ	similar
come‿I	similar

'The same thing happened to me.'†

---

* This text is an excerpt from a much longer recording of a conversation between Elsie and the late Mary George, recorded on 1 September 1997. Mrs. George's responses to Elsie, which were almost entirely interjections like "hmm," have been removed from this version.

† Here, Elsie is referring to a story that Mary George recounted prior to this excerpt. In her story, she heard the sound of a woman crying and walking around in high heels, and then subsequently lost one of her children to illness.

[čʼíˑyʋxʷč kʷšínʼ táʔʌ θíːčʌmtɛˑgʌns tᵊʔaˑyɛ́ʔoɬgʌ táʔʌ]

čʼiy-əxʷ ˍč		kʷ ˍ šinʼ	taʔa	θičim-tigan-s
hear-NTR ˍ1SG.INDC.SBJ		DET ˍDEM	DEM	back.woods-side-3POSS
heard.it ˍI		that	there	bush.on.its.side

tᵊ ˍ ʔayaʔ-uɬ ˍga		taʔa
1SG.POSS ˍhouse -PAST ˍMTG		DEM
my ˍformer.house		there

'I heard something come from over there right behind my house'

[sχʷóχʷoɬ]

sχʷux̣ʷuɬ
long.time.ago
a.long.time.ago
'a long time ago.'

[títoːlmot čúyʼ qʷayɪn naʔa kʷunʌs <<three month old>>]

titul-mut	čuyʼ	qʷayin	naʔa	kʷən-as	<<three	month	old>>
little-very	child	think	FILLER	INTRR-3CNJ.SBJ	<<three	month	old>>
very.little	child	I.think	(umm)	whether.it.is	three	month	old

'A very tiny baby. It must have been three months old.'

[ʔiˑ hóštgʌ táʔačiˑšʋ̀ɬ]

ʔiy	hu ˍšt ˍga		taʔačiš-uɬ
and	go ˍ1PL.INDC.SBJ ˍMTG		travel-PAST
and	go ˍwe		travelled

'We were on a trip.'

[hóˑhoˑguɬšt kʷáʔa pʼʌ́ƛ̓əm na: ƛʼáˑɬawʋm]

hu-h-ug-uɬ ˍšt		kʷaʔa	pʼəƛ̓-əm	naʔa	ƛʼaɬawəm
go-EPEN-PL-PAST ˍ1PL.INDC.SBJ		DEM	pick.fruit-MDL	FILLER	berries
plural.people.went ˍwe		there	to.pick.fruit	(umm)	berries

'We went picking berries.'

[héwtəmgʌ šɪms θóːʔ kʷšínʼ ʔiˑnám' kʷšínʼ (haːː)]

hiwtəm ˍga	šə ˍ ms ˍθu		ʔ ˍ kʷ ˍ šin'	ʔiy	nam'	kʷ ˍ šin'
before ˍMTG	DET ˍ1PL.POSS ˍgo		OBL ˍDET ˍDEM	and	similar	DET ˍDEM
before	our ˍgo		there	and	like	that

'Right before we went there, it was about this time of year.'

[qʷáyɪn nɛ́ʔ kʷna: č'ɛč'ʎχ kʷna: t'έʔɛnὲqʷ]

qʷayin	niʔ	kʷ‿naʔa	č'a‿č'əx̣	kʷ‿naʔa	t'in'iqʷ
think	be.there	DET‿FILLER	CJR ripe	DET‿FILLER	salmonberry
I.think	there.is	(umm)	probably‿ripe	(umm)	salmonberry

'I think it was about the time salmonberries ripen.'

[č'íč'χ qʷʊ̀l' kʷ t'έʔɛnὲqʷ]

č'ə-č'x̣		qʷəl'	kʷ‿t'in'iqʷ
IMPF-cook/ripe		come	DET‿salmonberry
they.are.getting.ripe		come	a‿salmonberry

'And the salmonberries are getting ripe now.'

[ʔíːmot t'ᶿók'ʷ nám' kʷšín']

ʔəy-mut	t'ᶿuk'ʷ	nam'	kʷ‿šin'
good-very	day	similar	DET‿DEM
it.is.good	day	like	that

'It was a fine day like today.'

[hʎhkʷaʔɪːt'ᶿʎč nɛ́ʔkʷ ʔásq']

ha-hkʷ-ay'-it'ᶿa‿č		ni?	kʷ‿ʔasq'
IMPF-hang-LIG-clothes‿1SG.INDC.SBJ		be.there	DET‿outside
hanging.clothes‿I		be.there	outside

'I was hanging clothes outside.'

[hɛːːw ǰaqa k'ʷáːq'ɛ́t kʷ čúy']

hiw	ǰaqa	k'ʷaq'<i>t	kʷ‿čuy'
very	AUX	cry<STV>	DET‿child
very		crying	a‿child

'Then, all of a sudden, a baby was crying.'

[č'íʸyʊx̣ʷč kʷ tíːːtol' čúy']

č'iy-əxʷ‿č		kʷ‿titul'	čuy'
hear-NTR‿1SG.INDC.SBJ		DET‿little	child
heard.it‿I		a‿little	child

'I heard a tiny baby crying,'

[k'ʷáːq'ɛ̀t nám' kʷ čɛ́ʔt ʔɛ́ʸʔaˑnàʔ čúy']

k'ʷaq'<i>t	nam'	kʷ‿čaʔat	ʔiʔanaʔ	čuj'
cry<STV>	similar	DET‿now	be.born	child
it.is.crying	similar	now	newly.born	child

'like a newborn baby crying.'

[kʷá:q'ɛ̀:t χʌ́χyɛ̀ hɛ́ tə ʔáyʔi:gə̀n ʔʌxʷ nɛ́ʔs táʔʌ č'í·yi·tʌn]

kʷaq'<i>t	χəχya	hi	tə ʔayʔiygən	ʔə xʷ niʔ-s	taʔa
cry<STV>	strange	it's	DET bush	CLF NOM be.there-3POSS	DEM
it.is.crying	strange	it.is	a bush	where.it.is	there

č'iy-i-t-an
hear-STV-CTR-1SG.ERG
that.I.heard.it

'It was crying and it was weird; I heard it coming from *the bush*.'

[hoy hóč na: χʌ́χyɛ gʌ tᵉ... nám'č'ot kʷqʷúl' háwegənθot ʔa·ǰú]

huy	hu č	naʔa	χəχya ga
then	go 1SG.INDC.SBJ	FILLER	strange MTG
then	go I	(umm)	it.is.strange

tᵉ ... nam' č ʔut	kʷ qʷəl'	hawigən-θut ʔaǰu
1SG.POSS ... similar 1SG. INDC.SBJ CLT	DET come	fool-CTR+RFL CLT
it.is.like I	come	be.confused

'I was going to ... it is funny why I ... it is as if I became confused.'

[hɛ́ tᵉ xʷáʔnópotən xʷʌ́čɛm nɛ́ʔ tʌ́n' kʷčúy' ʔáyʔi·gən nɛ́ʔ na: q'áq'ʎ'ʌm táʔʌ]

hi	tᵉ xʷaʔ	nup-u-t-an	xʷaʔ	čəm'-as
it's	1SG.POSS NEG	think-LV-CTR-1SG.CNJ.SBJ	NEG	why-3CNJ.SBJ
it.is.why	my not	I.would.think.of.it	not	

niʔ	tan'	kʷ čuǰ'	ʔayʔiygən	niʔ	naʔa	q'aq'ʎ'əm	taʔa
be.there	DEM	DET child	bush	be.there	FILLER	thick.bush	DEM
it.is.there	there	a child	be.in.bush	it.is.there	(umm)	thick.bush	there

'That is why it did not occur to me that there could not have been a child in the bush ... in the thick bush over there.'

[hó::č ʔi·na· hóč gʌ́ygiyɪt nam' táʔʌ]

hu č	ʔiy	naʔa	hu č	gay-giy-i-t
go 1SG.INDC.SBJ	and	FILLER	go 1SG.INDC.SBJ	PL-take.a.look-LV-CTR
go I	and	(umm)	go I	look.around

nam'	taʔa
similar	DEM
it.is.like	there

'I went and looked around there.'

[kʷtáyqa:θòt θo:kʷaʔʌʔaˑjʉ kʷnám' kʷáʔʌ]

kʷ‿tayq-a-θut	θu	kʷaʔa	ʔaju	kʷ‿nam'	kʷaʔa
DET‿move-LV-CTR+RFL	go	DEM‿CLT	DEM	DET‿similar	DEM
it.moves	go	there		like	there

'But the crying had moved to over there.'

[hɛ́ kʷšín' xʷ hósqǰí k'ʷá:q'ɛ̀t kʷčúy']

hi	kʷ‿šin'	ʔə‿xʷ‿hu-s‿qǰi		k'ʷaq'<i>t	kʷ‿čuy'
it's	DET‿DEM	CLF‿NOM‿go-3POSS‿again		cry<STV>	DET‿child
it.is	there	where.it.goes.again		it.is.crying	a‿child

'That is where the crying moved to ... the baby was crying.'

[ná:mmotʔot ʔʌ kʷčúy' ʔi: kʷiˑtθó:kʷi t'óˑsos]

nam-mut‿ʔut	ʔə‿kʷ‿čuy'	ʔiy	kʷit‿θu‿kʷi	t'us-us
similar-very‿CLT	OBL‿DET‿child	and	CLT‿go‿CLT	quiet-INC
it.is.very.similar	a‿child	and	go	become.quiet

'It was just like a real baby, and then it went silent.'

[tátʌwčgʌ tᶿnaː číˑčiˑyɛ̀ʔoɬ <<after>>]

ta-taw-t‿č‿ga		tᶿ‿naʔa	čičiyaʔ-uɬ
IMPF-tell-CTR‿1SG.INDC.SBJ‿MTG		1SG.POSS‿FILLER	grandmother-PAST
telling.her‿I		my‿(umm)	deceased.grandmother

<<after>>
<<after>>
afterwards

'Then I told my grandmother afterwards.'

[χʌ́χyɛmotɛw č'íːxʷʌn čúy' k'ʷá:q'ɛ̀t nɛ́ʔ kʷʔáyʔìˑgən nɛ́č]

xəχya-mut	hihiw	č'iy-əxʷ-an	čuy'	k'ʷaq'<i>t	niʔ
strange-very	very	hear-NTR-1SG.ERG	child	cry<STV>	be.there
it.is.very.strange	very	I.heard.it	child	crying	it.is.there

kʷ‿ʔayʔiygən	niʔ-i-t‿č
DET‿bush	say-LV-CTR‿1SG.INDC.SBJ
in.a‿bush	say‿I

'"I heard something really strange, a baby crying in the bush," I said.'

[hɛ́hɛw ɬʌ́χmothɛ́hɛw nɛ́:tʌs]

hihiw	ɬəχ-mut	hihiw	niʔ-i-t-as
very	bad-very	very	say-LV-CTR-3ERG
very	it.is.very.bad	very	she.said.it

'She said, "That is really bad.'

[k'ʷúnɛčxʷ θčí·čùy' k'ʷúnɛčxʷ θtígixʷʌɬ ná:θʌs]

k'ʷən-i-t ˍčxʷ	θ ˍčəy-čuy'	k'ʷən-i-t ˍčxʷ
see-STV-CTR ˍ2SG.INDC.SBJ	2SG.POSS ˍPL-child	see-STV-CTR ˍ2SG.INDC.SBJ
seeing.them ˍyou	your ˍchildren	seeing.them ˍyou

θ ˍtəgixʷaɬ	na-θ-as
2SG.POSS ˍchildren	say-CTR+1SG.OBJ-3ERG
your ˍchildren	she.said.to.me

'Watch your children. Watch all your children," she said to me.'

[čέʔma·sʌm kʷyέʔθots kʷšín']

čam'-as ˍsəm	kʷ ˍya?-θut-s	kʷ ˍšin'
why-3CNJ.SBJ ˍFUT	DET ˍdo-CTR+RFL-3POSS	DET ˍDEM
how.it.will.be	that.it.does	that

'"Something will happen to someone.'

[qʷúlč'ɛ táwθɛmkʷut tá·mʌs]

qʷəl ˍč'a	taw-θi-m ˍkʷut	tam-as
come ˍCJR	tell-CTR+2SG.OBJ-PASS ˍCLT	what-3CNJ.SBJ
they.probably.came	you.are.told	something

'They (spirits) just came and told you something."'

[gʌna·xʷmòt'ot hó:št tʌs kʷáʔʌ níʔji ʔʌms hó·naʔʌ šɛn' ƛ'óqʷowɩ hóšt p'ʌƛʌmò·wuɬ kʷáʔʌ ƛ'á·ɬawʊm]

gənaxʷ-mut ˍʔut	hu ˍšt	təs	kʷaʔa	niʔi	ʔəms ˍhu	naʔa
true-very ˍCLT	go ˍ1PL.INDC.SBJ	reach	DEM	far	1PL.POSS ˍgo	FILLER
it.is.very.true	go ˍwe	reach	there	far	where.we.go	(umm)

šan'	ƛ'əqʷuwi	hu ˍšt	p'əƛ-əm-uw-uɬ	kʷaʔa	ƛ'aɬawəm
DEM	summer	go ˍ1PL.INDC.SBJ	pick.fruit-MDL-PL-PAST	DEM	berries
there	summer	go ˍwe	plural.people.pick.fruit	there	berries

'It was really true. We reached our faraway destination, that is where we umm ... that summer, we went to pick berries.'

[ʔi·nɛʔ qéy' kʷšín' šɩtθ naʔa mémnàʔoɬ]

ʔiy	ni?	qəy'	kʷ ˍšin'	š ˍtθ ˍnaʔa	mi-mna-ʔuɬ
and	be.there	die	DET ˍDEM	DET ˍ1SG.POSS ˍFILLER	DIM-child-PAST
and	it.is.there	she.dies	that	my ˍ(umm)	deceased.small.child

'And my baby died there.'

[héyɛkʷa kʷut xʷ qʷúl's na:]

hiy ˏa ˏkʷa ˏkʷut	ʔə ˏxʷ ˏqʷəl'-s	naʔa
it's ˏQN ˏQUOT ˏCLT	CLF ˏNOM ˏcome-3POSS	FILLER
it.is	why.they.come	(umm)

'That is why, you see, they seem to ...'

[qʷúl' nám' kʷa táwθì:yʌm]

qʷəl'	nam'	kʷa	taw-θay-əm
come	similar	ˏCLT	tell-CTR+1SG.OBJ-PASS
come	like		I.am.told

'have come and told me.'

[hɛ́čgʌ q'áʔiˑ hɛwč q'áꞏimot hɛw gʌ́naꞏxʷakʷùt]

hi ˏč ˏga		q'ay'	hiw ˏč	q'ay-mut	hiw
it's ˏ1SG.INDC.SBJ ˏMTG		believe	very ˏ1SG.INDC.SBJ	believe-very	very
it.is ˏI		believe	very.much ˏI	really.believe	very.much

gənaxʷ ˏa ˏkʷut
true ˏQN ˏCLT
it.is.true

'I believed. I really believed it was true.'

[gʌ ʔʌ́xtaystòmɛt qʷúl']

ga ˏʔəxtay-stu-mi-(i)t	qʷəl'
if ˏsimilar-CAU-2SG.OBJ-SBR.PASS	come
if ˏthey.do.something.similar.to.you	come

'If they come and do that to you,'

[qʷáyɪn xʷaʔ q'áq'aymɛtìt kʷǰɛ́ʔʌm]

qʷayin	xʷaʔ	q'a-q'ay-mi-t-it	kʷ ˏǰaʔəm
think	NEG	RDPL-believe-RLT-CTR-SBR.PASS	DET ˏsome
I.think	not	it.is.believed	by.some.people

' ... well ... I do not think some people believe in them (spirits of this sort).'

[ʔi: gʌ́naxʷ hɛw gʌ́naːxʷmot]

ʔiy	gənaxʷ	hihiw	gənaxʷ-mut
and	true	very	true-very
and	it.is.true	very	it.is.very.true

'But it is true. It is really true.'

7

Teachings on Grief

I t's really important to acknowledge grief when we go through our many losses, and how to look after yourself and how to look after your family during a time of grief. Realizing that at the time of grief, at the time of loss – in particular your parents, when you've just lost your parents, one or the other or both, or your spouse. There's this – what is truly believed in by the ancestors, my great-grandparents and part of the practice – how to look after yourself at that particular time of loss, that you have very strong medicine powers. It's almost like a gift. You've lost someone, but you have this gift of healing that you could use in a good way, or it could be negative. But I always focus on the good, and advise people, remind them, "This is a time that's very powerful for you. You've just lost this person very close to you. It's a time for self-discipline. It's a time to take care of yourself. Be kind to yourself, be good to yourself." And if there's certain areas that you want to change in your life for the better, then that's the time to do it. It's a time to analyze your life and say, "Where do I go from here?" My grandmother used to say, "You are in this fork in your life. You're either going to go left or you're gonna go right. That's your choice to make. If you choose to go right, then that's the right way to go. It's gonna be hard work. It's gonna be tough. It's always easier to go left. Because you don't have to make any decisions. You don't have to work hard at it. You just allow your grief to take you. But if you choose the right road, and you struggle, you will struggle to make things work for you and for your children. It's going to be worthwhile. If you fall, you get up and you continue on. But if you had taken that left road, all you're gonna do is you're going to fall into – going to lay there and it'll be hard to ever come back from the road." And the belief is that you do this for a whole year, one year of self-discipline. If you have bad habits, you give up those bad habits, any kind of bad habits that you have. You were kept away from the community if you allow that to happen, to have your Elders help you. They advised you that you don't be out there and be visible. Sure, you're in mourning, but you're quietly in mourning. You're helpin' yourself. You're helpin' your family. You're careful about your activities. That you're not seen to be out there, I guess, being careless about your ways, your words. Be respectful how you talk to people, because your words are very powerful at that time that you've lost someone close to you. Your words can hurt people, so be very careful what you say. You control yourself. Control your temper, if you have a bad temper. You work. You work hard. Making sure that you're busy and that you don't become lazy and just lay around. So there's a lot of important teachin's around that, about self-discipline when you've lost someone. So it all ties in with that other grief I was talkin' about with cleansing every morning, askin' for guidance, askin' for direction, asking for the strength and energy, asking for your loved ones to help you – ask *them* to help you. So that all ties in together, that respect that you have for the teachin's. And you listen – you listened – you listen to your Elders that advised you at that particular time.

I was forty-four. Well, it was a very lonely time for me. It was quite sudden. And I felt I had to pretty much withdraw from activities that we shared together. Because our activities were around other couples. And we were going out to party here or, you know, just gatherings. I felt very odd and fifth wheel. I just didn't fit in. Because being alone and you're with couples, it just didn't sit right with me. So I just didn't go there. I pretty much isolated myself. But I kept working. I had a job then, as a social worker for the community, so that's pretty much what I did. I just went to work. I only took two weeks off when my husband died, and then I went back to work. So I went to work and back home and looked after my kids and back to work and that was pretty much it. Yeah, it was not an easy time. But there were certain things in my life that I felt that I changed. I wanted to change, re-membering my grandmother's teachin's. Sacrificin' my friends. So I just did not miss only my husband, but I missed the friends that we used to associate with. Because I just didn't fit into that anymore, to the outside activities outside of my family. So my focus was on my children, my immediate family. And I'm not sorry for that. It turned out okay. Yeah. It was important to do that for me. I think otherwise I would've, you know, if I didn't have that in the back of my mind, that you need to discipline yourself after a loss, 'specially your dad, your mother, or your spouse. It's a very powerful time. I guess that would apply to just about anything in life. When you decide, "I'll be strong, I'm going to do this," and you do it. It may mean sacrifices, but you're gonna do it. Yeah. It works. Worked for me!

So people were always guided by the Elders. Always guided by the Elders, that you – "You must not do that. This is what you do, you look after yourself." So it's a time to empower yourself. And your Elders made sure you did that, because if you didn't look after yourself, then grief is very powerful. It can destroy you. You can go so deep in grief to a dark place that you're not able to get up and walk. It can destroy you if you give in to your grief and cry and stay down. Crawl under your bed and cover your head, 'cause you don't want to face the world. You've lost someone. There's a lot of things to remember about that. You don't only consider yourself and your well-being when you're going through a grieving process. Or you've just lost – maybe your child, maybe your parents – someone close to you. If you allow yourself to grieve and cry and weep and never, ever see a good side or look for – "I've lost this child, it's gone to a good place, this child is an angel now, it's gone to join the ancestors." You have to look at that side. The ancestors have – or my brother or my sister or my parent, whoever that was – the ancestors are on the other side. They're in the spirit world. So when you lose someone, someone very close to you has died, which we all will someday, that's what we have to tell ourselves: "One day I will go there to that other place where all my ancestors are. And I trust that they will meet me and greet me." So that's where you have to put your faith in. That my loved one has gone to be with the other family that's on the other side. And take comfort in that. And that's how you start to look after yourself. If you don't do that and you hang on to your grief and cry and cry and always cry, the spirit of your loved one is never going to be able to go on its journey to the other side, because they now see you as grieving and they are going to be concerned. Because they're always around. The spirits of your loved ones are always gonna be around. And if they see you grieving and cryin' and you neglect the rest of your family – you could neglect the rest of your children, if it was your child that died – you have to go on living for the living. So you have to allow your loved one that's left to go and join the other family on the other side. So that's number one. That's so important! That's why we do a lot of brushing and cleansing around the time of the funeral. We have to allow that person to go. Before the burial, you say your final good-bye, and you say, "Go. Just go and be with your ancestors. I allow you to go. I'm okay. You go." So you're giving them their freedom as well to go. They'll go in a good way. And you're allowing yourself too to release that. So after the person has gone and you continue to look after yourself. If it's a time you want self-discipline, it's a time you need to do that. It's time to take care of that. Want to change your habits. If you've been eating too much, you want to stop that. You do a fasting. You discipline yourself to eat very little. And you do not face your children when you're eating. You face away from your children, because that's how powerful it was to the old people that as a widow or widower or someone that's lost a very close connection, you face away when you're eating, 'cause you're saying you've got so much power that you could be taking on the life of another person you're facing when you're eating. So I saw it when I was growing up, a lot of the old-timers, they would just face away and eat. That's how much they believed in that power at the time of loss and grief. Just things like that. That's just one of the things. And to brush yourself every morning, you know, 'cause you're not going to forget overnight that you've just lost someone. You're always going to be missing that person you've lost. There's always going to be an empty space in the house, or around the table. So you take care of that. It's always gonna be there. It's always gonna be hurting. It'll take time, you know, gradually get over it. But you'll never forget. But the first year is so critical. The first two years is critical. You're not gonna get over it in a month or two months. You're gonna remember that person, especially at the different seasons: "Now it's summer, oh ..." It's really hard. It hits you hard. "It's winter now and snow on the ground." All these things – just reminders. And it's painful reminders that your loved one is out there, out in the cold. Or they're somewhere where – just the things you used to do in the summer, it's all going to flash back to you. So that's when the tears come. So after the tears, you have to go wash your face, brush yourself, take care of – say, "It's okay, they're gone. I know they're in a good place." So you're constantly reminding yourself. You are constantly doing the discipline: "I'm not gonna be a glutton. I'm not gonna eat all this, and 'cause it looks good," and you become overweight or, you know. So it's a real discipline program. It's almost like a program you see today. People go on diets or whatever program to go into. But they keep falling off. But that was the time it was used, for people that wanted to give up any kind of bad habits. If you were a gossip or you were angry all the time, "Control that! You're not gonna be angry, you're gonna think before you open your mouth." Just so many different bad habits. You've got a long list, and you were advised, "You take care of that." So that good medicine is the cedar boughs that was used. Always cleansing. And I think I told this before about my grandmother's way, and how she would always go out early, early morning, and wash her face. She didn't go to the river or – sometimes cedar wasn't always available, but she used the water. The water was very powerful as well. Very, very powerful. It's cleansing and it takes away whatever you need to get rid of. The negative energy. So that's really important, that self-care is so important to let go, to remember that your loved one is gone to a good place. It's fine to grieve. Acknowledge that. But pick yourself up – keep going. There's so many different teachings around that, to respect that.

Because of that power you carry, that powerful medicine you carry, other people that know you and you've just become a widow or you've just lost someone – especially the parents, like, your mother, your father, or your spouse. There was, like, the three, actually, is the most powerful. And you would go, "Oh, so-and-so has the power. I really need to go and be taken care of." So you go – it's like going to a doctor. You go there and they will cleanse you and ask the ancestors to look after you and take care of you and brush you and put their hand on your head and your heart and – you know. And it just gives you that lift that gives you that will to live and to come away from your ailments, whatever that may be, if it's depression or you're emotionally upset all the time about something and it's dragging you down. Or it could be some people even with, I guess, maybe arthritis or aches and pains or whatever. And a lot of people go through heartache and broken heart. Whether it be broken relationships or whatever it may be, and you're grieving over those things. And you go to this person that's got the power to help you. And that person will help you in that way to talk to you and to give you that cleansing. And that was used in that way. Yeah. And I think a lot of it is you believe in it. If you go and expect that person to take it away from you, you got to co-operate. You have to co-operate. You have to be willing, 'cause nobody's going to help you if you're not willing to help yourself. It's like you could lead a horse to water but you can't make him drink, right? So that's that kind of mentality. You have to have that desire. And people knew how powerful that was, and they used it. And a lot of that is getting lost. And it's so important to remember that. You could use whatever is available today.

You know, myself, even though I remember all those teachings, sometimes I start to backslide and I start to feel sorry for myself and, "Oh, I'm getting old, I'm getting so old. You just can't do this anymore. I can't do that anymore." And that kind of gets you down. Kinda eats away at you. And if you allow it – if I allow that, I'm gonna sit here on my pity pot and, "Nobody ever comes to visit me and nobody ever does this for me and nobody ever –" and I tell myself, "Smarten up!" And I have this book, it's a daily meditation book. I will pick it up most every day, especially if I feel I need a boost, and I turn it to that page – "Oh, today is July the fifteenth, or July the sixteenth" – turn to that page, and lo and behold! There's always a message there that reminds me it's okay. I'm not going to worry about tomorrow – it's not here yet. I'm not going to worry about yesterday – that's gone. I'm here for today. And that's what's really important. I'm here and my children, my grandchildren might just drop in, and that's a gift. And a friend may phone me, and that's a gift. So I have to take each gift for that day as it comes. And if it doesn't come, I know it will be okay. So there's people that are in worse situations than I am. Maybe they're not able to walk. Maybe they're not able to feed themselves. So you have to think of all those other things in your life, instead of feeling sorry and "Oh, I got my knee problems and I can't walk that far," complaining or thinking about all the negative things. Think about other people that are worse off than you and where they are in life. Because they have got physical disabilities or, you know – it's important to think of those things too. Not just people with addictions or other traumas in their life, but physical disabilities that other people have. And to think about them and appreciate your own health. Appreciate what you're able to do. With your limited capacity, if you're gettin' limited capacity. So to me that's really important. Those are my reminders. I must remind myself every day to appreciate what I have, 'cause other people may not have that. Other people may be homeless. They may not have enough to eat today. What am I complaining about? I've got food in the house. I've got a family. I've got a roof over my head. And I should be thankful for that, and not to worry about what I don't have. So to me those are really valuable lessons for myself. I need to remind myself, I'm only human. And I tend to backslide sometimes, and I think, "Oh gee, I wish this, wish that." Well, it's fine to wish for things, but you don't always get your wishes. It'll come to you when it's ready. So I feel discipline is so important in one's life. Not only at the time of your loss, your immediate loss, or unexpectedly you will lose someone. It's always going to be a shock. Use the good medicine that the Creator gave you, that's around you: the very air you breathe, the water, the cedar, and all the teachings that come with that. Those are important.

The belief is that we are one with the animal kingdom. That we are one in spirit! And that's very, very strong – very, very important. They are living things, as we are. And so we are one with all the living beings, living things. So that's how people were so connected to the land, to the animal kingdom. People were very pure – very, very close to nature. Whenever a person, whether it be a young woman – especially the young men, when they reached puberty, they were sent on a quest, a vision quest, to go and bathe in the river, to go and bathe every morning in the river, get up before everyone else is up. That is *so* important. You go and bathe in the river, whether it was winter – summer and winter. Yeah. So that was really important. It's like a purification. And while you're there, doing your cleansing with cedar boughs and dippin' it into the water and just brushin' yourself, because again, there's so much good energy from the cedar boughs – that's a living thing – a living thing, it's cleansing. So when you're in the river, you're using that and brushin' yourself, like, "Help me today. Help me to be able to do the things I need to do. Help me to be productive today. Guide me today." Those are the words that are what is said in this morning ritual. And when you're finished brushin', then you either leave your bundles by the river, tie them up and leave them there – you hang them on the tree – or you can toss them in the river. So that way it drifts away. It's washed away. So that's all your laziness being washed down the river, all your ailments or whatever may be with you that you're carrying, all goes away from you. You are refreshed. And then you go on with your day. The ritual is called "sohoθot." "sohoθot" – it's what it's called in itself. You get up, your – whomever, your parents would say, "hoč sohoθot." "Go and do your cleansing!" That's it in a nutshell. That's what you're supposed to do. Because that's what the men in the family do. They go in the river and do that every morning. And it was an embarrassment if you didn't do that. If you are lazy, that was an embarrassment. If you were sleeping in, that was not a good image of you to your community. You're embarrassin' your family. So you need to uphold yourself. You need to uphold your family name. Otherwise people will talk, and ridicule your family because there's a lazy young man in the family. So those are the things that's really important in one's life. Especially the beginning of life. Going into manhood from a young boy, teen. It's puberty. And you gotta do *all* of these things now, to prove yourself – that you're trained to be strong, to do things that's tough, but it has to be done. You don't give in to being lazy: "Get up and go and do it."

There's just so much around that: the use of the cedar, the use of the river, the water. The water is very powerful, its energy, and that's always been recognized with our people. It's cleansing. It gives you life. If it wasn't there, then we would not survive. So therefore, it's used for that purpose, for helping you with your energy level. When I've gone away to take part in ceremonies, because some of the people that are there do actually go to a creek, or they go to the beach, like in December and January, and they go and bathe. And it's freezing outside. And I thought, "What? You went down the beach and had a dip in the ocean!" "Oh yeah. I've been doing it all my life and it feels really good. You don't feel it anymore. You don't hesitate. You just do it." So, there are still people that do it. And it works. It's something that's – it's medicine. It's a pick-me-up-er. You don't get anywhere – you don't start your day without doing that.

That kind of cleansing works for all kinds of things. The old people used to talk about, when you lose someone in your family, and you're grieving, you *really* need to focus on that cleansing. Otherwise you're going to carry your grief. Your grief is very heavy, and it'll make you sick. Or if you know that people have some resentments to you, or they're trying to hurt you in some way, with words, that's when you do that brushin' as well. Because people's words can be really hurtful. They can be really damaging to you. And if you don't take care of yourself, then you're gonna be feeling heavy. These words will penetrate through your skin with what was said, and it'll hurt you emotionally and mentally. So in your mind, when you're brushing yourself, you're getting rid of all these words that are stuck to you – they're penetrating you, these statements about you. "I don't have to take this. I don't need this. It's not mine. It doesn't belong to me," and you brush it away. The old people used to say that words from other people, sharp words or nasty words said to you, are like sharp objects, they're like needles, they're like little knives, they're penetrating your skin. You're bleeding, you're walking, you're bleeding. You don't see it, but you are. As you're walking wounded. So therefore, that's why you do the brushing. You don't own it – you push it away: "It's not mine to keep."

So, that's the importance of the brushin', and with women, it wasn't necessary for women to go to the river, but they did their own cleansing at home. In, like, a basin of water. Or if they have access to a little creek or something, that's where they would go and use that cedar boughs to brush themselves too, and especially if they're grieving, going through a hard time with different losses. I can only relate to my grandmother, in her time, of how many children she'd lost in her life. She had sixteen children in total, and she lost ten children, at various ages, and the eldest being ten years of age. She lost two children in one day. They were living up in Theodosia, and two of her babies were really sick. So they got on the boat to take the children to see the – there used to be a – called her an Indian doctor. She was a psychic. She was a healer. She lived on Cortes Island, on Klahoose reserve there. So she wanted to take the babies there, to this lady. So and – course they didn't have motor – they rowed or whatever, however means they went there. And before they got there, one of the children died. And so they got there and the other one died. It was too late to save. I don't know what kind of illness the baby had. But she lost a lot of her babies. Yeah, it was difficult times for people. There were a lot of baby deaths. Just through sickness and whooping cough and whatever other ailments, pneumonia, I guess. But even with all that, people took that in their stride, and that's how life was. Just dealing with it, and ... lettin' it go. And through her many losses, she grieved, and in constant grief, but this was how she took care of her grief, was by going and brushing with the cedar first thing in the morning – early, early in the morning. Breaking daylight, was when she would be up. And I would hear her cryin' and wailin' out there as she would take a basin of water and go out the back of the house and do her cleansing. And with us livin' up the coast, I always – I would hear her. She would cry out there and wail. And I think that was good therapy. For her it was really good therapy. And she'd just come in and tell us, "Okay, you all get up now." And she would talk to us: "You must have heard me cryin' out there. But I do that. That's my medicine. I have to release my pain in the morning. Otherwise, it's too heavy. It's a burden for me to carry that. Then I brush myself. I sweep myself with a cedar bough. I even take some of that water and I gargle, and then spew it out." And that's not only cleansing the surface of your body, your outer surface of your body, but you're cleansing your mouth – you're spewin' it out. You say, "Leave me. Go away." And you spew it in different directions, some of that water. So that's releasing? That was good medicine for her. And she'd come in and, "I've done what I needed to do," and get everybody up and get busy. And she would say, "It's okay to grieve. It hurts, because I've lost someone I love. But we don't stay in bed and cry all day. Life goes on. You have to get up and get things moving, get things done. We got a lot of work to do." So for her, it was fine. And we understood that. We all knew that! And it's quite different today that we've lost that practice. That quite often people will go to pharmacy and get sedatives and tranquilizers to deal with the pain they're carryin', which only covers the pain. You're going to have to deal with it sooner or later. And when you do it the way I remember seeing it done, then you're dealing with it right from the moment of your loss. You gonna keep on doing it. Another belief they had was that when you're holding on to your grief and you're not willing to let go of your grief when you've lost someone, whoever that may be, your parents or your children, your sibling – if you're holding on to that and you're not doing this work that's so important to do, the brushin', then you're going to be holding the spirit of that person that's just left you. You're holding the spirit back from going on its journey. You're keeping them. They're stuck in a place, because they see you as suffering. They see you suffering and you're in pain. So you're not giving them the permission to go. So there's, like, two sides to the coin: you're helping yourself, and you're helping your deceased relative to go. "Go on your journey. I give you permission. I'll see you one day." Because that's a very strong belief, is that one day we would meet with them again, when we go and join them.

And you give them that permission to go too. 'Cause it's been experienced by some people that the spirit will stay around in the home. And you'll hear little things. There's little signs, or little noises. You feel a presence, and you know that they're probably there. And I believe that. I had one experience after my late husband passed away and so I truly believe. When I say I've never seen a spirit or anything, I did at that one time. Although I didn't wake up to see him there, when I was waking up – it was just something that was there was leaving the room. And that was a real experience for me, if I wasn't a believer before – that the spirits like to hang around. He had been gone for two years. He died of a heart attack, and we had some unresolved issues before he left. And I always kind of grieved around that and thought about that. And all this, you know, what if, what if, what if? But two years went by. I *never* dreamt of him. I *never* – not even a dream about him or anything like that. Some people have dreams all the time about their – someone is gone on their journey and you'll have those dreams. But I never did. There was only *one* incident that I felt that he had come to visit the house. Where he used to sit, there's a lamp there. And he would sit there and watch TV or sit there and read. And it was kind of hard to get to that seat. I've remodelled my house since then. But you have to come in through a door, and another door into the living room. My children were still living at home and they were downstairs. And we'd all gone off to bed, and I woke up about three in the morning and the light was on in the living room. And I thought, "Oh. Wonder who's up." So I got up and I went, and nobody was there but the light was on. So it's one of those lamps you have to reach in under the shade to turn it off. So it wasn't just you turn on the switch. So I went back off to bed and the next morning I was asking my children that were there with me still, "Any one of you get up last night? Who got up? How come the light was on?" "No!" Nobody had gotten up during the night. And so we all found that really strange. 'Cause we all know, turn off the lights when you go to bed. So it got me thinkin', maybe he's come to tell me he's around. So not long after that, it was two years exactly to the time of his death – he died in May. And it's light early, early in the morning, like, five in the morning. And it was like I was in a dream, but yet I was awake. And he sat beside me on the bed. I was facing towards that way *[gesturing]* and he sat there, and I – it's really hard to explain. But it was like I was awake, and I said, "It's about time you come for a visit. I've been waiting for a long time for you to visit." And he sat there and he had his arm over across my shoulder like this. *[gesturing]* And just the way he spoke and just his body language, I saw all that. And he says, um – he used to always do that, take a real deep breath and he'd say, "Well, I've been here." He said, "I just came outside and had a drink of water at the tap outside." "Ooh." And then he leaned right over and his cheek touched my cheek. And I woke up! As soon as that happened, then I was fully awake. And then it was like this image, this, like, a shadow went out the door like that – out my bedroom door? So that was the *strangest* thing. I was awake but not awake, or I don't know, I sat up and it was just like something *real* had happened. I sat and it was like, "Come back!" You know, "We're not finished this conversation." I sat up – but it was gone. And then I just sat there and I *bawled* and I *cried* and I thought, "*Oh my God.*" So I had to pull my socks up and think, "What does that mean? Why did he come like that?" And I *know* he was here. I *know* as sure as I am sitting here, I *know* he was here. So I thought,

"Well, it's two years, you know. It's time I did an offering. Him saying he was thirsty – he came for a drink of water." So I made a food offering. I brought all my children together and told them about what had happened. And they all participated in the burning. They've always believed, 'cause I always have talked about it. They've always believed in our traditional way. And they're very good about that. And so when I invited them to come, I told them, "We're going to make this offering," and at the same time I wanted them to experience it too, to see it, and I wanted them to be all there. So they came, and my grandchildren were quite a bit younger then, but they came. And especially my adult children, they all were there, and they really had a good feeling about it. And I explained to all of them why we're doing this, step by step by step. And what you can get out of this and at the same time you're offering – in a good way, it's a way of letting go, it's a way of bringing closure. So that was really good for them, and for them as adult children – my children, some of them had, I guess, in their own way felt they never had a chance to say goodbye, and there were things they could have said to him or things they could've talked about. They all wrote letters. Each of them. Wrote letters that wanted to have some – very personal for each of them. They wrote letters and then they put it in the fire as well. So that brings peace too. So that was good. And I see a lot of people doing that. That practice is carried on in different healing centres too.[*] It was really good, and it just seemed to bring closure – after that it was like closure. Everything's fine now. So that was a good experience. I took that as a positive. Because I always wondered, 'cause there was some things about – we'd argue about things and all that kind of stuff and disagree and we're not speakin' for a long time and then all of a sudden he was gone like that. And I'm thinkin' we never did – we were not prepared for this moment, right? So to me, everything is okay. Yes, I truly believe in that kind of experience, or in the offering that followed that experience.[†]

And I have done it from time to time. Especially on our anniversary, or the anniversary of his death, around May, or somewhere close to June or Father's Day or something like that. Or I will do it in November

---

[*] Elsie has seen this done at Tsow-tun Le Lum, the treatment centre discussed in Chapter 10.
[†] For another account of burnings, see Dorothy Kennedy and Randy Bouchard, *Sliammon Life, Sliammon Lands* (Vancouver: Talonbooks, 1983), 54, 56-57.

for my grandparents too, 'cause the fish are coming up the river and we have an abundance of the fish that go up there. And I will do a feast for my ancestors. And I have called my grandchildren around that and – now that they're grown up and they can witness that – and they really *believe* in it. They really believe in it. And they really respect it, which I'm so thankful for. They don't treat it lightly. They really get something out of it, and they really appreciate it. Which I'm really proud of them for that. Yeah. It's a good feeling. Once you're done, you just feel really light. And around that time when we're around the fire, do the burning, we put the food out there. And then everyone turns away. You do your own meditation then. "For each of you," I tell them, "turn away. Don't be staring at the fire." Everybody turns away. And silence. No chattering. No chit-chatting. This time is very personal. And you think about all that you want to change in your life. What would you like to see change in your life? What would you like to fix in your life? It's a self-analysis. Where you've got some kind of pain or hurt or maybe you've got an illness or an ailment you want to – need help. And wherever you need help in your life! You asked the spirits that you're feeding, the ancestors, to be there for you, to give you the strength you need, or the direction you need to go. So when you're facing away from the fire, then you're meditating. Taking that time for yourself, for your own wellness. And when that's all done and the food has burned – you give it time to do that. And another reason why you turn away, too, from the fire, is that when you feed people, like if you feed people around this table, you know, and as a host you're not gonna stand there and watch people eat or stare at them eat. That's very rude. So you just put the food on the fire, you turn away, and you allow them to have their feast. So that's the other reason why you turn away.

You delegate someone from the other side, from the spirit world. You ask your grandmother or some Elder, or your late spouse: "You will look after this food. You make sure everybody gets some. So they'll have a feast on the other side." Making sure everybody gets some. And again, stressing the fact that there are people on the other side that may have been greedy in life, so therefore could be greedy on the other side. And they will take more than their share when other people don't get any, so that carries over to the other side. In your mind or your words, you talk to – "You will look after, you're the one in charge." So it's like if we have a banquet here, wherever: "You will do the serving. You're the person that's gonna make sure that everybody gets a fair share." So you do that to the spirit world. Yeah, that part is really important. And then the brushing again, and changing your clothes. So you could do burning any time of the year. I do it about twice a year in my family – I do a little offering. In the fall time I do it for my grandparents, because I know they loved the chum salmon that come up the river and every part of that chum salmon, the fish heads and the fish eggs and the smoked salmon and the t'ɛn, you know, that's barbecued fish, the t'ɛn. So I do it for them, thinking of my grandparents and all the other Elders, 'cause that was their favourite food, these things I'm preparing. So when I'm preparing the food on the table, I'm making sure it's all in your thoughts: "Grandmother, you will look after this. This is for you. And I know this was your favourite." You know, you talk to yourself! If there's no one there that you're talking to. If you have family you're teaching this to, you teach them those things as well. It's important to identify the foods you're burning and who it's for and separate the dish for the person that you've delegated to look after the food. But you can do a platter of other food for other people. But the person that you delegated to look after it will see that it's shared, so you do theirs last. It's like if you come into my house, I'm not gonna eat and you're sitting there and I don't feed you first. That's rude! So the same applies to the spirit world. You don't eat first. So that's why you burn offerings: "This is the last one. You've done your job. This is yours." Or just identify it in your thoughts and in your mind: "That's yours. You look after the others." So those are really important to remember.

Be focused on what you're doing. You can't just put it down. When I do a burning, I give myself a whole day so I can prepare myself from morning, and prepare the food, and when it's all done, you know – we usually do it about, um, I do it at noon. I feel it's okay. A lot of people, they would wait until almost three o'clock in the afternoon. They say that's when the spirits come up, is three in the afternoon. That's when the spirits are active, after three. But I've done it at noon. I've done it at eleven in the morning. So I justify that by saying, "Well, it's three o'clock somewhere else in the world." *[laughs]* I have my own ways! And I say, "Well, it's noontime here. That's when we usually have our meal." So I'm just great at justifying what we do.* *[laughs]* So when we're all finished and the food is all pretty much gone, burnt,

---

* Despite her joking tone here, Elsie later clarified that 3:00 p.m. really is the best time to do burnings because that is when the spirits come around, and that is when she tries to do them.

then we have cedar handy, available, and everyone gets a brushing. We brush each person. They do the circle or they make the turn. You brush them. Then they go away from the fire, don't come back. Just go. And everyone goes away feeling lighter, feeling good. Yeah. It's a good practice. It's very important. It's something that I find very, very important. It's good medicine. Yeah.

So I do it twice a year. So you pick your time. And once you've picked your time, I'm going to. "Oh, I think I'll do burning, uh, maybe next week, or maybe next month, or whatever" – it's not good. It could be harmful to you, because the spirits can read your mind. They can read you. As soon as you put that thought out there: "I'm going to do this." And if you don't do it, they're waiting. Then they're waiting again if you don't have a good excuse not to go ahead and do it. It's same thing as I invite you to come to my house, you come knock on my door and I'm not there. You're gonna be disappointed. And then I say, "Well, maybe next week." And you come again, I'm not there. And you're gonna get ticked off at me and you throw rocks at my house. *[laughs]* Yeah, so everything was explained in detail. Always. It's all part of growing up and the teachings. And you're watching the Elders do their thing and how they do it. Every aspect of life, from grieving to gathering to building a boat or making a basket. It wasn't in a school setting where you went every day to learn from a book. Mind you, that's nice, that's good. But this was how our people learned the ways of life and how to live life to the best of your ability. And share that knowledge, share the teachings, the taʔaw. That's your taʔaw. That's so important! Yeah.

And we cleanse the house too. We do the brushing of the house that the deceased person had lived in. Especially if it was a sudden death or whatever. You go and you brush with cedar, otherwise their spirit may be locked in the house. So you open the doors and you start brushing from – come in the door and you turn right and you brush. Especially it's a grandmother that always worked around the kitchen or whatever, make sure you brush the kitchen area and wherever they lived. In the bedroom, you will brush. And again you're talking to this spirit and saying, "You're gonna leave this place. You're gone on your journey. You're gone to another world. You're not gonna be here bothering your children or your family. Just go on your journey." So you're giving them permission, in a good way, to go. And people have felt spirits in different homes. They feel noises, they feel – they know someone's there, and they get scared. So they wonder, "What is going on?" Or somebody came and sat at the foot of my bed and there's no one in the house. There's just me and – things like that happen. And we'll go back then and we'll do another brushing. If it hadn't been done, that's especially when those things are happening. They hear the cupboard doors opening, or the door open and close, so we need to go there and cleanse the place out. And again taking the cedar, and you thank the cedar for the help of that cedar. You just don't go and take cedar anywhere and use it! You go to a cedar tree early in the morning and you get branches from there, 'cause that's what's going to help you, that's the medicine. So you offer prayers to that cedar tree and you say, "You're going to help me. And I'm going to do this work with your help. I don't mean to rob you of – but you've got the power." The cedar tree has the power, that energy. 'Cause it means so much to our people and how much we used it for everything, from our shelter, from our canoes, our paddles, our clothing. Weaving baskets and all kinds of things. Many, many uses. So you just don't go and take from the cedar without thinking. It's not gonna work. So you honour the tree. You humble yourself to that tree and you take what you need only. And that's what you will use. So you could either take that cedar, you could bundle it up and put it back to that same tree and thank the tree again. And as it's hanging there through the rain and all that, it's going to wash away your grief. It's going to take care of itself. It's going to go back to the earth. Or you could take it to the river and put it in the river and let it wash downstream. Or you could put it to the fire if you're doing an offering. When I brush people around the fire, I will take all the cedar and I'll burn that, you're offering it up to the universe, to the spirit world. And all that burns and goes up in smoke. And I like that. You know, for me that works. Yeah. So that's the house, right? You brush the people, and then you go brush the house. And it's a good feeling for the people in the house too, because the spirits are very strong. They'll always come around and maybe had unfinished business – whatever. They'll come around. So that's what we do with that.

Embracing loss, embracing death – that it's all part of life. And how important that is to recognize that, to accept that. You were born one day, and you're going to die one day. What I had always heard was that from the day you're born, your days were marked. You cannot argue – you cannot say it wasn't his time or her time to go. Only the Creator knows that. Only God knows that – that there is your day that you're gonna be called. And that you always be prepared, because you do not know when your time comes. You don't necessarily have to be an old person to die, or that you die of old age. You could be struck down. That was always really stressed to us. And one of the things about that, you don't stay angry at people. That forgiveness is really important, because when a – individual, a person, your loved one, your children, your spouse, whomever, within your family or your friends, it may be the last time you see them when you say goodbye to them. In your household, don't go to bed angry. Always thank the Creator for the day. Thank the Creator for your family, for your children, your grandchildren. Thank the Creator for all that he has given you. Appreciate what you have. Because maybe tomorrow you won't have that – you won't have some member of your family. So you always be careful not to be angry and carry your anger to bed at night. And again in the morning, thank the Creator for givin' you another day on this earth. And to be prepared for what the day brings. You put a lot of trust in the Creator. You put a lot of your trust in the hands of the Creator. Whatever happens to you, you have no control over it. When the Creator feels it's your time, or sees that it is your time, you will go. And you can't blame people. You can't point your fingers and blame people and do this: "If I'd only done this, if I'd only done that." Then it's a little too late for that, to be blaming yourself or other people. So it was just a matter of being prepared for whatever the day brings. Simply put, that's what it boils down to. To stop and acknowledge people and spend time with your family, your children. Really, really important. So you don't have regrets when you lose someone. I think all we can do at a time of loss is to say we've done our best, and I don't have any regrets. When an individual passes away, whether it be a sudden death, or whether it be through illness, that you don't question it, you accept it. You accepted it as the end of a life, and that you will meet again at another place, another time. That's very important is the belief in the spirit world, that the spirits will – their spirits will always come back to you and will be around you.

The things around respecting and honouring families when they've lost a loved one in the family, to be there to help them through their losses and their grief. Communities in the day were very, very supportive and respectful. Everything was shut down. People focused on the family. You just never mind your own work at home. You go and help that family. You bring them food. You go and help them prepare to deal with their loss. You stay with them throughout, 'cause that way you're taking the load off them, that they're not doing the work themselves. You go and you help dig the grave. You carry the body to the cemetery. It is our tradition to carry the body to the cemetery, to walk the casket to the cemetery, because that's the last journey on this earth for that person. And the teachin' was that one day someone will have to carry you there too. So you go and you help, even if it's just two or three steps that you've held that casket and helped carry that casket. You're putting your hand there. That's what they would say to you: "Go and put your hand over there. Go and help. Even if it's not much, but all hands workin' together makes for easier work." So those things are really, really important – important teachin's. To hold the family up by doing that work that you do around the family, it helps to wipe the tears. We still do it when we lose someone. We've pretty much brought that back again 'cause we didn't do it for quite some time. And I think the first time that we did it again was when I lost my husband thirty years ago. And I don't know what I would've done, 'cause I couldn't remember a lot of things around that time? I think I was just in shock, pretty much. But the community came together by some of my friends that put things together. I was not aware of all the things they were doing, and I don't know if I ever thanked everyone appropriately for all that work and time they put out there. But I was amazed at how much work was done. I didn't need to lift a finger, as somebody else took care of everything. And that really helped a lot. Someone gave me a CD – just a little while ago here within the month.* And someone was taping the service of my late husband. And the one person that spoke, and the choir, and I – I swear, I did not remember all that. I listened to the tape, and I'm thinking, you know, "Were they there?" They must have been there, 'cause they were talking about my late husband and the choir was from Sechelt, and I thought, "Oh my goodness, I didn't remember that." *[laughs]* So I think when you're going through a real bad time, you kind of go blank. You're not able to think properly. You're not able to function as well. So listening to that tape really, I think, reinforced for me the importance of being there for people like the teachin' says. To be helpful, to offer your help, and even if there's nothing you can do, just go and say, "I'm here for you, if you need me call me." Those things are so important.

People here used to make their own caskets. They always had the casket makers in the community. They never went through a funeral home. A funeral director never came out. So one of the casket makers was Dave Paul, that was my late husband's dad. And so was his dad.

---

* This refers to July 2007.

He was a casket maker in Church House. And so was Johnny Bob, that was my stepfather. So they had not designated, but maybe more like volunteers. 'Cause they knew how to make it, they would be the ones to be there building a casket. Just crude, just out of cedar planks they would nail together. And just wrap the person, the body, in a blanket and lay them in there. And we already had the cemetery of course here then. And they would just have the burial like that. It was really not an awful lot of fuss. This Chilean guy – he lived here and died here as an old man. I remember when he died. I was very young, but I remember going there to help cleaning the house. I remember people there – women there and some men there. My granny was one of them. Helping to bathe him, clean him, and get him ready for burial. So a lot of the things that people did here was just all volunteer and really self-sufficient and didn't depend on any outside help to help them. Like, you know, babies born at home, home births and aided by midwives, and right up to the death of a person – it was all taken care of in our own community. Yeah. So it was quite different, quite different setup then.

When we have our funerals, we have the wake. Preferably it's four days – after four days from the time of death that we have the wake. And people will stay up all night just to sit there throughout the night. People take turns, or just stay and visit throughout the night till daylight. In the morning, there are things that need to be taken care of with the family. And that's when an Elder, or a person that knows how to take care of these kinds of practices, beliefs in the healing of the cedar, the letting go. And at the first break of daylight, you go and you help people that have lost a loved one, for them to say their final goodbye to the individual. That they are brushed, and to send them away in a good way so that they're not going to be grieving and holding the spirits back from going on their journey. Because if you do that, if you are not willing to let go or you are not prepared to let go, then the spirit of your loved one is always going to be around. But not in a good way, because they see you grieving. They see that you're hurting. So therefore you need to let go. And this is why we do the very early morning ritual when our loved ones leave us. With the help of an Elder or some person that's done it before and knows how it's done. It's a very sacred time. It's a sacred ceremony. And the family members come up one at a time and stand by the casket and say their goodbye, and do their own meditation in their own heart. To do some soul-searching, and give permission for the spirit to go freely, and that we will meet again in another time. And

I've done that many times. I help people through that process: "Here's your dad"– or your mom, whatever. "He's going on a journey. You just say your goodbyes. Don't hang on to him." And then you talk to the spirit of the deceased person too and you say, "You're gonna go on your journey. Your children will be fine. Your family will be fine. So you can rest in peace and go on your journey." So those are real important – it's like a conversation. You're speaking on behalf of the person that's standing with you, and you're also speaking to the spirit of the deceased person. So you brush that person that's with you and they make a circle, stand in a circle, turn counterclockwise. And then they go out the door and another person is outside doing the same kind of work. And at that time, you will face where the sun comes up. And you're going into a new day. You're facing tomorrow or facing today. And this is a new beginning, this chapter in your life. And that's really important through all that process, to remember that.

In our community we have the Catholic church that's used by our people, and there's services and then the casket is walked up to the cemetery by pallbearers, and everybody puts a hand there. Could be women, you could go and put your hand there, help lift the casket, walk the casket all the way up to the cemetery. Because this is the very last thing you're going to do for that individual in their lifetime here with the families and their loved ones. It's your way of saying goodbye and letting go. Then walking up the cemetery, you have to walk on each side of the road. You don't just walk any way or be chatting. It's a time for silence and meditation and, while you bid farewell, you walk in two lines on each side of the road, one on each side of the road going up to the cemetery. That's allowing the spirits to walk through, so that you're not in the way. So you make room in the middle of the road. 'Cause if you're walking against the spirits, or you're walking among the spirits on this path where the deceased is going, then you're gonna need to be brushed, you're going to need to be cleansed. 'Cause when we do burning, offering of food, we do that – the brushing, the cleansing after we've done offering of food. That's important to keep in mind. 'Cause the spirits come there around the fire and you leave a path open, 'cause they're gonna be coming that way, right? So that was really important and you leave a path. It's like going into maybe the gym or wherever, a hall where there is a function. You know, you don't block the road. Other people are coming. You compare to that – the same idea.

At the cemetery we have men that go and dig first thing in the morning. They don't dig early – or they don't dig the day before.

Because the belief is that if you dig and leave the ground open overnight, that's inviting: it's like an invitation to other family members
to go on that journey. I know in some places they will have equipment
come and dig, and leave it open overnight. And according to the taʔaw
you don't do that. So this is why the ground is dug. It's all done by
hand, by our guys. It's not dug with a machine. And they use shovel
and picks and dig and that usually takes about maybe two, three hours
to do that. And the men are usually really good. They come out and
they're there, take turns – it's a big job. Especially in bad weather,
winter months, you know, they still go up there. And we always acknowledge those people that do that, to thank them. We thank them
at the cemetery. We tell them that they will get their reward. That
they will have the spirit of our loved ones that we've just put away.
That they will be there to help when you need the help. So everything
that goes around comes around. That is the belief. You've gone to help.
You've put your hand there – when they lower the casket into the
ground, it's all done by hand again, by the community members. They
take turns and they cover the ground, fill up the grave with the dirt
again till it's completed and it's finished. And I think by doing that –
that keeping up that tradition is really important. It completes the
work that needs to be done. It's a feeling of completion? That we didn't
depend on someone to come and do that work, or some equipment or
machine to do that. It's a good feeling – it's a feeling of letting go. ·

Then we usually have a lunch that people have donated all the
food. They've volunteered their time to prepare food. And our services
are usually quite long. If we have a service at ten in the morning,
sometimes it'll go till two and three in the afternoon because it's
lengthy – service is long, ceremony is long. Walking up to the cemetery
in itself is a long – could be a long haul. And then the final burial. So
then people have a meal together. The meal is not served until the
family get there, the immediate family. And they serve themselves
first, or they're served. And then there's another ceremony that takes
place: it is our tradition to help people in every way that we can,
and the last thing we do is to invite people to make a contribution. It
doesn't matter how little it is. It's out of your pocket. They call it
"wiping the tears away." To help wipe the tears away. It's not that
you're going to be indebted to people. People gave because they
wanted to do something for you, and they say, "Don't take this as
that you're indebted to me, but take it as a hanky. It's like a hand-
kerchief. It's to help wipe your tears away." So that's done every time

we have a funeral. That we have that practice. And that money could be used to whatever – wherever they need to, whether it be to the funeral home for a headstone, or they may have had to go out and buy an outfit or whatever for family members. But usually there's anywhere from, depending on the number of people that's there, it could be three hundred to three thousand dollars that is given and collected and documented and given to the family to do as they wish with that money. So that's one of the things we do at our funerals. It's very, very important.

And we take children to funerals. We don't deny them the right to know what is going on. Because for them it's an acceptance, too, of the cycle of life. You know, in some cultures, they discourage children from seeing a funeral, or be part of, or to be exposed, because it's gonna traumatize them. But our belief is that if you explain to your children what it's all about, you would say your goodbyes and not hide it from them. I think hiding it from them becomes more of a trauma to them in the long run. So I feel comfortable, you know. I've always taken my children to funerals. Ever since I was a little girl, I used to always go with my Elders, and be with them and to learn. How else would we learn if we don't watch how the Elders are doing the work that needs to be done? And the respect that is shown at a time like that. It's very humbling? You are not to be running around and be joyous or makin' a lot of unnecessary noise. You go about quietly and do what needs to be done. And it's a very sacred time. So those are the things that is all part of life, and we need to accept it at that. Hmmm.

Teachings around grief. It's very important, our taʔaw. "taʔaw" means "the teaching." That we all carry the teaching, what we learned from our ancestors, the traditional teaching, the traditional values. "ʔəms taʔaw" – "our teaching," that's what that means. So it's really important to keep that in mind, especially if we've lost someone in our family or a dear friend or whomever, is to be really mindful of ʔəms taʔaw. To follow those teachings. Because by hanging on to your grief, it only brings you down, and then it doesn't allow the spirit of your loved one to go freely, 'cause they'll always be there in spirit to see you suffering or grieving. You're keeping them away from going on their journey. So all of those things I've talked about before, but I just wanted to reinforce that and talk about that a little bit. How we conduct ourselves around funerals and during the wake and funerals and children and relatives. How we protect our children. Our children were exposed to the realities of life, about death and dying and being born one day and one day you're going to die. There's no two ways. So the children were taught at a very young age about that. So children accepted death as part of life. That one day Grandma will be gone, or Grandpa will be gone, whoever. It could be their pet, could be whatever is dear to them. Grief and how to take care of that. So especially around your parents or your spouse. And how you use the cleansing to get you through a bad time. Adults did it themselves. They did the cleansing themselves with cedar. Or you could get someone to do it if you're not able to do it yourself. But children were also brushed – small children – so that their spirit is not taken with the spirit of the person that's left. So children were kept close and they were cleansed as well, protected. You don't allow children to be around the open casket. You keep your children away. You hold on to them. Don't let them wander around. Don't step over the graves. They're sacred graves. There are people – deceased bodies of your family there. So you walk around and you don't ever step on top of other graves while you're in the cemetery. And pregnant women, they didn't go near the casket with no protection. So they always had a blanket around them or cedar. Cover your tummy with cedar, wear it on your belt or whatever, tucked into your clothing. That's to protect the fragile new life that's growing, 'cause they're vulnerable to the spirit world.

So you brush yourself, and if you've been crying over this loved one, your tears are falling onto their resting place, in a casket, whatever that may be. You're giving up your energy. Your tears are falling into that casket that it's gonna be buried with your loved one. And that weakens you. So you have to, at a time like that, take that back. That's why you do the brushing. You take that tears. There's always someone. I've done it, you know. When we have a funeral here, mainly Johnny Louie now who is our – he's a relative of mine – that's what his mother taught him. It was his grandmother that was a very, very spiritual woman. She was a healer and a psychic and she saw the spirit world, and so he got a lot of teachings through that. And learned a lot from her as well as his mother. His mother, she had a lot of teachings. She had a lot of teachings and was a very traditional person. Both from the Sliammon teachings, but she was also part Squamish, and she had a lot of their teachings too. And she combined it and so she taught her children all of these things. If you go visit her, she would remind you, remind you, remind you all the time. That was Rose Louie. Yeah, and she would go on, talkin' about the teachings, you know, taught him those things that's so important. And he carries it in a real good way. I'm very proud of him. So he's always there. He always makes sure there is cedar available. When the casket's now being closed before it goes to its resting place after the final goodbyes, he will brush the casket while it's still open. He will brush it and take back those tears so that it doesn't go with the deceased person. And that's really releasing and taking your power back, your life back. And that is protecting the family, the individuals that have gone there. You've said your final goodbye.

So when you're done at the cemetery and all the work has been done, you make sure you go and – in those days people went to bathe in the river. They would go and cleanse themselves in the river. Otherwise you will have a tired arm 'cause you've been digging, and that tired arm will become permanent. You'll always have that heavy, tired arm from digging. So that was really important. That's why when people are walking the casket up to the cemetery – and we still do that, we don't depend on the hearse to drive from the church to the cemetery, or from wherever, if it's from the house. The last journey, going up to the cemetery, is by walking the casket. And sometimes it's very heavy, so men just line up, and they take turns every few steps. Someone else is stepping in and replacing the carriers all the time. It's not just the pallbearers that are involved. It's the community that go and put their hand out and help during that walk to the cemetery. So you don't allow yourself to get tired when you're carrying the casket. That's why they're always doing that replacing – taking turns. If you get tired then it's always going to be that tired of feeling. So it's really important when you go to the river to – in your mind and in your thoughts and in your prayer, you're brushing that away. sohoθot. sohoθot. You would send your cedar down the river, and your cedar will drift away. It's taken all that tiredness and the grief and the sadness. It's gone down the river. That's why they use the river a lot. But if you're not near a river or anything, you just use the shower. And while you're in the shower you think those same thoughts. You know, all the negative energy – if there's negative energy on you, it'll go down that drain. So you have to keep that in mind and talk to yourself. It's so important to do this. Not just go in there to take a shower so you will be clean in body. You have to be clear in mind. You're clearing your mind. You're clearing your inner self. That grief, you're lettin' it go. You're allowing it to go. So those are really important teachings, ʔəms taʔaw. So all those that helped are, you know, it is suggested that they go and bathe or shower, or change their clothes.

And they usually will leave the clothes – if you've got a clothesline outside, you put it outside and air it out. Or just wash it, put it in the machine. But you don't walk around with the same clothes that you've been wearing through this day or from last night through the wake and that. Those are really important, 'cause you have to clean that too. Not just your body but what you've been wearing. And where else do I go? So the men are told at the cemetery that are helping with the digging to go and do that self-care. Because their arms maybe have gotten tired. They've been digging. They need to go and let that go in the river. Even if you don't jump in the river, you go into the cedar and you toss that cedar into the river, to take that heaviness away. Those are really important steps.

There was so much of it. There was a lot. Every step of the way there was so much meaning to the work that was being done. And it's very serious. It's not taken lightly. There was always someone that guided you through these times. And I think it happens in a lot of cases that we all say later on, "I should have listened. I should have paid attention to what my grandmother was saying or my grandfather was saying." Because back – earlier days, there was no documenting the teachings. It was all oral teachin's. You had to listen. So I think that's where a lot of it is lost now, because people are not listening or taking time to listen, or to share the teachings. That is so important. 'Cause it's not documented. A lot of it is not documented. There is a little bit documented, but not enough – all the little details. So those things are really important to remember.

SO GOING FROM TALKING about the teachings of how to keep well, how to let go of grief, how to deal with grief, and taking care of yourself, I'll use an example. And this was not all that long ago that this happened, in my grandmother's time, actually. And this was a brother of my grandmother's. He lost his only son. I'm not sure how old his son was, but he was probably around ten, twelve. He was young. When he lost his son, he lost the will to live. Up until then, my grandmother's brother was a very good provider. He was a good hunter, he was a good fisherman, he brought food into the home. He was always out being busy and doing things. He was just starting to teach his son to do all these things, taking him with him wherever he went. His son got sick and he died. And for a long time, he wasn't able to do anything with his life. He was grieving. He just kind of fell apart: everywhere he went, he was mourning, he was crying. Although he went hunting, he never caught anything. He was so absorbed in his grief. And wherever he went, if he was hunting, there was always the owl that was ahead of him, wherever he travelled in the forest, in the woods. And the owl will chase animals away, warning the animals away? – that is the belief. So whenever he went out in the boat to go fishing, he would see the sea lion instead, or the whale, or blackfish. That also chases the fish away. So he's not able to catch anything, or bring home anything. And this went on for quite a long time. He grieved so much. And one day, my great-great-grandmother's husband – that was her second husband, his name was Felix – they lived up in Theodosia, and he was one of two healers that was recognized in our community.* He was a very powerful man. He was a twin, this man. And the belief was that twins were very powerful? They carried a lot of good energy. And this man became a healer. He was psychic. He could see things that a lot of people could not see. He felt things. He was so much, like, in between the spirit world and the living world that he was so in touch. He was so in tune that he had gone to visit his family and after they ate, he felt ill. He got up and he went out and he got sick to his stomach. And he came back and he said, "Something's not right in this home. Someone is very ill. And I'm gonna go away and I'm going to meditate on this. And I will come back and I will tell you – identify who it is that is very sick in this room." So he went out and did some meditation overnight. This is how he meditated, was sitting by fire and chanting and going into his own little spirit world, asking the spirits to guide him, to help him. And he recognized the one that was sick. He came back the next day and he said to him, "You are the one that is very, very sick." He said, "You've lost your spirit. Your spirit has gone away from you, because you've been grieving for so long over your loss of your son. I was able to track your spirit. And your spirit is way up in Toba Inlet. Your spirit is on top of the highest mountain there at Toba Inlet. It's sitting right on the top there," he said. "If we don't bring it back, if you do not co-operate, your spirit will go to the other side of the mountain and there'll be no bringing you back. You're going to be dead. But if you co-operate and help bring your spirit back – it's entirely up to you – I'll help you. And then we'll work together." So this is what they did. Someone went out and got a seal, went hunting, 'cause this what the healer requested. This would be the offering for the return of the

---

* Felix was known as toqʷanən pɛlıks. Another story about him is shared in the section "Twins Are Gifted."

spirit. So that was all ready. Everything was gotten ready. And this all happened at Emmonds Beach. There was a village there – a lot of our people lived there. And so he had a little sweat. Nowadays you may see, like, a sweat lodge, but our people used to have individual small sweats. It was just enough for two people. So this was what they used. "And we are going to go in there and I'm going to pray. You gonna help me, ask the spirits to bring your spirit back. And it's going to take us all night in there." So they went out when it got dark, and he told him, "At the first breakin' of daylight, the white owl will bring your spirit back to you. We will know when you hear that from a great distance the owl will make its sound, will make his call. And then he will move and come closer, and the third time that we hear him, he will be sitting up in this tree above us." So that's what happened. They were there all night. It was just breakin' daylight. It was still dark yet. It was *just* a hint of light coming. And they heard that owl. Came closer. Then the next time they heard it, it was on the tree right above them. And these white owls, they're called "qʷoqʷoqʷ" in our language. Very powerful, very deep voice when they speak, when they holler and when they make that sound – hooting sound. They're so very loud, your hair will stand up on end. And it did that. And he could just *feel* that his spirit come back to him, right from the top of his head down to – it was a rush of this energy through him. So that was how he got his spirit back. And that day they had an offering of the seal meat. They cooked it and they got a fire going and they offered it to the ancestors, to thank the ancestors for bringing his spirit back. And my grandmother remembers that! And this is why I truly believe that this happened. Because this was in her family that was a generation up from her, that did this work – that were able to do that kind of work. That believed in that, and practised it. And it works! It worked for them. Because that was how they did things. That was how they looked after their spirit. And to me that's spirituality, the belief in spirituality: the belief that when you believe enough, it'll happen. That you call upon the spirit of your ancestors. They will help you. How did that white owl know to bring that back, as predicted by the healer? How did he know that? Because they are of one mind. They are of one spirit with that white owl. So that's powerful. *Very* powerful. And it wasn't something that was told out of nowhere to my great-grandparents. And that's a true story. My great-aunt used to tell that story to me. So did my grandmother and those sisters, you know, there's several sisters, my grandmother's sisters. And that's – that's a fact. That's a true story.

Painted photograph of Elsie Paul's great-great-grandparents and family, in Sliammon in the early 1900s. The photograph includes the medicine man and the man who lost his spirit, as described in Chapter 7. *Left to right, standing:* Teresa Tom (talɛsat), Chief Tom's daughter; Cecilia (child), talɛsat's daughter; Katherine Dominick, daughter of Bob George (tiyʔəpθot) and sister to Granny Molly; Louise Bob, Chief Tom's daughter; Emily Bob, Chief Tom's daughter; Bob George (tiyʔəpθot), Granny Molly's father. *Left to right, seated:* Felix (toqʷanən pɛlıks), medicine man and Elsie's step-great-great-grandfather; Ann, Elsie's great-great-grandmother and Granny Molly's grandmother; Jeannie Bob (čine), Granny Molly's mother; little girl next to čine unknown. *Seated in foreground:* Charlie Bob, the man who lost his spirit. Photo courtesy of Elsie Paul.

So I truly believe in things like losing your spirit when you lose a loved one. So that became part of the teachin' in our family. That when you lose someone, if you're grieving and you allow yourself to be crying all the time, you lose your will to live. You lose your will to take care of your family, or to take care of yourself – you become very sick. And once you've, I guess, hit rock bottom, then you'll just die. It's like it could kill you! So you have to be strong. When you lose someone in your family, you have to try to be really strong. Remember those teachin's. Remember the bathing, the cleansing, the getting up *early* in the morning and going outside and doing your cleansing. Greet the new day. And try to heal your spirit – to let your grief go. And by cleansing – you take water and you wash your face and you gargle some of this water, and you spew it out there. That's cleansing your inside as well. You want to feel lighter, 'cause you're heavy – the heaviness is there when you're grieving. So we were always reminded of that story: "Look at what had happened to this man, that he almost died because he let his grief get the best of him." So this is why this is a teachin' – it's a very important teachin' – that you look after yourself, take care of yourself. Because if you don't, nobody else is going to take care of you. That's a very personal thing, is grief, and nobody can come and take it from you. It's up to you to work on your wellness, to get yourself better. To get back to normal. Because if you don't, you're going to be down and you're not going to be good to yourself or to anyone else after a while. So that's a lesson learned from that. It wasn't a legend, it wasn't a made-up story. I *truly* believe in that. And they used to point out, "That's the tree that the white owl came and sat on." And what makes it more believable – makes it more factual, makes it more useful – that you could use it, because it was true! Doesn't get any better than that. So I truly believe in that. I just really believe in that – the importance of self-care. And especially at a time like that, you know, the loss of someone you love, someone you're close to. There was a lot of teachings around self-discipline, especially if you lost your husband, your spouse, or you lost your mother and your father, 'cause you're so closely connected to them. And that's the time to use those teachings about self-care. You don't get into bad behaviour or give in to, for an example, today – I know our people didn't have alcohol *years* ago – and what happened today is sometimes people will turn to alcohol or to medication to feel better, because they're grieving or they're hurting. They'll turn to something to make them feel better. But people didn't have those things, and this was how they took care of themselves. But they recognized that if you don't do this important work of self-care, then you're going to end up dead! Eventually. You're going to be no good to yourself or anyone else. You've developed this bad habit. You've become lazy. And become, you know, just a nothing. Although you were maybe a real good hunter or a good provider, your spirit leaves you. And you must protect that spirit. You must hang on to that.

8

Community Work

When the Band took over their own administration* and I got hired, I left my job at the hospital to come to work for the Band. And I started in social work without any experience, without any training. I was selected to do that work as a mature person, and so that was offered to me, like really, like, right now. Didn't have too much time to think about it. You'll be trained on the job, kind of thing. So that's what happened. I got the job and this fellow that used to work for the Department of Indian Affairs – his name was Ken Matsuni – he was a Japanese fella. He was the kindest man. He was such a nice person. And very patient and just showing me the very basic things I have to follow in the policy. So I'm given two books, one on policy and procedures, and the other book was on regulations and stuff. So he went through the book with me and, "This is what you do and this is what you have to follow," and just gave me some hints. Two weeks, he came and trained me. And from then on I just went off to different workshops.

Then after some time I really wanted to get my social work degree. So I went and I did upgrading at Malaspina College when they first came to Powell River. And they were just in a little building on Marine Avenue. So there was a group of us that took that program, and Karen Galligos was one of them. I can't remember, there was a few non-Native people in there. Upgrading. We had to upgrade first. I had to

---

* This took place in 1972.

305

upgrade first for my goal – what I wanted to do, what I wanted to achieve – in order for me to get my social work degree. So I passed by the skin of my teeth, I'm telling you. *[laughs]* It was really difficult for me. 'Cause at that time I was, like, a grade four level, after coming out of Sechelt Residential School and going to school here in the community, when we were in the community. So it was equivalent to grade four level. So I upgraded and took this upgrading course – barely passed. I managed to get my grade ten level. And it was funny how that happened. Because our instructor did our evaluation, our test. Then one of the questions – I can't remember what it was – I heard it one way and the question was asked in a different way than how I interpreted the question. So I failed on that, so I didn't pass the grade ten. But I went to talk to the instructor and I said, "This is how I heard this. This is why I answered this way." So we kind of talk around that for a while and he gave me a passing mark! *[laughs]* I must've looked sad. Pitied me and gave me a passing mark. So now I got my grade ten. So after that I started going to Vancouver on the weekends for – and the Band was good enough to pay my way to go back and forth on the weekends to UBC. By that time that I started taking these courses at UBC, Annie Hackett started working with me. So her and I started travelling back and forth on the weekends, and she was training too, in social work. So we'd go down midday Friday and go and attend classes that evening, all day Saturday, and then half a day Sunday, then we'd head back home. And so I got fifty credits for just experience – work experience. And I started accumulating the points that was given to you, taking these courses at UBC. It was something like four points, five points or whatever. So I did that for quite a while and then finally got to two hundred points, was what you needed to get in order to get your registered social work certificate. So, finally got it! I felt so good. So that's how I got to be a registered social worker. I don't think they do that anymore. *[chuckles]* You know, you'd have to go to school, right? Full-time, probably. So I was really glad to get that.

So I stayed on that job and I worked in my community for twenty-four and a half years on that job. I really wanted to get to twenty-five years, and I was going to walk away. 'Cause it was getting really hard and after doing that same kind of work for that many years, it gets really heavy. But at the same time, I really enjoyed it. I really enjoyed working with people. And there were a couple of times that I thought, "I can't do this anymore," but then I stuck it out. Well, twenty-four years, and I was getting really burned out and I just – that's it, I quit. It was starting to affect my health too. Then the posting came out for part-time Elders' worker, looking after the Elders' program. So I applied for that. And then I was on Council during that time. I was elected as a Councillor in the community. So there I was, first woman Councillor. And actually it was my second time around. Because when I was quite young I ran for Council and I got in, at that time, back in Bill Galligos's time. He was the Chief at that time. And my brother-in-law, George Blaney, was on Council with me. So we were small. There was really no business, no office, nothing. So it was just a matter of Indian Affairs coming or the Indian agent coming to the community and, "Oh, sign this. Sign this." And quite often the Chief would come to my house and say, "Can you sign this document? Indian Affairs needs this document." So it was really just in very early stages of looking after our own affairs. And it was small. So that was my first time around. Then I ran again and I got into Council again – for a year and a half I was in, the second time around. A two-year term. And so things kind of went sideways. Things were not working well and so that was a real difficult time, really hard time, doing social work and doing that as well. So our term ended after a year and a half as a group. Six Councillors, I guess at the time, 'cause the population was growing quite a bit. So we prematurely ended our term. But I stayed on in social work. I continued that work. So when I left that position in social work, I then went and applied for that position working with the Elders. So that was half-time. But I actually moved into the facility before that. Actually I occupied the building because it was decided by leadership at that time that that house was going to be given to a family. And I felt it shouldn't be used that way. I felt it should serve the community as a whole. So I dug my heels in about that, making that decision for a family to be moved there, which I felt was not necessary or it wasn't meant to be that. So I said, "Over my dead body you're going to do this." I said, "I'm holding the key. I'm gonna move in there." So I went against the Council as a whole. Came home, packed my bags, packed my belongings, and I moved in. And I stayed there. The leader at the time came to me and says, "I want those keys!" I said, "No way. No way am I giving you the keys to the lodge." So he's standing there like this over my desk. *[imitating]* I said, "And take off those glasses," I said to him. He was wearing dark glasses. And he really threatened me: "You're gonna be fired." But they didn't fire me. I managed to squeak by and ended up in the lodge and camped there – they're going to have to drag me out of here. So anyway, as it was we didn't finish our term 'cause things were happening that caused us to be, um, how did we put that? A group of community members decided things were not going right in the community, and asked for resignations. They didn't ask me for a resignation, but they named some of the Councillors, asked for their resignation. And they did, and I thought, "I'm going to resign too." I just handed in my resignation voluntarily. I felt I wasn't doing anything wrong. But I just felt we had to start over. So there was a real breakdown then in our system. But I continued to stay there and of course Indian Affairs intervened, like, what are we doing again, to save us from ourselves. So I continued to stay there and continued to work, and when I retired, then I applied for the Elders' position, 'cause I was already living there. Elders – a half-time position. So I was there for – how many years was I there? Was it nine years? In '99 was when I left there, 'cause my health got to a point where I needed to take care of myself. And that's when I left that that home. So while I was there I looked after the Elders programs, and I look after the house. I cooked for the Elders. I fundraised for the Elders. So it was more than full-time position. And I was quite comfortable in that big house. I lived alone there, but the days were very busy. The Elders would come and we'd have our social gatherings – almost every day the Elders were coming. And I was responsible for cooking their meals and lunches and entertainment. We'd just sit around. It was really a nice group of Elders we had. It was quite enjoyable, always planning for something to do. And I ended up doing most of the work, 'cause the Elders were quite elderly then. But it was really an enjoyable time. It was hard, but it was enjoyable. So when I started to get health problems, I left. I became quite sick for a while, but I wouldn't go to the doctor. I didn't want to go to the doctor. And that's when Honoré was staying there, and I didn't even tell Honoré how I was feeling.* And one day I just felt, I have to go see the doctor today. So I'm downstairs and I'm looking up the stairs, and I thought, "I've got to go tell Honoré where I'm going." I just didn't have the energy, so I hollered up the stairs, "Honoré!" Came out and, "Yeah, I'm going into town." So, just wanted him to know there's no one downstairs. Went to town and I got admitted into the hospital. I said, "Well, I

---

* Honoré Watanabe, the linguist who collaborated on this project and who has conducted work in Sliammon since the 1990s.

have to go move my car." I said, "I'm parked over there." And the nurse said, "Did you drive here?" I said, "Yes, I did." "You know, you could have blacked out on the road?" she said. "Your blood level is really low," she says. So I said, "Well, I'll phone someone to come and take care of my car." I got admitted. I was in the hospital for a couple of days. They were giving me blood transfusions. So that was the beginning of my deciding to quit and I went back, came out, went back, and then I was having the same problems over again. So I just finally quit 'cause I had to have surgery. And at that time that was it, you know, my family said, "That's it. You'd better go back home. Move home! Enough!" So I came out of the hospital. Was on September twenty-first – I always remember that 'cause I had the wristband for a long time. September the twenty-first, 1999, I came out of the hospital.* Came home instead of going back to the lodge! So that was that part of my life.

I was very fortunate to have a job in my own community, and I was glad to be here and able to keep my family together, raise my family in this community. At the same time it was difficult, especially after hours and before work hours and weekends. There's really no getting away from the work. It's always like you're standby – aside from your working hours, you're on standby, because people seem to take it that because you're right here, there's no such thing as five o'clock comes along and the office is closed. So they would phone. Or they'd come by, or people would come knockin' on your door or sometimes at night you're called. So in my job – my job description at first was a financial worker. And I think a financial worker is totally different from a social worker, but it was all rolled into one. So you did income assistance work and assessing the needs in that program, making decisions around that. But at the same time you were helping people, or assisting people: directing people to do a job search or give them forms to go and that tells me they've gone to look here and look there, which qualifies them if they need income assistance. So there's that and there's also the counselling. 'Cause people just called you any time because they just wanted to bounce some things off you – or the kids are misbehaving and, "Will you help me?" You know, "You're the social worker," or "My husband is not looking after the family," or whatever. So you were, like, jack of all trades, master of none. So you just had to do the best you can, and that's what I did to

---

* September 21 is Elsie's birthday.

assist people through hard times. Especially around loss in the family. Didn't matter what time of the day or how many days it takes to be with that family and help them, guide them, or give support to families. That's when it's a real critical time. Families really need that kind of support, outside support from their immediate family.

So there's so many different things you did outside of your job description. And I never said, "That's not in my job description so I can't help you!" I couldn't say that! Because being in a small community, it's hard to say that. I think it's different if you're working in the middle of some big city and you shut the door at five o'clock and go home. It's certainly not like that working in your own community, in a small community. You're living here. You're one of the people. So you know the people. You know their children. You know pretty much what goes on in the community. So you're right enmeshed into the fabric of your community. And in a lot of ways I found that enriching too, to have that privilege, or to be privileged for people to come to me and talk to me about their very personal kind of problems, or concerns – and confidentiality is a big, big thing, so you had to be really careful. And at the same time, you felt really isolated. I didn't go to social functions because people, when you're out in a social function, people bring up right away, "Why are you not doing this?" and "Why are you not doing that?" So they're kind of attacking. Or sometimes people come to you and they're praising you up and down and, "Thank you, thank you!" you know, "For this, that." And after you've been at a little social for a while, people will feel more free to talk about whatever! So I found that really uncomfortable. So I kept away from that scene. It was just not the place to be, 'cause what can you do when you're in that kind of setting? You can't make decisions or get into a conversation about issues or personal stuff. So those were kind of hard, dealing with those issues, those kind of concerns that came up. Then there's also the criticism from people that – for whatever reason, as people will – suspicious of what I have and what I bought. Or if I bought a new car, "Oh, she's robbing the program. She bought a new car." Or "She's robbing the Band. She bought a new –" whatever it may be. And my children felt the consequences of that, too. Whatever they wore, if they wore new shoes, "Oh, lucky thing for you, your mother's a band social worker." That's what hurt the most. That really hurt, 'cause that's something I can't defend. You just have to live with that, tolerate that, because I know in my heart I would never, ever use the program for my own use – there's no way you can do that. 'Cause you have to account for your clients, how many clients you have, and that's what I did. I never once misused the program to benefit my own family or to benefit myself. So that really hurt. Those kinds of comments and allegations and accusations and sometimes you got nasty letters, "How come you didn't help my so-and-so? And they came to you for help. It's fine for you, you're well-off." That kind of thing was really hurtful. And again, you can't stand up and defend yourself, because you don't get angry. You can't get angry at the people. It just would not be professional. So you learn to deal with that. You learn to live with that. You learn to take whatever. At the same time understanding where the people are coming from, why they are feeling that way. And I think for me in my life's lessons, that's one thing I learned is that people are coming from a place of maybe sometimes desperation, or a place of need. I don't think it's personal to me. It's not a personal attack, but it's an attack on the program, 'cause it's limited and it can only help so many people, or meet so much of their needs and no more.

So I just had to learn to separate my personal feelings, my life, from my work. And that's one thing Ken Matsuni taught me right at the very beginning: what is most important is you leave your work at work. When you go home, don't bring your work home. You've got a family. When you leave the office, go home to your family. And if you have personal issues or family problems at home, don't bring that to work, 'cause it's gonna affect your work. And I think that was a good piece of advice and I would advise that to anyone who deals with people, that you don't go to work grumpy and take it out on your clients or co-workers in the office that you're having a bad day and whatever it may be. Separate the two. Sometimes I would come home and I'm just totally beat and mentally exhausted, and I would just go to my room and shut the door for maybe ten, fifteen minutes and collect myself before I carry on with my home life. And there was another lesson learned when I first started in this work and I met this lady. She was at a workshop. And she used to be a band social worker for her own community up in the North. She said, "You're not going to last, Elsie," she said to me. "It's really difficult. You gotta really think about how serious you are about your job. I had to leave home. I tried it for two years, working in my own community. It's the most difficult thing to work for your own people and live in the community. So I give you two years," she said. "And you're going to quit. You'll be burned out," she said. So I thought to myself – 'cause she went on to work for the Department of Indian Affairs. She was a qualified, certified social worker. So I thought about that whenever I felt like I was getting burned out. 'Cause I never really knew what "burned out" was. A lot of people use that expression: "I really am burned out. I'm so burned out. I've gotta take a week off or I gotta take a month off, I'm burned out." And I used to think to myself, "What is that? What is it to be burned out?" And so when this lady told me that, that I would be burned out in two years at the most, I always thought of that. And I would think when I was feeling really stressed or agitated within myself and I don't know about this kind of work, and then I'd tell myself, "No way. I'm not going to go there." Just to prove to myself that lady was wrong when she said I was going to burn out in two years. So that made me more determined to work through my job. And it worked for me.

And there are many other issues, like, when I was on Council things happened that was very stressful for me. And at that time I just felt this is just too much, I'm gonna quit – but again, I thought, "No I'm not. I'm not giving up." And then I went to this program in Victoria. Leonard* was the one that encouraged me to go, my nephew Leonard, 'cause he had taken that program when he was working on the Island. It's called Pursuit of Excellence. And he said to me, "Auntie, you should go to that program, it's really going to help you." I was going through a real stressful time over that whole incident when I was on Council. And I felt like sometimes I was out of body and I just was not in a good place. 'Cause there was so much conflict and attack to me – attacking letters, anonymous letters and gossip in the community – and people taking sides and all kinds of things. "It's a weekend thing," he said. "You arrive there Friday night and you stay. There's a workshop Friday night and Saturday and Sunday evening it's done. But you stay with a group of people and go through this whole program." It's a non-Native program. I said, "Agh, it's too much! It's expensive. It's five hundred dollars." At that time it was five hundred dollars, maybe it is more now, and I said, "Oh, five hundred dollars. That's a lot of money." "Well, look at it this way," he said to me. "If you took a break from your job and you went on a one-week holiday somewhere, you might spend five hundred dollars," he said. "You'll come home, you'll still be tired, and you're still going to have to deal with the issues." So having heard that, I decided I'll try it. I was convinced that it would be really good for me. So I went off to Victoria, stayed through the whole program, and a lot of what that program

---

* Leonard Bob, mentioned also in Chapter 9.

taught me was the very same things that I heard as a child and growing up with my grandparents: what people can do to you to get you down, how you can take care of yourself. It was put in a little different way – they didn't talk about cleansing or brushing – but it was a lot of mental unloading, a lot of clearing your mind and getting rid of other people's garbage. And they talked a lot about carrying other people's burdens and how that can affect you and your health. And dealing with all kinds of issues. "Yeah," I thought, "I've heard all this before!" So during that period of time I had forgotten the teachings. It was there all the time, that I could've done more of that. I did it in little spurts, you know, like going to my room after a day's work and trying to collect myself. But I wasn't doing it all the time, and I didn't have it perfected. So after having gone there, it just felt really good. I felt like a different person altogether. I came back from Victoria, went back to work, and I just felt like I unloaded all this garbage over there. And that's what that program told you: "You've come here for a reason, and after this weekend, when you go home, you're going to be a different person." So we really had to follow a rigid program. And there was one exercise that you had to be quiet from, was it the Friday night? 'Cause we were only there two nights, Friday night and Saturday night. And one of those nights, what they instructed us to do was not to talk. Not to talk to anyone! Even riding with other people in the program, going back to your – we stayed with a family down there that took families in that were taking that program. So it was, like, a house, not a boarding house, but they took in a few boarders. And you don't even talk to your roommate. So that was kind of a tough exercise. And we all did it. You know, getting on the car and leaving that workshop, not to say nothing to the person you're riding with, getting to that house, have dinner, go to bed with your roommate is there and not to talk, get up in the morning, don't talk to anyone, have your breakfast, you all go back to the program by nine o'clock. And we did well. I don't know if there were others that didn't, but I managed to do that. It's like self-discipline. So that kind of reminded me of, like, the vision quest or the self-discipline that people went through to make themselves stronger. So that's what we did. So I was never sorry I took that program, 'cause I came home and I was able to carry on with work and managed to work twenty-four and a half years in that same job. Yeah.

One person was just so angry at me all the time, was an angry man, or demanding why I don't do this or why I don't do that. And trying to explain the reasons why just didn't sink in. And he came twice to my office and just was yelling at me and pretty much leaning over the desk with both hands on the desk and addressing me across the desk and, "You –" swearing and cussing that I'm not doing my job. And the second time he came and did that I lost it. I got really angry. I stood up, because he was towering over me. I stood up and I leaned across my desk with my hands on the desk and I said, "You listen here. You come in here shouting at me. You think my job is easy? You think the decisions that I make are easy for me to make? I'm sorry to disappoint you." I said, "If you think this job is so easy, you can have it." I said, "You come sit on this side of the desk and you see what it's like." He just kind of was startled. He kind of straightened himself and kind of, okay, and he walked out. Well, the next day he came back. He came back and apologized. He said, "Yesterday," he said, "the other time when I came in I know I was nasty and I didn't realize what I was doing to you." He said, "I'm really sorry." Shook my hand and left. I shook his hand and we were fine after that, whenever he talked to me he was quite okay with me. But that was the one and only time I did that. Yeah, I still remember it so clearly today, that he was so angry. And all of a sudden he was just like – *[gesture].*[*]

So it was not easy working in your own community. It's really hard. I don't envy people. Sure, they got a job, they got money coming in, but it's not easy when you're dealing with people in a small community. I think social workers and health care workers and whatever your position is within your First Nations community, it's tough. In these days, you have to have a lot of training, a lot of self-discipline. And respect for people. Because people are people – doesn't matter where they're coming from or what their background is, people have needs and it all depends on how you treat them as to how they're going to treat you too. So quite often you're quite humbled by people and not to be reacting all the time to people. That one time I reacted to this individual. It worked that time, but I wouldn't do that all the time. I never would! And that was twice someone did that to me – came shouting around in my office. Another one was a young woman. And just came in and went up one side of me and down the other. And I just sat there and I listened to her. She accused me of all kinds of things, "You're reporting me to the welfare system in town," and all that kind of stuff. And "Who do you think you are?" And "I know

---

[*] By this gesture, Elsie indicates that the man's anger suddenly evaporated.

you're stealing money from this department! And I heard you gave your old furniture to someone else and you bought new furniture from this program, but you gave your old furniture to this person that needed –" all those kinds of just – it was terrible. So when she finished yelling, I said, "Are you finished?" I told her, "You can come back when you're feeling calmer." I said, "Then we'll talk." So she left. And the next day she came back and she was ready to talk. That was funny. It was strange. "I'm sorry," she said, "I'm sorry about yesterday. It's just that people are saying this about you, and people are saying that about you." I said, "Well, do you believe everything you hear?" I said, "It's too bad that you have to take this gossip seriously." So after that she never came back. So that was twice that I really encountered that kind of real menacing face-to-face anger. And another time another man came into my office and he wasn't from this community – I'd never seen him before. I don't know how he ended up in the community. I guess he was transient or – I don't know if he was friends with anyone. But he came into my office just to vent about the system, about the program. He came and he shut the door, so I'm alone in this room with him. And the secretary I think seen him come in, and he was in my room a long time, and he went on and on and on about the injustices of his life, and why he's venting on me, I don't know. "You think you've got a good job, you're lucky to have this job! You're living well." And I didn't know how to deal with him, because I didn't know him at all, and I didn't know if I should stand up and ask him to leave or – "You know what!" he said, "I could kill you right here," he said, "and no one would be the wiser, 'cause it's just you and me in this room." He said that to me. Yeah, I think he had some mental issues. He wasn't drinking. I didn't smell liquor on him at all. So he vented and vented on me. He was in there for close to an hour, sitting there just venting. And so I thought the best I could do is to sit here and let him talk, and let him talk, and let him talk. So finally, he got up and left. I thought, "Phew!" So anyway, I went back and I talked to the chief administrator at the time. And he said, "You know what you should do?" He said, "We should have a button in your room. Anyone that's angry like that, we have no way of knowing what's going on in your office." So that was the one and only time I felt really threatened. And it was by a non-member – it was a non-Native person. Yeah. He wasn't there to make an application for assistance, but he was so mad at the system – he was angry at the system, he was angry at the government, and he was directing that at me. So that was the one and only time that I really felt threatened, like, physically threat-ened, 'cause he said that to me: "I could kill you right here, nobody would know."

Well, I was a justice of the peace for seven years. And that was when I was still in social work and after I was finished with that I was still involved in that, so it was over that period of time. And that just kind fell out of the sky for me, that I got a phone call offering me this job. And I was so afraid of, like, why? Justice of the peace, to me that sounds really scary. I don't know nothing about justice of the peace. So I was called in and invited to come in and the administra-tion there talked to me about it and, "Could you do this?" And, "These are the duties." And, "Oh, it's not hard, you can do it and just use your common sense. All it is, is common sense." Well, I was really nervous about it. I said, "I have to think about this." So they gave me a couple, three weeks to think about it. So I accepted that job. So that was seven years and then I turned sixty-five, so that's when it ended, 'cause they retire you at sixty-five from that position. But I really learned a lot from that position. It's not a full-time job. You're only getting stipend. You're not on a salary. It was a set amount that you got, just to pay for my gas, pretty much. It's pretty much a voluntary position back then. I don't know how it is now. So I did the week-ends. I would do the weekends, when there's no judge – or nighttime. That you go there when you are called by the police station. Come and deal with a show-cause hearing. A lot of times there was a lot of juveniles, and you can't lock up a juvenile unless there's real good reason to keep them there. So it took a few hours sometimes, couple hours that you're there trying to find a parent – you know, the police are phoning and where's the parents of this underage person that needs to be represented by a parent. Or if there's no parents around, they have to try to contact a social worker to come and represent and support the young person. And it was left at your discretion, should you just have them released with conditions? So this is what the show-cause hearing is about. You just go and, "This is the evidence, this is what the person did. And should we let him go home or keep him locked up?" 'Cause they could only keep you locked up for three days. If this happened on a Friday, they have to appear in court first thing Monday. "Or is he okay to be released?" According to my judgment. I'd have to use my common sense. Well, we did both. Sometimes the person ended up staying there. Sometimes they went home. And doing the search warrants. Or the police would just come to my door with a search warrant in so-and-so's house. So you had to look at the reason why they want to go there. You had to be really, really careful around that. Because things have changed so much, that people have rights. You can't just go crashing into a door and search the house if you don't know what you're looking for – go search the outhouse or the outbuilding or wherever. It had to be so specific to what they're looking for, and where is it in the house, and who gave that information – is that a reliable source that gave the information? A known, reliable source? So you had to really look at that. And if it didn't look enough to warrant a search, I would have to say, "I'm sorry. I can't sign that. There's not enough here to justify a search." 'Cause it really is invasive, you know, police do a false search in your house. It's intruding into your life. If there's not enough evidence – you don't see enough evidence to allow that to happen. So that rested on my head, on my decision. Yeah, so, and I had the right to refuse: "I'm sorry, I can't sign this." And I made it very clear at the beginning, when I was first hired, that I will not sign a search warrant for my own community, if it's for my own community, because I live here, I live with the people. Everybody knows I'm the justice of the peace – then they get a copy of the search warrant with my name on it! So I told them right at the beginning, I will not sign a search warrant for my own community members. So it was okay. Yeah. It was okay. It worked out well.

Yeah, and that's when Honoré used to come and stay. Well, when I was living at the lodge and Honoré used to live there – and then he lived here with me too in this house. And sometimes when he'd be sitting up late doing his work and I've gone off to bed, and I guess he would answer the phone, "Could I speak to Mrs. Paul, please?" kind of tone of voice, I guess, the officers talk. "Okay." He'd come and knock on my door: "Telephone for you." So I, "Okay" – take the phone – "Okay, I'll be right there," Get dressed and go. I never told him what I was doing. So he came to his own conclusion that I was seeing a man. And he had those thoughts in his head for a long time. I don't know what he thought of me! He must have thought I was this loose woman! It was funny when he finally told me about it. Oh! I laughed and laughed. It just never occurred to me to explain to him. Because you know, the work you do is confidential and you don't go talking about it. You just go and do your job, and so the few times that he answered the phone, he thought I was meeting a man some- where. That's what he told me! *[laughs hard]* He laughed, oh, he laughed about it. We both laughed about it. Never met this mysterious man that phones in the middle of the night. *[laughs]*

When I was still in social work, the justice program started to come to be. And Denise Smith was the justice worker at that time. And so as a committee we were developing how to go about – and the committee consisted of RCMP representatives and different people from the court system, probation, and the Chief at the time. Our community deciding what kind of justice system should we have. And that's when they were first, I think, really developing and putting Aboriginal policing into Aboriginal communities. So at that time the police offered to put a station here in our community – a police station, a substation, very small – just to introduce that to the community, that there is police presence in the community. And the Salish Centre was quite – it was early – I don't know how many years the centre had been there. But there were a couple of tiny little offices, just enough for a phone there. That's where it first started. That's where the police officer would go and sit and, you know – no bigger than a closet. That's where it first started. And Mary George was involved in cutting of the ribbon there. It was after a lengthy discussion and consideration: should it happen? And put it out to the community. A lot of people were opposed to it: "If they bring a police station onto the reserve, we're going to destroy it." Or there was threats around that, 'cause the people at that time were really anti-police and didn't trust the police at all. So it went ahead anyway, and surprisingly nothing happened. These threats didn't come about. So, I don't know if it was a year later, probably a year later that the substation was put there by the band office. So it's got a little office in there and police officer who would be the Aboriginal police officer would be there during his time within the community. But he also serves the larger community – he or she would serve the larger community. So if there's a crisis in town, then he'd have to leave and go and respond to that. But in his off time from the rest of the community, from Powell River, he would be here in our community.

So it just started that way, building relationships with the people and Council and the other workers within our community, working with those people. And we talked about a whole lot of things. We had meeting after meeting, trying to get involvement from the community. How do we approach – how do we handle situations, especially with juveniles? They're out late at night. What are they doing out at night? How can we enforce something that's really hard to enforce? Like, it's the parents' responsibility to keep their children at home and from getting into mischief at night, when they're out at night, teenagers. And how do you go about that? Should we put watchmen out there?

That's where that "wačman" logo came from, trying to get into that kind of a mentality – the watchmen did this in our communities a long time ago, and they were the, like, the watchmen that controlled and oversaw that kids didn't get into trouble or didn't get hurt. So a lot of discussion around that. It was really hard to get that running, 'cause we were not consistent enough. Or those of us that were involved in the planning just had other things – they're busy – and there wasn't a lot of interest in the community as a whole. So it was really hard to get that off the ground. Then we got to talking about the legal system, dealing with our own crises and not really serious matters, but small offences. Like young kids getting into trouble, if they're caught breaking into – causing vandalism, whatever. Then we developed a committee that would deal with that instead of them having to go to court. So we did that and we tried a few cases and at one time there was a plan to have regular court at the Salish Centre. One room would be set up. The judge would come and hear the cases. And that didn't fly. They had to hook up the sound system and all of those things. It just didn't fly. So we stuck to our divergent program pretty much, that a case could be diverted to an Elders' – we even had workshops. A person came from the university in Vancouver, came to give a workshop to the Elders, how to, you know, the legalities of – and it was really hard for the Elders to understand that. And at the same time they were really afraid of repercussions too. And how do we select an Elder? Who's going to sit in a diversion program? 'Cause we're so related, no matter where you look. And if those Elders – whether they're two or three Elders that sits in on any one case in particular, in a hearing – whatever their recommendation is would naturally become very unpopular to other families. So it was really difficult. It was really difficult for an Elder to be put in that position. And they didn't quite understand the legalities of the system. So that really didn't fly too well.

Personally, myself, I handled a few cases on my own that I sat and talked with the families, tried to come to some resolution. And that worked really well. Both families came together, in a couple of incidents where both families shook hands and it's resolved, where it could have meant this individual going to jail, serious jail time. Which would not have served anyone well, because the two families were connected in a way. And it was serious enough that the person would have served serious jail time. And resolved it in a way that the offender really humbled himself to the other family and gave his possessions away – just like they would have done years ago. But he did

it on his own. Other people didn't say, "You have to do this." He made
his choice. He gave a lot of his stuff away, like pictures and different
things. And I think he even gave a vehicle away. Just big things like
that. It really changed his lifestyle, changed his life. He ended up that
he didn't have to be sent away. And we did this not in the courthouse,
but in a room in the government building, downstairs, in a separate
room where we sat and listened to everybody's – the grandparents of
that family and senior members of the family, and the victim and the
offender. So, came to a resolution. The prosecutor was sitting in. His
lawyer was sitting in, and the Crown prosecutor. And it worked out
really well. Probation officer was there. So we talked and they all
talked. It was a real good ending. So I think that's an example of how
well it could have worked if we continued to do that. And we dealt
with a couple of kids, just the probation officer and myself and another
Elder, one of our workers in the community. And minor offence – only
minor offences. This other one I'm talking about was dragging on for
almost two years in the court system, where it wasn't coming to a
resolution. It got postponed, postponed, postponed – remanded and
all that kind of stuff. And when we did the minor offence with a young
person, you can't go back to the diversion program if you have broken
the rules. We only handle it once, and you don't have a criminal record. But if you commit the offence again or another similar offence,
then you have to go to the regular court system. So in a couple of
cases, that worked fine – that was okay. And I really don't know how
it's working now. But that was in my time.

Yeah, and then I became involved in the Aboriginal Policing Program. A committee where they had representatives of Elders – probably
about four Elders, myself and I think three other Elders that took part
in this Aboriginal policing. So it was Aboriginal people from Aboriginal communities working with Aboriginal policing. And I was involved
in that for a couple years. And then the system changed and they
decided I guess it wasn't working, but we met at different places. Going
to different meetings with this group. They came here at one time and
we went to some other community. We even went up to Dawson City.
That's when I flew up there in Elvis Presley's jet, *[laughs]* which was
now owned by the Aboriginal policing. Ah! That was the thrill of my
life! Beautiful little jet plane. Yeah. It was fun. And going up there.
It was quite an experience to go up there. We had to go and find an
Elder from way far out. You need an Elder from the community to do
the prayer when you go to their community, right? And this one lady
said, "I'll go get my mother." So, "You want to come along?" So I

came along. And went along with her. We drove and drove and drove. It got dark. And she was way out in a very remote, isolated little place. Really rugged road, bouncing all the way there and back again. We didn't get back till probably about ten o'clock at night. So that was quite the experience! Yeah. You really get to see different places and the different lifestyles. And I guess that's what I liked about my involvement in different committees like that. You get to see and experience how other people live. And it makes you appreciate what you have, and some people have it so hard, especially living in real isolated areas – how they still lived. And I remember some of our old, old people living like that: no plumbing, no electricity, little woodstove, no outhouse. No inside plumbing, you know, there's an outhouse. And there are people still living like that. This one elderly lady, living alone. But she was looking after a little grandchild about two years old, or a year old, and I was really amazed at that. She's still caring for a child at her old age. So that was really a reflection of how some of our Elders used to be, looking after children. Never, ever giving up on children. To me, I think that's a very valuable lesson in how caring the old people were. Whatever reason it was that this child was in their home. I remember the lady that brought me there saying to her mom, "Why are you doing this?" You know, "She's gotta look after her own child. You're getting elderly. You shouldn't be looking after this child." Oh no, it's like she actually embraced this child, 'cause she loved that child! Such as it was. Her humble, humble home. But she still cared. So that was to me a real – like, oh! I knew some Elders like that in my community! Yeah. So that was short-lived, my involvement with the Aboriginal policing. At home I guess they changed their roles, or however they run their operation. Where they're pushing more now to put more Aboriginal police in First Nations communities, and that's working well. I see that to be very positive.

For a long, long time throughout my life, I guess I've always had some involvement with the church as far as caretaking or making sure that the church is looked after, and there's no budget anywhere for the church within our band funds. So it's always been fundraising to upgrade or when it needs new flooring. And back during this time that I'm talking about, when it really needed new flooring, new covering for the floor – the tiles were breaking and falling, coming apart. And so at that time, I was working with Mary – we called ourselves the Altar Society Group, although we were not a society. But we called ourselves that. And so there was Marion Harry and myself and, of course, Mary George. She was always involved. And that's pretty much it. We were a small group. And then other people just kind of joined in when there was real work to be done. And so we organized rummage sales and bake sales. It was just really pathetic. We weren't making any money. Might've made, you know, twenty-five dollars in a rummage sale that we prepared all week for. We'd get all this donation. We ask for donations. And people even coming from town, bringing stuff that were not worth putting out for sale. So it was a lot of work and frustrating. So. And we really wanted to get a carpet for the church, especially around the altar area and down the aisle. So it wasn't long after that we had the new Salish Centre built and put in place there. And other people started using it to fundraise for soccer teams and stuff like that, having dances. So I thought, "Oh, that sounds good." They made couple thousand dollars, this group. And so decided, "Yeah, we should try that!" So we did. So we organized a dance and got the music all lined up, the musicians, live music. It was easy enough for me, because my son-in-law at the time was in the Band. So he was agreeable – so was his group, so we organized this dance with live music. Went and got a liquor licence and we were going to sell liquor at the dance. And you know, I'm already a social worker in the community. And I'm doing all this stuff. So I was told by other people that had organized the previous dances, first you have to go to the police station and get a permit, and then you have to fill out this form. So I went there, got this form done. I was given a copy of this form, this permit. And I was told then, you take this up to the liquor store, 'cause it itemized all the liquor I was going to get and the price of all the liquor, like, for a shot of whatever liquor they were purchasing. How many bottles of this, how many bottles of that, how many cases of beer. So that was all itemized. So I go with that to the liquor store. And had brought a couple of men with me. They loaded up the liquor. And I was supposed to get the licence at the liquor store. But nobody asked me that at the liquor store. I showed them my itemized list, but they didn't ask me – or hand me the licence. I was really naive about all that. I thought I had everything I needed. So we got our – I don't know how many cases of beer it was, if it was thirty cases of beer and couple cases of hard liquor. So we went on our way and set up the dance and people were supposed to buy their tickets in advance. Of course people don't always do that, so people were buying tickets at the door to come in. So the lady that was watching the door, she was the one that was taking admissions at the door, and I'm just kind of floating around making sure that everything is going well. Had my permit tacked onto the wall – I thought that's the permit. That it's okay. So people started arriving. Pretty soon we had a real full house. And it's only about ten thirty, going on to eleven, and it's just starting to pick up and people are starting to dance and well, lo and behold! I look over to the door where the admissions was and there's a couple of men standing there looking really – like, they're really officious looking, leather jackets on – talking to the lady that was sitting there. I thought, "Oh, I wonder what –?" And then she's pointing towards my direction, like to say, "She's the one in charge, go talk to her." I could see that's what she was doing. So these two men came across the hall to where I was: "We'd like to see your licence to run this dance and sell liquor." "Oh yeah, no problem. It's over here." So I go over there and show it to him. And he says, "That's not a licence. That's a permit." He said, "You should have got a licence from the liquor store." "Really?" I said, "Nobody told me that." "Well, you don't have the licence to operate this dance. And it's not only that. You're serving to minors, and you're selling booze tickets at the door. That's a no-no." What else did he say? "You have minors in this establishment where you're selling liquor." And they had run into some young teenager outside that had a case of beer and that teenager said, "I bought it from inside," which wasn't true. He must've brought it there himself and hoped to get into the dance. So there were about five offences. And he said, "This dance has to shut down. We're shutting this dance down." And by then more officers walked in. There were about two or three officers in one door, and another two, three officers at the other door. So they came really prepared to shut the dance down. And to press charges, 'cause it was not run the way it should. So, "You shut this dance down. There's no two ways about it." So I had to go up to the stage and had to go and talk to my son-in-law, who was the drummer. And he's drumming away there and they're going – and I had to go and interrupt their music. And I'm leaning over and whisperin' – talking – trying to shout in his ear, "I have to shut the dance down!" "Huh?" he's going. He keeps on drumming away at it. "I have to shut the dance down." "Oh" – finally, you know, stopped and everything stopped. Then they started to gather all the liquor. They backed up their big vehicle, you know, a wagon – big vehicle. Yeah. And they loaded up everything! They even dumped the booze or the beer that was open on the tables. And they loaded up everything and away they went. And people were really good. They were understanding. They cleared out. They didn't get mad or didn't demand their money back. So, "You'll hear from us. You will hear from us." Taking everything, shutting us down. Off they went. We were just dumbstruck, looking at each other: "How did this happen?"

So anyway, and Joe Mitchell was our Chief then. I went to talk to talk to him at the band office. I said, "I really got into trouble. I may be facing charges." "Oh!" He was really silent and just listened to me, and "I think the police is gonna be calling you," I said to him. "Oh, that's okay," he said, "I'll talk to him when he calls. Don't worry about it," he said. So about a week later, a police officer called. And Joe and I had to go to the police station. And boy! That police officer read us the riot act! Me especially. All the laws that I broke that night, and all the charges that I could be charged with. And he started talking about, he had just moved to this post, to this position, from some remote, isolated area where there was a lot of violence and a lot of liquor and minors drinking, and so he's comparing that that could happen here. "This is what happens when –" he went on and on and on about where he'd been, how rough it was in that part of the world. And here I am selling this to minors and whatever. So we had to eat humble pie, I'm telling you. I sat there and listened, and Joe and I looking at each other, like couple of bad kids, sitting there while we got this lecture. So with all that, I was given a chance to explain what happened and I didn't realize this was going on. Sure we were selling tickets, 'cause we hadn't sold enough before the dance, so tickets were sold at the door. And I knew that was wrong, but I wasn't denying that – but it was an honest mistake about the licence. I truly was under the impression that I got everything right. And we didn't sell to those minors. That kid outside was lying when he said he bought that case of beer from the hall. We wouldn't sell to kids. So anyway, he let me off the hook. And he says, "You can take back all the liquor." I said, "What am I going to do with all that liquor now?" I said, "Can I have a picnic or something, or sell it that way?" "No!" he said, so much as to say, "Are you stupid?" or "You think I'm stupid?" or, you know, that kind of look. He was really gruff-looking. "Oh," I said. "Well." So I took it home. So I stored it in a storage area here in my house. Stacks of beer, cases of beer. We couldn't return those to the liquor store 'cause they were all open and marked. But the hard liquor that was still closed, I could take that and get a refund on that. So we did that. So I thought, "What am I going to do with all this beer in my storage area?" Course everybody knew I had all this beer, in the community. So I started to sell it to the soccer teams – after a soccer game they wanted to have beer and so they knew where to go – they come here and I'd sell them a case of beer. So I was getting the money

Elsie receiving donation for the Sliammon Sacred Heart Church from the Knights of Columbus in the late 1970s. Photo courtesy of Elsie Paul.

back that we put out. Well, I got a reputation for being a bootlegger in Sliammon. I had to live with that for a long time. Elsie the social worker is a bootlegger. *[laughs]* Long after the beer was all gone, people were still knocking on my door, "Got any beer for sale?" "No! I don't. I'm not a bootlegger!" Oh, that was so embarrassing.

We didn't make any profit at all! Because we lost a lot of the beer that was dumped out, right? And the hard liquor – what was left of some of the bottles were dumped out. Only the sealed ones we were able to get – so we broke even, pretty much. So, so much for a quick buck for the church. *[laughs]* That was so terrible! Oh, I'd never do that again. Yeah. So the Catholic women – Catholic group in town, through the Knights of Columbus – I don't know if they heard about this or whatever, but anyway, they helped us out. They donated money for the carpet. Yeah. So. I have a picture of that, the head of the Knights of Columbus handing me a cheque – we're inside the church – to pay for the carpet. So that worked out okay, and they saved us. Saved me from – *[laughs]* Oh! That was hard. So it was quite an experience, I'm tellin' ya. Almost went to jail. Could've been charged. Could've had a criminal record. All for the church! I meant well! I had good intentions! *[laughs]*

We could talk about the importance of the language. We're trying to preserve as much as we can. So I have worked with different groups of people that are documenting the language. We're trying to document the language. And for its use, too, in the school system, 'cause it's taught in the school system now in our area. So for that purpose we've done a lot of documenting. And for the community as well, all the recording that we did around that. To try to interest the people in using that, encourage the people to listen to it and listen to it at their own leisure and be able to learn the language that way, or to revive the language. So it is a lot of work. It's no ending to that work, and I don't think it will ever end, because a lot of the people don't use the language anymore. A lot of people don't know the language anymore. So there's very few that use it or that know it or are fluent in it. But we do as much as we can for the sake of the school program, and hopefully it will work. I do a lot of just clarifying a lot of words with Betty that is very involved in the language program through the school. She quite often phones to clarify this word, or how can you phrase this or how do you say this in this context or whatever. So I have quite a bit of involvement and input into that area. Just for their own documentation with the school, so she records it in the orthography style of writing. But for myself it's really hard, because I don't understand the orthography, and that translation. And I think it's really important to the people that know the orthography, like Betty and Gail* and Karen Galligos and Marion Harry – they have a good understanding of the orthography. So they're the main ones that have really learned that, or trying to learn it to be able to use it, because the language is really difficult to document. So it helps them, because they know how to read the orthography and how to write that orthography. But I don't, so when I look at the material that I've helped put together and worked with different people, like the linguists that come around, and so that's all written in orthography – when I look at the written work, I have to look at the translation first and, "Oh, that's the English. Oh, okay. Now I can figure out what that word is." So in order to carry the language to its fullest and to its best, you pretty much have to be a linguist. To me it doesn't make a lot of sense, because where the sounds come from, from way back in your throat or through your cheeks or, you know. And it's really difficult teaching it, because when you're talking to a linguist – and I've talked to quite a few different linguists that try to capture the sounds, "Where does that sound come from?" And "Is this syllable – where's this syllable? How many syllables of that?" And "Can you repeat that again?" And they're looking right at you and lookin' at your mouth and so when

---

* Betty Wilson and Gail Blaney.

I slow down and I try to say something in the language, like, oh, just for an example, "sɑymot puh?əm," you know? "It's real windy." So I just say, "sɑymot puh?əm!" "Oh! Can you repeat that again?" "sɑy. mot. puh. ?əm." You know. So they're lookin' at your mouth and studyin' how your mouth is working. And the Elders had a real hard time with that, the fluent speakers that are now gone: "skʷičimot hɛhɛw. pɑpqʷosəm!"* They'd go like that, 'cause they're not used to people lookin' right at their mouth and staring at them, studying their mouth. "Where's it coming from? Is it coming from the roof of your mouth? Is it coming from the throat or it's coming from – ?" So they's studying your mouth, studying your face. And for a person – our Elders especially – that is not used to having that kind of a contact, it is rude! And so they'd get really mad. "χɑχyɛmot hɛhɛw!"† they'd go, "pɑpqʷosəm!"‡ Get really annoyed. Yeah. What are they saying? You could see Agnes and Katherine,§ "ɬəχmot hɛhɛw!"‖ Gettin' mad. And the body language tells you they're annoyed, and the tone of their voice. So it's time-consuming. It takes a lot of your time and a lot of patience.

So it's really hard. I really would like to see the language stay alive. But the reality? I don't know if it's possible. Because a lot of the words that we used in my grandparents' time, and my great-grandparents' time, the language they used is so different from how it's used today, even to the fluent speakers. A lot of words are not used, so consequently that's not passed on. Because of the different activities, different lifestyle. What tools they used for going clam digging or going fishing or gaffing fish at the river, or going hunting or setting the branches out to gather herring roe. What kind of branch – all these things have names and titles that we don't have today. We don't do those activities anymore. Sure, we go clam digging. We get a shovel and go down there. Well, people didn't have a shovel a long time ago, so they used something else. So all of those things are like past history, how do you begin to document that? And even myself, I'm forgetting a lot of those old, old words, those old terms. And Dave Dominick is the only one that I know now that remembers all of those. If I'm really stuck I'll talk to him and say, "What do you call this?" Just like that

---

* Translation: It's really irritating to be stared at (your face is being stared at).
† Translation: It's strange.
‡ Translation: Your face is being stared at.
§ Agnes McGee (Elsie's aunt) and Katherine Blaney.
‖ Translation: It is very bad.

he'll give me that word. He hasn't forgotten. So that's really something, that he hasn't forgotten. 'Cause he grew up with his grandparents and he grew up around Bill Mitchell and losε? and all of those older people from north of here. And they travelled a lot. So he knows all the place names of every little bay and every little point and inlet and mountains and rivers and creeks. He still knows that today! And animals! And birds. It just amazes me. He's never stuck. He may sometimes have to think a little bit, but he'll come back and tell you, "When you were asking me this, I remember now. This is what it is." Yeah, so that's real precious – precious stuff. How can you capture all his knowledge? He's like a dictionary. And he's getting elderly and he had a lot of health problems. So you don't want to put a lot of pressure on him. But he'll willingly tell you when he's good and ready. He'll tell you. If you ask him in a nice way, he'll tell you. And he would be another one that would not sit still to be interviewed, and it'll be hard to get him to co-operate and expect him to sit still and, "How many syllables was that?" and "How do you form your mouth?" and "Where does that sound come from?" Yeah, so as much as I'm concerned about keeping the language alive, I don't see it as a reality. And my reality is how my Elders spoke to each other and one another. That's the reality. I don't see young people having that kind of language or communication.

But I feel it's important to have some of it documented, or as much as we can. And it's important for the young people to know that was how our ancestors communicated. That was their lifestyle. That was what they did. So somewhere along the way – if it's possible to have that preserved, so that one day, my great-great-grandchildren – or hundred years from now someone will look at it and find it really interesting. You know, that was our ancestors, and that was how they lived. And it would be really, really interesting a hundred years from now for people then, it's almost like if you forget the language and the culture, you came from nowhere. That's what forms your identity: your roots, your culture. So I continue as much as possible to be involved and share what I know. And like I said, I'm forgetting a lot of the old, old words anymore, or the names of the birds and stuff like that. Yeah. So it's dying off and dying off, bits and pieces, so slowly. There are other people here in the community that – very few that can still speak – maybe as a couple, man and wife, they talk back and forth to one another using the language. But even some people at that age, maybe the ones that spent a lot of time away from families, have forgotten, or they lost it through the system. They lost it through time. But it's a real neat language and it's so much fun. I used to have a lot of fun talking to Agnes and Katherine and Mary George. And Honoré used to get a kick out of this. I guess he just listens, 'cause I don't pay attention myself the way he does about how we converse with one another. He'd say, "You know" – he's pointing this out to me – "Agnes and Katherine, Marion, you, you're talking. You're having a conversation and you switch over to English and you all switch over in English and then you switch back to the language and –" but we unconsciously do that. Why do we do that? You know, it's like – certain words. And instead of really sticking to just the language, 'cause we were all fluent together. And even amongst themselves, you know, Agnes and Mary, Agnes and Katherine, and she would talk in English to Katherine, and more Agnes than Katherine, right? Yeah. But they were fun ladies together, 'cause they made baskets together and – yeah. I think I was telling that story about how Katherine thought Agnes could understand Inuit language? They were sitting on the couch at Agnes's there, and of course they're doing basket, right? They have the TV on. And APTN is on. Agnes used to like to watch that. So, what do you call the – dubbed? – subtitle. Yeah, subtitle. Agnes, I guess, is watching. Of course Katherine's there.* Yeah. So she's telling Katherine what's going on: "Oh, it's interesting," going on and on. And so Katherine looks at her real puzzled. Agnes is explaining, but they're talking, but you could hear them talking, but you don't understand, so it's subtitles. So Agnes is able to read. She was good at reading – she was good. And Katherine said, "χαχγαmot hɛhɛw ʔaʔ̌juθmɛtʌčxʷ." She said, "Do you understand – you know their language?" And Agnes looks at her, and you know how Agnes used to crack up. And she laughed! You could see her throw back her head and laugh. So she had quite a time explaining that to Katherine: "No! nɑmɛt tiyʔtɑ – nɑnɑmɛt tiyʔtɑ!" "It's written there! I'm reading it." *[laughs hard]* Oh, that was hilarious. So I went there to visit and they were both laughing. And Katherine says, "χαχγαmot hɛhɛw." She said, "hɛhɛw χαχγαmot nɛʔɛt č gɑ ʔaǰuθ Agnes t'θɛt'θit'θoǰus!"† They were a pair, those two! I could see Katherine being real serious, too. *[laughs]* They're hilarious. They were so hilarious, those two!

---

* The humour of this story turns on the fact that Katherine was blind.

† Translation: It's strange – I thought Agnes understood their language – she's crazy!

Honoré Watanabe, linguist, with Sliammon elders (from left) Marion Harry, Mary George, and Elsie Paul. Honoré worked extensively with these three ladies over more than two decades and lived with Elsie during his stays in Sliammon. Marion was Elsie's "little sister" at residential school and worked with Honoré to transcribe and translate the selections in Sliammon language included in this book. Photo taken at the Sliammon Elders Lodge in 2001. Photo courtesy of Elsie Paul.

The work I do at the Powell River campus, I find it really interesting.* Again, when that work was offered to me, I felt that I'm not deserving of that – this is a university! And I'm asked to go work in a university to talk to students, and I really had to think about that. And in talking with Arlette about that, "Well, what you would be doing is this," you know. "Talking about the history and the students would love to hear the history! I'm sure they'd love to hear the history of the Sliammon people." And recognizing my abilities or my knowledge of the history. So I wasn't sure. I guess it takes other people to

---

* This refers to the Powell River campus of Vancouver Island University. Arlette Raaen, who collaborated on this project, is currently the principal of this campus.

tell you what you're worth. Because I couldn't see myself in a place like a university campus, to be a – not a teacher, but to share the culture. So it's two days a week. We started the first year and it was, like, half-time. I work Monday and Wednesday, and from September to end of June. Then last year I felt that towards the end of the year, that the campus is starting to clear out and it was really slack. Time was really slack. I just felt really bad. I felt, "What am I doing here?" You know, place is getting really quiet. So I talked to one of the ladies there in the office. I said, "I think we need to shorten my time here, 'cause I just feel like I'm wasting your money and my time. 'Cause there's very few students that are coming through right now, this time of the year." So she talked it over, I guess, with other people, and decided, okay. So this past year I only worked till the end of May – ending of May, third week in May – and so I was off in June. Yeah. They're really, really fine people that work there. They're all so good to me. I've never been in a workplace that people are so good to me and so respectful to me. They provided a little office for me: "Oh, and there's a computer!" Yeah, right! *[laughs]* "I don't do computers, I'm sorry." That's been really good. I've worked with students that, they have an essay to do. So what I do is I go and I talk in the – like, the history class or, you know, different classes – like, the seniors come there for different kinds of a class and they invite me to come and speak to seniors. And the seniors just really like it. They enjoy hearing about our history. And the craft class and they invited me to come in there, and I give a one-hour talk about our history and our lifestyle before contact and all those things. And the history of our people, and Powell River when I was a child, and the discrimination and the restrictions and – oh, some people feel – just feel really bad about that. They couldn't believe that that's how it was in Powell River. They didn't know that! And some of them have just moved to Powell River, right? Being the retirement town it is. So some of them are newcomers, or they've been here maybe thirty years or so. They still didn't know what our history was. About all the discriminations and the segregation. And they couldn't believe that. So I guess I serve the purpose because the young students themselves are really interesting. They do a paper on it, on my talk. And they come back and they read it back to me and ask, "Is it okay? Is that what I heard you say?" So I book appointments for that class and book their time with me, and they come into my office and we have this one-on-one. Pretty much the same kind of topic, but they have different questions too. So it's quite interesting. Yeah, I did a little film. One of the students

Elsie and close friend Arlette Raaen in August 2012. Arlette worked with Elsie at Vancouver Island University and was a main contributor to this book project since its inception. Photo courtesy of Arlette Raaen.

was really interested and wanted to do a short little film. I have it here somewhere. Yeah. He's quite an interesting young man. And he asked if he could do that film, little video clip. Yeah, so he's got that and I have a copy of it. I guess in a way I'm like a grandmother, and a lot of them say, "You remind me so much of my grandmother," or "You remind me so much of my auntie," or, you know.

So I guess it was through my work at Malaspina campus here that that I had met the president from the Nanaimo campus – Ralph* – and

---

* This refers to Ralph Nilson, president and vice-chancellor of Vancouver Island University (as of 2013).

him coming up here. And I'd met him a couple of times through other functions tied into Malaspina before I was working there. And I was in town on another function, and the mayor was there, and the mayor introduced me. And Arlette was there. So we kind of just chatted and so that was the first time I met him. And then he had come, since I had started to work at Malaspina campus here, that Powell River campus, that I got to know him there and did opening prayer and that. So obviously people had a conversation about me and decided that I would qualify for this doctorate degree. So I was quite shocked when I got a phone call one day, I think it would've been around November, and it was Ralph calling. And I thought, "Oh, why is he calling me?" And he talked about, "We have this doctorate degree that I want to know how you would feel – we're talking about honouring you and giving you this doctorate degree." And I didn't really know what he was talking about, because being who I am, I'm just this lowly person on the west coast! *[laughs]* Anyway. So we had this conversation and I said to him, "You know what?" I said, "Ralph, I don't have a formal education." I said, "I thought degrees like that were only handed to people that have had their bachelor's degree, their master's degree, and whatever else – all these degrees behind their name. That you have to work up to that through the education system." And he said, "Oh, no, no." He said, "Yeah, there's that. But," he said, "There's different categories. And with you," he said, "because of your knowledge of the history and the language and your culture, you have totally a different category to offer. You offer something special that deserves this doctorate degree." I thought, "Wow! I never thought of that." After pondering over that, I thought, "Okay, okay." So it was decided, I would accept that I had that nomination. He said, "I had a meeting with other Elders around the campus." 'Cause there's other Elders, like, I'm the Powell River Elder, right? And they have one in Nanaimo and they have a Cowichan. And so he talked to those people, or someone talked to them. They did a little survey amongst those Elders, "And they voted unanimously for you," he said to me. I said, "Wow!" So that's how I came to have that. And got back to me and it was going to be in January – January the twenty-sixth that I would get this degree.* So I kind of kept that under my hat for a while – just really didn't know how to take it yet. And Arlette knew about it, and obviously Ralph and her had been talking. It felt a little overwhelming

---

* This was in 2010.

▲ Elsie receiving an honorary doctor of letters from Vancouver Island University on 26 January 2010. *Left to right:* Shawn A-in-chut Atleo, chancellor of Vancouver Island University; Elsie Paul; Ralph Nilson, president and vice-chancellor, Vancouver Island University. Elsie's son Walter is in the background at right. Photo courtesy of Davis McKenzie.

▼ Family photo following Elsie's honorary doctorate ceremony at Vancouver Island University, 26 January 2010. Photo courtesy of Davis McKenzie.

for me. And I didn't even want to talk about it. So I don't know if any of my other family members knew, but they wouldn't say anything to me either. *[laughs]* So that was quite an honour. It was a real honour to get that kind of a recognition. So, went to Nanaimo, and convocation in January for all the students there, different categories and that. And so, it was at that time that I got that presented to me. The presentation happened then. Yeah. It doesn't make me feel any different. Quite often people ask me now, "How does it feel to have that degree, or that label put on you?" I don't even think about it. To me, if it's important to people, you know – sure I feel really humbled and honoured to have been given that title. But I'm not going to brag about it or boast about it, 'cause it's a very humbling experience. In my growing years, old people used to say, "If you do your work well, or if you live a good life and you treat the people well, but don't brag about what to do, don't boast, don't ever boast about what you're doing, it's other people that will see you and recognize what you do. And if you go around bragging about, 'Oh, I did this and I did that and I went out and I caught ten deer, or I went out and I –' just boasting and bragging about what to do in life, then people are not going to respect you. It's up to other people to recognize what you do or who you are or what you do in life." Yeah.

So I think I learned from a very early age that it's so wrong to boast or brag about – in our language it's called "šɛʔt qʷayigən."* "ɬəχmot šɛʔt qʷayigən. xʷaʔ čxʷ šɛtas kʷə θ qʷayigən" – "It's not good to be proud. It's not good to brag." So they'd repeat that over and over. They're always telling the kids that: "ɬəχmot šɛʔt qʷayigən." Like, your qʷayigən is your mind, your heart, your being. And "šɛʔt" means "high," right? šɛʔt qʷayigən. ɬəχmot – "ɬəχmot" means "no good." It's not good. So that's the kind of teaching that was imposed upon me, and a lot of people believed that way a long time ago. Or if you had money in your pocket come, you don't go flashing, "Oh gee! I'm rich. I got money. I've got –" you know. It's not good. When you have money, put it away! "Put it away!" – they'd go like that *[gesturing]* – "Don't be showing your money to people. That's bragging, that's boasting! Money's not going to stay with you if you do that. If you respect and honour your money or whatever possessions you have, be humble about it. You have to respect that money, otherwise money's not going to come to you. Money's got power." How do they know

---

* Translation: to be proud; to be a braggart.

that? How did they know that? Even if it's two dollars or whatever – coin. Tuck it away. Tuck it away. But don't brag about it. "One day that's going to be your friend. That's gonna help you when you really need help, and no one's around to help you. You're gonna go to your little stash and use that money in a critical time or whatever it is. You don't go run to the neighbour and say, 'Can I borrow money from you? Can I borrow your boat? Can I borrow this?' Nobody likes a person that does that. You'll have no respect in life if you live that kind of life." So it's really important teaching about respect and to be humble and not to be flashy or showing off. Just keep quiet and you don't have to go around telling people all the things you do in life. They used to talk about this guy that used to go hunting. They always talked about that, using him as an example. That was another thing, like, the animal life really sense what you're doing, what you're up to. And if you decide to go hunting, you take care of yourself first. You bathe yourself, you brush yourself, you cleanse your mind, you prepare yourself to go hunting, and you go. But there was this one man that used to say, "Oh, I'm gonna go hunting tomorrow! And I'm gonna this, and I'm gonna da-da-da." And he'd be going on and on. He'd go hunting and more often than not he'd come home with nothing. So, you know, community laughed at him because he was bragging he's gonna come home with all this. So I guess it's very much like today, you hear people like, "Oh! I've got this flashy car and I've got this –" big-shot kind of a guy and showing off. Which probably the bank owns the vehicle, like maybe forty thousand dollars or something. "It's not yours. It belongs to the bank!" *[laughs]* So that system of long time ago was, you taught your children to be humble. Don't be a show-off, 'cause you may regret it. Yeah, so. Anyway. Back to my degree and, you know, people ask, "How does it feel?" I don't feel any different. I'm still me. I really don't have anything to say about it except that I'm very honoured to have received that degree. And thank the people for their consideration of me. But I'm still me. Yeah.

Legends

MINK AND WHALE

I will tell another one about a whale: qayχ and Whale. When we were children, we were always told by the old people, "Respect things around you. Every living thing has life. The sea creatures, the whales, the salmon. Don't make fun of them. Don't think bad things of them, because they can read your mind. They can see. They can read you." So if you make fun of them, something will happen to you. So one day, qayχ is out there for a change. He's out searching for food. He's all by himself. He's jiggin' out there – sittin' in his boat and he's jiggin' away for cod. And it's a *beautiful* day. It's *so* hot! The waters are *so* calm. And he's not getting a nibble at all, no bite. And he'd been there a long time. Nothing! So he sees a whale surface from the great distance. He sees this sparkle in the water, some movement over there. Then he'd see it again. And he recognizes it as a whale: "Oh, that's a whale." And he's getting irritated by this point that he's not getting any cod or anything at all. So he gets mad at the Whale. He says, "Oh, Whale! You'd think you'd come over here and bite my line, you shiny-headed so-and-so." So he done that a couple of times, name-calling that Whale. Pretty soon that Whale surfaces, a *lot* closer. And he just ignores it and he's getting a little nervous. The next thing you know, the Whale surfaced right near his boat. Now he's getting nervous. Then the Whale surfaced again with its mouth *wide* open. And here he is in his small little boat, jiggin' away. And the Whale sucks him up with its big mouth, pulls the whole boat in with qayχ in that boat. Swallows it! Boat and all. So he ends up in the belly of the Whale. Totally dark in there and it's *really* hot. And he's still sittin' in his boat. And he feels something hitting him on the head, or his face. Something would hit him. He doesn't know what this is. So he reaches around for a sharp object, his knife, takes it and he grabs this thing and he cuts it off. And here it is, the heart. So the Whale dies. And qayχ is still there. And the Whale drifts ashore – gets drifted onto the beach. And men seen this Whale, dead Whale on the beach, and they

said, "Oh my goodness! Look at that whale." All the men ran down
there and they slit the Whale open, 'cause it's partly in the water still.
And all the guts and everything spilled out of the Whale, including
qayχ's boat and qayχ still in it. qayχ ended up in the water and he's
bald. He's *totally* bald, because he'd been in the Whale's belly, and
it's so hot in the belly. So he snuck away. He didn't want anyone to
see him. He was embarrassed. He was embarrassed to be bald. So he
snuck away, swam away, and ends up on the beach, and he slithers
off and goes to hide. So the moral of that story is that you don't make
fun of things. You don't make fun of people. This is what happens.
See what happened to qayχ. He was making fun of the Whale and
calling it, "You shiny-headed, baldheaded Whale." So this is what
happened to qayχ. He was swallowed by the Whale, 'cause the
Whale read his mind. So be careful what you say. Be careful how you
treat the animals, and anything, sea life, anything around you. So
that's that story around that, around the Whale. ⬢

MINK AND WOLF

So the next one I'm going to do is story about the Wolf. The Wolf was
a great hunter. He was always out lookin', gathering food. And he
lived with his mother, but he would go out for days on end hunting,
whereas qayχ, in his community, was so lazy. Everybody knew he
was lazy. And he was always envious of the Wolf. He was jealous of
the Wolf, 'cause everybody praised the Wolf: "Oh, he's so good. He's
such a great hunter. He's respectable." And he's always thinkin', "Oh,
what can I do to get even with him?" So one day Wolf was out hunting. Then he'd been gone longer than usual. He'd been gone for days.
People started to worry in his little community: "Why hasn't he come
back? He's been gone forever." And this went on for several days. One
day, qayχ is out there again, he's out jiggin', trying to catch a fish or
a cod. And he's quite a little ways from his community around a bay,
or few miles away. And Wolf comes down the beach. He finally found
his way down to the beach. He was *so* very tired. He'd been hunting
for days. And he sat down to rest. He reached the beach, and he was
glad to be there. And it was a long walk for him, still, to walk home.
So he sees this boat out here and he recognizes, "Oh, it's qayχ is out
there. He's jiggin'. He's fishing. I'll ask him for a ride. I'll ask him to
come pick me up." So he hollers at him, and qayχ heard him, he seen
him, but he pretended that he didn't hear him, or he didn't see him.

And again, the Wolf would holler, "qayχ! Come and get me!" And again he wouldn't look. Still there fishing, ignoring the Wolf. And the Wolf got angry and said to qayχ, "qayχ! If you don't come and get me – I know you hear me – if you don't come and get me, I'm going to shoot you." And qayχ turns around, "What? What? Who said that? Who said that?" He looks in the water. "Who's talking?" And he looks, "*Oh!* There you are! I heard you from the bottom of the ocean," he says – looks down there. He always had a smart remark. But Wolf knew that he was lying. So he came ashore, got him onto the boat, and he's *so* very tired. Wolf is *so* tired. "Well, I see that you're really tired," he says to Wolf. "Why don't you just lay down there at the bow of the boat. Just put your head back and go to sleep. We're a long ways from home." So the Wolf went to lay down, and he was kind of slumped over, slouched over. And qayχ says, "Make yourself comfortable. Put your head way back. Just relax! I'll wake you when we get there." So qayχ is paddling away, paddling away. Pretty soon Wolf is nodding off, he's falling asleep. And qayχ says, "I'm gonna test to see if he's really sleeping." So he shakes the boat – deliberately shakes the boat. And the Wolf wakes up: "What's that?" "Oh, don't worry. Go back to sleep! It was just a ripple in the water. Just go to sleep." The Wolf falls asleep. Pretty soon he wasn't waking up when he would shake the boat. So qayχ got his knife, and he went, snuck up on him, and he slit his throat. He killed the Wolf. He was mad at the Wolf because the Wolf had threatened to shoot him. So he goes home, he skins the Wolf, he takes the head of the Wolf and he hangs it above his doorway facing down, and he takes the fur, the hide, and he makes himself an outfit. Makes himself a jacket, and a tie. He's going to show the community that he's a better man than the Wolf.

So the Wolf's mother used to go around the community. She'd be selling things – dried salmon or dried meat, or dried clams, whatever. And she comes to his door and she's saying, "Oh, you wanna buy something here?" qayχ comes to the door and looks at her. "Oh! Saleslady. Why don't you look up above? Look above you." And she looks up and she sees her son, his head there, over the door. Well, she *just* wailed and she cried as she *screamed.* And she fell to the ground, and she was just wailing. And qayχ says, "Get out of here, old lady! Get out of here, salesperson. Go do your wailing somewhere else," adding insult to injury. So off she went, wailin' and cryin', and told the community what had happened. Well, the whole community knew qayχ for what he was. Everybody was *so* angry. And they said, "We're gonna get him for this. We're gonna kill him. We're going to capture him. How can we do this?" So they had a big meeting – all the community came together – and they made plans: "How are we going to do this? Well, qayχ likes to eat. If we put on a potlatch, and we invite the whole community, he will come. But we'll trap him. We'll have two guys standing by each side of the doorway, and when he comes into the building, we'll grab him." Well, they all gathered one day. Invitation was out. So everybody was in this building, except qayχ. He took his sweet time. They finally sent a little boy, "Go and call him. What is he doing? He's the only one that hasn't arrived." So, little guy goes running over there, "We're waiting for you! You're the only one that's not there. So they sent me to call you." "Oh," he says. "Oh, okay. Well, I'm still getting dressed. I'm still gettin' ready. I'm still putting on the Wolf's regalia." Little boy went running back, told the people. They got more mad. They were so upset. He was doing this to aggravate them further. And he still didn't come for a while. Then the little boy got sent again. "Oh yeah, I'm just about ready. I'm just putting on the Wolf's tie," he said. So the little boy went back. Well, people were fuming. They're gonna get him this time for sure. So he finally goes strutting over there, all dressed in Wolf's regalia. He knew they were out to get him. So he didn't just walk through that door. He leapt from right outside the door and right into the middle of the floor. And they couldn't catch him. They chased him all over this big house. And qayχ's grandmother was many things. She could be a knothole on the board. And he goes up to this knothole and he says, "Expand, knothole! Expand!" That's his grandmother. And the knothole expanded. And qayχ went through that knothole and he escaped. So he's gone. They missed him. He escaped.

So he's out and about again, and they're thinkin', "How are we going to get him? We have to get him." They eventually caught him, and they tied his hands. They tied his hands with a cedar rope. And tied his hands behind his back. And what they're going to do is, they're gonna take him out on this canoe, and they're gonna take him way out there, and they're gonna drown him. Once and for all, they're going to take care of him. So they tied him, but he says, "You know what, you guys? That's not very strong, that rope." He says, "You know, the sea grass is really a lot tougher, stronger. You just braid it and you'll have this rope. And when I go like this and try to rip it apart, it's not going to rip it all. But with that rope you're making, when I go like this it'll just break." And these people said, "Okay. We'll do that." So they braided the sea grass and made a rope. And then he made another request: "When we're going out there," he says, "I want two canoes, side by side. And then we'll do this chant as we're going out there. I will have one foot on one boat, and the other on the other. And the boat will be going. We'll go out there like that." That was his final request. So they're heading out there, and before they got too far out there, he dove into the water and broke the ties on his hands. And down he went. They could see him, his little feet – see them going way down the bottom. And they're all looking. They've got a long pole. And they started stabbing where he had gone under a big rock, or by a big rock. Then he takes a sea urchin, and he puts it out there. And this pole was hitting the sea urchin, broke the sea urchin apart. And, "Oh good! Good. Look at all that stuff," you know, with all blood and gore. "Yeah! We finally got him. He's dead. We finally got him." So they went back to shore. In the meantime, he went under water. He swam. He got to the other side of the bay. And he climbed up the bluffs, and he sat there and he's watching what's going on. All the men came back to the beach and they're really happy. They finally got him. And someone hollers from across the bay, "*Is that qayχ?*" he says, "*Is that qayχ?*" They all look over there. Sure enough, he's over there. He's mocking them. He's up in the bluffs. So they didn't get him after all. He got away again. And on and on it goes. That was the story of his life, that he always got away with these things that he did. A terrible little character. So that's the end of that.

Chi-chia (čičiyɛʔ)

9

Naming My Family

M y name, qaʔaχstɑles, was handed down to me from my grandfather, Jim Timothy. His ancestral name was lɑsɑ. And his mother was from Cape Mudge, so "qaʔaχstɑles" comes from Cape Mudge. We didn't have a ceremony around my name. All I remember is him giving me that name when I was living with my grandparents, when I was still a young, young woman. And he told me, "I want you to carry my mother's name." So that was that, there's no ceremony. That, to me, was good enough that he passed that name on to me. But I also share that name with a couple of my cousins, one of them being Annie Dominick, who was the granddaughter of Chief Tom Timothy. And Chief Tom Timothy and my grandfather were brothers, so they had the same mother. So she too has that name. And also Stella, my other cousin, got that name. And my grandfather actually wanted to give her that name too, so we shared that same name. And that's okay. It's okay to share a name within the family, because, I guess, today it's similar to how we share names, like you're named after your uncle or your aunt or your favourite cousin or whatever, or great-grandmother. So it's okay. But what's important is that name represents someone that's dear to the family and you carry that name out of respect for someone that was close to the family, whether it was a relative or an aunt, cousin, whatever – grandmother, great-grandmother. So there were a lot of ancestral names handed down before our people got the Christian names or the biblical names. All that changed and we lost a lot of the names, the ancestral names, because the names of my ancestors were replaced through the church and that.* So a lot of the names got lost and it's very unfortunate, 'cause a lot of the young people today want to give ancestral names for their children. And so what we do is we kind of assess the child and the person as the person's growing now, what their makeup is and what their personality is like. So that's the reason why we have the names that we do now.

Yeah, so that's how I got my name was through qaʔaχstales. And through that name I have met other people from Cape Mudge, from the Assu family. That's where qaʔaχstales originally came from was the Assu family in Cape Mudge. So I've talked with different people there, like George Cook, he's a distant relative of mine, 'cause he's – I believe he said it was his mother that came from that family. And he's an Elder. He's from Alert Bay but lives in Victoria now. So he says, "Oh, you're related to me." And other people that I've run into, like Wedłidi Speck – it was his great-grandmother. His great-grandmother was related to the Bob George side of the family. So we're sitting around we're talking and, "Oh yeah! I'm from that branch of that family!" and so on. So they recognize the name, and gave me their explanation of what that means, 'cause I didn't know what it meant, that name. It was a name given to me by my grandfather, so I didn't know the translation of how – what does that mean? What does that represent? So I've gotten that explanation from the people of that area, which I was really glad to get. 'Cause I often wonder, what does that mean really? Because people ask, "What does that mean?" when I tell them my ancestral name is qaʔaχstales. And Eugene Louie always says to me, "qəχ s talas!" he says to me. Yeah, 'cause in our language, "qəχ s talas" is you've got lots of money. He teases me, calls me "qəχ s talas." So what I'm told is that one interpretation is it means you always have your door open for people. It also means that you share your wisdom with people, you're knowledgeable. So it's later in life that I found that out, after I had the name given to me. So I must honour that name – I cannot disgrace

---

* Elsie learned in 2012 that the field notes of the anthropologist Homer Barnett contain a record of many ancestral names on her grandfather's side. Elsie's grandfather's brother, Chief Tom, explained łaʔamɪn name traditions to Barnett using examples from his own family. Homer G. Barnett, *The Coast Salish of British Columbia* (Eugene: University of Oregon Press, 1955), 140, 204; University of British Columbia, Rare Books and Special Collections, H.G. Barnett Fonds, Box 1, Folder 6, Field notes: "Mainland Comox (Slaiäman, Klahuse, Homalco), 1936" (hereafter cited as Barnett field notes, folder 1-6).

that name. And I feel good with it, because I feel I never turn anyone away from my door – doesn't matter whom. I make the time to get to know the person. Whatever brings them to my door, or to my house. So I'm quite satisfied with that name. And I will pass it on one day to one of my grandchildren. I don't know yet who, but it's not gonna die down. It's not gonna die with me! *[laughs]*

When people were asked to give up their names, their original names, they were given one name only. So it's like, my great-grandfather, I guess, would have been given one name, and that would have been Timothy. No other name. It was one name. And so that applied to all other families and the people of that day were given one name. So if you were given the name Timothy, then your son then would be Jim Timothy and Tom Timothy and Sandy Timothy. Would take these first names as your last name. Because you were only given that one name when you were baptized. I heard that the first baptism they did in all these communities when they were giving biblical names – these were grown-up people already, and they were all given names, they were lined up and all baptized at the same time. So, "You'll be John, you'll be Peter, you'll be Paul. You'll be Harry. You'll be a da-da-da." And then starts over again. So we have a lot of Harrys, we have a lot of Pauls, we have a lot of Georges, and so many people with the same names. Those were not our choices! We never chose those names. Our ancestors didn't choose those names, but they were all given these names. So quite often there's confusion when we're doing family trees, about which family does this one belong to then? And then the women were given names like Annie, Molly, Marie, and another Annie and Mary, and Marie, and Josephine, and so many of those names were the same. Madeleine, Martha, Theresa. In different family groupings, the same name carried to another family. And so we have Agnes – there's my aunt Agnes, and there was her cousin who was an Agnes. Their mother was Agnes. And so on and so forth. And the next branch of that tree carries those names as well. So there's a lot of confusion sometimes when we're talking about the family tree and who belongs to which family. And so many Maries and Mollys, and sometimes some are siblings. Like your sister and you have the same name. Yeah.

So like, with myself, for an example. My aunt Elsie – I was named after her by my grandmother. But there was another Elsie who was my half-sister. So there was three of us that shared the name. And my aunt Elsie was ten years older than I. And then my half-sister was about maybe seven years older than I. So when I was born I was not registered right away. Then I had an older sister – her name was Mabel, but she died as a baby. And somehow my registration with the Department of Indian Affairs got mixed up with hers. So she was born in 1931. September twenty-first, 1931, was when she was born. I came along one year later. I was born October eighth, 1932. I could not prove that I was born that year or that month or that day. It had been ongoing for years that I'm trying to prove that I was born in 1932 and not 1931. So when it was time for me to apply for my old age pension – well, I found out how difficult it was to change it after my last child was born. And the hospital records said – "It shows on record that this is your birthdate. Now why are you saying this is your birthdate?" I said, "I've always gone by this birthdate." "Well that's not what the Indian records says for you." So I'm stuck with 1931, and it went on and on for years. I researched, I sent away to New Westminster where they keep records of all the children that went to Sechelt Residential School, and our day school here in Sliammon. No one could give me any answer. So I got stuck with my sister's birthdate. I couldn't argue because I didn't have proof. So they're saying, "If you can prove it, if you have someone that's older than you that remembers events the day you were born, or another event on the day you were born, then we can give you a certificate to that. But you have to go through this tribunal." I can't do that! I don't know who was around in those days. My grandmother is long gone and she would not have been able to look back in her *journal* and say – *[laughs]* so, anyway – period! I didn't even have a birth certificate. I'm trying to get a birth certificate and I couldn't get one. So my daughter was in Victoria and she went to the vital stats office. And she didn't get anywhere with it. They couldn't help. I sent to, again, to New Westminster and to Sechelt 'cause they have this thick book there that still exists. But it's all mixed up 'cause it takes everybody in that went to the residential school and wherever the priest travelled, he came back with whatever he documented in there. I'm not even in that book! So I doubt sometimes I was even born! *[laughs]* Or that I'm even a citizen! So it wasn't until Gordon Wilson was our MLA that he helped me and, you know, he's known me for a long time. He's known people that have known me for a long time. So he got all this going – *finally* they accepted that I am a Canadian citizen. But my birthdate, I can't prove that. So I have my sister's birthday. And then I got a letter from Pensions or from Health Canada that says, "You will be getting your gold card next month when you turn sixty-five." I'm going, "Hmmm! I'm not sixty-five for another year!" That's when I gave up. I thought, if they want to give me my pension one year sooner than later, then I'll take it. I give up! Because the last correspondence I had sent off to New Westminster, they came back with my half-sister's birthdate on there. *No!* And I'm going, *no!* That's not me! So I have two birthdays. My grandson was asking me just yesterday, "How old are you going to be this year? And I said, "Well, on September the twenty-first, I am going to be seventy-six, but October the eighth I'm going to be seventy-five." *[laughs]* He knows about it – I've told him all that has happened around that. So I'm not the only one. I know many more other people that have a hard time proving their birthdate, because most of our people were not born in the hospital, back then. They were born at home or up the coast or wherever. And when they became registered it was like a guessing game, I guess, when the priest would come into the community and baptize the children. Then, I guess, it was kind of a guessing game, 'cause, you know, people didn't carry calendars. You quite often hear the old people, when I was little, they'd always say, "Well, the salmon was running up the river about that time when that person was born," or "The salmonberries were just getting ripe at that time when that person was born." They went by different events, or different seasons of the year: "There's a lot of snow on the ground when that person was born." So you know it was winter, but could be anywhere from November to March. So it was really guess and by-golly. Yeah. So they just went by the season.

And a lot of people tattooed themselves: each year they put another little mark on their arm.* My grandmother had – it's like a little line of marks on her hand. It was on the inside of her arm like that. *[gesturing]* It showed how old she was, and every year she'd get little mark there. And I've seen a lot of the older people like that. That's how they kept track of their age. One year and you – little mark there. Two seasons, another mark. Up until you got married. Then it was gone. You didn't do that anymore. So it tells you what age you were when you got married. Otherwise, you live to be a hundred, you're going to be pretty marked up! *[laughs]* I used to see a lot of the older ladies with marks – tattoos. Their name or – once they were given their names, I guess. I'm surprised that was not outlawed, doing tattoos. But they used just needle and thread, and black ash from the fire. And they would wet the thread and run it through the black coal so the

---

* See also Dorothy Kennedy and Randy Bouchard, *Sliammon Life, Sliammon Lands* (Vancouver: Talonbooks, 1983), 52; Barnett field notes, folder 1-6, 53.

thread is now black. Then they would insert the needle *just* under the flesh, pull it through, and there's your mark. Just straight, or if they were writing names – I've seen women with those kinds of tattoos on their legs. Yeah, just their initials or whatever – I don't know what possessed them to do that! My grandmother didn't have those. Just except for her age. But I've seen other women with tattoos on their legs. Guess that was their way of documenting something, their name or their age perhaps. *[laughs]*

A long period of time had gone without givin' names to our families, our children, and now they are adults and some of them in their fifties and sixties, and they didn't have an ancestral name handed down to them, so when they were given those names, it was a *big* to-do. That you invited the whole community plus other communities, perhaps, to come. So there's that difference in how it's done. It's either done in a small way with just one child, to be given a name and honoured, which is just as important. So it's really important. A lot of the names are lost, like I was saying, lost because they weren't able to use it. It was forbidden to use names other than biblical names. You were baptized as – named after some angel or saint or whatever! So that's all you used. It was forgotten. There's very few people that still carried it secretly and held on to those names. So that those are the only ones that were preserved and kept – but it was not used. Only when there was no one else around, then it was still used amongst the family. Yeah, it's just so unfortunate because of the loss of our practices, the loss of our culture. That a lot of things were lost – and because our people had never documented things. It was just orally handed down.

I went to Brooks school – my grandson was there – two of my grandsons were going to school at Brooks actually, at the time. And their project was on a family tree. And my two boys are – their dad is non-Native, their fathers are non-Native. And their dad and their ancestors from that side of the family come from Scotland and England and places like that. And so their family tree is recorded in some Bible or some document somewhere, where goes back generation after generation after generation. Whereas with us, I can only go back as far as memory serves me, to my grandparents, to my great-grandparents. And probably three, four generations. And then I'm lost. It's like a void is there. You can't see beyond that? Because it's not written anywhere. So I'm lookin' at this tree and I'm asked to help my grandson fill in one side of the tree that is our side. I'm saying, "This was so-and-so, this was my grandmother, my grandfather, his great-grandfather," and so on. And then there's nothing. On the other side it went on for *several* generations. And I said to the teacher that was workin' with our kids, I said, "This is just so small. Our side is just so small. Look at this! The tree is just so big on this side and this side is pretty skimpy." As far as recording goes? And I just felt that was really unfair somehow, it was so lopsided. And the teacher said to me, "Well, I think your culture is very rich. Although it's not ever been recorded or documented, the very fact that you remember all of these things which was orally handed down," he said, "is very meaningful. Whereas other people have always depended on documenting things as far as their history go." So I guess that kind of made me feel a little better. But it just goes to show how unbalanced that is, that whole system of documenting and verbally handing down information and names and places.

I think for a name to be chosen for you based on what kind of a person you are is a real honour. That name suits you just so. That is who you are. It's what you've become as an adult. Right from when you're a young adult, the Elders can see right away, people can see right away what kind of a person you are. If you're a gentle person, if you're hard-working, you're kind, you're giving, you got a big heart, and all of those good qualities. And people will see – "I see *that* person as being a hɑys qɑymixʷ."* That's what our people would say. They already recognize those qualities in you that you are that person that – all those things I mentioned. You're going to be the makings of a good Elder. And that's what they call "hɑys qɑymixʷ." It's a person of high esteem. So it's really important, I believe, for that person to have that name given to them, although they have a name, like, the biblical names again. So the namin' is very important. I know, years ago when you didn't honour your name – if you were given a name of high esteem that you have to live up to it – if you are seen not to be living up to that life, because you've had all these witnesses that witnessed that name given to you, any one of those witnesses can step forward and say, "You've disgraced the name given to you." And you could lose that name. It could be taken from you. And you can't dispute that, because they were witnesses at your naming: "This person got this name because of ..." So that's what the naming signifies, that's what it all boils down to is do you carry that name proudly? It's just unfortunate we lost the true names of our ancestors, 'cause that's going back, like, I guess, two hundred years.

---

* Translation: respected/knowledgeable person.

Actually, my nephew Leonard Bob, his dad used to be a funny man. He used to always say – 'cause there's no one living there now – but he used to always say, "Oh, I'm the Chief of Harwood Island," he used to say. Harwood Island belongs to us still. And that's "ʔaʔgayqsən." "ʔaʔgayqsən" is the name of that. And so he passed on about four years ago. So we gave my nephew – we had a naming with our families, and they gave him that name. So his ancestral name is ʔaʔgayqsən. So we tease him, call him "Chief ʔaʔgayqsən." There were four of them that we named that summer. That was about two years ago.* And one of them was Leonard, and the other was Joe Gallagher.† That was Norman's son. And he worked with treaty. He's a very smart young man. He's a visionary. He likes to think of the future and planning ahead all the time. So we gave him the name kʷʷʊnʔəmen. "kʷʷʊnʔəmen" is someone that's visionary – can see things that ordinary people like us don't see. So that's the name he got, was kʷʷʊnʔəmen. And his buddy that works with them, that's my nephew Roy, Roy Francis, is very friendly, outgoing – he's always got a smile. We call him "ʔayišnomot," that means "friendly." You're always smiling, just being friendly. And the other one is his brother, Lee, Lee George. And Lee is a real provider. He likes to go and hunt. He does a lot of things. He loves going fishing. But whatever foods he brings home, he's one of those very rare people that still gives out a lot of stuff he brings home. So when he comes home with a deer, he'll butcher it or his dad will butcher it, and he'll go and give some to the Elders. He's always giving this traditional food out. And salmon – anything he goes out for. So if we call him "nʌhnohom" – that means "someone that's always giving a feast." Or you could be just putting a table out in your home and you invite people to come in, that's "nohom." But how I see Lee is that he's nʌhnohom – he's giving, giving of food all the time. So that's how we came up with those names for these four people. But they knew nothing about the names when we were preparing the names for them, talkin' about names, 'cause the Elders and I sat together. And recognizing the people that these four people are, and their quality of life, and how they live their life, just their whole character. And that's how names were given to people, is based on how people thought you. You did not give yourself a name, or say, "I want to be called this." It was up to the Elders or the family heads to

---

* This naming ceremony took place on 17 August 2003.

† Joe Gallagher is now the spouse of Harmony Johnson. He is the son of Annie Hackett, mentioned in Chapter 8.

give you a name because of what you represent, who you are as a person. So when we sat and talked about this, we kept it very quiet from them. So we gathered them, said, "We want to do this." And they were excited: "Okay! What's gonna be my name?" "No, we're not gonna tell you." And it wasn't until it was time to do it, and boy did they ever look nervous! *None* of them knew what their name was going to be. It was announced right at the ceremony. So we did the ceremony at the hatchery there. That's where Lee George works. And they were sitting there, just like, "Do you know what you're getting? Do you know?" *[laughs]* They're just like kids at Christmastime. And so, as they were called up – this is going to be the name. For Joe Gallagher: "Your name is going to be kʷʊnʔəmen." It was really a neat day! Just fell into place. And the Elders were seated there. And so, by them getting names, they gave out gifts to the Elders. That's like a payment, like, to honour the Elders that gave them the name. And I had suggested to them this is what you do. So just like a little basket of fruit or some token gift to them. So that's how that happened. It was a very beautiful day – and just being around the hatchery and by the river – and the Elders really enjoyed that day. They enjoy being down there. Yeah. That was really nice.

The ancestral names that were lost, that was our identity. They say that it takes seven generations. That it took seven generations to lose our identity, our language, and our culture, but it's going to take another seven generations to heal, to get the language back, if we ever will. The language is most difficult to learn for the new speakers today, because it was lost for so long. It's really difficult for them, the young people especially. And since now we've lost a lot of our speakers, our Elders, the fluent speakers, the very traditional people – we've lost those over the last few years. So you can't turn your life around in one generation. It will take just as long to get our language back, if we ever will – our identity, our self-esteem, our pride, and our work ethics, our respect and honour. That was all lost with the loss of our identity. When we had our naming done several years ago – it's in '97, actually – what we had as a family, my family, was a naming for my immediate family. My own children and my grandchildren plus the nənqəm* dancers. They really wanted to carry a name because of the performances that they do out in the public. And to introduce themselves, they'd like to use their traditional given

---

* Translation: killer whale.

names. So that's really nice. It goes well with the things that they do, and some of these Annie Dominick's grandchildren that I've worked a lot with, Annie Dominick and Dave? And most of this group that came in with our family were related. I'm related to Dave Dominick and to Annie – Annie was my cousin. Actually, Annie and I share our ancestral name given by our grandfathers to us. The name is qaʔaχstales. So we are quite connected that way. So she gave her grandchildren names, her children who are involved with the dancers and the drummers: that's Jolene and her brother Nolan and some of their cousins. And Gail Blaney, who has a lot to do with the dance group. Her and Dorothy[*] do a lot of work with the dance group. They are very culturally minded ladies. And so they are very instrumental in forming the nənqəm dancers, as was Sue Pielle that helped those two ladies in the very beginning to pull this together. And it's a lot of work for them. They're having practices on a regular basis, and I think they started with Erik when Erik was just a little guy, and now Erik's a grown man, and course right now he's busy with going to school, but he still will do this whenever he's home – to put on a performance, drumming or singing. And his little brother Drew does a lot of this as well. And Sosan's a real good participant.[†] Very culturally aware, carries her heritage very well. Things like drumming, singing, weaving. She does a lot of weaving of hats with cedar and things like that. So they're a very nice family – I'm quite happy to see that some of our young people are carrying that on. Which I'm sure it'll only grow. And their mom, Gail – and Dorothy, the other mother – are very into the language. They're very interested in documenting and using the language a lot. So that's very pleasing, to see that happening. So when we had our naming, all of them had gotten names at that time. And we had it in Gail's yard, outdoors. It was a beautiful day, so we were outdoors, and we invited Elders and we had quite a few people there. Maybe, I don't know, eighty people, a hundred people. And they drummed and sang, and we had a speaker that introduced each and every one that was getting a name. And we all pinned money on the blanket that the speaker was wearing. So that is the way to honour the speaker, to thank the speaker for walking us through this. He's like a master of ceremonies, but in our way we call him the speaker, 'cause he knows the way. He's very traditional person. So that's how we did our naming, and the names that we gave our children, and

---

[*] Dorothy Louie.
[†] Erik, Drew, and Sosan (sosən) are siblings and the children of Gail Blaney.

grandchildren, most of it were made-up names, based on their character.

And I'm going to list down the names that were given to my family. My eldest son, Glen, I gave him the name hɛwtał. I gave him that name because he's my eldest son, and that's how you say in our language that he's your eldest son, is "hɛwtał." And his wife, Pauline, we gave her the name of her mother, mɑliyən was her name. Even back then we had lost the ancestral names, because those generations had gone to school and lost their name, so she had the name Marion. But our people couldn't pronounce "Marion," so anyone with the name Marion was "mɑliyən." So that's what she's got is her mom's name, mɑliyən. Their son, Tim, my grandson, he got the name qʷoχʷɛčɪn. "qʷoχʷɛčɪn" came from Tom Peddie. He was a very good friend of the Sliammon people, him and his wife, Rose. Very, very fine people. Our people pretty much adopted them into the Sliammon community. They were honorary members. At one time the Elders decided to give Tom Peddie an ancestral name because of his involvement with our people: he was always there with our gatherings and just being around, both of them. And one day the Elders were talking about giving Tom Peddie a name. Because he was such a big man. He's a very big man. And he lived in Southview, where there's a huge reef out from Southview. You see the reef out there at low tide. So one of the Elders – actually it was Johnny George, he's gone now – he says, "Well, he's such a big man and he lives in Southview there, and Southview is called 'qʷoχʷɛčɪn.'" And that covers Southview and the reef out there: qʷoχʷɛčɪn. So my grandson, Tim, he's quite a large young man. He's a big boy. And because we were good friends with him, we asked him if we could use his name and he gladly gave it. And his sister Sally, her great-grandmother's name was ʔalpɑsen. ʔalpɑsen lived in Toba for many, many years. They were the first people in Toba that actually lived there year-round. So we got permission from the Barnes family, that's where the Barnes family came from. They were Klahoose people, but they lived in Toba. So Sally's got ʔalpɑsen as her ancestral name. And her daughter, Crystal, we had a difficult time to find a name for her, but Crystal really likes her potatoes, so we called her "kʷiškʷiš" 'cause the blue jay really likes potatoes. So Crystal got that name. She still likes potatoes today, her favourite food. And Serena, Sally's sister – her great-great-grandmother also lived up in Toba from the same family, the Barnes family. And her name was k'ʊlk'ʊl. I'm not sure exactly the meaning of that, but that's what she was called all her life, "k'ʊlk'ʊl." And Serena's husband, Calvin, we called him "məgɑ."

"məgɑ" is a cougar. So that's Calvin's name, is a cougar. And his son Brighton, Brighton is "memgɑ," that's a baby, a baby cougar. So it's just məgɑ passed down, like a father to a son name. So when you're young, you're a memgɑ. And Byron is χaʔǰɛys. Byron is a real solid young man. It's always been since he was a little boy – very solid and just a heavy, solid person. And we called him "χaʔǰɛys." "χaʔǰɛys" is, like, a big solid rock.

Then we go on to my daughter Jeannie. Jeannie's great-grandmother was čine. Her name was Jeannie as well. So she had lost that name as well, the ancestral name. So people just called her "čine." So Jeannie was named after her great-grandmother, čine. Then her daughter, Harmony, because her name is Harmony, it's like music. So we called her "wuwumtən." "wuwumtən" means a song, or a melody. Her brother, Dillon, we named him toqʷanən, because toqʷanən, to me, is a very special place. That's Theodosia – "toqʷanən." I spent a lot of time when I was just a little girl, in toqʷanən. I barely remember being there. And many times through the years, we've gone back there. No one lives there anymore up in Theodosia. But it's very special to me. And because Dillon is very special to me, I thought, I'm gonna call him "toqʷanən." A lot of sentimental memories of toqʷanən. And his sister Kory, I call her "ʔuwčkɪna." When she was first born, she was just the cutest little baby – tiny little baby – and my first thought when I looked at her through the glass at the maternity ward – there was Kory, and first thought that came to mind was ʔuwčkɪna, ʔuwčkɪna. My grandmother tells me that when I was a little girl, if I seen something really tiny or something cute – and in my own words, I guess, wherever that came from, but that was my expression of something that was cute, whether it was a small canoe or some tiny little bug or whatever. I would say, as a child, "ʔuwčkɪna!" So there I went and said it to Kory as a baby, "ʔuwčkɪna!"

Then there's my son Walter. His name is šɛpates. That's a very ancestral name. He was given that name by his great-aunt, who was Emily Francis, from Homalco. šɛpates was her dad. šɛpates was a very nice man. He was so full of stories to tell. He was just very, very traditional. And he carried that name. His other name was Alec Paul, but he carried šɛpates all the time. So ʔɛmɛlɛ asked me quite a number of years ago if I would name Walter. "I want to give my dad's name to your son," she said to me one day. She said, "He really reminds me of my dad. Because he's really ʔišnomot." "ʔišnomot" means you're friendly and kind. So I got ready for about four years. I had to think about it a lot 'cause there's another family – great-grandchildren and children of šɛpɑtɛs. So we had to do a lot of consultation and think about it, and she would ask me from time to time, "When are you gonna give Walter that name? When are you going to make it official?" So four years later we did. And so that's his name, šɛpɑtɛs. And his wife, Noreen, she's got the name sosən. Noreen was pretty much raised by her grandmother, sosən. So sosən was very special to Noreen. Her name was Susan. We all called her "sosən." Everybody knew her as sosən, so Noreen took that name. Then her daughter Kylie, my granddaughter, I call her "qʷasəm." That's a flower, a beautiful flower. That's Kylie's name. And then Andrea, Walter's other daughter, her name is ʔɛmɛlɛ after his great-aunt, the great-aunt that gave him šɛpɑtɛs for a name. So it's carried down again, father and daughter name.

And then my daughter Ann, her name is q'aʔq'ɛʔɛt. We had to give a lot of thought, because the ancestral names were lost. So we gave a lot of thought to each person and as to their character and how they present themselves. What kind of a person are you? What is a suitable name for you? And Ann has always been very, very ambitious, very hard-working, very organized, very structured. She's never still, she's always busy. So we named her q'aʔq'ɛʔɛt. "q'aʔq'ɛʔɛt" in our language, that's what it means: a busy person. And her son Bryce, we called him "maksɛma." maksɛma was my great-uncle. He was lasa's brother, my grandfather lasa. That was maksɛma. Bryce loves to go fishing. He just loves being out on the water. So was maksɛma. He practically lived out there in the water. Every day, if he could, he'd be out there, especially in the summer, rowing and with his fishing line out. He'd be gone all day, almost every day. So I thought that was most suitable for Bryce, so he got maksɛma. And Davis got "ʔaǰɛmaθot," meaning "making a change." Cody Quinn was q'aykʷ. Yeah. "q'aykʷ" was "eagle." One day Cody was down at the beach, front of their place. And he had brought some leftover fish or fish guts, whatever it was, he brought it down there to feed the eagles. And this eagle swooped down and just touched him with his wing. It just came so close to him it touched him. So the eagle was always very special to Cody. So that's the name he's got, is q'aykʷ.

And then we have Cathy. We named Cathy after my great-aunt Katherine from Squirrel Cove. Well, she was originally from Sliammon, but she married into Squirrel Cove. And everybody just called her "kitlen." So Aunt Katherine was very special to me. I was very close to her. She was like a second grandmother to me. I spent a lot of time with her. So we named Cathy after her – named her after her great-aunt kitlen.

Elsie and her daughters on the day of the family's naming ceremony, in May 1997. *Left to right:* Elsie, Ann, Marlane, Jeannie, and Cathy. Photo courtesy of Elsie Paul.

Then there's Marlane. We named her hayhiyšɛwʊm. And that name is very suitable for her more and more in the line of work she does. But even back then when we did our naming, she was already very busy being a liaison person. She worked for the school district. She worked for the regional district office as a young person. And she went on to work for Centra Gas. Then she went to work for BC Ferries as a program person. She was a liaison person for Centra Gas. And she's still doing that same kind of work today. She's very busy going into different communities, First Nations communities, and bridging – there's always bridging. So "hayhiyšɛwʊm" means "bridging," or building a path, or building a road.

Then there's my son Clifford. "p'ahiykɩla" is his name, and that's a raven. Raven is very important to us. Raven is a messenger, and raven is a trickster. So Clifford is my youngest son. And he's always been the kind of person that is just so – he carries a lot. He takes a lot with him. He's always full of stories to tell us, and he can be quite the trickster as well. He always has everybody laughing and finding his stories so funny.

And at the same time, the Elders and I decided to give Denise Smith a name as well. Denise is my niece. Her mother was Irene, my sister, late sister, Irene. Denise is a very smart young person. She was our

Chief for two terms. She was the first woman chief in Sliammon. And she's very well-spoken. She's not afraid to speak her mind. She's the one that gets up and speaks for us. She comes back to the Elders and she said, "What would you like to see?" She always involves the Elders: "If I do this, am I doing it right?" So she's very well connected to the Elders, that generation. But yet she can go to the government level and be able to speak. So it is a *real* talent. So the Elders at that time decided, well, that's what she does. We'll call her "qʷaqʷayʔəmtomoɬ." That's how you say that: "qʷaqʷayʔəmtomoɬ." That's the one that speaks for us. So these names were all sanctioned by these Elders, as listed. There was Mary George – she's passed on now. And Emily Francis – she's passed on. Agnes McGee – she's also gone. Rose Louie's gone. Katherine Blaney, she's also gone. And Annie Dominick. So these Elders are all gone now. So we as a group had put together these names, and made it official.

So it took us four years and thinkin' about what names to give to all of them. So we did this and prepared as well, like, for a giveaway. Started collecting things like tea towels and bath towels and blankets or quilts or lap quilts, whatever. So it's very important, just the cere-mony. That we call people together – come together and share the day and to listen. And the time when we did this, I had asked Eugene Louie – his ancestral name is pələč'ɛw'txʷ, and he's a very traditional man. He was the son of Rose Louie. So at that time we asked him if he would be our emcee. And he did that very well, introducing each and every one of the people that got their names, and introducing the names that were given to them. So I was very thankful he was able to do that for our family. And then we had a little giveaway. We gave little gifts and that to the Elders and the guests that we had there. And it didn't have to be a lot of stuff. When people did their naming, years and years ago, and I've heard this through my grandparents and other Elders, that whatever they had in the day – this would be going back hundred years, two hundred years ago, probably more. When you were given a name it was very important, and you called your friends or your other Elders in the community to come and be witness to that name. So it was similar to a christening, when you gave your child a name. And at those times when those ancestral names were given, those names could be very special. They were ancestral names of your great-grandparents or your great-uncle or names of importance that was handed down. So the gifts that were given to the guests at that time would be what was leftover of the feast that you had. Whether it was dried deer meat or dried salmon or dried clams – it depends on what the family had. It depends on what was available. There was no money, no money given. Today it's quite different. When people do namings, they use what is available today. Where sometimes I've witnessed, going to other communities where there's ancestral names given, where they hand out flour, sugar, like, bags and bags of flour and sugar and just other foods, canned goods or material things, like towels and tea towels and just anything. You know, socks and gloves – and they give lots. And it depends on how wealthy you are. And you could give money to your invited Chiefs, if there's invited Chief there from other communities. So these people are seated in a special place, and they're given money. Could be a hundred-dollar bill to twenty-four Chiefs. That's a lot of money. I was at a naming in another community, and then they came out to the rest of the people that were all sitting in a longhouse, and Elders were given twenty-five dollars each throughout the whole building. Now that's a lot of money. I've not seen that in our community. But I've witnessed a giveaway where they've given a lot of the other things away, such as food and flour or other things – like a basket, hamper, and it's filled with all kinds of odds and ends, an assortment of things that's given to different Elders. So when I did my naming, we did it in a small way. And it was, like, these small plastic hampers that I used and filled it with a little bag of sugar, and a little bag of flour and jam and jelly and jarred fish and just anything like that – biscuits and cookies. So it's a token of your appreciation for the witnesses that you have that have come to honour you and to be witnesses to the names that are given. The giving of names is so important to people that they call upon witnesses to stand up and be recognized as a witness. And I see in other communities where they'll go up to the witness and give them – the family of the people given a name that day would line up and they would go give quarters to this particular witness, and another witness. If there's ten witnesses, they all get these quarters. So you walk out of there with a bag of quarters. And that's just a token, you know, in our language it's called "ƛ'ɛʔkʷuʔjɛt" – you put something in their hand 'cause you appreciate them being there. And these witnesses have a real serious role. I don't know how serious it is. But if a person that was given an honourable name went out and did something to discredit that name, or embarrassed the family, they've gone out and done something bad or maybe they got arrested or maybe just not living up to that name, then the name was taken away from them. If I was called upon as a witness and I seen someone that was given

Sliammon Elders and lifelong friends, circa 2000. *From left:* Annie Dominick (also named qaʔaχstales), Dave Dominick, Elsie Paul, and Sue Pielle. These four friends grew up together and, as Elders, spent many hours together working on Sliammon language and cultural work. Photo courtesy of Davis McKenzie.

a very special ancestral name, I would expect that person to live up to that name. And if I see that person is not living up to that name, then I have the right as a witness to go and say, "Look, you're not living up to that name. Therefore, I'm going to take it away from you." So that's how serious it was for people a long time ago. So that's pretty much the history, the story of the naming. It's quite important.

Ancestral names were lost over the years, of course, and we struggle now to find names. So this is why we've used names that were suitable to the person's character. If you go back a hundred years or more, two hundred years, it's just not there anymore. Nobody remembers what their great-great-grandfather's name was, or what their great-great-grandmother's name was, because it just was lost. And besides, when the language was lost, people couldn't pronounce those names – you couldn't write it down. When you pronounce these names that I've mentioned, it's just impossible to write it down. So people, like linguists, have studied all this and they are written down, the ones that we remember. But it's not always easy to document the language in English. So that's the part about the ancestral names.

10

Healing Work

I t's very recent. I think it's only been within the last ten years, eight years that it was first talked about in our community. And people were very shame-based as well, that they didn't want to talk to anyone about their abuses. And that's the reality. And some of them are so angry and hurting, they don't want to talk about it. They just want to forget about it. Yeah. So I think in my work in being involved with the healing centres, there's good work being done. These programs are run by First Nations people, and the people that go there to deal with issues come out of there feeling very good about themselves. They feel safe in that environment. Not from the beginning, but they're there for a while, and then they get to know the others in that same room that suffered the same abuses, so they start sharing and talking. And I see it as – it's almost like being reborn. They feel good. They can stand up straighter. They can look you in the eye and not havin' to cast their eyes down because they're shamed, or they're ashamed to tell their story. They *all* share the common story. Maybe different levels of abuse, but it's pretty much the same. Yeah. So I'm thankful for those programs that are in place. It's just the tip of the iceberg. It's not available to everyone, although a lot more people would like to take advantage of those healing programs. But there's just not enough. There's a waiting list and there's not enough resources out there, not enough money. The government keeps saying, "We're short of money and we don't know if it'll be running next year." So there's cutbacks – it's always about cutbacks. Well, I believe that healing has to go on for a lot longer, for many more years, 'cause there's a lot of people out there – a lot more people that haven't come through the doors yet. Took many, many years for our people to be beaten, beaten to the ground, pretty much. It's going to take a long time to learn to get up and walk again, and to deal with their issues. It's not an easy task. Gonna take time.

Well, I'm a strong supporter of healing and of healing programs, because I see first-hand the suffering, especially when I go to these two different centres that I'm involved in. And I've seen the work that happens. And I see the struggle of our people. I see the pain and the hurt and how *much* they get out of these treatment programs. Sometimes it doesn't just take the one session. They need to come back again to deal with other issues related to those abuses. So I strongly support those centres. I feel it's *so* important. And I feel it's not going to resolve – it's not going to bring us our language back, or things such as our own teachin's, because that's a huge thing. A lot of people have left their communities and are now living in urban areas. And they're lost in the system. But that doesn't mean they're not interested in finding out about their culture. But they've been away from their communities for such a long time that they've pretty much been living in the white man's world. But that doesn't mean they're not hungry to learn about their culture, or their identity, or to learn about history of residential school. I know off-reserve people living in urban areas – they have their resources, they have Native centres and groups of First Nations people workin' together. They have their social events and their whatever, powwows and things like that. So I know there's a lot of work going on all over the place, but it's in pockets, different pockets, right? But as far as supporting treatment centres, you know Tsow-tun Le Lum Treatment Centre, which is in Nanoose, I've been involved in that program for twenty-two years now. And I *strongly* support that centre, because I've seen for myself how much it has helped people. And also with Inter Tribal Health, that have their treatment program over on Quadra Island, and I strongly support that. I feel that is *so important*. Because the kind of programs they provide there is geared to our people. It's not just dealing with whatever issues you have or what you're going through in your personal life to go and talk to a psychiatrist or a therapist or whomever. These programs are meant to deal with a long history of abuse to our people through residential school. And I feel that needs to continue. It really needs to continue for a long time to come. It's a long ways to go yet. It's important for us because it's our own people that run those programs. Not to discredit therapists and psychiatrists and mental health. It's just that there's not enough time. One hour per week for ten weeks is not enough. So to me, it's a waste of time. They really need intense work – a lot of our people need intense work, by people that know them, by people that understand the issues. Yeah.

It would be nice to have pre-treatment program, where you have a place where people can be while they're waiting to go away for treatment. Like a safe house – safe environment. And after they come out of treatment too, sometimes they need a place to go to. Another safe environment for more support, post-treatment, carry on with the work that has happened. Because right now a person can go away for five to six weeks, comes home to the same environment, and you're not well enough yet to stand on your own. You need that connection, you need the resources within your own community. The resources we get in our communities are very limited. We have an addictions worker, we have a women's support worker, we have a men's domestic program. And we have the sweat lodge, that some people utilize that through the men's program. And basically that's all we have. And there's just so much work that needs more time. These people are workin' a lot of overtime without pay. They're out there. Because you're working on reserve, you shouldn't expect to be paid overtime. I found that out when I was workin' in social work, and I used to ask for another person for help in my program: "We need two people here!" "No, there's only enough dollars for one person." Then they finally went up to one and a half person – half-time person. There's *no* such thing as a half-time person. When you're livin' in the community, when you're workin' for your people, there's no such thing as half-time. People call you at night when there's problems. They don't look at the time first and say, "Oh, this person is not working." They will call you at night! 'Cause they're having very serious problems, and what can you do? You know them. You live there. You get up and go. But it's never, ever considered to be overtime as far as the program goes. You don't get that extra pay. In the morning you get up and go to work at your regular job! *[laughs]* Yeah. I did that for twenty-four and a half years and that was – it was difficult. Difficult place to be. It's hard workin' in your own community. If you can stick it out, it's because you care for your people. Our people know one another, they know the families. And I give them a lot of credit, the people that work in these programs. They're very dedicated. You could just see the tiredness and the stress. But they still keep going, because they're needed. It's a real demand. Yeah, we need better programs. We need more training. The government gives you this little bit of money and you're to stretch it, and stretch it some more. When you run out of money, you still work for the people, 'cause people don't stop having problems because the budget has run out. And if you care, you're gonna be out there, doing what you can to help the people that need your help. It's very important work. There's a lot of issues that need to be dealt with, and the follow-up. They need ongoing support.

Yeah, we're all only a part of the big problem. We're not the only community that's going through these kinds of issues, the losses and the struggles. It's huge. How do you deal with all that? How does each community deal? Where do you begin? I guess in time it'll all come together. It'll all come together. There's people that's of the mind that, "Why don't people get over this whole issue of residential school? When will people learn how to let go?" It's not that simple. I feel for people that are going through what they're going through. It's like that big elephant in the living room: it's going to be there as long as you don't deal with it. It's like that obstacle in the middle of the trail. You walk through that trail every day, and if you don't move that – whether it be a root system sticking out of the ground – you're going to trip on it every day you walk through that trail. And if you don't do anything about removin' it, you're gonna trip on it every day. You've got to deal with it. Then you'll be able to walk there and not be tripping, falling down. Yeah, it's something you just don't turn a blind eye to. You need to deal with it. You need to talk about it. I think some people are just ashamed to talk about it, or a lot of our people still don't want to talk about the abuse they suffered. They'd sooner just put it away in the back of their mind and, "I've lived through it. I'm not the only one." But your behaviour, the way you live is going to tell the story – that you're not totally over it. You're still living with the abuse. And you could become that abusive person, because that's how you were treated. Maybe they don't think about it consciously, but it's there. And it just worries me, you know, for the future generation. Because they don't know the history. They didn't experience that history of being removed from the parents. But yet they're carrying on the behaviours of maybe their parents or their grandparents that got taken away to residential school. It sure changes the pattern of life and how you live your life, how you treat other people. Respect is really important, and that has been stripped away. There's no respect for other people's property, other people's belongings, another person's space. There's no consideration. There's just so much going on right now within all communities with the alcohol and drug issues. It's really made things so difficult to deal with –

the problems that are handed down from history. So there's a long ways to go.

My involvement with various healing programs has been really interesting for me because I come in contact with a lot of different people from different parts of the province, and sometimes people coming from across Canada to come to a healing centre – some people from communities, First Nations communities, and also from the urban areas. So, you know, there's a large cross-section of people that come and join the healing program at – first of all at Tsa-Kwa-Luten. Tsa-Kwa-Luten is on Quadra Island, and it's run by Inter Tribal Health. So it's really done a lot of good work. They're been in operation for, gosh! I think it's going on to maybe eight to nine years. So it's during the winter months. It starts around October, mid-October, and it goes right through to April. We had a shorter year the last year I worked there, because of shortage of funding, so it was cut back by a couple of months. It started late and they ended early in the year. The people that come there are searching for healing. It's a little bit different than another program that I've been involved with for a long, long time, and that is at Tsow-tun Le Lum. That one deals with addiction. At the beginning it mainly dealt with addictions. And it's kind of like, I guess, a springboard to the next level, which is Tsa-Kwa-Luten. So anyway, what with Tsa-Kwa-Luten, there's different facilitators that come there, people like psychologists and people that do a lot of workshops. And depending on what program is offered at a particular time, a particular program, it could be anywhere from one week to ten days, or it could be three weeks. The last program that I was involved in was thirty-three days, but it was done in eleven days – eleven days we're there, then come home for two weeks, then go back for another eleven days. But it was the same people that went through that particular program. And I think even going through thirty-three days, it's like scratching the surface of all that people have bottled up within themselves for years and years. So it was good to get that break in between the three sessions. It gets very intense. And it takes people a long time to start to unravel, and start to go within the deepest part of their memory about what has happened to them through the years, especially with what they've gone through in that period of time when children were taken away to residential schools. So that had a huge impact on our people. Some were in residential schools so far away from home, like in remote areas, that it was not possible for these children to go back home for holidays. Some just practically grew up in the residential school. So it was the hardest, I think, for people that totally lost the connection with their families for long periods of time. Losing the language, losing the cultural practices, and losing their identity. So that was the hardest and most touching and most heartbreaking stories you ever heard. And it's so emotional. People were so traumatized, but for years people did not deal with all that trauma. And now people are really starting to want to deal. It's getting more acceptable to talk about your issues, whereas before many people – all people, I think – were so shame-based about a lot of things that went on in the residential school. But it wasn't their fault – they were children when they were taken away. So it took a long time, and there's still many, many people out there that haven't even gone there. That haven't dealt with their issues. And still shame-based, but maybe not even realizing it. And I think that's the toughest part, is not realizing that if they went and dealt with those issues maybe things would become easier, you know – issues easier to handle. And how to deal with certain issues, like trust issues or to be able to express love and become – to understand why they're angry. And how to deal with anger. I think those are so important. So those are the kinds of things that's dealt with at Tsa-Kwa-Luten.

So my involvement there was more of an Elder role. There would be two Elders for every session. And so there's quite a few Elders from Vancouver Island and myself from the mainland here. That there'd be maybe one male Elder and a female Elder. So if any of the female clients wanted to really get into talking about their issues, they would go to the female Elder, and the same as the men, 'cause men really are – I think, harder for men to express and share their feelings with another person. So it helped, I think, the men to talk to the male Elder. And there are quite a few of the male Elders that are still culturally active and remember their own teachings and their traditional teachings. So that program, I feel, really works. It's still going on.[*] For how much longer, I'm not sure. It depends on funding from the government. They thought maybe it was going to be another three years, and that was about three years ago that I was last there. So I sure hope the funding keeps on coming, 'cause there's so much more to deal with. There's so many people affected by the residential school era. A lot of lateral violence stems from that. So there is a lot of healing

---

[*] Elsie was speaking here in July 2010.

that needs to be done. And I really enjoyed going to Quadra. The healing lodge there sits on First Nations land of the Cape Mudge people. And that's where my great-grandmother came from, so I always have a sense of belonging. I feel really good when I go there. I just really feel connected to the land and to the spirit of the land. Knowing that the spirit of that side of my ancestors, my family, lived there, and people lived, actually lived, on that site where that healing lodge is.

So the healing lodge is used during the winter months, but in the summer it's used as a summer resort. So it changes in the summer. So a lot of people, tourists, go there. People just want to go on holidays. Or people wanting to utilize the place, rent the place for other types of workshops or retreats. So it has many, many uses. So we're so fortunate that we have a facility like that that our people can go to. And especially for people that come from the urban areas, and that have not had a home base, or maybe not even knowing how it is to live in a First Nations community, and losing their identity that way. And so there's quite a few that come from the urban areas. There's always a waiting list. And I guess what is interesting is the different programs that it offers. They offer programs for couples, man and wife, and I think it's so helpful for them to both go. But they would have, like, different Elders that they can both talk to. Or one of the counsellors that could help them individually and as couples. So I thought that was really good. I guess the only thing is that there's no programs for youth. Anyone under the age of nineteen is, you know, don't qualify. And that's the sad part. There's no help for the youth under nineteen. And I think they would really benefit by something like that. And there are singles. Single moms programs. And all-men programs, whatever their issues are, whether it's sexual abuse or the same as the women programs. So there's various types of programs that's offered. And I miss going there, 'cause when I left there to go and work in Malaspina University, in the Powell River campus – I left there – it was kind of a hard choice for me to do that. But I thought, you know, I'm closer to home, and I miss home too, and my grandchildren, when I'm away. So I decided to take this job with Malaspina, but I think about the people that I came in contact with and wonder sometimes, how are they doing out there? A lot of them came in so burdened. And you could tell how they walked in the place, it's like they're afraid. They're, like, ready to bolt and leave. But after they're there for even a couple, three days, they start to meet other clients there – and we call them "guests." Instead of referring to them as "clients," they're guests. So that kind of thing, those kinds of changes are happening too in treatment centres. What makes it easier for them and feel accepted. So instead of "I'm a client," it's "I'm a guest there." So they're accepted in a real good way, in a kind way, and that makes them comfortable. So I wonder sometimes how they're all doing.

I met some wonderful friends. I met a lady from the Yukon, and she came to stay with me between one of – when I did the thirty-three days, and there's two-week break in between. So for two weeks, one break, she came and stayed with me. Oh, we had a lot to share! About her culture, about their practices, and so it was really nice. She really enjoyed being here, and she really wanted to know about our culture, our practices, and it's not much different. It's not much different. They're just in a different location and grew up in a different location, and their livelihood was a little different – what was available to them as far as resources go, was, you know, what they have in their own territories. But it's just amazing, their crafts, the kind of crafts they make. The beading of the moccasins and things like that. It's really intriguing. It's so interesting. And at the same time she's interested to know about our work too. So that was really nice. I had a really good relationship with this lady. And I just hope she's doing well. I haven't heard from her. We kept in touch, but I haven't heard from her in a while. And she, too, has a lot of concerns about her own community, about going home and helping her people. So those that have come from different places, that's one of their desires is to learn how to first take care of themselves and learn how to be able to use the tools they learned there and go home and share that with their communities. 'Cause all our people that, I think, come to treatment programs have that same desire. To go home and be able to help your community, or help your children, your grandchildren, and your neighbours. So in that way it's reaching out to all the communities and maybe encouraging other people to go for treatment. And, "It's not that bad! It's good. Look at me! It's helped me." So I really support that. I just strongly support, you know, whatever way I could. If I could support that program to continue running, that the government will fund it and keep funding it until we're able to get a good balance in our communities – that we could set up our own kind of support systems in our communities, in a healing way, in a supportive way. And be able to just stay home and not always sending our people away to treatment. They come back and you fall back into the same kind of situation 'cause maybe your family is, or your friends are, still using or still unhealthy. So hopefully by more people taking advantage of the treatment programs that's offered, that they can use those tools to come back and help other people. So that's where I am with that program. I really support that program. It really has a – a big place in my heart.

Same as Tsow-tun Le Lum, which I have been involved with for more years. I think it's about twenty-three years. You know, I forget and I say eighteen years, nineteen years. No, no! When I was over at our last AGM meeting, yeah, it's twenty-three years! I thought, "Holy!" *[laughs]* But I've been involved in Tsow-tun Le Lum program before the building was even built. And it's been there twenty-three years. Because that's when I was in social work, and back then we had people that worked together, like the CHRs, they called them: community health workers. And drug and alcohol workers, addictions workers, and social workers, band social workers. So we had a committee of these people that worked together, or met and discussed the issues that we were faced with in our communities. And at that time we decided it would be so nice to have an all–Aboriginal peoples treatment centre. So it took a long time. Nobody took us seriously for a long time. It's like you're asking for the impossible. Because what the government would say or what the higher agencies would say is, "Well, you know, there's programs offered. Counselling programs. There's AA programs. And there's this program, that program." But it's run off-reserve, and it's run by people that are non-Native people that don't really know our people, our lifestyle, where we're coming from, and don't know us as a people, that we communicate differently. Back then it was really hard to communicate with non-Native people because of the discrimination and the lack of trust. You're not going to go and talk to a psychologist or psychiatrist and, you know, "Why would I go and talk to … what does he know about me?" So it was just almost impossible to get anyone to go for counselling or therapy. So I'm really thankful for Tsow-tun Le Lum – that it was established. That we finally got it, through the efforts of many people that were in our committee. So we begin to look for a place where it would be situated. Finally, Health Canada agreed and other funding sources agreed. It started smaller than it is now, like a pilot project. We have another one that I've not been involved with, but it's at the West Coast, that takes families. But only in the summer, pretty much, and it's more remote and removed. So this was so much more convenient for a lot of people, especially on this side of the coast. You know, that they're able to access these programs offered at Tsow-tun Le Lum, in Nanoose, just outside of Nanaimo. So we looked at several places and it just didn't work in this place or that place. And finally in Nanoose they welcomed the centre, which was really, really great. So it's up on the hill, just up off the highway.

And it's grown a lot. It takes in sometimes parolees so they can go back to their communities when they're paroled, or they're released from another institution – that they can ease themselves back into their communities instead of just going back there from wherever it is they've been away from the community for a long time. But they are screened very carefully. And that was a real concern for some people around the neighbourhood there: "Oh, there's parolees in that treatment centre," and like, not in my backyard kind of mentality. So that was a real challenge too. But I think people are now okay with it, because the people that come there are screened very carefully. Couple of the workers from the centre would actually visit the jails, the institutions, when a person was ready to be considered for parole. So they would go and do their interviews with them and, like, the warden or whoever is in charge. That was just not one visit, it was several visits, and see if that would be a candidate – that person would be candidate to come to Tsow-tun Le Lum. And that has worked. There are people that have gone back to their communities. It's a transition. And I think, if a person has been in jail for quite some time, how do they go back? It's like, just taking you, putting you out there. Maybe your community doesn't trust you for whatever reason and you're rejected. But this way, you get back with your own people, and your own First Nations people, and they make friends there. It's a wonderful thing. And they leave and they're so reluctant and scared when they first come there, as all the other clients that come there. But when they leave, it's almost like you hate to leave, 'cause you know, it's five-week programs, six-week programs. And there's some that are there for different types of programs – would be, maybe ten days, three weeks, that kind of program. Like trauma and just different kinds of programs, addictions programs. There's a policy that because there's such a long waiting list, you have to have the desire, or the willingness to go for treatment. So you get on a waiting list, and normally it's three months, because the waiting list is becoming longer. So they have other places that people can go for detox. But it's not recommended that you go there while you're detoxing. So you have to have that desire that you wanna be there. And so it's good. It's really working well.

We have a First Nations lady there that's been the administrator – now she's the administrator. She was the assistant administrator right from the beginning when the place was first built. And the first administrator was a non-Native person. And he was really, really good. Then he decided to retire. So the assistant took over that role. And she's from Nanaimo. Her mother's originally from Nanaimo. She's a wonderful lady. So now she's got an assistant and, well, I think she's had a couple of assistants. One had to move. Then there's a new assistant who's worked her way through. And the people that work there, and some of them have come from a place where they themselves have had issues, or addictions, and they've worked through that. They come there as a client and really got on a good, good path in life, and had that desire to help others. Because they themselves were helped through that centre. And they go back and go to school or upgrade and then get themselves a degree and come back and work in the centre. So we have quite a few on staff that are First Nations people, and from that area. So it's really nice to see that. We still have a psychologist that comes from the outside. That helps certain clients that need to see a psychologist that comes once a week. So that's a little extra. Once people are comfortable in going to a person like that within that building. And it works fine. It really works well. So the clients are well taken care of while they're there. The people that work there, the staff, are wonderful people. There's just so much empathy for people that come there, and they get nothing but kindness and understanding.

There's a spiritual room, built within the building right from the get-go. And Elders come there. There's always an Elder-in-residence during the week. And so they find time to go and sit with an Elder. The Elder goes and sits in the spiritual room in the morning for introductions and just to see how everyone's feeling in the morning. And at first clients are reluctant to say, "I'm feeling this way this morning." It'd be just, like, maybe, "Oh, I'm okay." And after they'd been there for a little while, you see so much difference happening, taking place during the time they're there. And the Elder would give a talk after everybody has gone around and introduced themselves. It's a semicircle – the room is semicircle, and so they're all seated around a semicircle. And the Elder sits with them. And prayers are said to open the meeting. Prayers are said at the end. Then they go off to their individual workshops where they go and sit, and the men go to a different workshop, the women go to a different workshop. And so there's a lot of programs offered there now, different types of programs.

So they have, like, for front-line workers, they go there too for maybe a week to deal with what they're dealing with in their own communities. And that to me is really good for them. I took one of the programs. I was a client there for – I think it was a week, or was it two weeks that time. So I got a feel of what it's like to be a client, and to walk a straight line and to be in a program and, like, you get up at this time, this is what you do, and it's like, it was kind of a different kind of feeling. It's like, "I'm not an Elder, I'm a client!" *[laughs]* And that was okay. You get to learn that feeling. You come to understand where your clients are, and you're sharing a room with three other ladies, right? Some of those rooms are, you know, there's three or four. There's bunk bed and two lower beds, single beds. So you're totally in a different place as an Elder. So that's pretty good. Yeah, I think it gives you a better understanding, even though it's humbling. You know, understand where people are coming from. Lights out! Ten o'clock! Yeah, so it's quite an experience. You get more understanding of how the clients must feel when they're there, where they first come in and they're sharing a room with strangers. But you soon get to know your roommates and it's good. 'Cause they could be from anywhere else, from another community, and other communities. So that's good.

There's a real demand for more programs and it's ongoing. The only time it shuts down is between Christmas and New Year. And then they clean house. They bring people to really clean house, 'cause there's no one there. So they clean the place from top to bottom. Get started in the new year again. The programs there are so well run. There's been accreditation done in the last few years, and I guess it has to do with the funding. So people come and interview even clients that are there, "How is this place?" And just interviewing people in how they feel when they're there and what kind of service they're getting. And then they interview staff: the cooks, the people that clean up, and the office staff and the administrator and the board of directors. We were all interviewed. So we all have an input on how the place is run, right down to the clients. And it takes a few months for the results to come back and, boy, it was glowing! So we got this huge plaque on the wall, you know, the accreditation – I think that's so important, to be acknowledged, and Tsow-tun Le Lum has a reputation that it's one of the best. Or it is the best. So I'm really proud to say that. I think it's a real credit to the people that run the place. Yeah, it's very successful. There may be a few that go out and, you know, it's hard for the centre to keep in touch with people that have left. The follow-up. But they do make that effort, 'cause there's not much you can do once people have gone back to their own communities. But they encourage people to keep in touch: "Let us know how you're doing when you go back home." And some have fallen on the wayside and have had to go back again for a refresher. And they eventually find the path, right? And I think it's successful in that way. Yeah, it's good for the coast people here because it's close. I know there's others, like Round Lake and that in the interior. There's another one in Alert Bay. But those are further away from people here on the coast. And, like, the urban people probably utilize Nanaimo or Nanoose. So in that way it's good. It's successful. It's as successful as it can be. If it's not a hundred percent, you know, people there give it a hundred percent. The effort they put into welcoming people and working with people and showing kindness and another way of life. With all respect that they could give them. It's a beautiful place! So I'm happy to say that I've had that privilege of being on the board of directors for twenty-three years now. And so I was suggesting – I was jokingly saying to the administrator, "One day you're going to have to start thinking about putting an addition onto this building – like a retirement home for the board of directors, 'cause some of us are getting old!" *[laughs]* She was laughing. She was saying, "Oh yeah, we'll do that." Yeah, so that's that. I've gone as an Elder a few times there in the summer when I'm available. Just for a week as an Elder-in-residence. And it's good. I look forward to it. It's another good change for me. Just to see how the place is running, too. Yeah, so I've been as an Elder-in-residence, I'm on the board of directors, and I've also been a client, so I kind of get to know the run of the place pretty much. And they run a balanced budget. It's incredible! They run a balanced budget. And now and then there's fundraising that the staff will do – a little committee to fundraise for other things that's needed in the place. So there's always that happening. And the people from the community, like Nanoose and Nanaimo, the closest communities, are welcome to come and use the facility, like the gymnasium. So that's used sometimes for other kind of events. So I think that makes it really more friendly too, to the community. So, that's pretty much it. Um-hmm.

The teachings are the most important. This is the reason why they have Elders come and be in residence, 'cause they want to know – a lot of people, especially in the urban areas, that have been away for a long, long time. And especially people that were raised in the system. Or they grew up in the residential school, then they went to foster homes, or they went – and quite often people ended up in other institutions. So they were never around the First Nations communities or been around people that practise the culture. So they learn a lot from there. It helps them to get in touch. And we encourage them to seek their own family background, if they can. Because we have different teachings in different communities. Like I was mentioning about the Elder from the Yukon, it isn't till you talk to a person from another community that you start to appreciate their culture, and respect that culture. So I, as an Elder, I do not impose my practice, my cultural practice and teachings on them. I may share my teachings with them and "This is the teachings I had" – how to look after myself, how to do the self-care using the resources we have in our own community. Like using the cedar is important for us, and the men going on a vision quest and all of those kinds of other things. The different types of training, the sweat house, the sweat lodge. And there's no one way of doing things, or the right way or the wrong way. Maybe people from the Prairies have different way of doing things. Maybe people from south Island do things a little differently than we do here on the mainland. And that's okay! We don't discriminate against that. That is their way, that is their beliefs, that's how they were brought up. So we encourage people that want to get back in touch with their culture to make that effort to find – if not their own grandmother or their own grandfather, but maybe an Elder from that community. So that's why there's different Elders that come from different places on the Island, and sometimes from Vancouver, Sechelt and Musqueam, North Van. They've come there. So they rotate the Elders, so they can share their knowledge and their culture and their traditional practices. And so not to discriminate or say, "This is the way, this is how I was raised, this is how you do this." And I've compared it to this story I heard about two individuals that were at a cemetery at the same time. One was a non-Native man – or woman, I'm not sure. But the other individual was a Chinese – Oriental person. And this person brought a bouquet of flowers to this grave of a loved one. And this Oriental person brought a bowl of rice and put it on the grave, and this non-Native person looked and was, like, "What is he doing bringing rice to this –?" you know, placing the bowl of rice on the grave. So he asked the Oriental man, "Is your friend gonna come up and eat that bowl of rice?" And he said, "Yeah, the same time as your loved one is gonna come and smell those flowers." And I think that's just so great! *[laughs]* I thought that was, you know – I always will remember that. When you think about, "Oh, they're not doing things right. They're from over there, wherever. This is the right way! My way is the right way!" And be really cynical and critical. And we've become – startin' to use things because how our people move now, or married into another community or another First Nations – could be from the West Coast, it could be from the north or it could be from somewhere else. Or someone's married into this community and will try to impose their teachings on us. And I always say, "I got my own, it's okay. It's okay. I got my own way of doing things. I will not impose my ways on you." So you know, just keep those lines. I'm really fussy about that. I take pride and I have a strong belief in what my elderly people originally from this community taught me, or I was raised with. I watched how the grandparents did it here. Such as the brushing, the cleansing, self-care, the sweat for the men, and vision quests and self-discipline. All of those things that was taught, that I grew up with here, and the stories told by the old people in my community. That's my traditional practice, those are my values. And it would not be fair to start using someone else's and say, "Okay, I'll use that," or "I need you to come and brush me," or "come and smudge me," or "come and –" whatever methods they use, whatever tools they use. I respect that. That belongs to them, the same as any other nationality. I'm sure every nationality has their ways of taking care of themselves, whether it's meditation or yoga, or whatever! You know? That's their belief. That's what makes them feel good. So for me, I guess I'm quite protective in my own teachings – my own values are mine. I'll share it with my family and leave other people to practise their way, of how their ancestors did it, of how their grandmothers did it. 'Cause they're different. There's differences! So I can't say one is better than the other. It's the same with the legends when I've gone and had that opportunity and that privilege to listen to other Elders from other communities, and they talk about legends. And we have fun. We laugh about it! And, like, at Tsa-Kwa-Luten or at Tsow-tun Le Lum or wherever Elders gather. And so we kind of exchange stories and we have a good laugh about it: "Oh yeah, we know that story too! But it was told this way." It's like the wild woman of the woods, and for us it was the wild man of the woods here – same story! The base is very same. You know how the wild man used to come and gather children and take them away, or kidnap the women and take them away. So it's the same thing. It's so funny. So a lot of it is really similar in our ways. And so I'm not gonna argue and say, "Oh no! It wasn't a woman!

No, it was a man!" "No, it was a –!" *[laughs]* So we could get into a big debate about this! It's okay. I understand. I think it's great that we can respect our neighbours and how they practise. And other Nations and what they believe in. How they dress, what is meaningful to them in their dress, in their regalias. It's very important to them. My way is important to me. And we need to understand that. We need to accept that, and not push our values onto someone else, or them to push their values on me, 'cause my bristles go up and I get upset when someone says, "You're doing that wrong." It's right for me! Yeah. So that's pretty much it. My views on cultural practices. *[laughs]*

Sliammon Narrative

č'ɛhč'ɛhʌ čxʷ k'ʷʌnɛtomoɫ
(You Thank the One Who Looks after All of Us)*

[X'ásʌm qʷáys qáymɪxʷ]

X'asəm	qʷay-s	qaymixʷ
strong-MDL	talk-3POSS	Native.person
it.is.strong	their.talk	Native.person

'People's words are powerful.'

[nám' kʷX̌óˑX̌op ʔʌnígi]

nam'	kʷ‿ X̌u-X̌up	ʔə‿ nəgi
similar	DET‿ IMPF-wound	OBL‿ 2SG.INDP
it.is.similar	wounding	you

'It is like they go right into you.'

[gʌ páyɛʔʌs ʔóˑɫoθɛm qáymɪxʷ]

ga‿ payaʔ-as	ʔuɫ-u-θi-m	qaymixʷ
if‿ always-3CNJ.SBJ	tell-LV-CTR+2SG.OBJ-MDL	Native.person
if‿ always	you.are.told	Native.person

'If people are always talking about you,'

[X̌óˑX̌op θó: ʔʌ nígi qʷáys qáymɪxʷ]

X̌u-X̌up	θu	ʔə‿ nəgi	qʷay-s	qaymixʷ
IMPF-wound	go	OBL‿ 2SG.INDP	talk-3POSS	Native.person
wounding	go	at.you	their.talk	Native.person

'then what they say will cut right into you.'

[héɫhi:t ʔʌθqʷúl' q'áʔt'aˑt'ʌm]

hiɫ ‿hiyt	ʔə‿ θ‿qʷəl'	q'aʔt'-at'-əm
it's ‿CLT	CLF‿2SG.POSS‿ come	heavy-INC-MDL
it.is	that.you	become.heavy

'It weighs you down.'

---

* This text was recorded on 18 March 1996.

[xʷáʔhiːt čéʔmʌs ʔi: hóčxʷhiːt ʔéˑɉɛmtʌnómot]

xʷaʔ ‿hiyt	čam'-as	ʔiy	hu ‿čxʷ ‿hiyt
NEG ‿CLT	why-3CNJ.SBJ	and	go ‿2SG.INDC.SBJ ‿CLT
not		and	go ‿you

ʔiǰ-am-t-ə-nu-mut
improve-MDL-CTR-EPEN-NTR-RFL
get.better

'You become unable to make any progress, unable to get better.'

[hégʌxʷ nám's tán' tʌθ θó sóˑsoˑhoˑθot payéʔ]

hi ‿ga	ʔə ‿xʷ ‿nam'-s		tan'	tə ‿θ ‿θu
it's ‿MTG	CLF ‿NOM ‿similar-3POSS		DEM	DET ‿2SG.POSS ‿go
it.is	why		that	that.you.go

su-suh-u-θut	paya?
IMPF-do.traditional.ritual-LV-CTR+RFL	always
doing.traditional.ritual	always

'That is why you always do your morning rituals.'

[páyčxʷʔʊt hóː sóˑsoˑhoθot kʷʊθ qʷúl'ʔíʔ kʷʊθ ƛʌƛiːčʼɛˑθot]

paya? ‿čxʷ ‿ʔut		hu	su-suh-u-θut
always ‿2SG.INDC.SBJ ‿CLT		go	IMPF-do. traditional.ritual-LV-CTR+RFL
always ‿you		go	doing.traditional.ritual

kʷə ‿θ ‿qʷəl'	ʔəy'	kʷə ‿θ ‿ƛə-ƛəyčʼ-a-θut
DET ‿2SG.POSS ‿come	good	DET ‿2SG.POSS ‿IMPF-go.through-LV-CTR+RFL
your ‿come	good	that.your.getting.through

'You always do your morning rituals in order to better yourself and to achieve the good things that will help you to be successful in your life.'

[ʔiˑ ʔúːkʼʷstám qʷúl' ʔíʔ nígi]

ʔiy	ʔuwkʼʷ-s	tam	qʷəl'	ʔəy'	nəgi
and	all-3POSS	what	come	good	2SG.INDP
and	all.	thing	come	good	you

'And everything will be all right with you (if you do your morning rituals).'

[táːm θóˑ yéʔqʼʌšɛxʷ tʌχʌmʔay táʔʌ kʷʊθθóː]

tam	θu	yaʔqʼ-aš-axʷ	təχəmʔay	taʔa	kʷə ‿θ ‿θu
what	go	use-TR-2SG.ERG	cedar	DEM	DET ‿2SG.POSS ‿go
what	go	you.use.it	cedar	there	you.go

'Whatever you use ... (like) cedar over there ...'

[hέwtəm' kʷʌθθó: χʷʌt'ᵉʌm tán' kʷʊθ xʷí·kʷɛ·θòt]

hiwtəm'	kʷə‿θ‿θu	xʷət'ᵉ-ʔəm	tan'
before	DET‿2SG.POSS‿go	break.off-A.INTR	DEM
before	you.go	break.off	that

kʷə‿θ‿xʷikʷ-i-θut
DET‿2SG.POSS‿brush.with.cedar.boughs-LV-CTR+RFL
you.brush.yourself.with.cedar.boughs

'Before you break off cedar boughs to rub on yourself,'

[č'έʰč'ɛʰʌčxʷt tʎχʌmʔay]

č'ah-č'ah-a-t‿čxʷ	tə‿təχəmʔay
RDPL-pray-LV-CTR‿2SG.INDC.SBJ	DET‿cedar
thank.it‿you	the‿cedar.tree

'you thank the cedar tree.'

[táwčɛxʷ (tʌ)θkʷú·ɬma tə náʔʌs...]

taw-t‿čaxʷ	tə‿θ‿kʷuɬma	tə‿naʔa-s...
tell-CTR‿2SG.INDC.SBJ	DET‿2SG.POSS‿borrow	DET‿FILLER-3POSS
tell.to.it‿you	that.you.borrow	the‿(umm)

'You tell it you are going to borrow ... (from it).'

[χʷʌt'ᵉʌmčxʷθó]

xʷət'ᵉ-ʔəm‿čxʷ	θu
break.off-A.INTR‿2SG.INDC.SBJ	go
break.off‿you	go

'You go and break off its branches.'

[č'έʰč'ɛʰʌčxʷ]

č'ah-č'ah-a-t‿čxʷ
RDPL-pray-LV-CTR‿2SG.INDC.SBJ
thank.it‿you

'You thank it.'

[gʎyɛčxʷgə kʷúk'ʷaθɛs]

gay-a-t‿čxʷ‿ga	kʷə-kʷʔ-a-θi-s
ask-LV-CTR‿2SG.INDC.SBJ‿MTG	IMPF-help-LV-CTR+2SG.OBJ-3ERG
ask.it‿you	it.is.helping.you

'You ask it to help you.'

[yíːʔχmɛθɛs]

yəyʼx̣-mi-θi-s

take.care-RLT-CTR+2SG.OBJ-3ERG

he.takes.care.of.you

'And to look after you.'

[ʔiˑ nám'sčxʷ ʔʊt qáʔyɛ]

ʔiy	nam'-s ͜čxʷ ͜ʔut		qay'a
and	similar-CAU ͜2SG.INDC.SBJ ͜CLT		water
and	make.it.similar ͜you		water

'And you do the same with water.'

[ʔúːkʼʷtám tíˑsxʷʌxʷ níš tέʔɛ gíʃɛ]

ʔuwkʼʷ	tam	tih-sxʷ-axʷ	niš	tiʔi	giǰa
all	what	big-CAU-2SG.ERG	stay	DEM	ground
all	thing	you.respect.it	those.that.stay	here	world

'You treat everything with respect in this world.'

[héwtəm' kʷʌθ θóˑ yέʔqʼʌš tətám ʔέɬtən tíˑtʌčuˑmɪxʷ]

hiwtəm'	kʷə ͜θ ͜θu	yaʔqʼ-aš	tə ͜tam	ʔiɬtən	titačumixʷ
before	DET ͜2SG.POSS ͜go	use-TR	DET ͜what	food	animal
before	you.go	use.it	whatever	food	animal

'Before you use an animal as food'

[gʌθáˑhʌxʷ máʔʌm kʷǰénxʷ]

ga ͜θa-h-axʷ	ma-ʔəm	kʷ ͜ǰanxʷ
if ͜go-EPEN-2SG.CNJ.SBJ	obtain-A.INTR	DET ͜fish
if.you.would.go	get	a ͜fish

'or if you go and get some fish,'

[čʼέʰčʼɛhʌčxʷ tán']

čʼah-čʼah-a-t ͜čxʷ	tan'
RDPL-pray-LV-CTR ͜2SG.INDC.SBJ	DEM
thank.it ͜you	that

'you thank it.'

[táwčὲxʷ]

taw-t ͜čaxʷ

tell-CTR ͜2SG.INDC.SBJ

tell.to.it ͜you

'You tell it:'

[q'ʷéymɛθčxʷʊm]

q'ʷiy-mi-θ ˌčxʷəm

feel.sorry-RLT-CTR+1SG.OBJ ˌ2SG.INDC.SBJ+FUT

feel.sorry.towards.me ˌyou.will

'"Forgive me.'

[xʷáʔčʔot háysən tᵊqéyθɛ]

xʷaʔ ˌč ˌʔut		hays-an	tᵊˌ qəy-θi
NEG ˌ1SG.INDC.SBJ ˌCLT		only-1SG.CNJ.SBJ	1SG.POSSˌ die-CTR+2SG.OBJ
not ˌI		no.reason ˌI	myˌ kill.you

'I'm not killing you for the sake of nothing.'

[ʔóʔoˑwuˑθòč ʔʌnígi]

ʔu-ʔuw-u-θut ˌč	ʔəˌ nəgi
IMPF-assist-LV-CTR+RFL ˌ1SG.INDC.SBJ	OBLˌ 2SG.INDP
helping.oneself ˌI	by.you

'You are going to help me.'

[héga tᵊtíː qʷúl' máːθɛ]

hi ˌga	tᵊˌ tiy	qʷəl'	ma-θi
it's ˌMTG	1SG.POSSˌ ??	come	obtain-CTR+2SG.OBJ
it.is	why.I	come	take.you

'That's why I have come to take you.'"

[nígiʔot (ʔʌxʷ)qʷúl's ʔíʔ]

nəgi ˌʔut	ʔəˌ xʷˌ qʷəl'-s	ʔəy'
2SG.INDP ˌCLT	CLFˌ NOMˌ come-3POSS	good
you	where.it.comes	good

'It reflects well on you as a person.'*

[xʷʊčémʌs qáqsɛmɛčxʷ tám tíˑtaˑčumɪxʷ níš ʔʌtéʔɛ gíʃɛ]

xʷaʔ	čam'-as	qaqs-im-(m)i-t ˌčxʷ	tam	titačumixʷ
NEG	why-3CNJ.SBJ	play-MDL-RLT-CTR ˌ2SG.INDC.SBJ	what	animal
not		make.fun.of.it ˌyou	what	animal

niš	ʔəˌ tiʔi	giʃa
stay	OBLˌ here	ground
it.stays	here	ground

'You never make fun of/waste any animal in this world.'

---

* Elsie reverted back to general "you" in this line. She means that thanking the cedar tree that one uses or the fish that one catches is the proper act because it is in accordance with the teaching.

[hɛ́ɬʔot tán' kʷúkʷʔa·θɛ]

hiɬ	ʔut	tan'	kʷə-kʷʔa-θi
it's	CLT	DEM	IMPF-help-CTR+2SG.OBJ
it.is		they	the.ones.who.help.you

'They are the ones that help you.'

[hɛɬʔʌθqʷʊl'hi:t ʔíʔ]

hiɬ	ʔə θ qʷəl' hiyt		ʔəy'
it's	CLF 2SG.POSS come CLT		good
it.is	how.you.become		good

'That is how you get better.'

[gəyíʔχmɛtʌxʷ tán' tot ʔú:k'ʷtá·mʌs]

ga yəy'x̣-mi-t-axʷ		tan'	tut	ʔuwk'ʷ	tam-as
if take.care-RLT-CTR-2SG.CNJ.SBJ		DEM	??	all	what-3CNJ.SBJ
if.you.take.care.of.it		that		all	things

'by looking after that and everything else.'

[hɛ́wtəm' kʷʌθθó: tá ʔa·čiš]

hiwtəm'	kʷə θ θu	taʔačiš
before	DET 2SG.POSS go	travel
before	that.you.go	travel

'Before you go travelling,'

[hɛ́wtəm' kʷʌθ θó: hɛ́qɛθòt]

hiwtəm'	kʷə θ θu	hiq-i-θut
before	DET 2SG.POSS go	cast.off-LV-CTR+RFL
before	that.you.go	cast.off

'and before you cast off,'

[č'ɛ́ʰč'ɛhʌčxʷ (kʷ) k'ʷʌnɛtomoɬ]

č'ah-č'ah-a-t čxʷ		kʷ k'ʷən-i-t-umuɬ
RDPL-pray-LV-CTR 2SG.INDC.SBJ		DET see-LV-CTR-1PL.OBJ
thank.him/her you		the.one.who.is.seeing.us

'you thank the one who looks after all of us.'

[hɛ́səm k'ʷʌnɛθ kʷʊtᶿ hó:səm hɛ́·qɛ·θòt]

hi səm	k'ʷən-i-θ	kʷə tᶿ hu səm	hiq-i-θut
it's FUT	see-LV-CTR+1SG.OBJ	DET 1SG.POSS go FUT	cast.off-LV-CTR+RFL
it.will.be.him	seeing.me	when.I.would.go	cast.off

'He will be watching over me when I cast off.'

[hót^eəm ʔówʊɬ tənúxʷɨɬ]

hu ‿t^eəm	ʔuwuɬ	tə‿nəxʷiɬ
go ‿1SG.INDC.SBJ+FUT	embark	DET‿canoe
go ‿I.will	embark.on.boat	the‿canoe

'I will get on the boat.'

[hóč táʔa·čìš]

hu ‿č	taʔačiš
go ‿1SG.INDC.SBJ	travel
go ‿I	travel

'I will travel.'

[č'ɛ́ʰč'ɛhʌčxʷ k'ʷúnɛtomoɬ]

č'ah-č'ah-a-t ‿čxʷ	k'ʷən-i-t-umuɬ
RDPL-pray-LV-CTR ‿2SG.INDC.SBJ	see-STV-CTR-1PL.OBJ
thank.him/her ‿you	the.one.who.is.seeing.us

'You thank the one who watches over us,'

[yí:ʔχmɛtòmoɬ]

yəy'x̣-mi-t-umuɬ
take.care-RLT-CTR-1PL.OBJ
(the.one.who)take.care.of.us

'the one who looks after us.'

[č'ɛ́hʌmčxʷ]

č'ah-am ‿čxʷ
pray-MDL ‿2SG.INDC.SBJ
pray ‿you

'You pray.'

[nám'ʔot gʌ θá·hʌxʷ ʔɛ́ʔa·mìš]

nam' ‿ʔut	ga‿θu-h-axʷ	ʔiʔamiš
similar ‿CLT	if‿go-EPEN-2SG.CNJ.SBJ	hunt
it.is.similar	if‿you.would.go	hunt

'It is the same as when you go hunting.'

[tú·mìš há·hʌs ʔɛ́·ʔa·mìš]

tumiš	hu-h-as	ʔiʔamiš
man	go-EPEN-3CNJ.SBJ	hunt
man	he.would.go	hunt

'If you were a man going hunting,'

[héyčxʷʔʊt č'ɛ́ʰč'ɛhʌt k'ʷúnɛtomoɬ]

hiya ‿čxʷ ‿ʔut	č'ah-č'a-t	k'ʷən-i-t-umuɬ
soon ‿2SG.INDC.SBJ ‿CLT	RDPL-pray-LV-CTR	see-STV-CTR-1PL.OBJ
soon ‿you	thank.him	the.one.who.is.seeing.us

'you would immediately thank the one watching over us.'

[hésəm yíʔχmɛθɛ (kʷθ) kʷčɛ́ xʷθó·θo·]

hi ‿səm	yəy'x̣-mi-θi	kʷ ‿ča	xʷ ‿θu-θu
it's ‿FUT	take.care-RLT-CTR+2SG.OBJ	where	NOM ‿RDPL-go
he.will.be	the.one.who.takes.care.of.you	where	go ·

'He will watch over you wherever you go.'

[héɬʔot qʷúl' χʌna·θɛ kʷ tám θʔéɬtən]

hiɬ ‿ʔut	qʷəl' ·	x̣əna-θi	kʷ ‿ tam	θ ‿ ʔiɬtən
it's ‿CLT	come	give-CTR+2SG.OBJ	DET ‿what	2SG.POSS ‿food
it.is	he.comes	give.to.you	whatever	your ‿food

'He will give you your food.'

[xʷʊčémʌs ʔi: xʷáxʷaʔsčxʷ kʷtá·mʌs ʔá·ʔa·ƛ'ìš kʷtá·mʌs ʔʌθʔéɬtən]

xʷaʔ čam'-as	ʔiy xʷa-xʷaʔ-s ‿čxʷ	kʷ ‿ tam-as
NEG why-3CNJ.SBJ	and IMPF-come.off-CAU ‿2SG.INDC.SBJ	DET ‿what-3CNJ.SBJ
not	and taking.it.off ‿you	whatever

ʔa-ʔaƛ'-iš	kʷ ‿ tam-as	ʔə ‿ θ ‿ ʔiɬtən
IMPF-throw.away-INTR	DET ‿what-3CNJ.SBJ	OBL ‿2SG.POSS ‿food
throwing.away	whatever	your ‿food

'You never discard or throw any of your food away.'

[x̣á·ƛ'ὲt ʔi·qʷúlčɛxʷ máʔʌxʷ kʷán']

x̣aƛ'it	ʔiy qʷəl' ‿čaxʷ	maʔ-əxʷ	kʷan'
difficult	and come ‿2SG.INDC.SBJ	obtain-NTR	DEM
it.is.difficult	and come ‿you	get.it	that

'You have a hard time getting it.'

[héga θtí·ʰsxʷ]

hi ‿ga	θ ‿ tih-sxʷ
it's ‿MTG	2SG.POSS ‿big-CAU
it.is.why	you.respect.it

'And that is why you treat it with respect.'

[níš kʼʷʌ́nɛ·tòmoɬ]

niš	kʼʷən-i-t-umuɬ
stay	see-STV-CTR-1PL.OBJ
he.stays	the.one.who.is.seeing.us

'There is somebody watching over us.'

[pá:yɛʔot nɛ́ʔ kʼʷʌ́nɛtomoɬ]

payaʔ	ˌʔut	niʔ	kʼʷən-i-t-umuɬ
always	CLT	be.there	see-STV-CTR-1PL.OBJ
always		it.is.there	the.one.who.is.seeing.us

'There is always somebody watching over us.'

11

Teachings on Spirituality

S
o our people believed strongly in the spirit world. That even people that have been gone for years and years, and generations ago, their spirit is still with us. So therefore when we really need help in whatever area, or we're troubled or we're lonely or we're hurting in some way, that's why we always call upon the spirit of the ancestors to guide you, to help you. I guess it's like the teachings of the church, that you always pray to God or to the angels or to whoever you're praying to, to watch over you and protect you. Well, First Nations people had that, all that.* They always called upon the spirit of the ancestors: ʔəms hɛhɛw', ʔəms hɛhɛw'. That's "our ancestors." Our hɛhɛw'. hɛ səm t kʷə ms hɛhɛw' k'ʷənɛθɛ – the ancestors will look after you. So there's a lot of respect to that. And they will always look after you and guide you. So, at the same time, the people believed that there were some spirits out there too that were not too kind – that they could harm you as well. And they used to say it's like the living people: you have your friends, your good friends, and they'll help you, but there are other people that may harm you. So it's the same

---

* Chief Tom drew an analogy between ɬaʔamɪn conceptions of the supernatural and the Christian trinity. Homer G. Barnett, *The Coast Salish of British Columbia* (Eugene: University of Oregon Press, 1955), 206; University of British Columbia, Rare Books and Special Collections, H.G. Barnett Fonds, Box 1, Folder 6, Field notes: "Mainland Comox (Slaiäman, Klahuse, Homalco), 1936" (hereafter cited as Barnett field notes, folder 1-6), 233-34.

in the spirit world, that there are people that could bring you harm or take the spirit of your children. So that's why we're always told, "Guard your children. Look after your children. Keep them away from – keep them close to you during this time." So after all of that, people's belief back then – like Auntie Katherine when she used to live with us, and my grandmother and other Elders of that age – the old-timers used to strongly believe in covering the windows when it got dark. 'Cause the spirits are more prone to come into your space when you don't close your windows or pull your curtains. Or don't leave food on the table when you go to bed. When you're finished eating you either cover food that's left or put it away, 'cause the spirits are hungry and they'll want some of that food. So you protected those things like that. Quite often the old people used to cook midday. That was their main meal. Then they put the food away. So what they did, like, in the evening it would be just, like, snacks. 'Cause if they're cooking anything or frying anything, that really draws the spirits from the spirit world to come – and may be hungry and touch the food and that could leave you really feeling sick or just feeling ill, 'cause they've touched that food. So the food was always protected and put away, always covered. The windows were covered at night. Even a mirror, if you had a mirror in the house – in later times when we had mirrors in our homes, we were always cautioned about taking your baby to the mirror, and, "Oh, look at the baby in the mirror!" And their spirit could be taken. "Don't do that!" they would say. "Don't do that to the baby." Because they felt there was something that might pull the baby into the spirit world or might be harmed. So the mirrors were covered at night as well, if you had a mirror in the house. And that was a no-no to have those exposed. So those are really important teachings.

For myself, my Native spirituality teachings are very important to me. This is what grounds me, is that I pray to the Creator, I pray to the spirit of my ancestors, I pray to the universe. That God is wherever you are, whether you're in a house, where you're travelling on water, wherever you are – you're on top of the mountain, you're in the woods, you're in the forest, you're on the beach – that God is where you are! God, to me, is the Creator, Creator of all things. And I use that in my prayer: "God, Creator of all things, show me the way. Help me! Help me. I need direction. I need help. I need to clear my mind. I need direction. Help me to be strong. Help me to be this or that," whatever the case is. To me that's very, very important. That's very, very meaningful. And I really struggle with Christianity versus my Native spiritual teachings. I would like to see one day that our Native spirituality and our teachings be incorporated into the church, whether it be the Catholic Church or other denominations. I know that Native spirituality is not always recognized in the church. And I do have a problem with that. I just feel in my heart that that's overlooked? Or not accepted in a lot of cases. That we should not be believing in other things, other than God. I do believe in God. But I also believe that God is generous, that God is forgiving, that God loves all people. And that God would not expect us to walk a very thin line, that this is the only way we're gonna get to heaven. My thoughts around that is that on this earth you live a clean life. You respect everything around you. You call on the Creator when you need help. You call on the spirit of your ancestors. My belief is that when we die, we're only going to go on another journey. We're going to the other side, is what my people would say: "We've gone to the other side." Our spirit lives, and will live among our people and be there for our children, will be there for generations. That's why I have a strong belief in praying to my ancestors. I call upon the spirit of my grandmother, my great-grandmother, all of those that have left us. I feel their presence. I know they're around. When I need them I call upon them. And to me that's very, very important. Because I know their spirit lives with us. Maybe some people will say the memory of our loved ones that have gone before. But I feel strongly the spirit is with us. So I need to, in my own mind, to me it's very important to pass that on to my children, to my grandchildren, that strong belief that I have, the strong belief that *my* grandparents had, that there is a spiritual world out there around us, that is what grounds us. This is why we take care of things when our loved ones pass on to the other side, that we look after things. We have a whole traditional practice that we do around that time. Taking care of their belongings, just making an offering, a burning of food. Why do we do those things, if that is not true beliefs? That's what we were raised with. I've talked to many people from other communities, Aboriginal people – doesn't matter where they're from, they have different traditional practices that's very related to how we do things. And the church may not recognize that. They may not see that as part of their belief. But that is our belief, and I think it's really important for us to carry on that and pass that on to the young people, to share that with them. That this is how our ancestors lived, this is how our ancestors believed, this is how they practised – that that be carried on. Because if you don't believe in that, what is there? There's no life after death? The church believes there's a resurrection. Maybe that's how they've determined that we will be resurrected one day and will come back to life. So be it. But I feel that our teachin' in our Native culture, to me, is the right way for me and my people in my community. So we need to get beyond this confusion about, some people will say, "Why do you bother to go to the church? Their teaching is something totally different. Why go to church if you're uncomfortable there?" I think we need to come together, the church and the people, and be able to work together and to incorporate our teachings and our beliefs into the church and how they practise and how they enforce their beliefs. I think we've come a long way, and we need to come back to our traditional teachings and practices and to feel free to practise those things within the church. And that be accepted by the church people, the people that – whether they be Catholic priests, or other – their Anglican priest or whatever other religion's out there. We need to be recognized in how we incorporate how we practise – the importance of that. That's healing for us? As long as we're confused about how we're going to travel that road of healing, and to be able to let go when we lose our loved ones, how are we going to heal? And to celebrate the life of that loved one, that that loved one has gone beyond, but we know the spirit lives with us. 'Cause we were a part of that person, whether it was your parent, your grandparent – you are another generation and the spirit lives with you, and always will. And it's been a struggle to – I know that churches are gradually coming around, but for me it's not quick enough? Our people have that desire, and they want their loved one to have some kind of service to go through the church, but I also know that people are uncomfortable at the same time. It's torturous, actually! *[laughs]* It is difficult. It is *really* difficult for – especially someone that – just being taught in a totally different system about who God is. The orders come from Rome, from the Pope, from that level, and we're coming from this whole other place.

Way back in the day when it was so strict, the regulations and the church policy just didn't allow for that. If you died and you were not married in the church, you were not allowed in the cemetery. You were ... outcast, discriminated against, I guess. If that's possible, to discriminate a dead person! *[laughs]* Yeah, when I think of that, and how difficult that must've been for people that, you know, going through the loss of a baby. Could've been a stillborn, could've been a – died few months old. Because they were not baptized, they were determined that they were not going to heaven. They were going to be in limbo somewhere. And to me, how I see, whether you're baptized as a baby or not, you're an angel. You've gone to a good place. But that's how the church viewed it at that time. That you're in limbo 'cause you're born with a black mark. You're born with a black mark. So you're not free to go to heaven. That part I don't understand. If people still believe in that today – I guess the church has changed its policy, because they pretty much had to. You can't go on with that kind of thinking, or that kind of a ruling. So when I think of parents that lost a baby, how traumatic is that? And how much more painful is that to be told your baby's not gone to heaven? He's gone to limbo. And they're not to be buried with people that are blessed. That must've been hard on a mother, as it is. And that's just one other thing that our people endured and lived with that, and accepted that. They had no choice but to accept that as the reality: "That's what happens. When this happens, this is what happens." We're told that's the way it's going to be. Yeah, so that was very unfair. Very painful, very hurtful. Yeah, just another thing to cause more pain. Yeah. That's the history of – part of the history.*

When our kids were taken away to residential schools, that's how they were taught: you prayed twenty times a day on your knees. And there are some people that are not going to like hearing this. And I experienced that when I went to residential school, is that soon as you heard that "clap clap" – the nun is at the door, in the dormitory door in the morning – you rolled out of bed and you knelt down by your bed and you prayed. And you got up and that was only the first prayer. You prayed here, you prayed there, you prayed before you left this room, you prayed as you enter the next room, you prayed comin' out of that room, you prayed – must have been thirty times a day you prayed. And that's their teachin', that's their belief. But it was so different from how we prayed. I feel that God walks with us, God is with us. No matter where we go, we need to respect that. The Creator is with us. We need to walk with other people, whatever religion they are. Where are all the people gonna go that are non-Catholics? Or they're non-this, or they're non-that? We're all going to the same place. And hopefully there is a forgiving God, that there is a Creator that as long as we have accepted other people for who they are, that's God's job in the final end. To judge, if that judgment day comes, if that's how it's going to be. I don't know that! I just know that the Creator put us on this earth for a reason. And that we respect

---

* Elsie notes elsewhere, "They've expanded our cemetery since then, and they've included that area. So it's become part of the main cemetery now."

one another, and not to be judgmental or to put people down or to hold ourselves higher than someone else. So I cannot accept the fact that there's only one way to worship. I have my way – to me that's important, for me. And I'm sure other people have their way that's important to them. I would like to see the day that we can go to that church and be able to interact as a people within the church. Not to just go there and be silent and – as it is now, we do not interact, we don't have input. We don't have that conversation. Sure, we sing. And we pray according to this book. We sing this one, this hymn, or that hymn, or the song. Some things are not acceptable. We have our Indian hymns that we sing in church, but because not too many people speak the language now, there's just a few of us that can carry on, and those are nice. The words in there are very nice. But the young people don't understand it. So, because people have lost an interest to be consistent, to come to church on Sundays, because of all the other activities in their lives, in their busy lives – they're out there takin' their kids to soccer games, to whatever else is going on. There's so many other things that is important to the families? But I just feel that there's gotta be a way that we're not so divided. That people say, "I don't need to go to church. I don't believe in church." But what do you believe in? You have to have something to believe in. You've got to have a stabilizing tool. You've got to have that lifeline, that anchor, something that anchors you down. A belief in something is that lifeline. We believe that there is a Creator, but we need to work with that. It's very important that we share the teachin's of our ancestors. The importance of believing that around us is the spirit of our ancestors – the spirit of the Creator is there, our guide, our light. And that's what we pray for when we pray. When I offer prayers, I pray in my own words. Whatever the occasion may be, I pick my words accordingly. Whatever the event may be, I pick my words accordingly. So it's just not one way of praying that you speak to the Creator. You speak to God from your heart. So it's not just one way of prayin' – "Okay, I must kneel down and pray, and bow my head," and, you know – you just pick your own words. It has to come from the heart. And how to ask God to help you, or to help your friends, or your people, to help your children. You talk to God! To me, that's religion, that's my belief in my spiritual teachin's. Maybe not right for other people, but for me it's right.

Any time. From the moment you get up, "Thank you, Creator, for this day. Thank you for giving me this day. Creator, watch over my children today." Whenever! Whatever you're doing! And I don't get on my knees. Of course my knees are bad – I can't kneel down anyway. But I spend that moment, when I first wake up. When I go to bed at night, I thank the Creator for this day that I've had. So the other day I was havin' a bit of a conflict with myself about just the events of the day, and it wasn't starting out the way I would've liked it to go. Things were not coming together, my plan for the day, 'cause it involved other people. And I thought, "Oh my gosh, this is not –" you know, I'm starting to feel that agitation, that little bit of "I don't have control." And that's really important, is that control – we sometimes feel we have to have that control. Sometimes you need to let go of that control. And I think that's all part of prayer. It's not your God-given ability to control other people and other things around you. Things will happen, and you have to just go with the flow. Not that you're going to accept it, but it's out of your hands, right? So the other morning when I was feeling somewhat frustrated, and this is so important work that I need to do today, and it had to do with the loss of a relative, and after the work that needed to be done. It just wasn't coming together. I'm sitting there and I'm going, "Oh!" I'm getting agitated. And I have this book which is my, um, I guess like a spare tire for me! *[laughs]* I don't know how else to put it. When all else fails, and it's as obvious as the nose on my face that I should trust that there is a Creator, that there is someone – that I cannot control all things. So I pick up this book. It's called *Each Day a New Beginning*. It's like a affirmation book. And I flip the pages, "What day is this?" and then I come to, "Okay, this is the date," and I read that. And I thought, "Okay! Okay. It's out of my hands. Just calm down. Settle down." So I had to give myself a talkin'-to. Otherwise I'd be lashing at people, and sayin', "Why aren't you doing this? Why aren't you –" and da-da-da. I just needed to ground myself to calm down. So I really like that book. It really helps me. And it's *so* connected to our teachin'. It's very similar. So I just sometimes need those reminders for myself. It helps me not to fly off in every direction. It helps to calm me down and ground me.

The old people would say, "Never mind! Don't be hurt. nɛ? ʔot kʷ kʷənɛtomoɬ" – "Leave it to the one that oversees everything." So it's like, don't fret about that. Someone is watching over. There's nothing you can do about someone else. That kind of a message. Yeah, nɛ? ʔot kʷ kʷənɛtomoɬ – just leave it alone, kind of thing. Someone else will – yeah, that's one of the teachings that I've heard through my life – you know, just leave it alone. šɛʔtɛgus.* nɛʔ ʔot kʷ kʷˈʷənɛtomoɫ. Leave it to the higher power to deal with that. Which is good! It makes a lot of sense.

So that's just an example of, we need to use the tools that's there. Different people have different ways. They offer different things. They have different tools to offer to us. We just need to look at other people's tools and how they use those and how it helps me, as I can offer my tools to someone else that may be able to use them. It's sharing of our resources, and it's a way of helping people. As I would like for them to help me when I need direction. It's amazing how just maybe a few words can help a people – another person's outlook. And how they view things. Just sharing of a word here and there. And that's very helpful. So getting back to how I – in my own conflict, I guess, with the very rigid teachin's of the church, which I don't agree with. I don't think it should be that rigid. That's what's keeping our people away from coming to the church. If it was more inviting, more caring, more personalized, then I believe people will come. We need to take our armour off, and not be so untouchable, and hard to reach. That's how I see it. There's this wall. It's not inviting. It's not welcoming. And I really feel for the people. That's my concern. I feel for my children and my community and our people as Aboriginal people – that our teachin's, our beliefs be respected. It's happening, but it's slow, slow. Because I've seen it in other communities I've gone to, that it's more acceptable. There's evidence in the building that – good, you know. They use drumming in the church, they use sweetgrass, or they use cedar. We can use cedar now in our church, whereas before it was un-thought-of. We have different vestments in our church that has a Native design on it, and that's really nice. It's nice to see that. But still needs – it's fine to see those, they're visible. But it's in what's in the heart and desire to learn more about our teachin' and to incorporate that, our practices. So that's the part, that's the link that we need to work on. For it to come together, that the church is more accepting of our culture. It's hard to be told, "No, that's not accepted in the church. You cannot use that blanket on the casket because it's not acceptable at a church. You cannot sing that song. It's not acceptable to this church." Our people are comfortable with that particular song. And I just cringe 'cause I feel that resistance. It may not be spoken, but I feel it. I just know that it's not – it's like the look, you know?

---

* Translation: Creator/Lord.

And I just, like, "Agh!" *[sighs]* I guess when I say "armour," it's that whole structured teachin' with the church. It's not just one person that's got the armour. It's the messengers that bring that teachin' to our people. They need to be more open and accepting of our traditional ways, our traditional teachin's, and who we are as a people and where we come from. They need to know who we are, but they don't take the time to do that? We are to know their teachin', not them knowing our values and our traditional practices. So I don't know if it's an armour or a wall! A solid, concrete wall. *[laughs]*

I think it was not difficult for our people to make that kind of transition to saying, "Okay, we know there's someone in higher power," when it was introduced as God is the higher power. So it's šɛʔtɛgus ʔəms man.* God, our Creator, our Father – there's different names that is used. I guess after Christianity was introduced to the people, they used the word "šɛʔtɛgus." But that's "God," right? šɛʔtɛgus. So "šɛʔt" is "high." "hegus" is "leader." "šɛʔtɛgus" is what they use. So in church that's what is used too. Like if you're praying, you use "šɛʔtɛgus." "šɛʔtɛgus ʔəms man" – "our Father." Our Father is – "man" is your father. But you put it together with "šɛʔtɛgus ʔəms man." That's what's used normally. I think before that they would use, um, "kʷʷənɛtomoł," "the one that watches over us." Because they always believed there was someone watching over you, and there's some higher being. So that's what they would have used before "šɛʔtɛgus" came along as introduced by the church as God.

I think our people adapted quite readily to Christianity because they were always believers of a higher power, that there's a Creator. And regrettably, I think that was used in such a way that it was not good for our people. To abuse their faith, in a way that a lot of our people had to let go a lot of their own practices of wellness and believing in a Creator. Because those things were taken away. And it became narrow and strictly geared to the church and "This is how you must believe!" They brought a lot of sin into the picture, and punishment and cruelty and all of those things that it's a sin if you do this, that, and the other. So I can see myself, looking back, that that was a conflict for our people. But they were so taken in and overcome by this new practice in the name of God that fear was instilled in our people. Forgetting about our culture, or burying it. Because it was a sin to do the things that my grandparents did, or

---

* Translation: Creator/Lord, our father.

their parents. They continued the teaching. They never lost the teaching. They never lost the practice. That they still continued the practice. Maybe not as obvious, but they still continued, and used it. And I'm really thankful for that. I'm really thankful for that. That our culture was a rich culture. And it can still be. You need to work it. And to appreciate all the things that's out there. I don't know what it was in the beginning that replaced that. I sometimes have a hard time to try to figure that out. Why that was replaced. I know my grandmother was a quick learner, I guess. You know, she – they introduced what is called the Chinook language, and she was a little girl then, she tells me. Young girl. And the priest taught her to interpret or translate what the prayers were about to the congregation, because she learned Chinook really quickly. So from the priest to the people, she was like the one that was doing the translation. So I don't know how she learned Chinook, where that came from. Yeah, people lost a lot of their practice, during that time of contact. It's been really difficult to incorporate that now into the church.

I always say that the way our people prayed, and the way that I still pray in my own time, is praying to God's creation. Praying to the universe. Praying to our Creator that built all this. And be thankful for that. To me, that's the church. That we didn't just create out of nothing. I'm a firm believer in that. That if I go walk in the woods, I'm thankful for the birds – I'm thankful for everything that's around me. I go out in a boat – you know, how did this happen? How did this come about? To me, I thank God, or a Creator, for all of that. And if God is going to punish me for thinking that way, then – I don't think so. I really don't. I think God is not a punishing God. So when I still hear things today, "You're gonna be punished for this! You're gonna be punished for that!" I don't really buy that. It's not to encourage people – you know, "God will forgive you," or "Whatever you wanna do is okay!" But I think a lot of it is built around respect and appreciation of all of God's gift. Therefore, that's where you come to be the person that God meant you to be! To be honest, to be truthful, to be respectful. And take care of yourself and other people around you.

SPIRITUALITY TO ME MEANS something that's been passed on for years, as long as our people have been here. Something that our people have always – it's a way of life, it's a daily practice, it's a lifestyle, is spirituality to us. It teaches about respect. It teaches about boundaries. It's really important, the spirituality aspect. It's just as important if not more important than other things I always believe in. The four directions and your physical well-being, your mental well-being, your emotional well-being, and most importantly is your spiritual well-being. And that's something I always tell people that I'm talking to. To me that is so – it's very deep. It's very important to me to reflect on spirituality. Otherwise everything else doesn't matter, really. I always say you could be the most physically fit person, or you're fit in every aspect, but if you're weak or you don't have spiritual beliefs then you're really crippled. It's so important. The spiritual beliefs of our people, or how they practised before contact, and how they believed in the supernatural or that there's another side where we go to when we die – the importance of the spirits of our ancestors and everything – the whole universe. I think if you believe in those things and take it to heart, that these things are so important, that you offer prayers of thanksgiving and appreciation for all that you get. That's all part of the spirituality. So to me that is really the basis of our existence. 'Cause to me it's really the basis of our existence is the belief, to trust that there is a Creator, that there's a higher power. Some people would call it energy. Well, to me spirituality is energy, good energy. Where else are you going to go to if you're troubled? Where else are you going to go to when you're lookin' for guidance? You can't go to the store and buy it. You have to believe. You have to believe in it. That there is good energy out there that you can call upon. And trust in the spirit of your ancestors that knew all about the spirit world. I believe in that. I truly do. It's powerful. It's very powerful. And it works – for me it works! So if it works for me, it's gonna work for other people! *[laughs]*

A lot of it is around respect, boundaries, lookin' after yourself, your mental well-being, your emotional well-being, your physical well-being, your spiritual well-being. So much of that is incorporated in the stories. So it wasn't one thing you learned about spirituality, or "Now today's lesson is about physical" – everything was *all* combined. It was not identified separately. In everything these four things are *so* important. The physical, the mental, the emotional, the spiritual well-being is all one – it's all rolled into one. When one is missing, if you're not practising one aspect of those four things, then your life is not going to function well. Especially if you're not going to be honouring your spirituality, which is the most important thing. Your emotional well-being's gonna suffer. Your mental well-being's gonna suffer. Your physical well-being is gonna suffer. So, foremost and most important for me is your spiritual well-being, to take care of yourself. You take care of things around you. That's part of being spiritual. You take care of every livin' thing in your life, and the rest will fall into place. All those other things aren't going to happen if you're just going to go to the gym every day and exercise and be physically fit. If you're not looking after your spiritual well-being, then you can be as fit as you can be physically, but emotionally, mentally, you're not going to be. So you need to encompass the whole thing. All those four corner posts are so important.

And it's not to say that I get on my knees and pray every day. To me, spirituality is about thanking the Creator for who I am or what I have. Thanking the Creator when you have a meal. Thanking the Creator for my healthy grandchildren. Thanking the Creator for the rain! Thanking the Creator for the sunshine! All those things that is put on this earth or put in my path that I have no control over. It happens. That's life. And you need to appreciate everything in life and to recognize that in each of our lives that the rain falls. We can't always have sunshine. The rain brings something else. And we have to recognize that we are born one day, and we go through life with everything that comes to you, whether it be sorrow mixed in there, or pain, or illness, or hardship, it's there for a reason and you – not gonna complain about those things. You make the best of what the Creator gave you. You do the very best that you can in life. And to have ownership of your own well-being. You are responsible for your own well-being. And not to expect other people to make you well. You don't blame other people if your life is going down the wrong way. It's your job to look after yourself. To be well from inside and to teach that to your children, to teach that to your family, to set that example. When you listen to these stories, or the legends, or examples, and you apply that to your life. That's why you're the one that's responsible for the direction your life takes you.

I USED TO HEAR about, "It's time to go and" – we called it "qɛsɛθot." It's a vision quest. It was not just only to young men, but to older men as well if they're needing to do a vision quest to alter their life somehow, or to look for their power, their spirit power. Then they would go off on their own. Or sometimes, something has happened in their life in the community that was frowned upon. Then you have to prove yourself. And you go off and go and be gone for as long as it takes for you to find your spirit power, and come back when you're ready. So it's like being sent to the corner as a little child, right? You stay there until you learn how to behave. Or come back and apologize, if you've offended someone. They used to tell this story about this one man, and this happened in Theodosia area, in toqʷanən, where this man who was a relative of the Bob George family – that's my grandmother's side of the family. Bob George was her dad. And it was through that family. One of the guys in that family was doing that. He needed to do that, to go and find his vision. So he went on this vision quest around a lake and he was bathing every day in the lake. And he was doing the whole circle around the lake. Don't know which lake it was. But it was in that area, in Theodosia area. And he stayed there and every day he'd do a bundle and get in the lake and brush himself. Leave it there – leave his bundle there. Leave another bundle. Every day he'd move on, until he'd complete that lake. Living off the land. And he would start getting these dreams, how it's going to come to you, how your spirit power is going to come to you. So he started getting these dreams about, "You will find it in the water. Your power will come out of the water. Don't be frightened when it comes to you. Don't be afraid of it. You'll touch it. And you'll get your power transfer from that" – whatever is going to come out of the water. So he'd been doing this for quite some time and he'd almost completed his journey, his vision quest. And he's bathing in the lake one day and all of a sudden something popped out in the lake. It was beyond his reach. He couldn't touch it, but he was afraid to go deeper to touch it. He got scared. And it was huge. Water just *swwwissh!* – swished up like that. And this thing, it looked like it was a box of sort. And then he turned around, "How am I gonna reach that?" He was told in his dream, you're gonna swim out and grab it when it comes. And he turned away and he reached for – looking for something to hook it to shore to him, and as he did that it – *swwwissh!* – went under again. So he lost it. He didn't get it. So his vision quest was for nothing. So that was always used as an example. That's what happens when that time happens. Not to be afraid. It's gonna come, it's gonna be scary, but it's going to be yours. That's your power. That's your spirit power. It's gonna come to you. So there's different ways of going about how they will get strong and how they will achieve what they went out to do, whether it's just to come back and be a good provider and have that courage and that power in a good way.[*] So that was really important teaching for the young men. The women didn't do that. It was just the

---

[*] Homer Barnett recorded a similar story told by Chief Tom about the importance of not being afraid when one's power appeared. Barnett, *Coast Salish*, 94; Barnett field notes, folder 1-6, 21.

men, the boys, that did that – the boys and men. Wherever needed that to be done. sohoθot. "sohoθot" is cleansing with, like, cedar boughs. qɛsɛθot. "qɛsɛθot" is – is the word for, um, how can I say it in English? qɛsɛθot. *[pause]* Lookin' for a word. It's like to aim for something. It is a vision quest, right? You want to – you go for it, and it'll come to you. So you have to work for it. By bathing in the lake, and sacrificing. And, like, for an example if you are fasting, is "q'aʔaθot," so that's sacrificing your meals, q'aʔaθot. "qɛsɛθot" is your whole being, like you're sacrificing something to achieve your goal. Yeah and I guess it's, like, anything, you know, you're qɛsɛθot. It's a sacrifice.

Some of the coastal people, I think, like our neighbouring communities – the big sweat houses are for more, like, prayer-y kind of buildings – they're big, they'll hold anywhere from four, six to maybe twelve people. That's big. But what we had here was more of a private sweat. And it would hold two people at the most. So like, if a young boy, young man and maybe his dad would go together and use that. Or just one person. It was a one-man thing. And people would have it in their own – wherever their buildings were. If it was here or Okeover or Theodosia or, you know, anywhere – wherever they had their cabins or wherever they were living at the time, they always had their own. So they could go in there and use it whenever they felt they needed that. To cleanse themselves, purify themselves. So the new sweat house type of things now, and there's sometimes controversy around that: "Which is the right way? What is the right way to do sweat?" The prairie people have their big ones, and some people say we should have that here. But I think if our way was the more private, personalized, then that's how we should stay. Use it like that, because they say that if you're in a closed area and you're trying to purify yourself, your body and your mind, that you're collectin' all the other sweat and the negative issues or whatever you're sweating. You're there, you're sweating and so you're sharing all this sweat and steam from all the other people there that are there. And you didn't occupy the same sweat as a woman. Women around here never used a sweat. Now I hear of women using the sweat. And they enjoy it. I guess it's like a sauna. But I've never been in a sweat myself, so I don't know what it would feel like. But women in the old days did not use the sweat. It was more personal and, you know, if people chose to have one in their backyard, that was a preference, that was how they did it. But they used to have them along the river and nobody ever bothered – every person knew where theirs was. It would be all along the river. People said they used to have them around the river area so they could go in the sweat and then jump in the river afterwards. Yeah. So that's our style of sweat, now I see more and more of it used the other way. You know, it's a form of meditation while you're in there. You know, clearing your mind, clearing your body. I think it's good. Time for reflection. Yeah.

As I SEE IT and how I've heard it through my ancestors, is that we are all one and part of nature. Of any living thing, 'cause those things, to us, is very connected to us. We're very close to all these things. That's what's here in our territory. Those things are to us very important, and we're connected to that. But I can't say that I can claim it and only I can claim it, as mine in my family. Because there are many families on the coast that I'm sure would share those same feelings that they are the eagle, the whale, or salmon or wolf. They used to actually see – with the people that were very visionary, that had psychic powers – that the wolf, the owl, the whale, or the blackfish are all one spirit. And the eagle. They're all one spirit. They share the same spirit. They used to talk about – we have a burial ground in Okeover or outside, close to the mouth of Okeover Inlet. And we have a burial ground there that our ancestors used. And quite often you seen whales or blackfish around that area, or the owl is there. And at one time this healer, or this psychic, seen a whale swimming there, around the island. Then it went up onto the beach and became a wolf on the land. And then it went back into the water and it was now a blackfish again, going towards the other side of the inlet. And it got to the other side and it got on the beach and it was a wolf again, going up to the beach. And then there's the owl. So it transforms one to the other? And I truly believe that. I have no reason not to believe that, because that's what I had always heard, and I believe it! That we're very connected to the owl – especially the white owl. You don't see them often, but when you see them, you hear them, it touches you. They're very powerful. The same as the owl, the regular owl – big owls. They're very much connected to the people. Our people see them as the spirits that are on the other side. The spirit of our ancestors – when they come close and hang around your house, they're messengers. They're bringing you something. They have something to tell you. So, and when that happens, you be cautious. You look after your children, look after yourself. There's a messenger hangin' around. People will see it. They're perched near your home. They're bringing a message. And it is believed that whenever that happens, that something will happen. It could mean someone's going to get hurt or someone's going to fall, or someone's going to die. That's why the owl's there, 'cause they know someone's very vulnerable. You can say, "That's why that owl's been hanging here." And the same as the blackfish. When they're around, you know they're messengers. So it's all connected to those things. The wolf is connected in its own way to these beings. The eagle. The raven. It's all connected.

So when people ask me, "What clan are you?" I cannot say, "Oh, I'm the wolf clan," or "I am the eagle clan," because all of those things together are one, to me. And I know I'm a salmon person, because to me salmon is very close to us. That's what sustains us. That is our main diet, is salmon. We use a lot of it in our community. So to me that's really important. My cape that has a salmon designed on the back, my daughter made that for me, because she sees me as a salmon person. Ann made that for me, and I didn't realize she was making it for me. I knew she was making the cape. And she put a lot of work into it, a lot of months of work, and one day she gave it to me. She said, "I've made this for you." And I was, like, "Holy!" I was just so touched. I was in tears! I'm tellin' you. But it's a beautiful salmon design on the back. It's a black background, and it's bordered, it's got red in there. But the huge salmon, it's got eggs coming out of it, like, the buttons, they're sewn on the blanket. And around the edges of the blanket itself is hide, deer hide, that she had had cured, and it's so soft and it's beautiful. And it ties to the front – it laces up on the front. So that's very special for me because of my connection and my respect for the salmon. And for her to have picked up on that and she said, "As long as I remember, since I was little, I've always seen you cut fish and smoke fish and dry fish and I've also seen you skinning deer and preserving the meat, put it in jars and –" you know, I know how to butcher a deer and so I do all those things. And so she saw that as, that's how she saw me. So I'm very proud of that blanket. It has so much meaning in it because she put so much work into it, and so much thought into it. So I know that other people can be really sticky about ownership of what their clan is. And sometimes I don't know what to make of that. I don't know exactly how to, um, I just kind of shied clear of that. I just need to be who I am. I need to have my own thoughts and my own beliefs of who I am, and what I see is what's close to me, what is meaningful to me and my family and my own people. I don't claim I'm the only one that owns the spirit of all of these things, the salmon or the blackfish or the owl. I believe it belongs to all of us. So I guess if anyone were to ask me, "What is your clan?" I would say I'm a salmon person. You know? But it's not strictly mine, it belongs a lot of people. So that's my feelings on that.

PEOPLE HAD A LOT of respect for nature. And anything that is put on this earth that the Creator gave us. We always were taught to thank the Creator, to thank Mother Earth for anything we took from there. This morning we had a ceremony – we're gonna have a new health building built here in our community.* So John Louie and I went and asked permission to use that property – whatever things there may be there, whether it's birds or other living things that's in that little bit of area that's going to be cleared. Bulldozers will go there and clear the land and knock down some trees and dig up the ground. And that's what we did this morning. We went to ask permission so that – and to apologize that we're going to disturb this piece of property there. And also to thank the Creator, and to ask the Creator to bless this property where this important building is going to sit on, which will be our health centre, that a lot of our people – programs come out of there – that they'll be working in a healthy environment. And so we have to humbly ask the Creator to bless that, at the same time asking for forgiveness for disturbing life that's there. So that was the practice of our people. And we want to maintain that. You just don't go and clear off a piece of land not thinking about "What was that land used for?" Ask our ancestors to guide us, 'cause their spirits are here. We ask them to guide us and to look after what we're doing, to show us the way so that we're not doing things we shouldn't be doing. To do things in a good way and a respectable way. To ask the Creator to help these people that are coming to do the building. That they will do a good job. So that's what we did this morning. I was glad that's done. So that we can be grounded in the work we do. So that we can be focused and not go in there and be scattered. So we bring people, key people, and you get into a circle, and you hold hands, and ask for that blessing. It's very powerful. It's very rewarding. It's very meaningful. To me it is. And I was glad to see that happen. It's only the beginning. Once the clearing is done and the foundation is laid, we're going to have another little ceremony again. And then once that's done and it's completed, then we'll have our opening ceremony. So in different stages we kinda stop and acknowledge what's been done. Stop and give thanks. It is very, very important.

---

* This refers to March 2005.

And that's what my grandmother did every morning. We'd get up and thank the Creator for this new day. Thank the Creator for giving us what we have. A lot of that thankfulness, that appreciation, on a daily basis goes a long ways. For what little you have, you thank the Creator for that. And that's how we did. We thanked the Creator before we went up Rivers Inlet, that we'll come back safely, and ask for guidance – and come back and thank the Creator you've returned. That's really the number one in life for me is to be thankful and to be appreciative of all that we have. Whether we have a lot or we don't have very much, it's still something that we need to be thankful for. When we look around our lives and every day to wake up and just to hear the birds or to hear the wind or just to look out and thank God for where we live, thank God for God's creation. That's what's really important. To be thankful and to appreciate and ground yourself first thing in the morning. You always started your day with thanksgiving. When you got up in the morning, you just need to get grounded and think of what that day is going to be for you. Not to dread getting up in the day. We all need to learn to be thankful for a new day and to greet the new day with "What am I going to do today? What worthwhile thing am I going to get done today?" and that's really important, to think of those things. It gives you a purpose in life. Hmmm. I guess as I get older and have a lot of plans for every day, but sometimes I don't always accomplish those things now. But nevertheless, I think we have to take every minute of every day and put it to good use. And not to have regrets about what we didn't get done today, but there'll be another day to do that.

I THINK WHAT IS missing today is that spirituality. And I know that young people are interested and they want to know, and they will listen when you talk to them. But because it's been kind of out of practice, they grew up with other kinds of teachings. That it's lost its richness. The importance of brushing, cleansing, taking care of yourself, taking care of yourself from within. What makes – I guess what makes you complete and whole. In the trust in a higher power. That life can be good. And you also accept when you have losses in your life that there is a way to take care of yourself. To rise from that and not to stay down and get lost in your grief. Our people knew how to do that. Our people had resources that took care of their every need. Our people had self-government! They had their leadership! They had their watchmen! They had their advisers. They had their healers. They had their spiritual leaders. They relied on all of these things to help them through good times and bad times. They took care of themselves. They took care of one another. They had a lot of respect for one another. They respected nature. They respected everything that the Creator gave them, or gave us. And that's something we need to relearn, is to appreciate what the Creator gives us, what the universe gives us, what the spirit world brings to us. I strongly believe that when we lose our people, that they are here in spirit. And that is my own resource. When I'm really down, or when I'm confused, or when I'm feeling lost, I call upon the spirit of my ancestors: "Give me some guidance and show me which way to go. Help me." To me that is so important. Because when you go out there, you don't know what you're going to run into. You always ask for guidance. You always ask for that help. You pray for guidance for your children, your grandchildren, when they're off on a trip, wherever. Or when they're out – going out hunting or fishing or, you know. Young people were taught, "When you go and do these things, don't forget. Be appreciative of whatever you bring home, that you're gonna catch out there and bring home. Things will come easier for you if you thank the Creator, thank the animal family for giving us the food that we need. Don't waste. Don't waste things." Those are very important teachings. Very, very important. I think today a lot of things just come too easy for people. Like there's the conveniences we have today. We've forgotten how to be thankful, to appreciate. It's easy just to go to the store and pick up what you need. It's not like going out into the ocean or going out into the forest to work for those things. Sure, people have to work. They have to earn the money to go to that store. But do people ever stop and think that one day maybe we won't have these resources? The hard times will come. And be prepared for that. Yeah, I think we've become so wasteful with our resources. We don't think about the future – future generations to come. It's a gradual thing, but we need to stop and think: Where are we going? How can I improve what the Creator gave us? All the waste. What is there for my great-grandchildren? Or future children or – what is the future for our people? Not only my own people but other people. Yeah.

Thoughts about Ma

~

On May 22, 2013, Elsie's son p'ɑhiykɪla (Cliff Paul) passed away suddenly as a result of a heart ailment. As described by Elsie in this book, p'ɑhiykɪla was a very funny man and was growing into an exceptionally gifted stand-up comedian – if Cliff was in the room, you knew that you were in for a good laugh. He loved being ɬaʔamɪn and endeavoured to learn the language and ɬaʔamɪn teachings. Cliff particularly embodied the teachings regarding family and community, creating and nurturing an urban community among ɬaʔamɪn citizens residing off-reserve and advocating for off-reserve inclusion and access to cultural resources.

p'ɑhiykɪla (Cliff Paul) in 2012.
Photo courtesy of Hank and Emily Taylor.

Following his passing, a number of remarkably insightful writings were found in Cliff's belongings. The following, "Thoughts about Ma," is particularly fitting for this book.

Had the privilege of having a truly remarkable wonderful person for a mother ... for years I live(d) in Vancouver when I would come home we would sit and talk for hours. I remember one of our many conversations. I told her about how I would often get a real sense of wellness when I would be able to develop a good relationship with the clients I worked with in my role as a person who worked with people who lived in the DTES* ... she spoke to me about her work at Tsow-Tun Le Lum and the importance of understanding human nature...and paying attention as to how you interact with others and to think before you speak ... small things are what people remember being ignored or brushed off can totally ruin a person's day sometimes. how a kind gesture are the things that people remember ... something as simple as listening, being non judgmental, how everyone comes deserves to be treated with dignity. one thing she taught me was that showing kindness and love becomes a habit. quite often people who are angry ... picked up these qualities and developed them over time as well ... when my ma speaks at a family function or a gathering she always asks us to take care of ourselves and one another ... A GOOD SOUL ... PATIENCE AND CARING ...

~

---

* This refers to the Downtown Eastside of Vancouver.

Additional Readings

The following is a selected list of readings related to topics raised in this book. It is by no means intended as a full survey of the relevant literatures. For each chapter a separate reading list is arranged by topic in the order in which it is discussed in the chapter. Additional readings for the "teachings" chapters (Chapters 3, 5, 7, and 11) have been combined into a single section at the end.

INTRODUCTION: LISTENING TO ʔəms taʔaw

For more extensive references to particular scholarly literatures discussed in the introduction, see the notes to the introduction.

The ethnohistorical literature on ɬaʔamɪn is small. See the following:

Barnett, Homer. *The Coast Salish of British Columbia.* Eugene: University of Oregon Press, 1955.

Clapperton, Jonathan. "Desolate Viewscapes: Sliammon First Nation, Desolation Sound Marine Park and Environmental Narratives." *Environment and History* 18, 4 (2012): 529-59.

Kennedy, Dorothy, and Randy Bouchard. *Sliammon Life, Sliammon Lands.* Vancouver: Talonbooks, 1983.

Patrick, Lyana Marie. "Storytelling in the Fourth World: Explorations in Meaning of Place and Tla'amin Resistance to Dispossession." MA thesis, University of Victoria, 2004.

Washington, Siemthlut Michelle. "Bringing Traditional Teachings to Leadership." *American Indian Quarterly* 28, 3 and 4 (2004): 583-603.

The literature on Coast Salish peoples and places is extensive and includes the following monographs and essay collections:

Barman, Jean. *Stanley Park's Secrets: The Forgotten Families of Whoi Whoi, Kanaka Ranch and Brockton Point*. Madeira Point, BC: Harbour Publishing, 2005.

Bierwert, Crisca. *Brushed by Cedar, Living by the River: Coast Salish Figures of Power*. Tucson: University of Arizona Press, 1999.

Carlson, Keith Thor. *The Power of Place, the Problem of Time: Aboriginal Identity and Historical Consciousness in the Cauldron of Colonialism*. Toronto: University of Toronto Press, 2010.

Harmon, Alexandra. *Indians in the Making: Ethnic Relations and Indian Identities around Puget Sound*. Berkeley: University of California Press, 1998.

Miller, Bruce G., ed. *Be of Good Mind: Essays on the Coast Salish*. Vancouver: UBC Press, 2007.

–. *The Problem of Justice: Tradition and Law in the Coast Salish World*. Lincoln: University of Nebraska Press, 2001.

Miller, Jay. *Lushootseed Culture and the Shamanic Odyssey: An Anchored Radiance*. Lincoln: University of Nebraska Press, 1999.

Oliver, Jeff. *Landscapes and Social Transformations on the Northwest Coast: Colonial Encounters in the Fraser Valley*. Tucson: University of Arizona Press, 2010.

Roy, Susan. *These Mysterious People: Shaping History and Archaeology in a Northwest Coast Community*. Montreal/Kingston: McGill-Queen's University Press, 2010.

Suttles, Wayne Prescott. *Coast Salish Essays*. Vancouver: Talonbooks, 1987.

Thrush, Coll. *Native Seattle: Histories from the Crossing-Over Place*. Seattle: University of Washington Press, 2007.

The "told-to" literature on Indigenous individuals – and analysis thereof – is very large. The following two works give a sense of early directions and recent developments, respectively, in critical analysis of told-to narratives:

Bataille, Gretchen M., and Kathleen M. Sands. *American Indian Women: Telling Their Lives*. Lincoln: University of Nebraska Press, 1984.

McCall, Sophie. *First Person Plural: Aboriginal Storytelling and the Ethics of Collaborative Authorship*. Vancouver: UBC Press, 2011.

Told-to narratives about Coast Salish women:

Maracle, Lee. *Bobbi Lee: Indian Rebel*. New ed. Toronto: Women's Press, 1990. First published 1975.

Peter, Susie Sampson. *Aunt Susie Sampson Peter: The Wisdom of a Skagit Elder*. Transcribed by Vi Hilbert. Translated by Vi Hilbert and Jay Miller. Recorded by Leon Metcalf. Seattle: Lushootseed Press, 1995.

Shelton, Gram Ruth Sehome. *The Wisdom of a Tulalip Elder*. Transcribed by Vi Hilbert. Translated by Vi Hilbert and Jay Miller. Recorded by Leon Metcalf. Seattle: Lushootseed Press, 1995.

Told-to narratives about Coast Salish men:

Baker, Simon, and Verna J. Kirkness. *Khot-La-Cha: The Autobiography of Chief Simon Baker*. Vancouver: Douglas and McIntyre, 1994.

Pennier, Henry. *Call Me Hank: A Stó:lō Man's Reflections on Logging, Living, and Growing Old*. 2nd ed. Edited by Keith Carlson and Kristina Fagan. Toronto: University of Toronto Press, 2006. First published 1972.

Individual Indigenous women's told-to narratives:

Alfred, Agnes. *Paddling to Where I Stand: Agnes Alfred, Qʷiqʷasuʼtinux̌ʷ Noblewoman*. Edited by Martine J. Reid. Translated by Daisy Sewid-Smith. Vancouver: UBC Press, 2004.

Blackman, Margaret B., and Florence Edenshaw Davidson. *During My Time: Florence Edenshaw Davidson, a Haida Woman*. Seattle: University of Washington Press, 1982.

Harris, LaDonna. *LaDonna Harris: A Comanche Life*. Edited by H. Henrietta Stockel. Lincoln: University of Nebraska Press, 2000.

Moran, Bridget. *Stoney Creek Woman: The Story of Mary John*. Vancouver: Arsenal Pulp Press, 1988.

Mountain Wolf Woman. *Mountain Wolf Woman, Sister of Crashing Thunder: The Autobiography of a Winnebago Woman*. Edited by Nancy O. Lurie. Ann Arbor: University of Michigan Press, 1961.

Mourning Dove. *Mourning Dove: A Salishan Autobiography*. Edited by Jay Miller. Lincoln: University of Nebraska Press, 1990.

Red Shirt, Delphine. *Turtle Lung Woman's Granddaughter*. Lincoln: University of Nebraska Press, 2002.

Snell, Alma Hogan. *Grandmother's Grandchild: My Crow Indian Life*. Edited by Becky Matthews. Lincoln: University of Nebraska Press, 2000.

Underhill, Ruth M. *Papago Woman*. New York: Holt, Rinehart and Winston, 1979.

Wiebe, Rudy, and Yvonne Johnson. *Stolen Life: The Journey of a Cree Woman*. Toronto: Vintage Canada, 1998.

Individual Indigenous men's told-to narratives:

Assu, Harry, and Joy Inglis. *Assu of Cape Mudge: Recollections of a Coastal Indian Chief*. Vancouver: UBC Press, 1989.

Bird, Louis. *Telling Our Stories: Omushkego Legends and Histories from Hudson Bay*. Toronto: University of Toronto Press, 2005.

Blue Spruce, George, Jr. *Searching for My Destiny*. As told to Deanne Durrett. Lincoln: University of Nebraska Press, 2009.

Mihesuah, Henry. *First to Fight*. Edited by Devon Abbott Mihesuah. Lincoln: University of Nebraska Press, 2002.

Nowell, Charles James, and Clellan S. Ford. *Smoke from Their Fires: The Life of a Kwakiutl Chief*. Hamden, CT: Archon Books, 1968. First published 1941.

Rios, Theodore, and Kathleen M. Sands. *Telling a Good One: The Process of a Native American Collaborative Biography*. Lincoln: University of Nebraska Press, 2000.

Robinson, Harry. *Living by Stories: A Journey of Landscape and Memory*. Edited and compiled by Wendy Wickwire. Vancouver: Talonbooks, 2005.

–. *Nature Power: In the Spirit of an Okanagan Storyteller*. Edited and compiled by Wendy Wickwire. Vancouver: Talonbooks, 2004.

–. *Write It on Your Heart: The Epic World of an Okanagan Storyteller*. Edited and compiled by Wendy Wickwire. Vancouver: Talonbooks, 1989.

Sewid, James. *Guests Never Leave Hungry: The Autobiography of James Sewid, a Kwakiutl Indian*. Edited by James P. Spradley. New Haven, CT: Yale University Press, 1969.

Wilson, Waziyatawin Angela. *Remember This! Dakota Decolonization and the Eli Taylor Narratives*. Translated by Wahpetunwin Carolyn Schommer. Lincoln: University of Nebraska Press, 2005.

Compilations of told-to narratives:

Bussidor, Ila, and Ustün Bilgen-Reinart. *Night Spirits: The Story of the Relocation of the Sayisi Dene*. Winnipeg: University of Manitoba Press, 1997.

Byrne, Nympha, and Camille Fouillard, eds. *It's Like the Legend: Innu Women's Voices*. Toronto: Women's Press, 2000.

Cruikshank, Julie, Angela Sidney, Kitty Smith, and Annie Ned. *Life Lived Like a Story: Life Stories of Three Yukon Native Elders*. Lincoln: University of Nebraska Press, 1990.

Dauenhauer, Nora Marks, and Richard Dauenhauer. *Haa Kusteeyí, Our Culture: Tlingit Life Stories*. Classics of Tlingit Oral Literature, vol. 3. Seattle: University of Washington Press, 1994.

Innu Nation and Mushuau Innu Band Council. *Gathering Voices: Finding Strength to Help Our Children*. Vancouver: Douglas and McIntyre, 1995.

Kulchyski, Peter Keith, Don N. McCaskill, and David A. Newhouse. *In the Words of Elders: Aboriginal Cultures in Transition*. Toronto: University of Toronto Press, 1999.

Matthewson, Lisa, Beverley Frank, Gertrude Ned, Laura Thevarge, and Rose Agnes Whitley. *When I Was Small, I wan kwikws: A Grammatical Analysis of St'át'imc Oral Narratives*. Vancouver: UBC Press, 2005.

Silman, Janet. *Enough is Enough: Aboriginal Women Speak Out*. Toronto: Women's Press, 1992.

Wachowich, Nancy, Apphia Agalakti Awa, Rhoda Kaukjak Katsak, and Sandra Pikujak Katsak. *Saqiyuq: Stories from the Lives of Three Inuit Women*. Montreal/Kingston: McGill-Queen's University Press, 2001.

Weiss, Gillian, ed., with Pearl McKenzie, Pauline Coulthard, Charlene Tree, Bernie Sound, Valerie Bourne, and Brandi McLeod. *Trying to Get It Back: Indigenous Women, Education and Culture*. Waterloo: University of Waterloo Press, 2000.

The historical literature on Indigenous women is diverse in subject matter and methodology. The following collections of essays offer just a sample:

Anderson, Kim, and Bonita Lawrence, eds. *Strong Women Stories: Native Vision and Community Survival*. Toronto: Sumach Press, 2003.

Carter, Sarah, and Patricia A. McCormack, eds. *Recollecting: Lives of Aboriginal Women of the Canadian Northwest and Borderlands*. Edmonton: Athabasca University Press, 2011.

Kelm, Mary Ellen, and Lorna Townsend, eds. *In the Days of Our Grandmothers: A Reader in Aboriginal Women's History in Canada*. Toronto: University of Toronto Press, 2006.

Krouse, Susan Applegate, and Heather Howard-Bobiwash, eds. *Keeping the Campfires Going: Native Women's Activism in Urban Communities*. Lincoln: University of Nebraska Press, 2009.

Mihesuah, Devon Abbott. *Indigenous American Women: Decolonization, Empowerment, Activism*. Lincoln: University of Nebraska Press, 2003.

Miller, Christine, and Patricka Chuckryk, eds. *Women of the First Nations: Power, Wisdom, Strength*. Winnipeg: University of Manitoba Press, 1996.

Monture-Angus, Patricia, and Patricia McGuire, eds. *First Voices: An Aboriginal Women's Reader*. Toronto: Inanna Publications, 2009.

Perdue, Theda, ed. *Sifters: Native American Women's Lives*. New York: Oxford University Press, 2001.

Pickles, Katie, and Myra Rutherdale, eds. *Contact Zones: Aboriginal and Settler Women in Canada's Colonial Past*. Vancouver: UBC Press, 2005.

Valaskakis, Gail Guthrie, Madeleine Dion Stout, and Eric Guimond, eds. *Restoring the Balance: First Nations Women, Community, and Culture*. Winnipeg: University of Manitoba Press, 2009.

Williams, Carol, ed. *Indigenous Women and Work: From Labor to Activism*. Urbana: University of Illinois Press, 2012.

On Indigenous women and feminism, see the following:

Brownlie, Robin Jarvis, and Valerie J. Korinek. *Finding a Way to the Heart: Feminist Writings on Aboriginal and Women's History in Canada*. Winnipeg: University of Manitoba Press, 2012.

Green, Joyce, ed. *Making Space for Indigenous Feminism*. Black Point, NS: Fernwood Publishing, 2007.

Moreton-Robinson, Aileen. *Talkin' Up to the White Woman: Indigenous Women and White Feminism*. St. Lucia, Australia: University of Queensland Press, 2000.

Ouellette, Grace. *The Fourth World: An Indigenous Perspective on Feminism and Aboriginal Women's Activism*. Black Point, NS: Fernwood Publishing, 2002.

Suzack, Cheryl, Shari M. Huhndorf, Jeanne Perreault, and Jean Barman, eds. *Indigenous Women and Feminism: Politics, Activism, Culture*. Vancouver: UBC Press, 2010.

For critical discussions of Indigenous and/or decolonizing methodologies see:

Absalom, Kathleen. *Kaandossiwin: How We Come to Know*. Black Point, NS: Fernwood Publishing, 2011.

Archibald, Jo-ann. *Indigenous Storywork: Educating the Heart, Mind, Body, and Spirit*. Vancouver: UBC Press, 2008.

Brown, Lesley, and Susan Strega, eds. *Research as Resistance: Critical, Indigenous, and Anti-oppressive Approaches*. Toronto: Canadian Scholars' Press, 2005.

Chilisa, Bagele. *Indigenous Research Methodologies*. Los Angeles: SAGE Publications, 2012.

Denzin, Norman K., Yvonna S. Lincoln, and Linda Tuhiwai Smith. *Handbook of Critical and Indigenous Methodologies*. Los Angeles: SAGE Publications, 2008.

Kovach, Margaret Elizabeth. *Indigenous Methodologies: Characteristics, Conversations, and Contexts*. Toronto: University of Toronto Press, 2010.

Kuokkanen, Rauna Johanna. *Reshaping the University: Responsibility, Indigenous Epistemes, and the Logic of the Gift*. Vancouver: UBC Press, 2007.

Mihesuah, Devon Abbott, ed. *Natives and Academics: Researching and Writing about American Indians*. Lincoln: University of Nebraska Press, 1998.

Mihesuah, Devon Abbott. *So You Want to Write about American Indians?* Lincoln: University of Nebraska Press, 2005.

Mihesuah, Devon Abbott, and Angela Cavender Wilson, eds. *Indigenizing the Academy: Transforming Scholarship and Empowering Communities*. Lincoln: University of Nebraska Press, 2004.

Regan, Paulette. *Unsettling the Settler Within: Indian Residential Schools, Truth Telling, and Reconciliation in Canada*. Vancouver: UBC Press, 2010.

Smith, Linda Tuhiwai. *Decolonizing Methodologies: Research and Indigenous Peoples*. London: Zed Books, 1999.

Wheeler, Winona. "Reflections on the Social Relations of Indigenous Oral Histories." In *Walking a Tightrope: Aboriginal People and Their Representations*, edited by Ute Lischke and David T. McNab, 189-213. Waterloo, ON: Wilfrid Laurier University Press, 2005.

Waziyatawin and Michael Yellow Bird, eds. *For Indigenous Minds Only: A Decolonization Handbook*. Santa Fe, NM: School of American Research Press, 2012.

Wilson, Shawn. *Research Is Ceremony: Indigenous Research Methods*. Black Point, NS: Fernwood Publishing, 2009.

Wilson, Waziyatawin Angela, and Michael Yellow Bird, eds. *For Indigenous Eyes Only: A Decolonization Handbook*. Santa Fe, NM: School of American Research Press, 2005.

CHAPTER 1: THE TERRITORY AND PEOPLE

On the history of reserve policy and the corresponding lack of historical treaties in British Columbia, see:

Harris, Cole. *Making Native Space: Colonialism, Resistance, and Reserves in British Columbia*. Vancouver: UBC Press, 2002.

Harris, Douglas. *Landing Native Fisheries: Indian Reserves and Fishing Rights in British Columbia, 1849-1925*. Vancouver: UBC Press, 2008.

Tennant, Paul. *Aboriginal People and Politics: The Indian Land Question in British Columbia, 1849-1989*. Vancouver: UBC Press, 1990.

On the Roman Catholic "Durieu system" in British Columbia, see:

Gresko, Jacqueline. "Durieu, Paul." In *Dictionary of Canadian Biography*. Vol. 12. Toronto/Montreal: University of Toronto/Université Laval, 2003.

On the British Columbia Treaty Commission process, see:

McKee, Christopher. *Treaty Talks in British Columbia: Negotiating a Mutually Beneficial Future*. 3rd ed. Vancouver: UBC Press, 2009. First published 1996.

Penikett, Tony. *Reconciliation: First Nations Treaty Making in British Columbia*. Vancouver: Douglas and McIntyre, 2006.

Woolford, Andrew. *Between Justice and Certainty: Treaty Making in British Columbia*. Vancouver: UBC Press, 2005.

On the Indian Act, particularly its relationship to band governance and its impact on women, see:

Alfred, Taiaiake. *Peace Power Righteousness: An Indigenous Manifesto*. Don Mills, ON: Oxford University Press, 2009.

Canada. Royal Commission on Aboriginal Peoples. "The Indian Act." Chapter 9 in *Report of the Royal Commission on Aboriginal Peoples*. Vol. 1, *Looking Forward, Looking Back*. Ottawa: Minister of Supply and Services Canada, 1996.

Green, Joyce. "Sexual Equality and Indian Government: An Analysis of Bill C-31." *Native Studies Review* 1, 2 (1985): 81-95.

Lawrence, Bonita. *"Real" Indians and Others: Mixed-Blood Urban Native Peoples and Indigenous Nationhood*. Lincoln: University of Nebraska Press, 2004.

Sayers, Judith, Kelly A. MacDonald, Jo-Anne Fiske, Melonie Newell, Evelyn George, and Wendy Cornet. *First Nations Women, Governance, and the Indian Act: A Collection of Policy Research Reports*. Ottawa: Status of Women Canada, 2001.

Walls, Margaret Elizabeth. *No Need of a Chief for this Band: The Maritime Mi'kmaq and Federal Electoral Legislation, 1899-1951*. Vancouver: UBC Press, 2010.

On epidemic diseases on the Northwest Coast, see:

Boyd, Robert. *The Coming of the Spirit of Pestilence: Introduced Infectious Diseases and Population Decline among Northwest Coast Indians, 1774-1874*. Vancouver: UBC Press, 1999.

Galois, Robert. "Measles, 1847-1850: The First Modern Epidemic in British Columbia." *BC Studies* 109 (1996): 31-43.

Harris, Cole. "Voices of Smallpox around the Strait of Georgia." Chapter 1 in *The Resettlement of British Columbia: Essays on Colonialism and Geographical Change*. Vancouver: UBC Press, 1997.

On the history of toqʷanən, see:

McKenzie, Davis. "Right Past Wrongs: Restoring Toh Kwon_non," *Neh Motl*, 1 September 2005, 1-2. Accessed 30 April 2013. http://sliammontreaty.com/documents/news/Newsletter_2005_09.pdf.

Patrick, Lyana. "Storytelling in the Fourth World: Explorations in Meaning and Place and Tla'amin Resistance to Dispossession." MA thesis, University of Victoria, 2004.

On logging's impact on salmon streams in British Columbia more broadly, see:

Rajala, Richard. "Forests and Fish: The 1972 Coast Logging Guidelines and British Columbia's First NDP Government." *BC Studies* 159 (2008): 81-120.

–. "'Streams Being Ruined from a Salmon Producing Standpoint': Clearcutting, Fish Habitat, and Forest Regulation in British Columbia, 1900-45." *BC Studies* 176 (2012/13): 93-132.

For the hundredth-anniversary issue of *Powell River Living* that Elsie refers to, see:

Powell River Living (July 2010). Accessed 13 January 2012. http://www.prliving.ca/content/1007/index.html.

For early descriptions of ɫaʔamɩn territory as "desolate," see:

Clapperton, Jonathan. "Desolate Viewscapes: Sliammon First Nation, Desolation Sound Marine Park and Environmental Narratives." *Environment and History* 18, 4 (2012): 529-59.

CHAPTER 2: LIFE WITH MY GRANDPARENTS

On the history of logging in British Columbia, see:

Felt, Margaret Elley. *Gyppo Logger.* Seattle: University of Washington Press, 2002.

Pennier, Henry. *Call Me Hank: A Stó:lō Man's Reflections on Logging, Living, and Growing Old.* 2nd ed. Edited by Keith Carlson and Kristina Fagan. Toronto: University of Toronto Press, 2006. First published 1972.

Rajala, Richard A. *Clearcutting the Pacific Rain Forest: Production, Science, and Regulation.* Vancouver: UBC Press, 1999.

On the introduction of brass bands by missionaries, see:

Neylan, Susan, with Melissa Meyer. "'Here Comes the Band!': Cultural Collaboration, Connective Traditions, and Aboriginal Brass Bands on British Columbia's North Coast, 1875-1964." *BC Studies* 152 (2006/7): 35-66.

On the introduction of potatoes on the Northwest Coast, see:

Suttles, Wayne. "The Early Diffusion of the Potato among the Coast Salish." Chapter 8 in *Coast Salish Essays.* Vancouver: Talonbooks, 1987.

On Indigenous plant use and ethnobotanical knowledge on the Northwest Coast, see:

Deur, Douglas, and Nancy Turner, eds. *Keeping It Living: Traditions of Plant Use and Cultivation on the Northwest Coast of British Columbia.* Seattle: University of Washington Press, 2005.

Turner, Nancy, and Dana Lepofsky, eds. "Ethnobotany of British Columbia: Plants and People in a Changing World." Special issue, *BC Studies* 179 (2013).

Turner, Nancy. *Food Plants of Coastal First Peoples.* Vancouver: UBC Press, 1995.

On trading and work in the wage economy, see:

Knight, Rolf. *Indians at Work: An Informal History of Native Labour in British Columbia, 1848-1930.* 2nd ed. Vancouver: New Star Books, 1996. First published 1978.

Lutz, John. *Makúk: A New History of Aboriginal-White Relations.* Vancouver: UBC Press, 2008.

McCallum, Mary Jane Logan. *Indigenous Women, Work, and History: 1940-1980.* Winnipeg: University of Manitoba Press, 2013.

Muszynski, Alicja. *Cheap Wage Labour: Race and Gender in the Fisheries of British Columbia.* Montreal/Kingston: McGill-Queen's University Press, 1996.

Newell, Diana. *Tangled Webs of History: Indians and the Law in Canada's Pacific Coast Fisheries.* Toronto: University of Toronto Press, 1993.

Raibmon, Paige. *Authentic Indians: Episodes of Encounter from the Late-Nineteenth-Century Northwest Coast.* Durham, NC: Duke University Press, 2005.

Williams, Carol. "Between Doorstep Barter Economy and Industrial Wages: Mobility and Adaptability of Coast Salish Female Laborers in Coastal British Columbia, 1858-1890." In *Native Being, Being Native: Identity and Difference: Proceedings of the Fifth Native American Symposium,* edited by Mark Spencer and Lucretia Scoufos, 16-27. Durant: Southeastern Oklahoma State University, 2005.

Williams, Carol, ed. *Indigenous Women and Work: From Labor to Activism.* Urbana: University of Illinois Press, 2012.

On an earlier period of Chinese-Indigenous relations in British Columbia, see:

Barman, Jean. "Beyond Chinatown: Chinese Men and Indigenous Women in Early British Columbia." *BC Studies* 177 (2013): 39-64.

On the Japanese in Canada during World War Two, see:

Oikawa, Mona. *Cartographies of Violence: Japanese Canadian Women, Memory, and the Subjects of the Internment.* Toronto: University of Toronto Press, 2012.

Roy, Patricia E. *The Triumph of Citizenship: The Japanese and Chinese in Canada, 1941-67.* Vancouver: UBC Press, 2007.

CHAPTER 3: TEACHINGS ON LEARNING

Additional readings for this chapter have been combined with those for the other teachings chapters and appear at the end of this section.

CHAPTER 4: RESIDENTIAL SCHOOL

The literature on residential schools is extensive. For general studies, see:

Canada. Royal Commission on Aboriginal Peoples. "Residential Schools." Chapter 10 in *Report of the Royal Commission on Aboriginal Peoples*. Vol. 1, *Looking Forward, Looking Back*. Ottawa: Minister of Supply and Services Canada, 1996.

Miller, J.R. *Shingwauk's Vision: A History of Native Residential Schools*. Toronto: University of Toronto Press, 1996.

Milloy, John S. *A National Crime: The Canadian Government and the Residential School System, 1879-1986*. Winnipeg: University of Manitoba Press, 1999.

Truth and Reconciliation Commission of Canada. *They Came for the Children: Canada, Aboriginal Peoples, and Residential Schools*. Winnipeg: Truth and Reconciliation Commission of Canada, 2012. http://www.attendance marketing.com/~attmk/TRC_jd/ResSchoolHistory_2012_02_24_Web posting.pdf.

On child apprehension:

Crey, Ernie, and Suzanne Fournier. *Stolen from Our Embrace: The Abduction of First Nations Children and the Restoration of Aboriginal Communities*. Vancouver: Douglas and McIntyre, 1997.

For stories about the experiences of individual Indigenous women at residential schools across Canada, see:

Grant, Agnes, ed. *Finding My Talk: How Fourteen Native Women Reclaimed Their Lives after Residential School*. Calgary: Fifth House Books, 2004.

On residential schools in British Columbia:

De Leeuw, Sarah. "'If Anything Is to Be Done with the Indian, We Must Catch Him Very Young': Colonial Constructions of Aboriginal Children and the Geographies of Indian Residential Schooling in British Columbia, Canada." *Children's Geographies* 7, 2 (2009): 123-40.

–. "Intimate Colonialism: The Material and Experienced Places of British Columbia's Residential Schools." *Canadian Geographer* 51, 3 (2007): 339-59.

Fiske, J. "Life at Lejac." In *Sa Ts'e: Historical Perspective on Northern British Columbia*, edited by Thomas Thorner, 235-72. Prince George, BC: College of New Caledonia Press, 1989.

Furniss, Elizabeth. *Victims of Benevolence: The Dark Legacy of the Williams Lake Residential School*. Vancouver: Arsenal Pulp Press, 2000.

Glavin, Terry, and Former Students of St. Mary's. *Amongst God's Own: The Enduring Legacy of St. Mary's Mission*. Vancouver: New Star Books, 2002.

Haig-Brown, Celia. *Resistance and Renewal: Surviving the Indian Residential School*. Vancouver: Arsenal Pulp Press, 2010.

Jack, Agnes, ed. *Behind Closed Doors: Stories from the Kamloops Indian Residential School*. Penticton, BC: Theytus Books, 2006.

Kuper Island: Return to the Healing Circle. DVD. Written, produced, and directed by Peter C. Campbell and Christine Welsh. Victoria/Vancouver: Gumboot Productions/Moving Images Distribution, 1997.

Raibmon, Paige. "'A New Understanding of Things Indian': George Raley's Negotiation of the Residential School Experience." *BC Studies* 110 (1996): 69-96.

Sellars, Bev. *They Called Me Number One: Secrets and Survival at an Indian Residential School.* Vancouver: Talonbooks, 2013.

On residential schools outside of Canada:

Child, Brenda. *Boarding School Seasons: American Indian Families, 1900-1940.* Lincoln: University of Nebraska Press, 1998.

Jacobs, Margaret. *White Mother to a Dark Race: Settler Colonialism, Maternalism, and the Removal of Indigenous Children in the American West and Australia, 1880-1940.* Lincoln: University of Nebraska Press, 2009.

Lomawaina, K. Tsianina. *They Called It Prairie Light: The Story of Chilocco Indian School.* Lincoln: University of Nebraska Press, 1994.

On the intergenerational impact of residential schools:

Ing, N. Rosalyn. "Dealing with Shame and Unresolved Trauma: Residential School and Its Impact on the 2nd and 3rd Generation Adult." PhD dissertation, University of British Columbia, 2000.

–. "The Effects of Residential Schools on Native Child-Rearing Practices." *Canadian Journal of Native Education* 18 (1991): 65-118.

Stout, Roberta, and Sheryl Peters. "kiskinohamâtôtâpânâsk: Inter-generational Effects on Professional First Nations Women Whose Mothers are Residential School Survivors." Project #236. Winnipeg: Prairie Women's Health Centre of Excellence, 2011. http://www.trc.ca/websites/trcinstitution/File/pdfs/kiskino_Intergenerational%20Effect%20of%20IRS%20on%20Prof%20Women.pdf.

Tait, Caroline L. *Fetal Alcohol Syndrome Among Aboriginal People in Canada: Review and Analysis of the Intergenerational Links to Residential Schools.* Ottawa: Aboriginal Healing Foundation, 2003. http://www.ahf.ca/downloads/fetal-alcohol-syndrome.pdf.

On the health of Indigenous people in residential schools and under colonialism in British Columbia more broadly, see:

Drees, Laurie Meijer, ed. *Healing Stories: Stories from Canada's Indian Hospitals.* Edmonton: University of Alberta Press, 2012.

Kelm, Mary-Ellen. *Colonizing Bodies: Aboriginal Health and Healing in British Columbia, 1900-50.* Vancouver: UBC Press, 1999.

For works on reconciliation and healing projects in the wake of residential schools, see the works listed under Chapter 10: Healing Work.

CHAPTER 5: TEACHINGS FOR MOMS

Additional readings for this chapter have been combined with those for the other teachings chapters and appear at the end of this section.

CHAPTER 6: MARRIED LIFE

On logging in BC, see the works listed under "Chapter 2: Life with My Grandparents."

On the history of "relief" to Indigenous peoples, see:

Lutz, John. *Makúk: A New History of Aboriginal-White Relations*. Vancouver: UBC Press, 2008.

Shewell, Hugh E.Q. *"Enough to Keep Them Alive:" Indian Social Welfare in Canada, 1873-1965*. Toronto: University of Toronto Press, 2004.

For additional readings on Indigenous peoples and the wage economy, see the works listed under "Chapter 2: Life with My Grandparents."

On the regulation of liquor in British Columbia, see:

Campbell, Robert A. "A 'Fantastic Rigmarole': Deregulating Aboriginal Drinking in British Columbia, 1945-62." *BC Studies* 141 (2004): 81-104.

–. "Ladies and Escorts: Gender Segregation and Public Policy in British Columbia Beer Parlours, 1925-1945." *BC Studies* 105/106 (1995): 119-38.

–. "Making Sober Citizens: The Legacy of Indigenous Alcohol Regulation in Canada, 1777-1985." *Journal of Canadian Studies* 42, 1 (2008): 105-26.

–. "Managing the Marginal: Regulating and Negotiating Decency in Vancouver's Beer Parlours, 1925-1954." *Labour/Le Travail* 44 (1999): 109-27.

Schlase, Megan. "Liquor and the Indian: Post WWII." *British Columbia Historical News* 29, 2 (1996): 26-29.

Several popular histories of Powell River have been written, a number of which are compilations of oral interviews with residents:

Lambert, Barbara Ann, ed. *Old-time Stories: Billy-Goat Smith, Powell River Co. Xmas, Mr. Dippie and Others*. N.p.: Trafford Publishing, 2006.

–, ed. *Powell River 100: The Largest Single Site Newsprint Manufacturer in the World*. N.p.: Trafford Publishing, 2009.

–, ed. *Rusty Nails and Ration Books: Great Depression and WWII Memories, 1929-1945*. Victoria: Trafford Publishing, 2002.

Levez, Emma. *People of the White City: Stories from the Powell River Mill*. Powell River, BC: Norskecanada, 2002.

Powell River's First 50 Years. Powell River, BC: Powell River News, 1960.

Southern, Karen, and Peggy Bird. *Pulp, Paper and People: 75 Years of Powell River*. Powell River, BC: Powell River Heritage Association, 1988.

Thompson, G.W. *Once upon a Stump: Times and Tales of Powell River Pioneers.* Powell River, BC: Powell River Heritage Association, 1993.

Recently, a study has been conducted into the positive working relationship between the Sliammon First Nation and James Thomson Elementary school:

Pearson, Christine Joanne. "First Nations Parent Involvement in the Public School System: The Personal Journey of a School Principal." PhD diss., University of British Columbia, 2007.

Chapter 7: Teachings on Grief

Additional readings for this chapter have been combined with those for the other teaching chapters and appear at the end of this section.

Chapter 8: Community Work

For a small sample of literature about Indigenous women and their roles as community leaders, see:

Anderson, Kim. "Female Chiefs and the Political Landscape." In *Restoring the Balance: First Nations Women, Community, and Culture*, edited by Gail Guthrie Valaskakis, Madeleine Dion Stout, and Eric Guimond, 99-123. Winnipeg: University of Manitoba Press, 2009.

Castellano, Marlene Brant. "Heart of the Nations: Women's Contribution to Community Healing." In *Restoring the Balance: First Nations Women, Community, and Culture*, edited by Gail Guthrie Valaskakis, Madeleine Dion Stout, and Eric Guimond, 203-35. Winnipeg: University of Manitoba Press, 2009.

Kenny, Carolyn, and Tina Ngaroimata Fraser, eds. *Living Indigenous Leadership: Native Narratives on Building Strong Communities.* Vancouver: UBC Press, 2012.

Kirkness, Verna J. *Making Space: My Life and Work in Indigenous Education.* Winnipeg: University of Manitoba Press, 2013.

Tsosie, Rebecca. "Native Women and Leadership: An Ethics of Culture and Relationship." In *Indigenous Women and Feminism: Politics, Activism, Culture*, edited by Cheryl Suzack, Shari M. Huhndorf, Jeanne Perreault, and Jean Barman, 29-42. Vancouver: UBC Press, 2010.

Voyageur, Cora. *Firekeepers of the Twenty-First Century: First Nations Women Chiefs.* Montreal/Kingston: McGill-Queen's University Press, 2008.

For a thoughtful, first-hand account by a non-Indigenous social worker on the BC coast (including Homalco territory) in the 1960s and 1970s, see:

Gibson, John Frederic. *A Small and Charming World.* Smithers, BC: Creekstone Press, 2001. First published 1972.

CHAPTER 9: NAMING MY FAMILY

Jane Cook, who carried the same ancestral name as Elsie Paul, is the subject of a book:

Robertson, Leslie A. *Standing up with Ga'axsta'las: Jane Constance Cook and the Politics of Memory, Church, and Custom.* Vancouver: UBC Press, 2012.

For two books that situate Indigenous naming practices at their centre, see:

Alia, Valerie. *Names and Nunavut: Culture and Identity in the Inuit Homeland.* New York: Berghahn Books, 2007.
Roth, Christopher F. *Becoming Tsimshian: The Social Life of Names.* Seattle: University of Washington Press, 2008.

CHAPTER 10: HEALING WORK

Elsie discusses her involvement with healing work in the following documentary film:

Keepers of the Fire. VHS. Written, narrated, and directed by Nola Wuttunee. Edmonton/Kelowna/Richmond: Great North Productions/Filmwest/Image Media, 1993.

For analysis of attempts at culturally specific justice systems, see:

LaRoque, Emma. "Re-examining Culturally Appropriate Models in Criminal Justice Applications." In *Aboriginal and Treaty Rights in Canada: Essays on Law, Equality, and Respect for Difference,* edited by Michael Asch, 75-96. Vancouver: UBC Press, 1997.
Miller, Bruce G. *The Problem of Justice: Tradition and Law in the Coast Salish World.* Lincoln: University of Nebraska Press, 2001.
Milward, David. *Aboriginal Justice and the Charter: Realizing a Culturally Sensitive Interpretation of Legal Rights.* Vancouver: UBC Press, 2013.
Monture-Angus, Patricia. *Thunder in My Soul: A Mohawk Woman Speaks.* Black Point, NS: Fernwood, 2003.

For examples and analyses of health, healing, and reconciliation, particularly in the wake of residential schools, see:

Canada. Royal Commission on Aboriginal Peoples. *Report of the Royal Commission on Aboriginal Peoples.* Vol. 3, *Gathering Strength.* Ottawa: Minister of Supply and Services Canada, 1996.
Castellano, Marlene Brant, Linda Archibald, and Mike DeGagné, eds. *From Truth to Reconciliation: Transforming the Legacy of Residential Schools.* Ottawa: Aboriginal Healing Foundation, 2008. http://www.ahf.ca/downloads/from-truth-to-reconciliation-transforming-the-legacy-of-residential-schools.pdf.

Chansonneuve, Deborah. *Reclaiming Connections: Understanding Residential School Trauma Among Aboriginal People.* Ottawa: Aboriginal Healing Foundation, 2005. http://www. ahf.ca/downloads/healing-trauma-web -eng.pdf. http://www.ahf.ca/downloads/healing-trauma-web-eng.pdf.

Henderson, Jennifer, and Pauline Wakeham. *Reconciling Canada: Critical Perspectives on the Culture of Redress.* Toronto: University of Toronto Press, 2013.

Kirmayer, Laurence J., and Gail Guthrie Valaskakis, eds. *Healing Traditions: The Mental Health of Aboriginal Peoples in Canada.* Vancouver: UBC Press, 2009.

Regan, Paulette. *Unsettling the Settler Within: Indian Residential Schools, Truth Telling, and Reconciliation in Canada.* Vancouver: UBC Press, 2010.

Reimer, Gwen, Amy Bombay, Lena Ellsworth, Sara Fryer, and Tricia Logan. *The Indian Residential Schools Settlement Agreement's Common Experience Payment and Healing: A Qualitative Study Exploring Impacts on Recipients.* Ottawa: Aboriginal Healing Foundation, 2010. http://www.ahf.ca/downloads/cep -2010-healing.pdf.

Stout, Madeleine Dion, and Gregory Kipling. *Aboriginal People, Resilience, and the Residential School Legacy.* Ottawa: Aboriginal Healing Foundation, 2003. http://www.ahf.ca/downloads/resilience.pdf.

Stout, Madeleine Dion, and Rick Harp. *Lump Sum Compensation Payments Research Project: The Circle Rechecks Itself.* Ottawa: Aboriginal Healing Foundation, 2007. http://www.ahf.ca/downloads/newest-lsp.pdf.

Waldram, James B., ed. *Aboriginal Healing in Canada: Studies in Therapeutic Meaning and Practice.* Ottawa: Aboriginal Healing Foundation, 2008. http:// www.ahf.ca/downloads/aboriginal-healing-in-canada.pdf.

CHAPTERS ON TEACHING:
CHAPTER 3 (TEACHINGS ON LEARNING), CHAPTER 5 (TEACHINGS FOR MOMS), CHAPTER 7 (TEACHINGS ON GRIEF), AND CHAPTER 11 (TEACHINGS ON SPIRITUALITY)

A diverse and growing literature draws upon and shares Indigenous teachings, traditions, and methodologies. For examples, see:

Alfred, Taiaiake. *Wasáse: Indigenous Pathways of Action and Freedom.* Peterborough, ON: Broadview Press, 2005.

Anderson, Kim. *Life Stages and Native Women: Memory, Teachings, and Story Medicine.* Winnipeg: University of Manitoba Press, 2011.

–. *A Recognition of Being: Reconstructing Native Womanhood.* Toronto: Sumach Press, 2000.

Archibald, Jo-ann. *Indigenous Storywork: Educating the Heart, Mind, Body, and Spirit.* Vancouver: UBC Press, 2008.

Atleo, E. Richard. *Principles of Tsawalk: An Indigenous Approach to Global Crisis.* Vancouver: UBC Press, 2012.

–. *Tsawalk: A Nuu-chah-nulth Worldview.* Vancouver: UBC Press, 2004.

Borrows, John. *Drawing Out Law: A Spirit's Guide*. Toronto: University of Toronto Press, 2010.

Dion, Susan. *Braiding Histories: Learning from Aboriginal Peoples' Experiences and Perspectives*. Vancouver: UBC Press, 2008.

Doerfler, Jill, Heidi Kiiwetinepinesiik Star, and Niigaanwewidam James Sinclair, eds. *Centering Anishinaabeg Studies: Understanding the World through Stories*. Winnipeg: University of Manitoba Press, 2013.

Gonzales, Patrisia. *Red Medicine: Traditional Indigenous Rites of Birthing and Healing*. Tucson: University of Arizona Press, 2012.

Kovach, Margaret Elizabeth. *Indigenous Methodologies: Characteristics, Conversations, and Contexts*. Toronto: University of Toronto Press, 2010.

Kuokkanen, Rauna Johanna. *Reshaping the University: Responsibility, Indigenous Epistemes, and the Logic of the Gift*. Vancouver: UBC Press, 2007.

Simpson, Leanne. *Dancing on Our Turtle's Back*. Winnipeg: Arbeiter Ring Publishing, 2011.

Simpson, Leanne, ed. *Lighting the Eighth Fire: The Liberation, Resurgence, and Protection of Indigenous Nations*. Winnipeg: Arbeiter Ring Publishing, 2008.

Turner, Nancy. *The Earth's Blanket: Traditional Teachings for Sustainable Living*. Vancouver: Douglas and McIntyre, 2005.

Wilson, Waziyatawin Angela. *Remember This! Dakota Decolonization and the Eli Taylor Narratives*. Translated by Wahpetunwin Carolyn Schommer. Lincoln: University of Nebraska Press, 2005.

Index

Printed and bound in Canada by Friesens

Set in Eidetic Neo, Charis, and Gentium by Artegraphica Design Co. Ltd.

Copy editor: Sarah Wight

Proofreader and indexer: Cheryl Lemmens

Cartographer: Eric Leinberger